Roman Law and the Idea of Europe

Europe's Legacy in the Modern World

Series Editors: Martti Koskenniemi and Bo Stråth
(University of Helsinki, Finland)

The 19th century is often described as Europe's century. This series aims to explore the truth of this claim. It views Europe as a global actor and offers insights into its role in ordering the world, creating community and providing welfare in the 19th century and beyond. Volumes in the series investigate tensions between the national and the global, welfare and warfare, property and poverty. They look at how notions like democracy, populism and totalitarianism came to be intertwined and how this legacy persists in the present day world.

The series emphasizes the entanglements between the legal, the political and the economic and employs techniques and methodologies from the history of legal, political and economic thought, the history of events, and structural history. The result is a collection of works that shed new light on the role that Europe's intellectual history has played in the development of the modern world.

Published

Historical Teleologies in the Modern World, Henning Trüper, Dipesh Chakrabarty and Sanjay Subrahmanyam
Europe's Utopias of Peace, Bo Stråth
Political Reform in the Ottoman and Russian Empires, Adrian Brisku
European Modernity: A Global Approach, Bo Stråth and Peter Wagner
The Contested History of Autonomy, Gerard Rosich

Forthcoming

Caesarism in the Post-Revolutionary Age: Crisis, Populace and Leadership, Markus J. Prutsch
Social Difference in Nineteenth-Century Spanish America: An Intellectual History, Francisco A. Ortega

Roman Law and the Idea of Europe

Edited by Kaius Tuori and Heta Björklund

BLOOMSBURY ACADEMIC
LONDON • NEW YORK • OXFORD • NEW DELHI • SYDNEY

BLOOMSBURY ACADEMIC
Bloomsbury Publishing Plc
50 Bedford Square, London, WC1B 3DP, UK
1385 Broadway, New York, NY 10018, USA

BLOOMSBURY, BLOOMSBURY ACADEMIC and the Diana logo are trademarks of Bloomsbury Publishing Plc

First published in Great Britain 2019

A catalogue record for this book is available from the British Library.

A catalog record for this book is available from the Library of Congress.

ISBN: HB: 978-1-3500-5873-6
ePDF: 978-1-3500-5874-3
ePUB: 978-1-3500-5875-0

Series: Europe's Legacy in the Modern World

Typeset by Deanta Global Publishing Services, Chennai, India
Printed and bound in Great Britain

To find out more about our authors and books visit www.bloomsbury.com and sign up for our newsletters.

Contents

List of Illustrations

Editors

Heta Björklund has a PhD in Classics from the University of Helsinki, Finland. She has previously worked as an editor at the Classical journal *Arctos*.

Kaius Tuori is Associate Professor of European Intellectual History at the University of Helsinki, Finland. He is the author of *The Emperor of Law: The Emergence of Roman Imperial Adjudication* (2016) and *Lawyers and Savages: Ancient History and Legal Realism in the Making of Legal Anthropology* (2014). He is also the co-editor of, with Paul J. du Plessis and Clifford Ando, *The Oxford Handbook of Roman Law and Society* (2016).

List of Contributors

Lorena Atzeri is Lecturer in Roman Law at the Università degli Studi of Milan, Italy, and Honorary Research Associate of the Byzantine Legal Sources Research Centre of the Academy of Sciences of Göttingen. She has carried out research in the fields of Roman law in late Antiquity, Roman law sources and their transmission and the history of Roman legal science in the nineteenth and twentieth centuries. She is the author of *Gesta senatus Romani de Theodosiano publicando. Il Codice Teodosiano e la sua diffusione ufficiale in Occidente* (2008).

Tommaso Beggio works at the Faculty of Law of the University of Trento, Italy. He has mainly written on legal epigraphy, Roman criminal law and Paul Koschaker and Roman law under the totalitarianism. He is the author of the chapter 'Epigraphy' in the *Oxford Handbook of Roman Law and Society* (2016), of the article 'Paul Koschaker und die Reform des romanistischen Rechtsstudiums in Deutschland. Ein unveröffentliches Dokument' for the *Zeitschrift der Savigny-Stiftung* (2018) and of the monograph *Paul Koschaker (1879–1951). Rediscovering the Roman Foundations of European Legal Tradition* (2018).

Stefan Berger is Professor of Social History and Director of the Institute for Social Movements at Ruhr University Bochum, Germany. He is also Executive Chair of the History of the Ruhr Foundation and an honorary professor at Cardiff University, UK. He is the author, with Christoph Conrad, of *The Past as History: National Identity and Historical Consciousness in Modern Europe* (2015), and he is also co-editor, with Mario Carretero and Maria Grever, of the *Palgrave Handbook of Research in Historical Culture and Education* (2017).

Cosimo Cascione is Full Professor in Roman Law at the University Federico II of Naples, Italy. He is the author of the monographs *Tresviri capitales. Storia di una magistratura minore* (1999), *Consensus. Problemi di origine, tutela processuale, prospettive sistematiche* (2003), *Manuale breve – Diritto romano* (2007), *Studi di diritto pubblico romano* (2010) and of a hundred of articles and essays in the field of ancient law and Roman law tradition.

Johann Chapoutot is Professor of Modern History at the University of Paris-Sorbonne, and author of *Le national-socialisme et l´Antiquité* (2008). His latest book is *La révolution culturelle nazie* (2017).

Paul J. du Plessis holds the chair of Roman law at the University of Edinburgh. He is a legal historian whose research focuses predominantly on the multifaceted and complex set of relationships between law and society in a historical context. His main field of research is Roman law (with specific reference to property, obligations and, to a lesser extent, persons and family). Within this field, he is mainly concerned with the contexts within which law operates and the extent to which modern socio-legal methodologies can be applied to historical material from the Roman period in order to further our understanding of Roman law. He is the author and editor of many works on Roman law, the medieval *ius commune* and early modern conceptions of law.

Ville Erkkilä is a post-doctoral researcher in the Center for European Studies at the University of Helsinki. He has published, among others, on history of historiography and feminist history. His book on *Conceptual Change of Conscience: Franz Wieacker and German Legal Historiography 1933–1968* is forthcoming.

Jacob Giltaij is a university researcher at the Centre of Excellence in Law, Identity and the European Narratives at the University of Helsinki. His forthcoming book is titled *Fritz Schulz (1879–1957): Reinventing the Principles of Roman Law.*

Dina Gusejnova is Lecturer in Modern History at the University of Sheffield. She is the author of *European Elites and Ideas of Empire, 1917–57* (2016) and the editor of *Cosmopolitanism in Conflict. Imperial Encounters from the Seven Years' War to the Cold War* (2018).

Hans-Peter Haferkamp is Professor of Private Law and Legal History at the University of Cologne, Germany. He is the author of *Die Historische Rechtsschule* and *Georg Friedrich Puchta und die Begriffsjurisprudenz*, and co-editor of the second edition of the *Handwörterbuch zur deutschen Rechtsgeschichte*.

Magdalena Kmak is Associate Professor in Minority Studies at the Åbo Akademi University and University Researcher and Team Leader at the Centre of Excellence in Law, Identity and the European Narratives at the University of Helsinki, Finland. She is a co-editor, with Dorota A. Gozdecka, of a book *Europe at the Edge of Pluralism* (2015) and author of numerous publications focusing on migration and citizenship.

Diego Quaglioni is Full Professor in History of Law at the University of Trento, Italy. He has written widely on the doctrinal tradition of the *ius commune*, legal humanism, early modern parliamentary history and state sovereignty. He is the author of *La concepcion pré-moderne de la justice* (2003), *La sovranità* (2004) and *Machiavelli e la lingua della giurisprudenza* (2011). He is the co-editor, with Gerhard Dilcher, of the three volumes *Die Anfänge des öffentlichen Rechts* (2007, 2008, 2011). He is also the editor of the Italian version of Harold J. Berman's *Law and Revolution, II* (2010).

Bo Stråth is Professor Emeritus in Nordic, European and World History. He held chairs at the University of Helsinki, the European University Institute and the University of Gothenburg. He has written widely on conceptual history, the history of European integration and global modernity. His recent publications include *Europe's Utopias of Peace: 1815, 1919, 1951* (2016), *A Brief History of Political Economy. Tales of Marx, Keynes and Hayek* (co-authored 2016) and *European Modernity. A Global Approach* (co-authored 2017).

Acknowledgements

This book is the culmination of the research project Reinventing the Foundations of European Legal Culture 1934–1964, generously funded by the European Research Council under the European Union's Seventh Framework Programme (FP7/2007–2013) / ERC grant agreement n°313100. The editors would like to warmly thank all of the contributors of the book for not only their marvellous chapters but also for the insights and discussions at the authors' meetings in Helsinki in 2016 and in Rome in 2017, which shaped the book into its final form. In addition, we owe a debt of gratitude to Martti Koskenniemi and Bo Stråth as the editors of this series for accepting it and Rhodri Mogford and Beatriz Lopez at Bloomsbury for their efficient help in getting the book from proposal to a finished work. We would like to also thank Christopher Goddard, Mark Shackleton and the proofreaders of the University of Helsinki Language Services for their patient and meticulous proofreading.

Introduction

Kaius Tuori

This book explores the controversial role of ancient Rome and its legal heritage, Roman law, in the making of the idea of a shared European legal tradition. This derives from the use of the memory of the classical past in the political upheavals of the early twentieth century. For example, the classical civilization was often used to provide legitimacy to contemporary political causes by seeking parallels between historical examples and current policies. This reaching to the past for guidance for the future has, as a phenomenon, a long history, especially in times of crises. This book argues that a group of émigré scholars who fled totalitarianism had a crucial role in the formation of the European project that lead to integration after the war. While the Nazi and fascist states had legitimated their rule through references to the classical past, in the field of law and the example of ancient Roman law, these scholars would reinterpret the past to demonstrate how the Roman legal heritage was in fact in complete opposition to the totalitarian theories of law.[1]

One of the most beloved historians writing about the ancient world, Jérôme Carcopino (1881–1970), published in 1940 his still popular *La vie Quotidienne à Rome à l'Apogée de l'Empire* (*Daily Life in Ancient Rome*) during the height of the Second World War. In it, he paints an engaging picture of life in ancient Rome during its height, describing it from the viewpoint of the individual on the street. What is less known is that after the fall of France in June 1940, Carcopino became a supporter of the Vichy regime that collaborated with the German occupiers. Carcopino was made minister of education and he would scrupulously see that the programmes and policies of the Vichy regime that were often racist and anti-Semitic were enforced. Jewish members of academia were expelled and ultra-nationalist ideology was promoted. Antiquity and its civilization became for many across the political spectrum a touchstone in turbulent times. The past or at least glorious images of the past were seen as providing a vision of the future.[2] This book is about such visions and how the uses of the past to provide legitimacy for ideas.

Carcopino was, however, at the same time, shielding from dismissal the historian Marc Bloch (1886–1944), a Jew who became an active member of the Resistance.[3] The vision of Carcopino was that Europe and France were the true successors of ancient civilization. The example of Carcopino is fitting in another respect that is central to this book; it shows how when approached at an intimate level, contradictions and inconsistencies push aside neat categories of friend and foe. While the stories of a great turn towards enlightened ideas of justice and the European heritage after the catastrophe of the Second World War may appeal to our conscience, what we want to demonstrate is how upon closer inspection there are inconvenient continuities and awkward pasts that bring the history into sharper relief.

The rise of totalitarianism in Europe during the interwar period was felt acutely in academic scholarship because the totalitarian dictatorships in Germany and Italy, not to mention the Soviet Union, were intent on controlling the production of knowledge. The field of Roman law, which had traditionally enjoyed prominence in Continental legal academia, faced very different challenges. In Germany, the Nazi regime had declared the eradication of Roman law as one of its aims,[4] while in Italy Roman law enjoyed the same favour that was accorded to the classics, as a part of the hallowed *Romanità* that the fascists idealized. At the same time, Roman law faced a crisis in the reforms of legal education, where the advent of modern codifications led to its teaching being cut. For professors of Roman law who were of Jewish ancestry or politically opposed to the new regimes the crisis was equally a personal one. They faced expulsion from office and exile, often ending up in places (such as the United States or Britain) where the expertise they had was in very little demand. Numerically, this group of professors was not very large. To Britain, there came Fritz Pringsheim (1882–1967), Fritz Schulz (1879–1957), David Daube (1909–99) and Arnold Ehrhardt (1903–65). Of those, the last mentioned ended up finishing his academic career and becoming a vicar in Manchester. To the United States, there went Ernst Levy (1881–1968), Adolf Berger (1882–1962), Ernst Rabel (1874–1955), Hans Julius Wolff, (1902–83), Eberhard Bruck (1877–1960), Richard Honig (1890–1981) and Gerhart Husserl (1893–1973).

In contemporary scholarship, Roman law is widely considered to be the foundation of European legal culture and an inherent source of unity within European law. The purpose of this book is to explore the emergence of this idea of Roman law as an idealized shared heritage, tracing its origins among exiled German scholars in Britain during the Nazi regime, as well as the German and Italian scholars who either stayed behind or joined totalitarian regimes. The book follows the spread and influence of these ideas in Europe after the Second World War as part of the larger enthusiasm for European unity. The central claim is that the rise of the importance of Roman law was a reaction against the crisis of jurisprudence in the face of Nazi ideas of racial and ultra-nationalistic law, leading to the establishment of the idea of Europe founded on shared legal principles. The aim is to trace the crisis and rebirth of Roman law from the 1930s onwards in Europe in its intellectual context. At its centre are a group of émigré scholars who fled Nazi persecution to Britain and began to reinvent the role and nature of Roman law in European history. Equally important were the ones who stayed on the Continent, adapting their scholarship to the wishes of the new regimes, or remaining purposefully apolitical (a position often described as inner exile), such as Paul Koschaker or Franz Wieacker. They too would write about Europe, but of a Europe of exclusive Western culture in opposition to communism and Eastern influences, replicating trends of both Nazi and fascist propaganda. What the book argues is that after the war they would find a new cause in the European character of Roman law, leading to its revival as the roots of European legal tradition. In Britain, the influx of top-level specialists in Roman law led to a renaissance in the field, one that eventually sought to link even Britain to the Roman law tradition.

The book will demonstrate how the post-war beginnings of European integration brought a new urgency to the ideas of shared European traditions, and Roman law was in a privileged position to take the role of a shared origin for European jurisprudence in these discussions. At the same time, it seeks to critically engage with the narratives of European heritage and questions the teleological constructs of the European idea and its past. A major part of the controversies about history, law and culture continues to be the use of the past for present purposes. Classical culture and the legacy of ancient civilizations were enthusiastically embraced by authoritarian nationalists like Carcopino or Italian fascists, but equally by the Europeanists seeking to find a counterpoint to the totalitarian ideas.

The discussions over the European legal heritage have a large number of conceptual peculiarities that have different connotations in various historical layers. One example is the concept of Roman law itself. In European legal history, Roman law meant the law of the ancient Roman Empire, but more importantly it was used as a code word for the European legal tradition, also known as civil law. This tradition had as its common denominator that which was derived from the foundations laid by ancient Roman legal writings. Roman law was not only a legal system; but due to its emphasis on commerce and property rights, it also had distinct ideological underpinnings in the Continental European debates from the nineteenth to the twentieth centuries. In these discussions, Roman law was presented as a system that promoted capitalistic oppression and dismissed the ideas of social civil law such as the protections of weaker parties in contractual relations or the safeguarding of land rights. While elements of Roman law could be used to promote a liberal or a reformist agenda, most often it was resorted to by conservative authors.[5] This was due to the easily conservative nature of tradition, which meant in this case that if the content of the law was drawn from the past, the law could easily be petrified and ossified. Legal and social reform, especially one that could be realized through legislative acts, could be stymied by referring to the tradition. Not coincidentally, this resistance towards legislative reform was a reason why Roman law was popular in many authoritarian regimes, from apartheid South Africa to some military juntas in South America.

After the war and the reorientation of Europe as a bastion of liberal democracy against totalitarian communism, the idea of Europe and the cause of freedom and justice were accepted on both sides of the political spectrum, with different overtones (Duranti 2017). The relevance of these debates today stems in part from the currency that the idea of a shared European legal heritage has for the European project. Influential authors have depicted the European tradition as a foundation on which a new unity of European law may be built. Beginning from the 1990s, different strands of the so-called European private law project have sought to make this vision a reality. The project sought to extend the European unification to the realm of private law, advancing the harmonization of the law between Member States. A part of this quest has been to create a new understanding of the different kinds of European legal traditions and their linkages.

Among others, Reinhard Zimmermann maintained that the emerging common law of Europe should be informed by the shared heritage of the reception of Roman law, if not ancient Roman law itself. This meant that Roman law, through its history, could lead the way in showing how a common legal tradition may be established through an intellectual unity. Therefore, Roman law has both nothing and everything to do with the new common law. Rather than laws or norms themselves, Zimmermann speaks of a shared legal culture that was based on legal science. This vision is one of past unity in law, born through a series of exchanges and transmissions, where both scholars and texts were moving on a European scale. Of particular importance in his theory is the shared historical past and influences between English private law tradition and the European heritage. In his vision, inspired by this precedent, a new *ius commune* could be formed based on shared values, methods and principles (Zimmermann 2011). This vision of the past unity has been heavily criticized by opponents claiming that national traditions have been even more influential and the Europeanist vision is a false hope.[6]

Other critics have noted how the concept of European private law projects its historical vision as a kind of teleology, a projection rather than a statement of fact. This teleology works as a kind of a long process of harmonization of private law of the past and the future simultaneously.[7] At the same time, the whole vision of a European private law has come under fundamental criticism from the historical side, where, for example, its historical precedent of *ius commune* has itself come under new scrutiny (Wijffels 2000).

The historical debate of a shared European legal heritage has thus become something of a hostage to the contemporary debate over the future of the European private law project and the drive for a European civil code. However, the concepts of unification are not themselves in harmony, with many disagreements on how to proceed with unification, from the bottom up or top down or with initiatives like Lando's *Commission on European Contract Law*, Bussani and Mattei's *Trento Common Core Project* or the *Study Group on a European Civil Code* presenting different visions for the future.[8]

In these endeavours, the historical past has a somewhat uneasy position as a legitimator and the source of the idea of the shared roots. For example, in their influential criticism on the Draft Common Frame of Reference, Eidenmüller et al. (including Zimmermann) recognize how legal historians have 'helped us to recognize the common ground shared by Europe's modern national legal systems'.[9]

Zimmermann's work on the Roman legal tradition and its relationship with the European legal development has been a conspicuous presence in the European legal discourse since the 1990s. Zimmermann's defence of Roman law echoed that of Paul Koschaker, even to the extent that one of his articles had the same title. While he emphasizes the European character of law, he remains careful to insist that as in all European culture, there is a mixture of unity and plurality which prevents a simplistic model of continuities to be applied. Rather, there is a common groundwork laid by the Roman jurists, especially in the field of private law, which is evident in all European legal systems. While the British legal system has, at least by the accounts given by nationalistic authors, lived in splendid isolation, this was hardly the case as influences and interpretations travelled across Europe, including the common law. The tracing of the shared roots of common law and civil law has led to a lasting interest in mixed legal systems, for instance those of South Africa or Scotland, which both have a significant element of Roman law influence.[10] Whatever implications these ideas would then have for the European private law projects or even the harmonization of law is, even for Zimmermann, a matter of dispute. Especially now with the repercussions of the Brexit vote, it remains to be seen whether the inclusion of Britain to the European legal ambit proves to be solely of historical relevance.

In addition to the importance of Roman law in the justification of the unification of private law, the legal foundation it provided was an important reference point to the issues of tradition and governance. Even though both the modern state and the ancient Roman Empire were founded on the basic principle that the state was in theory sovereign and thus exercised unfettered power, the European heritage of constitutionalism operated on two basic principles: liberty and rule of law. The first meant in its most basic form that men were free persons, not the property of their ruler. The second meant that even though rulers would have power, they were still bound by the legal order, if not by the state law then a legal order derived from God or nature (Pagden 2002: 4). In a democratic or even in a constitutional order, these principles were mere theoretical musings. However, with the advent of the totalitarian states, they were subject to an unprecedented attack. Especially after the beginning of the war, the Nazi and fascist states turned law itself into an instrument of terror. While the formalities of law were observed, in practice the result was the 'devaluation of historic legal norms and the perversion of traditional judicial procedure' that evolved from an 'explicit rejection of principles underlying both common and Roman (civil) law systems' (Rachlin 2013: 80). Against such a reversal of the ideas of justice, equality and the rule of law, the references to the tradition based on Roman law shared by most of Europe were a call to fundamental values.

One of the impacts of the scholarly exodus precipitated by the rise of totalitarianism in Europe was the spread of new ideas and conceptions. In this book, the foundational value of Roman law to the European legal heritage was one of these ideas. This was not to say that Roman law and its cultural value were not familiar in Britain and the United States, but rather that such a conviction was not spread to a similar degree. Thus, beginning from the nineteenth century, there existed a lament that the greatness of the Roman law tradition was not recognized and known in Britain. For example, Tomkins and Jencken wrote in their 1870 work on Roman law that they had a 'hope of awakening an interest in this country in the study of the Modern Roman Law', the 'feebleness' of which had been noted even on the Continent. In their view, Roman law was the root which was then passed on to the legal systems of the 'European and Transatlantic nations' (Tomkins and Jencken 1870: ix–xiii). It is uncontroversial that the influx of émigrés to Britain led to a new flourishing in the field of Roman law, where much of the subsequent generation of scholars, such as Tony Honoré, Alan Watson or Peter Stein, was trained by these exiles. In addition to a new and extraordinarily well-trained group of scholars, the émigrés brought with them ideas about the role of Roman law in modern society and law.

However, even within the European countries where the legal system was based on Roman law, there was continuing discourse on the value of Roman law in the legal system, be it in legal education or the interpretation of law. This discourse had come to a head in the much-discussed crisis of Roman law that had reigned from the early 1900s onwards and which only intensified with the Nazi revolution after 1933. In part, the issues that were facing Roman law scholars in the 1930s were the same that had troubled Roman law scholars earlier, namely how to link Roman law and modern law. For example, Johannes Voet (1647–1713), one of the most celebrated jurists of the so-called *usus modernus Pandectarum*, grappled with similar questions in his works. Voet maintained that Roman law should be used and studied because it offers solutions, models and principles that help in resolving contemporary issues. However, it also gave models and principles through which disputes between jurisdictions could be solved by applying principles that were acceptable to both parties, that is, the rules of Roman law (Voet 1955: 4–6). The famous notion of Goethe about the influence of Roman law in European history compares it to a duck. Sometimes it is eminently visible, swimming on the surface, sometimes invisible under the surface, but always it is there (Eckermann 1971: 313). The simile about ducks though hides something of the usages of Roman law, where Roman law has, in addition to its own uses in the field of law, been displayed for the benefit of ulterior motives. As with the definition by Voet, Roman law could be seen as a secondary source of law with superior qualities and prestige. However, it could equally be seen as a supranational corrective to the power of the state, an inherently correct law like natural law, or more recently, human rights.

These early twentieth-century revivalist ideas of Roman law took place in a period where considerations of law and society were in a state of flux both in Europe and North America. Legal realism and other critics of formalism such as Marxism raised social facts before legal norms, while in totalitarian regimes there was a stated preference for power (or politics) over law. Even within the democratic states, the expansion of state power and the extent of state interventions grew at an extraordinary pace. Arguably, this constitutional process had begun already with the First World War, but the triumph of the executive powers during the fascist years marks a true revolution in that sphere (Thornhill 2014). This led to the simultaneous need to reinforce the position of the individual and, arguably, to the emergence of human rights as the prime concept in the modern relation between state and individual.

One of the testaments of the malleability of the Roman law tradition is that it could be used with equal effectiveness in liberal, conservative, authoritarian or even totalitarian contexts. Even in the countries of Eastern Europe where a system of historical Marxism was adopted in legal education, the position of Roman law suffered only a minor setback. Even though the Communist regimes were in theory committed to the idea that the political and legal systems were inseparable and thus the ideology of the regime was primary to the doctrine of the law, the system of private law remained in countries like Poland, Hungary and the Soviet Union, tied to the old Pandectistic system derived ultimately from Roman law. Only in some of the most doctrinaire of the communist people's democracies, such as the DDR or Czechoslovakia, was the reform to expunge all vestiges of the old system.[11]

How does the book contribute to the debates?

The issues of law, totalitarianism and tradition are ones that have motivated scholars of law, history and politics in many ways. The book touches upon three important debates on intellectual history: (1) the use of the past in totalitarian regimes, (2) the impact of émigré scholars and (3) the emergence of the European project.

The contemporary significance of the study of ancient culture has been the subject of increasing scholarly interest.[12] The political importance of classics in the twentieth-century totalitarian regimes has been an important subfield, where researchers have discussed how the totalitarian regimes, especially the Fascists in Italy, used ancient Rome as an example and justification for their policies of militarization and aggression (Nelis 2007). For the study of the classical past, this meant that the object of their study was made to conform to the expectations of the present, sometimes in very confusing and contradictory ways, such as precursors to racial policies. Important studies have demonstrated how the position of Roman law varied from being under threat to being co-opted by the regime (Miglietta and Santucci 2009), but concerted study of the impact in the field is still lacking. In the current volume, the chapters by Chapoutot and Cascione, among others, offer important starting points for this.

The scholarship on émigré intellectuals is a fast-growing field, in which the first generation consisted mostly of purely biographical studies of émigrés, for example, the some 20,000 intellectuals (among whom were some 2,000 professors) who left Germany in the 1930s. The second generation of studies has explored the impact that this transfer had in Britain and the United States, where new areas of research were born and others were revitalized with the influx of new talent from Germany and Italy (Fermi 1968; Ash and Söllner 1996; Rösch 2014). For legal scholars, the study has thus far been concentrated on the biographical aspect, with works like *Jurists Uprooted* (2004) detailing lives of émigré legal scholars, including some Roman lawyers like F. Schulz and D. Daube. Beyond that, the impact of their work in Britain, the United States or Germany after the war is still mostly unexplored.[13] The chapters of Tuori, Kmak, Giltaij and Atzeri follow the process of change and adaptation through several examples.

Of the vast scholarship on the European integration or the idea of Europe, there have been only a few works that investigate the history of the turn to Europe in historical scholarship after the Second World War (Kaelble 2001; Schulz-Forberg and Stråth 2010). While the European project has always presented itself as a counter reaction to totalitarianism, critical studies such as *Darker Legacies of Law in Europe* (2003) have showed how Nazi legal thought held many of the same ideas as the European integration.[14] With regard to the impact of Roman law in the European project, the more prominent works have dealt with the way Roman jurisprudence actually influenced different European legal cultures[15] rather than with how Roman law was used as part of the European project. In the current volume, the works of Beggio, Quaglioni, Stråth and Berger offer important points on how the concepts of history, culture and crisis were utilized in the workings of the European discourse.

In conclusion, the book seeks to fill an important lacuna in the academic debate and brings together scholarship that addresses the issues of the use of the past and totalitarianism, knowledge transfer and emigration and the birth of the European idea as a reaction to the totalitarianism of the 1930s. The main contribution of this book is that it presents for the first time the development that led to the shared conviction that Roman law is the common foundation of European legal culture. The book will demonstrate how behind that development there are coincidences and human tragedy and how the idea of the role of Roman law was in part a political statement against totalitarianism. However, what it argues is that the vision they offered was a deeply conservative one, an idea of turning to the past in a period of tremendous social, economic and political upheaval. While works like *Jurists Uprooted* have shown the importance of the exiles and their work, what we are adding is the crucial connections that the exiles still had both in their countries of origin and, as importantly, in their new homelands, the network of people who aided them, read their work and promoted their cause in desperate times. As works like the *Darker Legacies of Law in Europe* were instrumental in establishing crucial continuities from the totalitarian regimes to the present Europeanist discourse, the present work offers a different take, one that seeks to step back from the value judgement and to discuss the individuals on their own terms.

The chapters of the book follow a broadly thematic order, from the conflict of ideas in the 1930s to the totalitarianism and exile experience and finally the roots of the European thought. The first half of the book will explore the exile experience and its implications in knowledge production about the meaning and understanding of history between the Continental and the Anglo-Saxon traditions. The second half will address the Nazi and fascist ideas of Europe and the culture of the past and their role in the making of the European historical narratives.

In Chapter 1, Magdalena Kmak examines the effects of exile with a study on the experiences of legal scholars exiled by Nazi Germany and their impact in British and American legal academia. She maintains that the exile process is a complex cultural exchange where the exiles could act as bridges between academic cultures, but that the position of legal scholars in exile was extraordinarily hard due to the national insularity of the profession. Despite this, within the vast scale of the scholarly exodus, she points out the number of exceptional characters, such as Franz Neumann or Otto Kirchheimer, whose experience in exile produced important contributions to the theory of law and totalitarianism. Kaius Tuori continues, in Chapter 2, on the impact of the exile experience in Britain on three prominent Romanists: Fritz Schulz, Fritz Pringsheim and David Daube. He argues that the exiles were forced to reimagine their work in a new context, speaking to a new audience and leading to the working through of their experiences and observations both in Germany and Britain. The result was a surge of unconventional and creative scholarship that redefined the field.

In Chapter 3, Lorena Atzeri examines the fundamental role of Francis de Zulueta in shaping the attitudes towards Roman law and totalitarianism in Britain and the reception of exiled Romanists there. An important figure in the resurgence of Roman law in Britain, de Zulueta was a controversial figure, a Spanish conservative and supporter of Franco who nevertheless dedicated himself to aiding exiles from Nazi Germany. Jacob Giltaij, in Chapter 4, compares the contradictions between the legal ideals of Schulz and Franz Wieacker, a younger Romanist working with the Nazis but later fundamental to the creation of the idea of the European legal heritage. Giltaij focuses on the image of the Roman jurist in the works of Schulz and Wieacker, presenting them as opposites in the political spectrum but at the same time sharing a fundamentally similar conception of the Roman jurist as a creative vehicle behind legal change, a central theme in the idea of a shared European legal heritage. In Chapter 5, Dina Gusejnova illustrates how the percolation of contemporary issues through the classical world was not limited to German émigrés in Britain, but was part of a larger academic culture. She raises the example of Baron Taube, a Russian exile writing on the Roman and Byzantine roots of legal internationalism as a counter narrative; Taube was actually an exile in Nazi Germany, not from it.

Beginning the second half of the volume, Johann Chapoutot, in Chapter 6, examines the complicated path of Roman law in Nazi Germany and its development in relation to the alliance with Italy. He demonstrates how the resistance to Roman law stemmed from the ideas of communality and shared ownership of land that were thought to be the essence of Germanic culture. In Chapter 7, Cosimo Cascione shows how the Italian fascists used Rome as their foundational idea and projected that into the national and legal discourse and how it influenced Roman law. Cascione illustrates how the Roman law foundation played a contradictory role in the fascist reverence of *Romanità* and the will to enact a legal revolution and to reject liberalism. In Chapter 8, Hans-Peter Haferkamp takes an example of the principle of fidelity and how its Roman and Germanic roots were balanced during and after the Nazi era in German legal thought. Using the discussions on the principle of *aequitas* and the role of Pringsheim in them, he establishes how the debate on general principles was ongoing even before the Nazi takeover. The fears of the risks that reliance on the general principles would have to the rule of law were then largely realized in the Nazi jurisprudence, where these principles were then utilized to revert the meaning of law. In Chapter 9, Tommaso Beggio focuses on Paul Koschaker, who first presented the common legal roots of Europe as a source of cultural unity. Koschaker is a central character in the formulation of the idea of the crisis of Roman law in the 1930s and equally in creating the response to the crisis in the idea of a cultural unity in law. Far from presenting him as a committed Europeanist, Beggio critically evaluates how Koschaker skilfully navigates between the earlier Europeanist discourses and the Nazi conceptions of European civilization in his defence of Roman law. In Chapter 10, Diego Quaglioni takes a different example of the sense of crisis in the legal tradition in the writings of famous Dutch historian Johan Huizinga. A stern anti-fascist, Huizinga would see the European crisis as a sign of the weakening of Western civilization, and only the restoration of the ideal of humanity and law would create a moment for the restoration of Europe.

Balancing between the themes of rupture and continuity, in Chapter 11, Ville Erkkilä focuses on the thinking of Franz Wieacker and the position of Roman law and legal history in the development of law. He traces the changes in Wieacker's theories after the war years and his re-foundation of law as wisdom, where civilization and heritage were the marks of the advance of rationality and the correct law. Wieacker's theories of the historical nature of law and the legal profession were later fundamental in the formation of the idea of the European legal heritage. In Chapter 12, Paul du Plessis takes a similar stance in Britain, where he traces the way the foundational role of Roman legal tradition was conceived in Scotland in contrast to England. Dismissing the Europeanist theories of Scots law as a model for European integration, du Plessis demonstrates how independent and peculiar the development of the Roman law tradition was in Scotland. In Chapter 13, the connection of history and nationalism takes centre stage as Stefan Berger examines how the search for authenticity and national uniqueness in nationalistic historical writing conflicted with the rise of Europeanist thought after the Second World War. Berger maintains that claiming to be special continues to be a very common theme in nationalistic historiography around Europe; but the linkage between historical writing and identity has evolved in unprecedented ways since the Second World War. What remains to be seen is how these nationalistic conventions of identity and history can be combined with a European narrative.

In the concluding chapter, Bo Stråth presents crisis as a continuum of Europeanist thought, setting the different crises such as the economic crises, value crisis and the crisis of science as generative moments, where responses such as Husserl's crisis of European science create the path forward. Starting from the roots of the European crises of the 1930s, as a value crisis that influenced science, economics and political thought, Stråth presents movements like the Roman law revivalism and ordoliberalism as attempts to find a new path between law, economics and politics in Europe. In his final point, Stråth presents a gloomy picture of the future of Europe in the face of the current financial crises and shows how both ordoliberalism and a retreat to a shared legal heritage are both insufficient: yesterday's answers to a new kind of crisis.

Due to the continuing interest in the history of Nazi Germany and Fascist Italy as well as the roots of the European project of unification, the relevance of these issues extends much beyond the boundaries of Roman law scholarship. The book seeks to move beyond the purely biographical work, attempting to encompass the breadth of the migration of jurists and the intermingling between exiles and those who stayed, their interactions before and after the war. The second critical input the book seeks to make is to address the reaction, largely inspired by Carl Schmitt, to the enthusiasm of the 1990s on European unification. While those works presented a criticism of the enthusiasm of the 1990s (a theme evident in *Darker Legacies of Law in Europe*), this book attempts to provide a critical analysis of the multifaceted consequences of the crisis and reformulation of the European legal heritage. Due to the ongoing crises, there is a clear opening for this kind of argument on the uses of the past and the influence of exile on scholarship. Through both the crisis of the European project and the influx of refugees, the issues analysed have gained a new relevance.

The idea of a return to a shared European legal heritage, one characterized by its foundations in Roman law and the civilian tradition, emerged as a response to a crisis. This crisis was not only brought about by Nazism and fascism; it was equally a response to the crisis of modern society and its values. This response, of looking backwards to see the future, was in many ways conservative and focused on the legal profession as a privileged segment of society. Its original framers, the exiled lawyers and scholars, were concerned with the impact of unchecked political power, not only of tyranny but also of demagogic democracy, in the field of law. The lure of tradition, civilization and culture was in part in their anti-modernity, in the return to a simpler and more refined era. During the post-war years, this traditionalist movement coincided with the European integration and was pushed into the limelight. Resorting to the past as a way to the future was also beneficial to the European project that was struggling with the stubbornness of national traditions and legislation. By resorting to the past, one could gain legitimacy for the project without resorting to references to the legislation emanating from Brussels.

Notes

1 This process of reinterpreting the past for the remaking of the future may be understood through Assmann's term *Mythomotorik*, the complex of narrative symbols and evocative stories that influences the understanding of the present and the future. See Assmann 1992, 2008, 2010.

2 See the different portrayals, for example, in Corcy-Debray 2001 and Grimal, Carcopino, and Ourliac 1981. The Vichy 'National revolution' was defined by anti-communism, anti-Semitism and Anglophobism; its definition of Europe was defined by the same characteristics. See Corcy 2005. After the war, Carcopino was imprisoned and tried, but acquitted due to 'services to the resistance'.

3 Fink 1989: 251. The protection of Marc Bloch has been attributed to the fact that Bloch's father had been Carcopino's teacher. In 1944, Bloch, who had refused to go into exile, was arrested by the Vichy police. He was questioned and shot by the Germans shortly afterwards.

4 Paragraph 19 of the NSDAP party programme from 1920 called for the abolition of 'materialistic' Roman law and its replacement with German national law.

5 Whitman 2003.

6 Just one example is Legrand 1999: 76–7. More groundbreaking is Osler 2007, which exposes the political agenda and its implications for the history of reception.

7 See, for example, Hondius 2011: 3.

8 For a rare level-headed introduction to these different initiatives, see Miller 2012.

9 Eidenmüller et al. 2008. The aim of these projects is the future final Common Frame of Reference that would function as a framework for the harmonization. On the national side, see Comparato 2014.

10 The main points are outlined in Zimmermann 2007. For more emphasis on the tradition, see Zimmermann 2001. On homonymy, see Zimmermann 2002.

11 Wołodkiewicz 2009.

12 See, for example, Tziovas 2014; MacMillan 2009.

13 Beatson and Zimmermann 2004, see also Graham 2002: 777; Lutter, Stiefel and Hoeflich 1993; Breunung and Walther 2012 (second volume forthcoming).

14 Joerges and Ghaleigh 2003. Even more pointedly, Laughland 1998.

15 Zimmermann 2001; Stein 1999; Wieacker 1996. Critical scholars have expressed doubts about the role of Roman law as a foundation for European legal culture; see Wijffels 2013; Osler 1997.

References

Ash, M. G. and Söllner, A., eds. (1996), *Forced Migration and Scientific Change: Émigré German-Speaking Scientists and Scholars after 1933*, New York: Cambridge University Press and the German Historical Institute.

Assmann, J. (1992), 'Frühe Formen politischer Mythomotorik. Fundierende, kontrapräsentische und revolutionäre Mythen', in D. Harth and J. Assmann (eds), *Revolution und Mythos*, 39–61, Frankfurt: Fischer.

Assmann, J. (2008), 'Communicative and Cultural Memory', in A. Erll and A. Nünning (eds), *Cultural Memory Studies: An International and Interdisciplinary Handbook*, 109–18, Berlin: Walter de Gruyter.

Assmann, J. (2010), 'Memory, Narration, Identity: Exodus as a Political Myth', in H. Liss and M. Oeming (eds), *Literary Construction of Identity in the Ancient World*, 3–18, Winona Lake, IN: Eisenbrauns.

Beatson, J. and Zimmermann, R., eds. (2004), *Jurists Uprooted: German-Speaking Émigré Lawyers in Twentieth Century Britain*, Oxford and New York: Oxford University Press.

Breunung, L. and Walther, M. (2012), *Die Emigration deutscher Rechtswissenschaftler ab 1933*, vol. 1, Berlin: De Gruyter.

Breunung, L. and Walther, M. (forthcoming), *Die Emigration deutscher Rechtswissenschaftler ab 1933*, vol. 2, Berlin: De Gruyter.

Comparato, G. (2014), *Nationalism and Private Law in Europe*, Oxford: Hart.

Corcy, S. (2005), *La vie culturelle sour l'Occupation*, Paris: Perrin.

Corcy-Debray, S. (2001), *Jérôme Carcopino, un historien à Vichy*, Paris: Éditions L'Harmattan.

Duranti, M. (2017), *The Conservative Human Rights Revolution: European Identity, Transnational Politics, and the Origins of the European Convention*, Oxford: Oxford University Press.

Eckermann, J. P. (1971), *Conversations with Goethe*, London: Dent.

Eidenmüller, H., Faust, F., Grigoleit, H. C., Jansen, N., Wagner, G. and Zimmermann, R. (2008), 'The Common Frame of Reference for European Private Law - Policy Choices and Codification Problems', *Oxford Journal of Legal Studies*, 28 (4): 659–708.

Fermi, L. (1968), *Illustrious Immigrants: The Intellectual Migration from Europe 1930–1941*, Chicago: University of Chicago Press.

Fink, C. (1989), *Marc Bloch: A Life in History*, Cambridge and New York: Cambridge University Press.

Graham, K. (2002), 'The Refugee Jurist and American Law Schools, 1933-1941', *American Journal of Comparative Law*, 50: 777–818.

Grimal, P., Carcopino, C. and Ourliac, P. (1981), *Jérôme Carcopino: un historien au service de l'Humanisme*, Paris: Les Belles Lettres.

Hondius, E. (2011), 'Towards a European Civil Code', in A. Hartkamp, M. W. Hesselink, E. Hondius, C. Mak and E. Du Perron (eds), *Towards a European Civil Code*, 4th edn, 3–25, Alphen aan den Rijn: Kluwer Law International.

Joerges, C. and Ghaleigh, N. S. (2003), *Darker Legacies of Law in Europe*, Oxford: Hart.

Kaelble, H. (2001), *Europäer über Europa: Die Entstehung des europäischen Selbstverständnisses im 19. und 20. Jahrhundert*, Frankfurt and New York: Campus Verlag.

Laughland, J. (1998), *Tainted Source: The Undemocratic Origins of the European Idea*, London: Sphere.

Legrand, P. (1999), *Fragments on Law-as-Culture*, Zwolle: Tjeenk Willink.

Lutter, M., Stiefel, E. C. and Hoeflich, M. H., eds. (1993), *Der Einfluß deutscher Emigranten auf die Rechtsentwicklung in den USA und in Deutschland*, Tübingen: Mohr Siebeck.

MacMillan, M. (2009), *The Uses and Abuses of History*, London: Profile Books.

Miglietta, M. and Santucci, G., eds. (2009), *Diritto romano e regimi totalitari nel '900 Europeo*, Trento: Università degli Studi di Trento.

Miller, L. (2012), 'The Notion of European Private Law', in M. Lobban and J. Moses (eds), *The Impact of Ideas on Legal Development*, 265–85, Cambridge and New York: Cambridge University Press.

Nelis, J. (2007), 'Constructing Fascist Identity: Benito Mussolini and the Myth of *Romanità*', *Classical World*, 100: 391–415.

Osler, D. (1997), 'The Myth of European Legal History', *Rechtshistorisches Journal*, 16: 393–410.

Osler, D. (2007), 'The Fantasy Men', *Rechtsgeschichte*, 10: 169–90.
Pagden, A. (2002), 'Introduction', in A. Pagden (ed.), *The Idea of Europe: From Antiquity to the European Union*, 1–31, Cambridge and New York: Cambridge University Press.
Rachlin, R. D. (2013), 'Roland Freisler and the *Volksgerichthof*', in A. E. Steinweis and R. D. Rachlin (eds), *The Law in Nazi Germany: Ideology, Opportunism, and the Perversion of Justice*, 63–87, New York: Berghahn Books.
Rösch, F. (2014), *Émigré Scholars and the Genesis of International Relations: A European Discipline in America?*, London: Palgrave Macmillan.
Schulz-Forberg, H. and Stråth, B. (2010), *The Political History of European Integration: The Hypocrisy of Democracy-through-market*, London: Routledge.
Stein, P. (1999), *Roman Law in European History*, Cambridge and New York: Cambridge University Press.
Thornhill, C. (2014), 'Fascism and European State Formation: The Crisis of Constituent Power', in M. Madsen and C. Thornhill (eds), *Law and the Formation of Modern Europe: Perspectives from the Historical Sociology of Law*, 29–76, Cambridge: Cambridge University Press.
Tomkins, F. J. and Jencken, H. D. (1870), *A Compendium of the Modern Roman Law, Founded Upon the Treatises of Puchta, von Vangerow, Arndts, Franz Moehler, and the Corpus Juris Civilis*, London: Butterworths.
Tziovas, D., ed. (2014), *Re-imagining the Past: Antiquity and Modern Greek Culture*, Oxford: Oxford University Press.
Voet, J. (1955), *The Selective Voet; Being the Commentary on the Pandects, Paris Edition of 1829, and the Supplement to that Work by Johannes van der Linden*, Durban: Butterworth.
Whitman, J. Q. (2003), 'Long Live the Hatred of Roman Law!', *Yale Law School, Public Law Working Paper No. 36.*
Wieacker, F. (1996), *A History of Private Law in Europe: With Particular Reference to Germany*, Oxford: Clarendon Press.
Wijffels, A. (2000), 'A New Software-Package for an Outdated Operating System?', in M. Van Hoecke and F. Ost (eds), *The Harmonisation of European Private Law*, 101–6, Oxford: Hart.
Wijffels, A. (2013), 'Le ius commune européen: Mythe ou référentiel indifférencié des discours sur la formation d'un droit européen?', in B. Bernabé and O. Camy (eds), *Les mythes de fondation et l'Europe*, 87–101, Dijon: Editions Universitaires de Dijon.
Wołodkiewicz, W. (2009), 'Il diritto romano nei paesi del "socialismo reale" ed il cambiamento delle opinioni dopo il crollo del sistema totalitario', in M. Miglietta and G. Santucci (eds), *Diritto romano e regimi totalitari nel '900 europeo. Atti del seminario internazionale (Trento 20–21 ottobre 2006)*, 145–73, Trento: Università degli Studi di Trento.
Zimmermann, R. (2001), *Roman Law, Contemporary Law, European Law: The Civilian Tradition Today*, Oxford: Oxford University Press.
Zimmermann, R. (2002), 'Europa und das römische Recht', *Archiv für die civilistische Praxis*, 202: 243–316.
Zimmermann, R. (2007), 'Römisches Recht und Europäische Kultur', *JuristenZeitung*, 62 (1): 1–12.
Zimmermann, R. (2011), 'Roman Law and the Harmonization of Private Law in Europe', in A. Hartkamp, M. W. Hesselink, E. Hondius, C. Mak and E. Du Perron (eds), *Towards a European Civil Code*, 4th edn, 27–54, Alphen aan den Rijn: Kluwer Law International.

1

The Impact of Exile on Law and Legal Science 1934–64

Magdalena Kmak[1]

Introduction

According to the survey 'List of Displaced German Scholars' compiled by the *Notgemeinschaft deutscher Wissenschaftler im Ausland* together with the London Academic Council, as many as 1,639 German scholars lost their positions in the first half of the 1930s. This number grew to over 2,000 after the German annexation of Austria (Krohn 1993: 12; Ash and Söllner 1996: 7). Over a hundred of those who lost their academic positions were lawyers, which constituted about 26 per cent of the law faculties' staff (Beatson and Zimmermann 2004: 51). About 60 per cent of scholars dismissed from German universities in the 1930s went into exile (Krohn 1993: 15).

Despite assistance by individuals and refugee relief organizations, scholars in exile were often forced on arrival to cope with anti-Semitism and the impact of the Great Depression, both of which significantly influenced universities' ability and willingness to accept them. Thus for many, exile meant not only loss of scholarly prestige and academic position but also often loss of livelihood, impoverishment and the need to remain at the mercy of others. In addition, émigrés had to overcome not only the language barrier and differences in education and teaching traditions but also a more general rejection of German culture as broadly understood due to its association with the rise of Nazism and fascism (Greenberg 1987; Coser 1984; Fermi 1968). This experience had a significant transformative impact on the work of émigré scholars.

This chapter constitutes an attempt to achieve a more comprehensive understanding of these scholars' experience of exile and its role in the development of scientific legal thought. That task requires a focus on the conditions of knowledge production and the way disciplinary methodologies were transformed under the circumstances of exile. This approach necessitates going beyond the perception, long dominating in exile studies, that treats the transfer of knowledge under exile as one-sided and static. Instead, and without forgetting its traumatic circumstances, exile needs also to be perceived as a formative and dynamic process (Konuk 2005: 32; Burke 2016: 39). In other words, we need to treat exile as a practice through which knowledge is produced and to understand the workings, effects and implications of exile in relation to the life of émigré scholars and their scientific work (see Aradau 2014: 8). The point of departure for a study of the impact of exile on scientific thought is the theory of acculturation, broadly understood as a mutual process of cultural interchange between minority and majority cultures (Strauss 1991: 82; Ash and Söllner 1996: 12), leading to the deprovincialization of thought and knowledge (Tillich 1961: 139). In particular, a scholar's exposure to alternative styles of thought and exposure of the host society to new ideas and knowledges constituted, according to Burke, double deprovincialization (Burke 2016: 40). This approach, however, needs to be expanded to encompass other aspects of exile, including, for instance, its political context or the fact that scientific and cultural exchange happened not only between the exiles and the staff of the host universities or society in general but also between the exiles themselves in such institutions as, for instance, the University in Exile (Camurri 2014).

This chapter follows the journey of émigré scholars and introduces the reader to the reasons, mechanisms and repercussions of exile on legal science, taking as its main case study émigré law scholars from Nazi Germany to the UK and the United States. To be sure, the experience of scholars from Germany is one of many in the twentieth century (see, for instance, Fermi 1968; Camurri 2014). However, the choice of focus for this study is based, on the one hand, on the breadth of available archival and secondary materials, which allows us to undertake the difficult task of tracing the role of exile in the development of scientific thought. As Kaius Tuori points out in Chapter 2 of this book, the difficulty of such a study lies in the fact that in most cases the émigrés themselves have not reflected on the impact of forced displacement on their work. For that reason, access to archival materials such as private correspondence or existing biographies and studies and scholarship itself is crucial. On the other hand, however, despite the vast array of research on immigration from Nazi Germany in general, and on the fate and impact of German refugee scholars in particular that has already been conducted, many aspects of exile remain unstudied (see Camurri 2014). Even though some studies of the impact of exile on particular disciplines and the role of exile in fostering new knowledge have recently been published (Rösch 2014) existing scholarly analyses of the impact of émigré scholars on law have primarily been conducted in the form of biographical studies (Mattei 1994). For example, *Der Einfluß deutscher Emigranten auf die Rechtsentwicklung in den USA und in Deutschland* contains chapters focusing on thirty-nine individual scholars and their impact on American law (Lutter, Stiefel and Hoeflich 1993) while *Jurists Uprooted* presents biographies of sixteen refugee and émigré legal scholars and their impact on the development of English law (Beatson and Zimmermann 2004). Chapters usually focus on individuals' concrete scholarly achievements and their dissemination within the discipline (Lutter, Stiefel and Hoeflich 1993). Overall, these studies are fragmented and lack a carefully elaborated socio-legal framework. They are also often written by scholars' students, who display a tendency to glorify their teachers. This article, however, shifts the focus of the study from individuals to the phenomenon of exile itself. It is grounded in the claim that the practical experience of exile has had a critical impact on the development of legal thinking and on shaping post-war Europe. Such an impact of exile on science has also been acknowledged by migrants themselves. Many asserted that they would not have accomplished as much as they had if they had remained in their home countries (Fermi 1968: 16; Hughes 1975: 3). Moreover, it has been this 'interstitial or boundary situation' that stood behind their creative force (Fleming and Bailyn 1969: 8). For instance, Paul Tillich pointed out in a lecture how exile had deprovincionalized him and his thought (Tillich 1961: 139), and Theodore Adorno remarked that due to exile in the United States he became 'inclined … towards critical scrutiny' (Hughes 1975: 3). Additionally, the most recent study on the impact of the experience of exile on historiography underlines the 'potential of exile for fostering innovation and cross-fertilization' (Berger and De Baets 2016: 16), which occurs in three dimensions: 'mediation between the cultures of the exile's homeland and the host country; distanciation from both cultures, especially liberation from the conventional wisdom current in the host country; and the hybridization of different styles of thought resulting from these cultural encounters' (Burke 2016: 39 and 44).

However, to understand the scope of the impact of exile on development of law, one needs first to analyse the different aspects of the exile experience (Camurri 2014). For that reason, the first part of this chapter focuses on the reasons for and mechanisms of exile, the loss of position and expropriation of property, the processes of leaving, the networks and societies that helped scholars before leaving and while in exile and their personal integration in their receiving countries. Secondly, one needs also to understand the relationship between exile and science, the latter to be approached not only from the perspective of a scientific discipline but also from the perspective of the individual intellectual trajectory (Ash and Söllner 1996: 14). Therefore, the second part of the chapter traces the academic careers of legal scholars in exile. The focus there is on the academic integration of émigrés, the role of their intellectual heritage and scientific agenda, as well as the impact of American legal thought, academic culture and scientific methodologies and, finally, political developments in influencing the directions of their research (see, for instance, Rösch 2014: 6). In particular, this part of the chapter focuses on scholars coming to terms with their experience and striving to understand the development and operations of the totalitarian state and the threats it poses for the future. Here, the perception is of a marginalized position and the need to start afresh, without the support of one's own scholarly environment, as critical for development of émigrés' scientific thoughts. In concrete terms, this approach points towards the need to unearth a shift in the academic work and career of émigré scholars as a result of exile and to identify the influence of this intellectual turn on scholars' work and understanding of their own discipline.

The mechanisms of exile

Exile can be understood as an embodied condition of forced displacement from one's own country requiring a search for safe havens elsewhere. According to Camurri, 'The meaning of exile in the 20th century essentially indicates the experience of fracture, of displacement from the motherland, of alienation lived as a loss, an injury' (2014). Despite the fracture or loss brought about by exile, the process of exile itself also constitutes an intermesh of various mechanisms of leaving, travelling, arriving and coping. This part of the chapter looks at the mechanisms of exile from Nazi

Germany. The focus is, on the one hand, on the social, political and legal reasons for leaving the home country and the mechanisms of doing so and, on the other hand, on mechanisms facilitating arrival and personal integration, including networks of assistance, institutions and organizations that helped those in exile.

Dismissals and expropriations

Even though Hitler's political support in November 1932 had dropped to 32 per cent, he was not marginalized as predicted but through a number of legal and extra-legal measures took over power in Germany. His rise to power brought to surface the anti-Jewish sentiments permeating German society. Discrimination and boycotts of Jewish shops, offices, doctors and lawyers started immediately after the elections of 5 March 1933. Expropriations, arrests and emigration followed (Neumann 1966). Many of those who did not support anti-Jewish measures remained silent under social pressure. The Act 'for the restoration of the professional legal service' (*Gesetz zur Wiederherstellung des Berufsbeamtentums*, shortened to *Berufsbeamtengesetz*) and other decrees that followed effectively eliminated Jews from public life (Beatson and Zimmermann 2004: 3–6; Neumann 1966: 111–20).

These measures culminated in the Nuremberg Laws in September 1935 stripping Germans of Jewish origin of citizenship of the Reich and aiming to protect German blood and German honour by instituting the crime of race defilement. These laws were also accompanied by expropriations of material possessions and measures aiming to liquidate available sources of income. Jews found themselves without income and material resources after the *Reichkristallnacht* on 7 November 1938 and the decree on 'elimination of Jews from German economic life' (*Verordnung zur Ausschaltung der Juden aus dem deutschen Wirtschaftsleben*). Even those leaving the country were obliged to pay a special tax on account of leaving Germany. It is estimated that emigrating Jews during 1933–7 lost from 30 to 50 per cent of their assets and during 1937–9 from 60 to 100 per cent (Beatson and Zimmermann 2004: 34–6; Neumann 1966: 116–20).

The Nazi takeover also had an immediate impact on the German universities, including the law faculties. Even though some scholars, for instance those serving in the army during the First World War, were protected by exceptions to the Law for the Restoration of the Professional Civil Service (*Gesetz zur Wiederherstellung des Berufsbeamtentums*), many were dismissed or forced to retire, while others resigned in protest. One of the first victims of these policies at the University of Berlin was professor of Roman law Fritz Schulz (focused on in greater detail in Chapters 2 and 4 in this book). His salary was reduced and he was asked to stop giving lectures and holding seminars. The final measure against him was early retirement. Despite this discrimination, many distinguished scholars did not emigrate until the last moment. For example, Schulz left only in April 1939 for the Netherlands, from where he left for the UK four months later (Beatson and Zimmermann 2004: 47).

Unlike in the case of these older and more established professors, the situation was different for younger scholars and those termed by Krohn as *double outsiders* – scholars of Jewish origin holding socialist or liberal views. For them, the beginning of the 1930s meant living in constant uncertainty in a non-tolerant Weimar Republic. For instance, both Otto Kirchheimer and Franz Neumann, scholars active in the labour unions and Social Democratic Party, began studying English intensively as early as 1932 to prepare themselves for emigration. These individuals were among the first to leave the Nazi Republic after 1933 (Krohn 1993: 15). The chairs and positions vacated by Jewish scholars were given to their Aryan colleagues, none of whom protested against the dismissals. Finally, any resistance to these actions from the university leadership stopped after the introduction of the principle of Führer leadership (*Führerprinzip*) in all academic institutions in October 1933. This resulted in changes in higher university positions for those politically sympathetic to the new regime (Beatson and Zimmermann 2004: 31).

Overall, according to reports by aid committees, about 1,200 academics lost their jobs in Germany during 1933 in consequence of the Nazi takeover. This number rose to 1,700 after inclusion of those who lost their positions towards the end of the 1930s and to 2,100 after the annexation of Austria. With other academic professionals this number amounted to 7,500, and with artists, writers and other freelancers the number possibly amounted to as many as 12,000 (Krohn 1993: 12).

Emigration

As a consequence of these changes, Jews and political opponents of National Socialism started to leave Germany from 1933. 37,000 left in 1933 alone, and many tens of thousands left in the following years, peaking at 78,000 in 1939. Fewer people were able to leave during the war: These numbers amounted to some 30,000 between 1940 and 1945. In addition, many Germans were leaving for political reasons. However, unlike Jews, who seemed to be encouraged to leave Germany, the Nazis did not want their political opponents abroad and in consequence they were under heavy surveillance by the Gestapo, kidnapped or assassinated (Beatson and Zimmermann 2004: 43–4). Overall, even though it is very difficult to make precise statements about the extent of emigration after 1933, the high commissioner for refugees estimated the numbers of all exiles as approaching 500,000 by the time the Nazi Reich collapsed (Krohn 1993: 15).

Before the 1930s the main motive for scholarly emigration was an opportunity to find teaching and research positions due to their limited availability in Europe. However, after Hitler's rise to power increasingly large numbers of European scholars and intellectuals were forced to leave due to dismissals and persecution. It is assumed that 60 per cent of scholars dismissed in the 1930s went into exile (Krohn 1993: 15). In the case of law faculties, the number amounted to sixty-nine individuals, of whom sixty were of Jewish faith or origin. Eight out of twenty-eight of those who did not emigrate returned to the universities after the war. The others died. Out of forty-four legal scholars removed from office for political reasons, nine decided to emigrate. Of the twenty-eight who remained in Germany, eighteen survived and twelve went back into law teaching after the war, mostly to their old posts (Beatson and Zimmermann 2004: 53).[2] Overall, about 2,000 German scholars left the country (Krohn 1993: 12; Ash and Söllner 1996: 7; Fermi 1968: 13). The exodus of German scholars was often compared to the exodus of the Greek upper classes after colonization of the Byzantine Empire by the Ottomans. Indeed, in such disciplines as social sciences and economics, dismissals and exile often meant the expulsion of entire research traditions (Krohn 1993: 13).

The emigration path of those who escaped led first to neighbouring countries – France, the Netherlands or Czechoslovakia. For instance, before reaching the United States, Hannah Arendt, after being arrested by Gestapo for helping her Marxist friends and colleagues, escaped to France, where she ended up being detained in the women's concentration camp in Gurs (Coser 1984: 191). For those wanting to escape Continental Europe, the route through Spain and Portugal was for a long time the only way to do so. In particular, those caught in southern France were forced to cross the Pyrenees to reach Lisbon. The United States admitted 1,300,000 persons, while 759,000 ended up in Latin America. The UK sheltered 80,000 refugees, while 55,000–60,000 emigrated to Palestine. Additionally, some 100 scholars found positions in Turkey, where Kemal

Figure 1 An immigration officer checks the names of refugees escaping Nazi persecution. Photo by Bettmann via Getty Images.

Ataturk had introduced a programme of modernization and Westernization of Turkish universities, based largely on the German scholarship tradition (Konuk 2005: 35). However, some countries, such as Switzerland, Sweden and South Africa, closed their borders to refugees immediately or later on. Finally, the Soviet Union accepted only communists (Beatson and Zimmermann 2004: 40–1).

The emigration of Jews from Nazi Germany met a mixed reception in the receiving countries. For instance, whereas British migration policy remained, with some exceptions, unchanged after 1933 so that Germans and Austrians did not require a visa to go there (Beatson and Zimmermann 2004: 41–3), in the United States the National Origin Act of 1924 introduced the principle of national origin (which after heated debate entered into force in 1929), creating an obstacle for those in need to leave. According to the principle, the maximum number of visas issued to immigrants from all countries except the Americas was set at 150,000. The Act, however, allowed for exceptions and grant of non-quota immigrant visas to ministers of any religion, bona fide teachers of higher education who would be teaching in the United States, and to their families allowing them to obtain a visa to the United States more easily. These measures tipped the balance from immigration by the unskilled to immigration by the educated. Those immigrants became, in the words of Fermi, 'doubly privileged' (Fermi 1968: 24–6). However, despite these exceptional measures, commentators point towards a strong resistance to immigration in the US State Department, which was also creating obstacles to the grant of visas to refugee scholars. These sentiments did not change even after a request from President Roosevelt himself to treat refugees with special consideration (Krohn 1993: 87–8).

Consequently, even though the United States became the most popular country of destination for refugee scholars, most of them decided to first stay in Europe, in particular in the UK, or went to Palestine or Turkey. The strict laws, the small number of positions for émigré scholars and the scholars' own negative attitude and scepticism towards the United States and American culture influenced scholars' choices (Krohn 1993: 16). These approaches changed, however, as a result of problems with integration and belonging in European countries, which turned out to be less of a problem in the United States (Neumann 1961: 18). Additionally, excitement about the New Deal and an increase in assistance from donors and foundations (for instance the Rockefeller Foundation) influenced scholars' choices. Geographically, in the United States, the journey of most scholars ended at the US East Coast, which ever since the seventeenth century had traditionally functioned as the final destination for German-speaking immigrants. It was also there that assistance for refugee scholars was the most developed and where such scholarly havens had been created as the University in Exile at the New School for Social Research or the Institute for Advanced Study at Princeton University (Coser 1984; Fermi 1968; Krohn 1993).

Arrival and support

Rescue operations and assistance agencies both in Europe and beyond supported refugees to a remarkable extent (Camurri 2014). Internationally, assistance to refugees from Germany was provided to a certain extent by the League of Nations, which in

1933 established the institution of High Commission for Refugees from Germany. The Commission not only pursued diplomatic negotiations with Germany but also provided documents to refugees such as residence and work permits, identity and travel documents. Additionally, the Committee of Experts for Academic and Kindred Refugees from Germany was established with the aim of coordinating national academic committees. In practice, however, the Commission was not legally or organizationally part of the League of Nations, and in reality it exercised only moral authority (Krohn 1993: 25–6). In consequence, the first high commissioner, James G. McDonald, resigned due to dissatisfaction with the League's failure 'to remove or mitigate the causes which create German refugees' (Fermi 1968: 71). It was therefore for national agencies and institutions to assist refugee scholars.

In Europe the main assistance agencies included the *Notgemeinschaft deutscher Wissenschaftler im Ausland* (Emergency Assistance Organization for German Scientists), which was formed by German Scholars in Switzerland. Funding for its activities came from contributions from displaced scholars themselves. The organization's most widely known achievement was a detailed list of 1,639 German scholars displaced from their posts, published in 1936 by the Rockefeller Foundation. A second agency was the *Comité International pour le Placement des Intellectuels Réfugiés* (International Committee for Placement of Refugee Intellectuals) in Geneva, consisting of representatives of many Western countries, including the United States. The Committee's competence was not limited to scholars only (Fermi 1968: 62–3). In addition, a number of support bodies were created in countries such as England, France, Belgium, Holland, Denmark and Sweden. In England, the Academic Assistance Council was established with the aim of assisting 'those university teachers and investigators who, on grounds of religion, political opinion or race, were unable to carry on their work in their own country'. In practice the Committee acted as a specialized employment agency. Its role was to collect data on exiled scholars and to pass those data to other organizations and institutions of higher learning (Krohn 1993: 27). By November 1938 the Council had placed 655 scholars in both permanent and temporary positions in 36 different countries including the United States (Fermi 1968: 63). The Committee also paid a small living allowance to refugees without employment. Funding for its operations was raised from among the public and academia. Many members of British and American universities as well as émigrés already in Britain voluntarily taxed themselves (from 2 to 5 per cent of their salaries) for this purpose. The Council helped not only German scholars but also scholars displaced from other countries such as Austria, Hungary, Czechoslovakia, Italy, Poland and Spain. It even bypassed official American institutions and sent scholars directly to the United States. By 1935 the Academic Assistance Council had registered 1,200 names and by 1939, 2,541 (Fermi 1968: 64–5).

Turkey presents an interesting example of support to refugee scholars from Nazi Germany after Ataturk's decision to westernize Turkish universities. In 1933, the new University of Istanbul employed around fifty German scholars for a period of five years. Additionally, the new University of Ankara employed another group of German scholars. In total, a hundred academic teachers were placed in different universities in Turkey. At the beginning, many of the academic positions were negotiated with the Turkish government through the *Notgemeinschaft* organization. However, later nominations had to be agreed on by the Nazi government, which limited the chances of refugee scholars to obtain positions. However, most of the Germans could not adjust and left Turkey after their contracts expired (Fermi 1968: 66–70; Konuk 2005: 33–6).

In the United States, excitement at receiving quality scholars competed with the effects of economic depression. To explain the situation in contemporary terms, strong push factors clashed with a general lack of pull factors. Very often, lack of available funds to employ émigrés was often combined at the universities with xenophobia, in particular among unemployed, mostly young, scholars (Fermi 1968: 72). In consequence, the United States received proportionally the least number of refugees in comparison to European countries. In opinion polls, over two-thirds of respondents were against relaxing the immigration rules, which did not happen, even after the defeat of France in 1940. For that reason most of the aid for refugees was in private hands, including numerous Jewish organizations and Christian churches, Quakers and other charity organizations (Krohn 1993: 26).

However, thanks to the involvement of these individuals and donors, a number of institutions providing assistance to refugee scholars had been created. First, in 1930 Abraham Flexner established the Institute for Advanced Study at Princeton. The Institute first focused on assisting scholars of mathematics and economics (for instance it recruited Albert Einstein). However, after 1933 it opened its doors to the humanities as well. The idea behind the Institute was to balance between American and foreign scholars (Fermi 1968: 73).

Another famous institution, the University in Exile, was established in 1933 by Alvin Johnson within the New School for Social Research and was able to operate thanks to private and institutional donations. The main purpose of the University in Exile was to allow continuation of the German research tradition in social sciences. Again, the initial focus of the University on economists was later expanded to other disciplines, and by 1939 the University in Exile was employing thirty-three émigré faculty members (Coser 1984: 102–9). Unfortunately, the efforts of these two institutions to provide safe havens for émigré scholars were not emulated by other universities, which did not wish to accept immigrants. One such example was Harvard University, with its established quota for Jewish students and its professors often expressing pro-Nazi opinions (Krohn 1993: 59–76). In addition, some American universities actively welcomed pro-Nazi scholars on their campuses (Norwood 2011).

These sentiments were, however, mitigated by another institution – the Emergency Committee in Aid of German (Foreign) Displaced Scholars, established in 1933 and consisting of presidents of universities and educational institutions – aiming to coordinate activities supporting persecuted European scholars. The Committee provided scholars with temporary positions of from one to three years at universities across the United States. Thanks to funds raised from private donors and foundations, the Committee helped 335 individuals, contributing financially to scholars' salaries (Fermi 1968: 76–8; Krohn 1993: 27). Finally, the Emergency Rescue Committee for Refugees was established after the fall of France, initiated by those émigrés who were already in the United States. It conducted underground work in Marseilles with the aim of bringing scholars and intellectuals to the United States and rescued up to 1,800 refugees before the office closed in 1942 (Fermi 1968: 85).

One of the most important donors supporting the activities of rescue and relief organizations was the Rockefeller Foundation, which allocated 1.4 million dollars to help displaced scholars. This sum constituted half of the funding raised in the United States for assistance to refugees. One-third of the Foundation's funding went to scholars outside the United States, and in terms of disciplines the biggest share of funding went to the social sciences (for instance 540,235 dollars went to the University in Exile). However the Foundation's considerable financial support provided during the first few years after 1933 did not result in increased numbers of scholars placed by the Foundation with US universities. This was because the Foundation supported scholars in Europe through its office in Paris. However, the Rockefeller Foundation, supporting such institutions as the Frankfurt School, with many Jewish scholars, was also trapped between the wish to support innovative research and the fear of having a negative effect on public opinion in Germany. After 1933 the Foundation's employees were even expressing pro-Nazi sentiments (Krohn 1993: 31–6).

To sum up, despite existing anti-Jewish sentiment, support for scholars was quite extensive. However, this support decreased after 1937 and 1938 when the number of scholars from other countries such as Austria, Czechoslovakia and Poland grew rapidly. Official channels, however, were not the only way of obtaining assistance – personal relations were also of great importance when selecting foreign scholars. Those who had been in the United States on a previous visit had the best chance of obtaining an academic position. In addition, personal connections with those already in America, who could provide some support or reference letters, were very helpful. In practice, those scholars with established professional or family contacts were subjected to less strict selection processes (Fermi 1968: 82–4). On the other hand, young scholars were in the most difficult situation because of the fear of encroaching on professional opportunities for young American scholars. Therefore, assistance was restricted to scholars over thirty years old. Only the Oberlander Trust did not follow this rule and gave small grants to younger émigrés (Krohn 1993: 29).

The impact of exile on legal science

Assessing scientific change under circumstances of exile requires not only analysis of the mechanisms of exile but also its relationship with science. According to Ash and Söllner, the most interesting scientific change occurred not within scientific disciplines but 'above' and 'below' them, a change that can be traced in detail only on the level of research groups or individual biographies (Ash and Söllner 1996: 14). This approach corresponds with the understanding of exile as individualized experience. As underlined by Turton studying forced displacement, 'By emphasising the common experience and common needs of forced migrants, we risk seeing them as a homogeneous mass of needy and passive victims. The truth is that there is no such thing as the "Refugee Experience" … and there is therefore no such thing as "the refugee voice": there are only the experiences, and the voices, of refugees' (Turton 2003: 7). For that reason, to avoid simplification (see Camurri 2014), over-interpretation and projection, research into the impact of exile on science requires extensive archival research of scholars' private correspondence, courses and lecture notes or notes from meetings and conferences, in addition to scrutiny of their scientific writings.

Coping and integration

Every individual copes with the experience of exile and loss in a different, idiosyncratic manner. Scholars, while no exception, are forced to grapple not only with human and material losses but also with the loss of intellectual territory, language, audience or status (Neumann 1961: 12). German-speaking scholars had in addition to redefine their relationship to German legal culture and scholarly tradition, which had often been renounced in the United States as complicit in the rise of Nazism and fascism (Greenberg 1987). Finally, Jewish scholars had also been subjected to anti-Semitism in their countries of arrival. As a result, many were unable to acquire the same status as in their home country, which often constituted a source of frustration. Scholars were also themselves widely diverse in relation to their backgrounds, political opinions and racial origins, which affected their adaptation (Coser 1984: 4).

Émigré lawyers and legal scholars in particular suffered the greatest difficulties (Fermi 1968: 79) due to minimal resemblance between German and American legal traditions and education. Indeed, as pointed out by Graham, by the end of the 1930s placing foreign jurists in US law schools was nearly impossible (Graham 2002), and most of them were in practice faced with the need to start afresh. In her detailed study of intellectual migration from Europe to the United States, Fermi devotes only one-and-a-half pages to those legal scholars who found academic posts at US law schools. According to her, the successful ones were specialists in branches of law that were of interest in the United States such as comparative, Roman or international law, mentioning only six names: Eberhard Bruck, Adolf Berger, Arthur Nussbaum, Friedrich Kessler, Max Rheinstein and Hans Zeisel. Other sources mention additional names but the list remains rather short (Stiefel and Mecklenburg 1991). Excepting these few, scholars who eventually found academic positions in law had first to re-educate themselves and complete law studies in the United States. For instance, Edgar Bodenheimer (who obtained his doctoral degree from the University of Heidelberg and in 1966 became professor of law at the University of California, Davis), after arriving in the United States, completed basic law studies at the University of Washington (Stiefel and Mecklenburg 1991: 56–7). Other scholars – the biggest group – rebranded themselves and took positions at political or social sciences departments (Coser 1984: 6). Indeed, out of sixty-four émigré scholars that Söllner identifies as holding a teaching and research position in political science in the United States, thirty-three obtained their doctorates in law (Söllner 1996: 250, 271).

For example, Hans Kelsen was able to find a stable position in US academia only at the department of political science in Berkeley. In the words of his Austrian friends, 'In America he has not done as well as in Europe and is not as highly regarded or widely known' (Fermi 1968: 351). Yet what Scheuerman refers to as 'Professor Kelsen's Amazing Disappearing Act' (2014) did not pertain to Kelsen alone. Superficially it indeed seems as if the German legal tradition simply vanishes into thin air when coming into contact with its American counterpart. But a closer look at the lives and work of the émigré scholars reveals that their legal background continued to underlie and orient their scholarly work. More importantly, this turn had a tremendous influence on the development of law and on the understanding of the role of law in society.

According to statistics, of sixty-nine legal scholars from Germany, forty-eight were able to continue their academic career in the host country (mostly the United States or the UK) (Beatson and Zimmermann 2004: 54), and they were mostly active in areas other than doctrinal fields of German private law, public law or criminal law. For instance, both Franz Neumann and Otto Kirchheimer, who in Germany were practising lawyers specializing in labour law, joined the Frankfurt Institute of Social Research in exile, first in London and later at Columbia University (Ruckert 1993), subsequently obtaining academic positions in political science at the New School and Columbia University (Stiefel and Mecklenburg 1991).

Finally, research on law was not only the domain of legal scholars working in both law and political science departments. Another group of scholars did not come from the legal tradition but started to work on law as a result of their exile experience. One of those persons was Hannah Arendt, who in exile in the United States wrote extensively about exile, political justice and human rights (Arendt 1999, 2006). Her writings clearly indicate her turn from philosopher to political scientist deeply interested in such questions as the origins of totalitarianism and the role of human rights.

So, what were the conditions of personal and academic integration and acculturation for scholars in exile? First, immigrants met a mixed reaction and often anti-Semitic sentiments, both at universities and in society in general. In the UK, refugees other than lawyers and doctors were in principle welcomed. Even though a societal tendency to accept anti-Semitic stereotypes has been noted by commentators, this was mitigated by the characteristically British stance of 'moderation and tolerant compromise' (Beatson and Zimmermann 2004: 78–9). Nevertheless, many German refugees, including such scholars as Fritz Schulz and Fritz Pringsheim, were interned on the Isle of Man as 'enemy aliens'. Additionally, many scholars, such as Franz Neumann, who spent their first years of exile in the UK, quickly realized that employment opportunities in the UK were severely limited (Jay 1986: xi). In the United States, despite better opportunities, both competition for academic positions and anti-Semitic prejudices were quite prominent. Here the situation was paradoxical. On the one hand, many in the United States believed that the country should quickly reach and invite the best scholars to its own universities as the German education system enjoyed a very high reputation (Greenberg 1987). This approach clashed, however, with isolationism, limits imposed on immigration, anti-Semitism and a difficult economic situation at the universities resulting from the great depression (Krohn 1993: 26). On the one hand, those scholars who in the UK were perceived as 'insufficiently suitable' due to their inability to adapt were often told to try their chances in the United States, where acculturation was much easier (Ash and Söllner 1996: 12). On the other hand, German scholars were perceived with particular suspicion as competitors, especially by younger American scholars. In consequence, many universities deliberately sabotaged efforts to welcome more German scholars. Arriving professors were often caught in what Krohn describes as the 'double handicap' of being both Jews and migrants. In the words of Heilbut,

'Racism was a central fact of American life; below the Mason-Dixon line, it was law.' According to Heilbut, racism seemed so endemic that Franz Neumann even declared that the United States was more anti-Semitic than Germany. 'This was Neumann's way of asserting that the character of his homeland was essentially benign – he contended that Hitler was an aberration – but his statement also expresses the belief, widespread among émigrés, that most Americans shared the Nazis' prejudices' (Heilbut 1997: 50).

Coping mechanisms were also affected by the level of similarity between the home universities and the science and intellectual requirements in exile. Many scholars could not display their talents, skills and achievements in a new language, in a new environment and under the new 'rules of the game' defined by native scholars: 'They often found themselves in the paradoxical situation of feeling superior to the members of the group whose approval or esteem they sought, while the members of the new group frequently perceived them as inferior for not knowing the rules of the game' (Coser 1984: 5).

Coping in a new environment also depended on transferability of skills and knowledge within different disciplines. Adaptation was much easier for natural scientists, or for instance for economists trained in mathematics or those with a neoclassical orientation rather than those trained in historical economics. Besides, scholars representing areas in which they filled a need not previously met, such as psychoanalysis, or in areas where they could relate to an already established tradition, such as social psychology or philosophy, found themselves to be most influential (but see Ash and Söllner 1996). In many cases, however, Americans rejected the orientations of Europeans if there was little in common between German and American science, as occurred, for instance, in the case of gestalt psychology in psychology dominated by behaviourism. In general, scholars outside the natural sciences and engineering (except such well-known figures as Thomas Mann or Albert Einstein) were forced to lower their expectations in order to find any position at all.

Finally, the age and position of scholars constituted another factor in their path to integration. In principle, the older generation was in a much more difficult position than younger scholars, despite the restrictions on admitting scholars younger than thirty. Whereas the latter found it much easier to find their place in American society and, for instance, to acquire new academic degrees, the former struggled to build networks to help them learn about opportunities and navigate between their own demands and societal expectations (Coser 1984: 6–9). This is visible, for instance, in the case of legal scholars such as Edgar Bodenheimer, mentioned earlier, who did not shy away from completing a basic law degree upon arrival in the United States, despite holding a German doctorate in law.

In addition to external conditions, scholars themselves adopted different approaches to their situation in exile and to local scholarship. According to Coser, differences among refugee scholars were quite prominent between 'locals' and 'cosmopolitans' in their professional orientation (Coser 1984: 5). Indeed, analysing the coping mechanisms of scholars in American scientific life, Franz Neumann identified three degrees of scholarly involvement in academia: (1) abandonment of previous intellectual positions and acceptance of a new position without questioning, (2) attachment to own old thought structures with an attempt to change American patterns or, if that failed, retreating into own circles and (3) integration of old tradition and new experiences. According to Neumann, the third position was not only the most difficult but also the most rewarding solution for a scientist. Moreover, the best setting for development of the third type of scholar was in a mixed environment of native and refugee scholars, where émigrés could serve as 'bridges' between the old and the new (Neumann 1961: 20). In such environments, thanks to personal interactions between émigré and local scholars, not only could ideas be exchanged but also the 'tacit knowledge' of modes of working (Ash and Söllner 1996: 13). Unfortunately, some scholars never recovered from the shock connected to the exile experience and remained uprooted and isolated (Krohn 1993: 7). On the other hand, these peculiarities of life and work in exile, coping mechanisms, a marginalized position and the need to start afresh, without the support of one's own scholarly environment were critical for development of émigrés' thought (Rösch 2014: 3; Fleming and Bailyn 1969: 8; Hughes 1975: 2–3).

Scientific developments

The multifaceted relationship between exile and legal scientific thought is visible, for instance, in biographies of scholars focused on in other chapters of this book. They appear for instance in Kaius Tuori's inquiry into the change in scholarship and scientific approaches under the influence of Nazism and exile in the UK in the work of Fritz Schulz, Fritz Pringsheim and David Daube. The shift happened despite scholars' lack of self-awareness and often resulted from the unintended consequences of a move to a different scholarly tradition and work in a different language. The remaining part of the chapter provides initial reflections on how the experience of exile and the need to understand the development and operations of the totalitarian state influenced scientific work. As mentioned earlier, though, more work is needed to fully understand the impact of exile on individual intellectual trajectories of émigré scholars.

As a result of exile, many scholars, including lawyers, felt the need to come to terms with their shocking experiences and to understand the developments that had led to the victory of National Socialism in Germany (Krohn 1993: 130). As noted by Berger and De Baets, 'Those who are on the losing side of history – those defeated in war, those victimized by human rights violations and indeed those forced to leave their homelands – develop an acute sense of the past' (Berger and De Baets 2016: 13). In order to do so they had not only to confront their own intellectual heritage, which, as often claimed, resulted in creation of a totalitarian state (Greenberg 1987) but also to react to various scholarly methodologies and approaches to law and political science developed in the United States, also as a result of war. For instance, lawyers arriving in the United States found themselves in the midst of the debate between legal realists and 'rational absolutists'. This debate, accelerated by the Second World War, often linked legal realism with totalitarianism and marked a shift towards natural-law thinking. Many scholars believed that some sort of 'supralegal moral standard' was needed as a basis for moral judgements (Herget and Wallace 1987: 437). In political science, behaviouralism was the prevalent paradigm, and similarly many émigrés became avid critics of the 'behavioural revolution', turning towards pre-modern ideas such as Christianity or natural law (Ash and Söllner 1996: 248).

A shift to natural law resulting from the experience of totalitarianism and exile is visible, for instance, in the scholarly work of Edgar Bodenheimer. His doctorate, completed in Heidelberg in 1933, focused on the principle of equality in corporate law (Bodenheimer 1933), but already in 1940 he published his best-known treatise in legal philosophy: *Jurisprudence: The Philosophy and Method of Law* (Bodenheimer 1974). According to Durham 'Whatever Bodenheimer's attitude towards natural law may have been before Hitler's rise to power, he has been a dedicated devotee of the doctrine ever since' (Bodenheimer 1993: 136). Bodenheimer continued his work on natural law, justice, rule of law and legal civility until his death in 1991. He clearly saw the link between the positivist denial of values and the risk that 'the human race will fall back into a condition of barbarism and ignorance where unreason will prevail over rationality, and where the dark forces of prejudice may win the battle over humanitarian ideals and the forces of good will and benevolence' (Bodenheimer 1974: 168).

On the other hand, for Schulz and Pringsheim, the experience of persecution in Nazi Germany prompted a turn towards the rule of law, and such virtues as humanism, individualism and freedom stemming from the principles of Roman law, which contrary to the Nazi law they experienced, was oriented towards justice. They were also inclined towards praising the classical Roman legal tradition and its value that was under attack in Nazi Germany (see Chapter 2 in this book).

Besides the focus on questions concerning the origins and characteristics of the totalitarian state and the role of law there, the relationship between law and politics, or the nature of the *Rechtsstaat* or the rule of law, has been enhanced by the turn of many lawyers towards political theory. To be sure, even though political science did not exist as a university discipline in the Weimar Republic, one can notice the politicization of the legal tradition in the work of many scholars of *Staatswissenschaft* (study of public administration), which then formed part of jurisprudence (Ash and Söllner 1996: 248). In addition, before the war many German-speaking scholars maintained scientific contacts with American scholars of political science. However, it seems that only the experience of exile enhanced the turn of lawyers to political science already established as a discipline in the United States.

In particular, it would be hard to imagine Franz Neumann's and Otto Kirchheimer's shift from law to political science without the exile experience. For instance, Neumann's publications before their exile focused on labour law and jurisdiction and constitutional aspects of freedom of association (Neumann 1929, 1931, 1932), but in exile turned to political and legal theory (Neumann 1935, 1936, 1964, 1984, 2009). According to Jay, this turn in Neumann's work would not have been possible without his stay at the London School of Economics under the direction of Harold Laski. The move from Germany to London resulted in lifting Neumann's 'horizons from purely legal questions to more broadly theoretical ones, while at the same time in a more radically leftward direction' as exemplified, for instance, in Neumann's essay 'The Change in the Function of Law in Modern Society' (Jay 1986: xi). And in the United States, it was the tension between Marxism and democratic liberalism that, according to Hughes, constituted the source of Franz Neumann's influence (Hughes 1975: 8).

Despite this turn, both Neumann and Kirchheimer did not renounce their legal background. For instance, Neumann's famous book *Behemoth: The Structure and Practice of National Socialism 1933–1944* (Neumann 1966) – a detailed account of the governmental workings of Nazi Germany – suggested that the Nazi organization of society involved the collapse of traditional ideas of the state, of ideology, of law and of underlying rationality. As he diagnosed, 'In any event, National Socialism is not concerned with legal conformity to the prevailing constitutional system. It substitutes the claim of "legitimacy". A system is "legitimate" when it has an intrinsic justification for existence, in this case, the success of the National Socialist revolution. In other words, the justification of the new constitution lies in its success' (Neumann 1966: 53).

Additionally, as pointed by Donna E. Arzt, 'With Franz Neumann … Kirchheimer added a legal and political focus to the Frankfurt School's analysis of Nazism, which otherwise concentrated on cultural and psycho-social phenomena' (Arzt 1993: 36). His main work of 1961, *Political Justice: The Use of Legal Procedure for Political Ends* (Kirchheimer 1961), controversially grouped together such totalitarian states as Nazi Germany and Stalinist Russia with the United States. As noted by Arzt, this book brought together Kirchheimer's 'knowledge of law and ability to make socio-political sense of legal institutions and processes' (Arzt 1993: 44). In this sense, both Neumann and Kirchheimer themselves acted as a 'bridge' between the science of home and host countries.

Other scholars in exile also focused on the question of totalitarianism. In particular, in her most famous book, *Origins of Totalitarianism* (1985), Hannah Arendt (who turned from philosopher to political scientist interested in questions of the origins of totalitarianism or the role of human rights) dealt with similarities between the political regimes of Nazism and Stalinism, despite their different political and ideological background.

Finally, since émigrés were considered of paramount assistance during the war and in the post-war reformation of Western Germany (Greenberg 2014: 11) and Europe in general, their scholarship and expertise was not only politicized but also used for political purposes (Ash and Söllner 1996: 12–13). A number of scholars such as Herbert Marcuse, Franz Neumann and Otto Kirchheimer were involved in research conducted by the Research and Analysis branch of the Office of Strategic Services (OSS), a US military intelligence organization established during the Second World War. Their role was to write a series of reports on war crimes, de-Nazification and post-war military government. The OSS team, working under the leadership of Neumann (and later Kirchheimer), was responsible for preparation and supervision of various briefs prepared by Justice Jackson's prosecution office. It has been claimed that the theory of anti-Semitism advanced by Neumann at that time heavily influenced the work of the prosecutor's office (Salter 2000: 197–8). According to commentators, the experience of exile described in this chapter often left émigré scholars 'catastrophe-minded' (Coser 1984: 193). Many saw the conditions that would allow a reversion to dictatorship and totalitarianism still firmly in place and feared such a reversal (Hewitson and D'Aura 2012: 71). In particular, many scholars saw the link between Nazi ideology and communism so that in consequence anti-communism often became the ultimate goal of their work for US agencies (Hewitson and D'Aura 2012: 70) or at European universities (Lutter, Stiefel and Hoeflich 1993).

Conclusion

The aim of this chapter was to introduce the reader to the reasons, mechanisms and repercussions of exile through the experience of émigré law scholars from Nazi Germany in the UK and the United States. The chapter has shown the origins, mechanisms and effects of exile and reflected on its impact on academic scholarship. In particular, it perceived a marginalized position and the need to start afresh, without the support of one's own scholarly environment, as critical for development of émigrés' scientific thinking.

Tracing the shift in scientific work to the result of exile is difficult as it is embedded in various events and experiences, starting not only with scholars' scientific achievements and their position in academia but also with their personality, adaptability to new circumstances and sometimes connections and sheer luck. Despite the complexity, this chapter reflected on such aspects of the shift among scholars of law in the UK and the United States as the need to come to terms with persecution and war experiences, the need to understand the role of law in the totalitarian state and the political role of scholarship in preventing totalitarian regimes in the future.

In this chapter, exile is treated as a practice of knowledge production or a lens through which the scientific work of émigrés can be observed and analysed. This approach departs from and develops the theory of acculturation, allowing treatment of exile not only as a loss but also as a dynamic process which can contribute to the advancement of scientific scholarship. However, more research is needed, in particular archival research and research within the field of law as well as the methodology of exile, in order to understand the role of exile in development of science.

Notes

1 This research has been partly funded by the European Research Council under the European Union's Seventh Framework Programme (FP7/2007–2013) / ERC grant agreement n°313100 (Reinventing the Foundations of European Legal Culture 1934–1964).

2 The statistical information is quoted after *Jurists Uprooted: German-Speaking Émigré Lawyers in Twentieth Century Britain*, where it is gathered from multiple sources. For detailed information, see Beatson and Zimmermann (2004: 53).

References

Aradau, C., ed. (2014), *Critical Security Methods: New Frameworks for Analysis*, 4th edn, Abingdon, Oxon and New York: Routledge.

Arendt, H. (1985), *The Origins of Totalitarianism*, New York: A Harvest Book, Harcourt Inc.

Arendt, H. (1999), *The Human Condition*, Chicago: University of Chicago Press.

Arendt, H. (2006), *Eichmann in Jerusalem*, London: Penguin Classics.

Arzt, D. E. (1993), 'Otto Kirchcheimer: Critic of the Administration of Justice', in Marcus Lutter, Ernst C. Stiefel and Michael H. Hoeflich (eds), *Der Einfluß Deutscher*

Emigranten Auf Die Rechtsentwicklung in Den USA Und in Deutschland, 33–56, Tübingen: J. C. B. Mohr (Paul Siebeck).

Ash, M. G. and Söllner, A., eds. (1996), *Forced Migration and Scientific Change: Émigré German-Speaking Scientists and Scholars after 1933*, Cambridge: Cambridge University Press.

Beatson, J. and Zimmermann, R., eds. (2004), *Jurists Uprooted: German-Speaking Émigré Lawyers in Twentieth Century Britain*, Oxford and New York: Oxford University Press.

Berger, S. and De Baets, A. (2016), 'Reflections on Exile Historiography', *Storia Della Storiografia*, 69 (1): 11–26.

Bodenheimer, E. (1933), *Das Gleichheitsprinzip im Aktienrecht*, Mannheim: Bensheimer.

Bodenheimer, E. (1974), *Jurisprudence: The Philosophy and Method of the Law*, revised edn, Cambridge, MA: Harvard University Press.

Burke, P. (2016), 'Silver Lining: On Some Intellectual Benefits of Exile', *Storia Della Storiografia*, 69 (1): 39–48.

Camurri, R. (2014), 'The Exile Experience Reconsidered: A Comparative Perspective in European Cultural Migration during the Interwar Period', *Transatlantica: Revue D'études Américaines. American Studies Journal*, 1 (July). https://transatlantica.revues.org/6920.

Coser, L. A. (1984), *Refugee Scholars in America: Their Impact and Their Experiences*, New Haven and London: Yale University Press.

Durham, W. C. (1993), 'Edgar Bodenheimer: Conservator of Civilized Legal Culture', in Marcus Lutter, Ernst C. Stiefel and Michael H. Hoeflich (eds), *Der Einfluß Deutscher Emigranten Auf Die Rechtsentwicklung in Den USA Und in Deutschland*, 127–44, Tübingen: J. C. B. Mohr (Paul Siebeck).

Fermi, L. (1968), *Illustrious Immigrants: The Intellectual Migration from Europe 1930–1941*, Chicago and London: The University of Chicago Press.

Fleming, D. and Bailyn, B. (1969), *The Intellectual Migration: Europe and America 1930–1960*, Cambridge, MA: The Bellknap Press.

Graham, K. (2002), 'The Refugee Jurist and American Law Schools, 1933–1941', *American Journal of Comparative Law*, 50: 777–818.

Greenberg, K. J. (1987), *The Mentor Within: The German Refugee Scholars of the Nazi Period and Their American Context*, New Haven and London: Yale University Press.

Greenberg, U. (2014), *The Weimar Century: German Émigrés and the Ideological Foundations of the Cold War*, Princeton: Princeton University Press.

Heilbut, A. (1997), *Exiled in Paradise: German Refugee Artists and Intellectuals in America from the 1930s to the Present*, London: University of California Press.

Herget, J. E. and Wallace, S. (1987), 'The German Free Law Movement as the Source of American Legal Realism', *Virginia Law Review*, 73 (2): 399–455.

Hewitson, M. and D'Aura, M. (2012), *Europe in Crisis: Intellectuals and the European Idea 1917–1957*, New York and Oxford: Berghahn Books.

Hughes, H. S. (1975), *The Sea Change: The Migration of Social Thought, 1930–1965*, New York: Harper and Row.

Kirchheimer, O. (1961), *Political Justice: The Use of Legal Procedure for Political Ends*, Princeton: Princeton University Press.

Jay, M. (1986), 'Foreword: Neumann and the Frankfurt School', in F. L. Neumann (ed.), *The Rule of Law: Political Theory and the Legal System in Modern Society*, ix–xiv, Oxford: Berg Publishers.

Konuk, K. (2005), 'Jewish-German Philologists in Turkish Exile: Leo Spitzer and Erich Auerbach', in *Exile and Otherness: New Approaches to the Experience of the Nazi Refugees*, 31–47, Oxford: Peter Lang.

Krohn, C.-D. (1993), *Intellectuals in Exile, Refugee Scholars and the New School for Social Research*, trans. R. Kimber and R. Kimber, Amherst: University of Massachusetts Press.

Lutter, M., Stiefel, E. C. and Hoeflich, M. H., eds. (1993), *Der Einfluß Deutscher Emigranten Auf Die Rechtsentwicklung in Den USA Und in Deutschland*, Tübingen: J. C. B. Mohr (Paul Siebeck).

Mattei, U. (1994), 'Why the Wind Changed: Intellectual Leadership in Western Law', *The American Journal of Comparative Law*, 42: 195–218.

Neumann, F. L. (1929), *Die Politische Und Soziale Bedeutung Der Arbeitsgerichtlichen Rechtsprechung*, Berlin: Laub.

Neumann, F. L. (1931), *Tarifrecht Auf Der Grundlage Der Rechtsprechung Des Rechsarbeitsgerichts*, Berlin: Allgemeiner Deutscher Gewerkschaftsbund.

Neumann, F. L. (1932), *Koalitionsfreiheit Und Reichsverfassung. Die Stellung Der Gewerkschaften Im Verfassungssystem*, Berlin: Heymann.

Neumann, F. L. (1935), *Die Gewerkschaften in Der Demokratie Und in Der Diktatur. Probleme Des Sozialismus*, Karlsbad: Graphia.

Neumann, F. L. (1936), *European Trade Unionism and Politics*, New York: League for Industrial Democracy.

Neumann, F. L. (1961), 'The Social Sciences', in Franz L. Neumann (ed.), *The Cultural Migration: The European Scholar in America*, 4–26, New York: A Perpetua Book.

Neumann, F. L. (1964), *The Democratic and the Authoritarian State*, New York: The Free Press.

Neumann, F. L. (1966), *Behemoth: The Structure and Practice of National Socialism, 1933–1944*, New York: Harper Torchbooks.

Neumann, F. L. (1984), *The Rule of Law: Political Theory and the Legal System in Modern Society*, Oxford: Berg Publishers.

Neumann, F. L. (2009), *Behemoth: The Structure and Practice of National Socialism, 1933–1944*, Chicago: Ivan R. Dee.

Norwood, S. H. (2011), *The Third Reich in the Ivory Tower: Complicity and Conflict on American Campuses*, Cambridge: Cambridge University Press.

Rösch, F., ed. (2014), *Émigré Scholars and the Genesis of International Relations*, Basingstoke: Palgrave Macmillan.

Ruckert, J. (1993), 'Franz Leopold Neumann (1900–1954) – Ein Jurist Mit Prinzipien', in *Der Einfluß Deutscher Emigranten Auf Die Rechtsentwicklung in Den USA Und in Deutschland*, 437–74, Tübingen: J. C. B. Mohr (Paul Siebeck).

Salter, M. (2000), 'The Visibility of Holocaust: Franz Neumann and the Nuremberg Trials', in *Social Theory after the Holocaust*, 197–218, Liverpool: Liverpool University Press.

Scheuerman, W. E. (2014), 'Professor Kelsen's Amazing Disappearing Act', in F. Rösch (ed.), *Émigré Scholars and the Genesis of International Relations*, 81–102, Basingstoke: Palgrave Macmillan.

Söllner, A. (1996), 'From Public Law to Political Science? The Emigration of German Scholars after 1933 and Their Influence on the Transformation of a Discipline', in Mitchell G. Ash and Alfons Söllner (eds), *Forced Migration and Scientific Change: Émigré German-Speaking Scientists and Scholars after 1933*, 246–72, Cambridge: Cambridge University Press.

Stiefel, E. C. and Mecklenburg, F., eds. (1991), *Deutsche Juristen Im Amerikanischen Exil (1933–1941)*, Tübingen: J. C. B. Mohr (Paul Siebeck).

Strauss, H. A. (1991), 'Jewish Immigration in the Nazi Period: Some Aspects of Acculturation', in Werner E. Mosse, Julius Carlebach, Gerhard Hirschfeld, Aubrey Newman, Arnold Paucker, and Peter Pulzer (eds), *Second Chance: Two Centuries of German-Speaking Jews in the United Kingdom*, 81–95, Tübingen: J. C. B. Mohr (Paul Siebeck).

Tillich, P. (1961), 'The Conquest of Theological Provincialism', in Franz L. Neumann (ed.), *The Cultural Migration: The European Scholar in America*, 138–56, New York: A Perpetua Book.

Turton, D. (2003), 'Conceptualising Forced Migration', *RSC Working Paper No. 12*, University of Oxford.

2

Exiled Romanists between Traditions: Pringsheim, Schulz and Daube

Kaius Tuori[1]

Introduction

The purpose of this chapter is to investigate the way Romanists exiled by the Nazis reacted and adapted to new scholarly traditions in their writings. Though ancient Rome and Roman law remained their primary focus, for scholars in exile, the changing of circumstances often meant that they would need to take into account the different approaches, focuses of attention and methodologies popular in their adopted countries. In Britain, they were also faced with a new kind of political culture and ideals, many of which appeared strange while others, such as liberalism and individualism, were seen as welcome contrasts to the German tradition taken over and corrupted by the Nazis.

The transformation of scholarship due to exile is a phenomenon that has been recorded in numerous studies on exiled scholars.[2] In many cases, there was little or no change. The theoretical physics done by Einstein at Princeton was perhaps not substantively different from the work he had done as a director of the Kaiser Wilhelm Institute of Physics in Germany. In a similar way, the art historians recruited to the United States were perhaps not prompted to change the content of the work they had been doing. For the most extreme example of how the experiences of deprivation, persecution and exile affected scholarship, one may look at political scientists such as Franz Neumann (who was originally a jurist) or Hannah Arendt (who wrote at length about totalitarianism and dictatorship). For lawyers in general, transitioning to a new environment was especially hard because the black letter law tends to be so national, making it almost impossible for a German lawyer to practice or teach in Britain or in the United States beyond a few disciplines.

In order to address the issue of exile and scientific change on Roman law scholars, I will focus on three scholars: Fritz Pringsheim, Fritz Schulz and David Daube. The reason for the choice is in part obvious, as they were the best known of the Roman law scholars who moved to Britain. They also provide a chance to observe important variations in political inclinations and age. With all of them, there is the added benefit that there are fairly recent biographies of each of them, allowing us to focus on the change in their scholarship.[3]

For the most part, investigating reactions to new surroundings would demand either a control group or a way of investigating what particular influences were received and why. However, no such luxury is available to us, because the numbers are quite small, and a control group not affected by the Nazi regime is not available, for obvious reasons.[4] In general, it has been observed that legal scholars going to exile in the United States, such as Hans Kelsen or Franz Neumann, tended to end up working in political science departments (Ash and Söllner 1996). Another common trajectory is that towards comparative law (a favourite among foreign scholars in US law schools even today). Some famous names, for example, Ernst Rabel, had, of course, made the transfer already much earlier. Then we have Hermann Kantorowicz, who began to collaborate with scholars in the United States and the UK earlier on, but died fairly early, making the tracing of a transformation even more difficult.

Age and linguistic skills were often a determining factor in acclimatization. The young could re-educate and gain necessary skills and contacts to make a new career, while the middle-aged and older often struggled. The ones who already knew English or had the capacity to learn languages had a clear advantage, but as with learning in general, age is a determinant here as well. In this case, Daube was the most likely to succeed, having both age and language skills, but both Schulz and Pringsheim were polyglots (as all Roman law scholars by necessity are), and, despite their age, able to learn. What is equally clear is that the conditions and cultural receptivity of the place of exile were of enormous importance. A settler society such as the United States was accustomed to people from diverse backgrounds and due to the enormous scale of earlier German immigration, had a ready social context into which the exiles could assimilate. While some countries were extremely homogenous and insular and thus difficult to come into, Britain was in the 1930s a society that was for all its insularity accustomed to exiles and people from different backgrounds. Despite this, the social isolation that many suffered was considerable. For Schulz and Pringsheim, Oxford was perhaps easier than some other places might have been, as they were in an environment where they still enjoyed some respect due their academic achievements and where knowledge of foreign languages was more common. With Daube, despite his Orthodox background, the effect of training in Britain eased his transition into British academic life.

Another way of observing change is that of looking at instances where a scholar picks up traits from the scholarly tradition of their adoptive countries. In Roman law, this is also not unproblematic. Can one say that there was a particularly British or American style of Roman law scholarship or a preoccupation peculiar to those areas (apart from the interest in *lex Aquilia*)? In the case of the move of some of the brightest minds of German Roman law scholarship to the UK, is this question equally one of their influence in Britain, the fact that their emigration brought forth a new generation of Roman law scholars in Britain, people such as Peter Stein, Tony Honoré, Alan Rodger or Alan Watson? As we will see, much of the change in approach was due to the fact that there was virtually no audience for the highly technical work they had done in Germany either in the UK or the United States. While many of the writings in exile can be grouped under the heading of 'advertisement for Roman law', as superficial texts intended to make the audience favourable to the subject, we will equally see how some of it was fascinating reinterpretation of matters to a new audience.

The aim of this inquiry is to observe changes in scholarship and scientific approaches with each of our examples, the way that they reoriented their scholarship in exile. As such, the results are inevitably contentious and tentative, as people are not simple receptacles of ideas or tendencies, and one must not reduce a scholarly change to changes in external circumstances. We struggle even to grasp what the experiences of persecution and exile meant for these scholars, let alone how it affected their work. Despite these challenges, I hope to be able to demonstrate some tentative suggestions on how the contrasting experience of Nazism and exile in Britain may have influenced them. As we will see, whatever changes are observable, they are essentially more nuanced than the works of political scientists who launched into an inquiry of the nature of the totalitarian state.

Fritz Pringsheim: An officer in exile

The journey into exile was not easy for Fritz Pringsheim. A German patriot, an officer and a conservative, he was not known as an easy person to get along with. He was also over fifty when he left, a time when people rarely are at their most flexible and open to new ideas. This all meant that, on the face of it, Pringsheim's prognosis for adaptation to new surroundings was not promising. The fall from a high-status position in Germany to poverty combined with an unyielding mentality is rarely indicative of the flexibility and unprejudiced attitude that getting a new start normally requires.[5] But appearances can be deceptive.

Pringsheim's orientation towards Britain took place already in the early 1930s. Pringsheim's first recorded visit was a lecture tour in Oxford under the invitation of Francis de Zulueta in 1930, then three years later a stay with William Buckland in Cambridge. These visits also led to a series of publications in British journals such as the *Journal of Roman Studies*.[6] Thus while Pringsheim only moved into exile in 1939, in his scholarship the transfer appears much earlier.[7]

Pringsheim's aversion towards the totalitarian regimes, be they communist or national socialist was clearly evident already in his writings from the 1920s (of these in more detail, see Chapter 8 in this volume). There, he warned against the dangers of general principles and political aims, because when given too much weight they could be used to circumvent the law (Pringsheim 1930: 160–2). When the Nazis took power in 1933, Pringsheim criticized their legal policies early on in his lectures. He would go as far as writing an open letter to Carl Schmitt, at that point the main legal ideologue of the Nazi regime, about the role of Roman law in Germany. The Nazi policy had been to replace Roman law with Germanic people's law, but Pringsheim wrote that this was clearly wrong as Roman law was an organic part of the German legal tradition. Though openly challenged, Schmitt was unenthusiastic about the confrontation and no consequences resulted.[8]

The way that Pringsheim was treated in Germany got progressively worse during the 1930s. He was, early on, protected from dismissal (under the Nazi law for the Restoration of the Professional Civil Service on 7 April 1933) by his status as a *Frontkämpfer*. (During the First World War he had served as an officer on front-line duty both on the Western and Eastern fronts.) This privilege was later abolished and in 1935 he was removed from his teaching duties as professor. Rather than dismissed outright, professors who were removed were often placed on different kinds of administrative leaves or moved to different universities where they were not given students or salaries. In the case of Pringsheim, in 1936 he was given a position in the research project at the Prussian Academy of Sciences working on an edition of the Basilika. The task was one that he had been interested in already when working with Ludwig Mitteis as a student (Honoré 2004: 6; Breunung and Walther 2012: 410). What this meant was that he no longer had the protection of his loyal students, because the Nazi policy was to remove all Jewish scholars from positions of teaching and influencing students.

One of the surprising effects of Nazi repression was the way that the impact of repressive measures rippled into the society at large as individuals and institutions began to anticipate the limitations and sanctions. Thus, even though publishing works by Jewish scholars was not prohibited, journals stopped taking them and removed Jews from positions of authority. As a result, Pringsheim's last publication in Germany was in 1934. The ban on Jewish authors was implemented through self-censorship and the implied threat of losing publishing subsidies that most scholarly publications in Germany relied on. In addition to not publishing works by Jewish scholars, they were not to be quoted except in a negative fashion.[9]

Possibly thinking that his social and professional standing would protect him from harm, Pringsheim would not go into exile until the last minute. Even then, the deprivations of being taken to a Nazi concentration camp in Germany was repeated in a sense when he was also arrested and taken to a prison camp in the UK. After *Kristallnacht* on 9 November 1938, Pringsheim was arrested and put into a concentration camp. He was released three weeks later. However, his mother had died during the ordeal, just two days after *Kristallnacht*. Like many others, Pringsheim had searched for an academic job in Britain, but the opportunities were not good. The shock of incarceration meant that he would accept a less than satisfactory offer from Merton College in Oxford. Even Oxford proved to be hazardous. After being arrested for suspicious activities (listening to the radio with his sons), Pringsheim was interned on the Isle of Man (Honoré 2004: 15–16; Breunung and Walther 2012: 425).

In the case of Pringsheim, his work contained much that was potentially politically sensitive in the Third Reich, even though it is not that obvious. What could be political about Greek law of sale? For the most part, the change in scholarship from the Basilika to the Greek law of sale was prompted (as noted by Honoré) by the lack of materials available in Oxford. This is not to say that the topic was not political. In fact, what the research implied was that many of the principles that were dear to the German legal science were in fact the products of the hated post-classical Roman law.[10] This was a long-standing debate that had been exacerbated by the focus on interpolationism. For Nazi scholars and even many conservatives in academia, the very idea that the texts of Roman law as they were now known were not purely Roman but rather the product of Greek, Hellenistic or even Semitic scholars who had edited them was a matter of great importance and passion. For conservatives like Salvatore Riccobono, the idea of oriental origins laid doubt on the whole legitimacy of Roman law as the product of pure

Figure 2 Public shaming of Jewish women in Linz, Austria, during the *Kristallnacht*, November 1938. Photo by Galerie Bilderwelt/Getty Images.

Roman spirit. For Nazis like Ernst Schönbauer, the oriental roots would have meant that the law would be racially impure (Riccobono 1925–6; Schönbauer 1939: 390–1).

One may also see an interesting counter-narrative to the Nazi ideas of law in some of Pringsheim's earlier texts. For example, in an article published in 1934, he would present Rome as an empire of peace, prosperity and law, where even the lowliest people are guaranteed their rights, and the rule of law would be safeguarded by an independent legal profession. Even those with limited rights such as slaves would be protected against abuse (Pringsheim 1934: 141–53). What Pringsheim did was to raise cosmopolitan Rome as an ideal, as a model of a society and its treatment of others. This painted a stark contrast towards the nascent legal policies of Nazi Germany, where rights were not universal but rather determined by racial and ethnic heritage. According to the Nazis, law was subordinate to political expediency in that the will of the Führer was the highest law (Lepsius 2003; Koontz 2003; Stolleis 1998). In 1934, the last vestiges of legalism had been removed from the acts of the Nazis; with the purge known as the night of the long knives in late June and early July, even the most ardent supporters had to contend with the fact that the party would not shy away from openly murdering its own supporters.

As Honoré writes in his biography, Pringsheim was not a good fit for British legal academia, but much of the blame was due to his personality, which appeared haughty and Prussian to the British. What is equally clear is how rooted in the German tradition his work remained, meaning that the intake of new ideas was fairly limited. The praise he gives to the Roman jurists and their method can be seen as a reflection of the type of scholarly approaches to legal science that had been the style of German scholarship from the nineteenth century onwards.[11] He sought parallels between Roman and English law, appreciating the practical, problem-oriented nature of English jurisprudence. Fairly soon after the war, he started to return to Freiburg periodically, helping in the reestablishment of the university. At the same time, he cultivated students both in Oxford (the most famous of them Honoré himself) and in Freiburg. He would even help Franz Wieacker, who had become deeply involved in the Nazi movement, to be rehabilitated after the war.[12] Pringsheim's position became thus progressively stronger both in Britain and in Germany, enabling him to advocate a return to normality and the resumption of the study of classical Roman law.

The example of Pringsheim shows a distinct turn of scholarship, but less so in the attitudes towards politics and science at large. It is clear that Pringsheim as a lawyer was deeply committed to law and jurisprudence and saw the dangers of excessive political power to the law. This conviction only solidified during the Nazi years and in British exile. In his published works, British exile meant the loss of a specialist audience of Continental Romanists, with whom he had numerous combative exchanges on very specialized subjects, and forced him to address more fundamental issues. He had to publish pieces that were aimed at a general legal audience, perhaps in order to gain more support for himself and the subject of Roman law. However, despite his illustrious students at Oxford, Pringsheim remained a German nationalist, and his prime reference group was in Germany. Even the book he wrote in exile about vulgar law was published in Germany, not by Oxford University Press (Pringsheim 1950). He would take a forgiving stance towards the former Nazis, perhaps out of necessity, since they were so numerous and usually kept their positions in academia even after the war. Pringsheim's letters show that he considered return and taking an active part in the reorganization of the Freiburg University as a crucial part of his efforts to guide German students towards the ideas of justice, democracy, and rule of law and to prevent the resurgence of Nazism. Freiburg was after all in the French zone of occupation where the repressive and punitive measures were harsh and caused hostility.

Fritz Schulz: From interpolationism to the freedom of law

Our second case is Fritz Schulz, who was roughly the same age as Pringsheim and left Germany two months after him. What is different between them is that while Pringsheim returned to his chair in Freiburg after the war, Schulz never did.

Schulz's story of emigration has recently been told in detail by Ernst, but we can recapitulate the most important points here. Schulz had been selected as a professor of Roman law in Berlin in 1931, two years before the Nazi takeover, after chairs in Freiburg, Kiel, Göttingen and Bonn. Pringsheim and Schulz may have already been considered to have peaked in their careers; Schulz was fifty-four years old when the Nazis came to power. Like Pringsheim, Schulz was not Jewish but of Jewish ancestry and thus a target of the racial laws. He was also a member of the DDP, or the Deutsche Demokratische Partei, one of the primary opposition parties before it was banned. Unlike Pringsheim, who was protected by his status as a front soldier, Schulz was early on faced with the inquiries of the Nazi bureaucracy and the deprivations of status and wealth that went with this. The way that these things worked was that one was not simply dismissed, but various means of removal were used. For Schulz, he was first forcibly transferred to Frankfurt am Main in 1934, but not assigned any teaching, but finally he was given early retirement from Berlin in 1935. Finally, in 1936, he lost his right to teach in Berlin and later he lost his access to libraries. The persecution of Schulz was chiefly the work of Carl Schmitt and Karl Eckhard, a young legal historian. The Schulzes first sent their children to Britain and, following a short stint in Holland, left for Oxford with the help of his editor at OUP, Kenneth Sisam, and his former student F. A. Mann.[13]

As a scholar, Schulz's main work before the Nazis' taking of power was tied to the interpolationist school. He had worked for the great *Index interpolationum* project, which sought to trace the post-classical interpolations from the preserved texts of classical jurists. In the same vein, Schulz produced other works of textual interpretation, such as the Epitome of Ulpian or the Sabinus fragments.[14]

These works were mainly exercises of textual criticism, of removing the encrustations of post-classical authors from the works at hand and revealing the authentic texts. Interpolationary criticism has since fallen out of favour, mostly because the aim was thought to be unreachable. The reason for this was that the textual criticism of a single compilation such as the Code of Justinian was not a reliable method. The rejection of texts and their parts relied on various criteria, such as textual or substantive criticism. Among purely textual grounds were things such as grammatical structure and its dating or word selection and its likelihood at a given time. The substantive criticism was based on dogmatic issues, whether a rule was typical of classical law, and so forth. There is probably no need to delve deeper into the intricacies of interpolationary research and the considerable passions that were involved to fairly soundly pronounce that they were hardly considered to be of political significance.

What emerged, however, in Schulz's writings after 1933 is a completely different approach. He wrote three main works under distress or in exile: *Principles of Roman Law* (1934, English translation 1936), *History of Roman Legal Science* (1946), and *Classical Roman Law* (1951). These books are to a greater or lesser degree books with agendas.

In the *Principles*, Schulz outlined his understanding of the underlying principles of Roman law, such as the autonomy of law from politics or liberty. He depicted Roman law as a creature of the rule of law, maintaining that it was a non-political protector of individual freedom. Many of the principles that Schulz presented, such as humanity, freedom and trust, may be understood as liberal ideas against the principles of national socialist law, the way that law was subjected to national political aims. As a whole, the book may be seen as a defence of the position of Roman law in Western civilization and an attack on the Nazi doctrine that sought to displace it, a remarkable work in the light of the situation it was written in.

The *History of Roman Legal Science* was initially a chapter for a general book on the history of legal science, but the end product was a full-blown glorification of the Roman jurists. If the *Principles* was a book addressing the value of free legal discourse and the idea of freedom and justice against the Nazi oppression and the strategic use of law, the *Legal Science* was another type of cross-cultural endeavour altogether. Its idea of jurisprudence as the science of law was purely of German origin, one of systematic *Rechtswissenschaft.* Yet, its execution and its spirit were quite British. His heroes are the 'creative geniuses and daring pioneers' (p. 99) of the Roman Republic. It sought to present the practical genius of Roman jurists that manifested itself in the *responsa* given to clients. A jurist would abstain from advocacy, a profession Schulz considered below the legal profession, nor would he 'suffer the noisome weed of rhetoric' (p. 55). The science of law gained its scientific credentials from Greek philosophy and its dialectic method. Another Greek import was that of individualism, the foundation of law on the 'basis of freedom and individualism' (p. 84) (Schulz 1946: 85, 112, 119). There is thus much of the same in Roman jurisprudence and British legal scholarship: the concentration on practical legal solutions, the abstention from grand theories, and the recusal from advocacy. Of course, this was by no means a sign that Schulz had conflated the Roman and British jurists. It is perhaps possible that working within the British system, he had simply elaborated on the points that appeared relevant for his audience there.

The third and final book (Schulz's main works are books) was *Classical Roman Law* (1951). In it, Schulz continued to deepen the thesis of classicism, humanism and liberalism as the great foundations of the Roman legal tradition. In all of the books, the great uniting factor is (beyond the continuing belief in interpolationary research) the separation between law and politics: of the harmfulness of needless legislative inputs and the interference of political power in the law.

Within the praise of the Roman legal achievement, there were still elements that may be understood through the background of Nazi racial laws, for example, his exaltation of the Roman law of marriage:

> The classical law of marriage is an imposing, perhaps the most imposing, achievement of the Roman legal genius. For the first time in the history of civilization there appeared a purely humanistic law of marriage, viz. a law founded on a purely humanistic idea of marriage as being a free and freely dissoluble union of two equal partners for life. (Schulz 1951, 103)

Recent scholars have questioned the accuracy of Schulz's idealistic interpretation (Urbanik 2016: 483). While the Nazi legal machinery regulated marriage with the aim of the preservation of racial purity and the continuation of the race through procreation, Schulz's Roman marriage was its complete opposite, a radical alternative to not only the Nazi marriage laws that forbade marriage between unsuitable partners such as Jews and 'Aryans' but also the modern European laws that were founded on the legal oppression of women and the obstacles placed on divorce.

Schulz never returned to live in Germany, preferring to stay in Britain. Alongside Pringsheim, he had sought and gained British citizenship in 1947. His family had left Germany for good, many of his children ending up in the United States, and despite the continuing financial hardship the prospect of a permanent return was not enticing. He was offered teaching positions, honorary doctorates and other possibilities to come back to Germany, but he held on to a fairly tenuous position as a tutor in Oxford.

Despite this, Schulz's influence continues to be significant in German Roman law scholarship, mostly due to his single student, Werner Flume.

Like Pringsheim, Schulz was a thoroughly international scholar to begin with, and thus the issue of tradition and influence of exile remains elusive. In his Roman law scholarship, he remained very much tied to the German style of research, with strong links to Italy. However, what the move to Britain meant for him was the necessity of applying a more general approach in scholarship and stepping back from the interpolationist school that was losing steam at the time. Instead, he would turn to the ideas of legal science and the self-referentiality of jurisprudence. One should not underestimate his influence in Britain, especially on the ideals of freedom and science in law and legal scholarship. The change in Schulz's scholarship was forced by the exile experience, by the forced removal from his zone of comfort both scientifically and socially. In the end, Schulz reprocessed the learning he had into a new kind of synthesis, one that was again significant when brought back to Germany. (*Legal Science* was translated into German only in 1961.)

David Daube: An outsider who thrived

Our two previous examples, Pringsheim and Schulz, were driven to exile at the height of their careers. They were widely known and respected scholars who were settled in their ways and universities. In contrast, our third example is that of David Daube, a man three decades the junior of Pringsheim and Schulz. For the development of Roman law scholarship in Britain, Daube was to be the most consequential. Born in 1909, Daube was exiled already in 1933 and made his career first in Britain and then in the United States, at UC Berkeley. The example of Daube is one of interest since he was one of the great success stories of the German diaspora. If one compares him with, say, Hans Julius Wolff, the difference is huge. Wolff (born in 1902) would go into exile in 1935 in Panama and work his way around the United States during the 1940s and early 1950s, in places such as Tennessee or Oklahoma but without having a great impact. Only on his return to Germany would he rise to the professorship and make a splendid career. In contrast, Daube would begin a new education in Cambridge and ultimately became the Regius professor of civil law at Oxford.[15]

Though Daube had had his basic training in Germany with some very good people such as Otto Lenel, Pringsheim and Wolfgang Kunkel, he did his doctorate at Cambridge under Buckland. In his biography, Rodger describes Daube as being the ideal age for an emigrant, able to have gained the rigorous training of German academia but young enough to be able to learn the English language properly and to adapt to the different style of scholarship (Rodger 2004: 234–5). His introduction had been Otto Lenel, his teacher at Freiburg, who had written in July 1933 to Jolowicz in London, while Pringsheim had written to Buckland at Cambridge and de Zulueta at Oxford. Ultimately, Daube moved to Cambridge in 1933, but continued to visit Germany. In 1938, with the help of Cambridge friends, he arranged the flight of his family from Germany to Britain.[16]

In the case of Daube, the change in scholarship due to the experience in exile is thus total – one of immersion and refashioning. Before exile, he had published just a couple of articles, meaning that there was no real comparison of before and after. According to Carmichael, Daube would credit his success to the exile experience, that the itinerant life from Germany to Britain and the United States was a key reason for the extraordinary fecundity of his work (Carmichael 2004: 124).

Apart from age, another great difference between Daube and the two older professors, Pringsheim and Schulz, was one of social standing and religion. While Pringsheim and Schulz were prosperous and assimilated members of the *Bildungsbürgertum* and their families had converted to Christianity, Daube was an Orthodox Jew from financially precarious circumstances.[17] Even when he left Germany, Daube was an outsider.

Daube was a scholar of Roman law, but his other main area of interest was religious law, both Talmudic and New Testament. It would have naturally been impossible for him to continue his career in Germany during the Nazi period, given that while the regime had an adverse attitude towards Roman law, it was even less inclined to grant additional resources to the study of Jewish law. Beyond the fact that the regime was opposed in principle to the subjects that Daube was interested in, his scholarship did not have similar traces of content criticism as is detectable in Pringsheim and Schulz. What Daube, who was by most accounts an apolitical person uninterested in making a political point through scholarship, has are numerous references to the moral choices present in the Third Reich and the Second World War.

In his book *Appeasement or Resistance* (1987), Daube takes up several examples, for instance, the 'Sophie's choice' situation of the mayor of Strasbourg during the war. His sons had been arrested and due to be executed in retaliation for the actions of resistance fighters. The German commander offers him a chance to save one of his sons, but he is unable to choose and both are executed. Daube compares this to the games of tyrants in classical literature, who made fun out of placing people in impossibly cruel dilemmas. In another example, the protagonist is not unknown: Daube's own teacher Wolfgang Kunkel, one of the leading scholars of Roman legal history. Kunkel was a military judge on the Eastern Front in 1943, where he was presented with a case of two captains, where one had denounced (out of jealousy of the other gaining a promotion) the other for listening to Moscow Radio, a capital offence. Rather than sentencing the man to death, Kunkel managed to demonstrate via clever legal reasoning that the sentence did not apply (Daube 1987: 51–2, 76–7). Though Kunkel is the hero of this story, he is equally clearly shown as a part of the Nazi machinery of terror. These kinds of stories were completely absent from the writings of Pringsheim and Schulz, who would refer to the Nazi years only in an oblique fashion. This is perhaps due to the general trend of discussion; before the 1960s the Nazi years were not discussed so openly and after that only Daube was around to do so.

Daube would hesitate to judge those who had joined the Nazis and instead stressed the need to understand the circumstances in which these choices were made.[18] Like many Germans, he was critical of the Nuremberg trials and the conception of retroactive justice it embodied. He would make a distinction between those who had joined the regime or the party because of anti-Semitic conviction and those who were opportunists or just making ends meet. Of course, Carmichael met with Daube only when he was in his fifties and time had possibly mellowed his feelings. Nevertheless, issues of resistance to and collaboration with tyranny remained a constant theme in his writings (Daube 1965; Carmichael 2004: 53, 82–3).

Even in Britain, Daube did not feel completely safe. He too was interned on the Isle of Man in June 1940, an experience that he later described as horrifying because it would have made it possible for a defeated Britain to easily collaborate with the Nazis and hand over the Jews collected there. This later recollection shows how deeply the existential threat was felt even in Britain. Unlike Pringsheim, Daube was of military age, which could explain why he was treated more harshly. He would spend four months in the camps and was freed only after petitions from powerful friends.[19]

Like the older professors Pringsheim and Schulz, Daube was a bridge between the Continental and the British traditions of scholarship, but unlike them he would become fully acclimatized to the new surroundings. Daube's links to Germany endured during his career, and in his bibliography one sees continuously articles written in German for German journals. With his methods and approaches, Daube became considerably more Anglo-American, moving freely between law, classics and theology. While for the older generation, the events that took place during the Nazi years were a clear aberration and signified the destruction of the academic life they had grown accustomed to, for Daube, the permanent attachment to a scholarly environment was formed only in Britain. Due to his Orthodox background, Daube did not have a similar high status in Germany, and due to his younger age the drop in social standing and salary was much less than among his older peers.

Making sense of the Nazi years

In the studies of exile scholarship, numerous theories have been presented about the way scholars adapt to new circumstances and how they change their approaches and form new theories on the basis of their experiences in exile. Some, such as Hannah Arendt, dedicated their entire careers to understanding the experience of the *Shoah*, leading to celebrated works like *The Origins of Totalitarianism* (1951), detailing the mass movement and its relation to social conditions and ideological elements like anti-Semitism. Others, for example, Franz Neumann, would tackle the totalitarian state in the *Behemoth* (1944). Beside these celebrated scholars and the very obvious way that they were forced to confront the Nazi ideas, the examples dealt with here show a similar tendency of engaging the ideological challenge presented by the Nazis.

The challenge of the Nazi order was nothing less than existential for people such as Pringsheim, Schulz and Daube. The Nazis not only wanted to exterminate them and their families but also disparaged and wanted to abolish their object of study: Roman law. The Nazis forced their colleagues to turn on them and stripped them of their status, livelihood and occupation. Their relatives were brutally murdered en masse. After the war, they were faced with the prospect of reencountering the same people that had forced them out of the profession. The fact that they were able to do that is nothing short of extraordinary. In the case of most of the exiles who went to the United States, for example, Neumann and Arendt, a similar rapprochement never took place.

Both Pringsheim and Schulz would write in defence of what they considered to be the true law, the foundation of Western legal culture: Roman law. However, the Roman law in their writings becomes enmeshed with virtues and qualities that are more at home with the modern rule of law or the values inherent in liberalism. Humanism, individualism, freedom and giving each their due were ideals that they saw to be inherent in the works of Roman jurists. Unlike Nazi jurisprudence, which emphasized the primacy of the national interest, the political will and racial destiny, their Roman law was oriented relentlessly towards justice.

For the exiles, reaching out to the history of law and to Roman law was not simply a matter of what they did naturally; the kind of search for meaning that they went through was quite out of character. Especially with Schulz, his earlier works had been focused on the purely technical analysis of textual transmission that had no greater significance, at least openly stated. They operated purely within the tradition. On the other hand, during the exile process and in exile, they were to a certain degree outside the tradition and the circle of communication that would have understood them. Thus, the tradition takes on a different role; it signifies the loss of culture that Germany and they personally have gone through. The legal tradition was broken; Nazi totalitarianism had not only taken over the law but also subdued the very people who were supposed to defend it, the lawyers. By reaching into the past, to the tradition beyond the Nazi menace, they were recreating the ideals of law.

In contrast, the work of Daube shows no sign of a similar need to work through the issues of law and justice, but distances itself from the whole German experience. The way they are presented is largely as examples of totalitarianism and perversions of justice, a negation that is in and of itself quite obvious. It is impossible to say whether the fear that had gripped Daube, even in Britain, about being turned over to the Nazis was something that haunted Pringsheim and Schulz, but it is not possible to say that they would have been too idealistic about Britain.

What all of them have in common is praise of the classics of Roman law, the uplifting of the Roman legal tradition and its value that was under attack. Much of the work they had published, especially some of the minor pieces by Schulz and Pringsheim, must have appeared as superficial and bland generalizations to their former peers in Germany. In the culture of Roman law scholars in Germany and Italy, there existed a widely shared understanding, rarely uttered beyond the festive speeches and ponderations of the crisis of Roman law, of the value and meaning of the study of Roman law. Within that shared understanding, scholars could concentrate on the technical work on the intricacies of legal dogmatics. Since a significant amount of the interest was highly technical and based on the relevance provided by the said legal rules in the interpretation of the German Civil Code or Bürgerliches Gesetzbuch, there was equally a tendency towards sterility, the separation of the law from the life. What made the writings of someone such as Schulz or Pringsheim so important was that they were able to convey not only the technical side but also the meaning of the study of Roman law in the big picture, the development of the Western legal tradition. Whether they appreciated the style that they had to adopt for writing to a new audience unaccustomed to the scholarly style, I would be highly sceptical. Nevertheless, it was enough to prompt their students to embark on a novel type of research in Roman law.

The very fact that the exiles would write about the matters of legal heritage that reflected their experiences of exile was a rarity. When discussing exile legal scholars, one often mentions persons like Bodenheimer or Neumann who would take up the

Nazi past and analyse it. In contrast, the vast majority never did openly discuss their painful experiences. This may be a similar phenomenon as that of the soldiers who never discussed their wartime experiences. A comparison of sorts is the case of the Jewish refugees who fled to the United States and were assigned teaching positions in historically black colleges in the South. In her remarkable history of these scholars, Gabrielle Edgcomb notes that of these dozens of people, none wrote a single line of what must have been a surreal experience moving from the persecution of Nazi Germany to a different kind of persecution in the Jim Crow South (Edgcomb 1993).

For our scholars, Schulz, Pringsheim and Daube, despite their tribulations, the movement to exile was one of privilege. They were at the apex of German academic life and would stay there beyond the Nazi period itself. When subjected to a new tradition, they did that in the comfort of Oxford, helped by innumerable friends who sought to aid them. Their contact with the British tradition was not unproblematic, and it is not sure that they really overcame their sense that the legal and academic culture they had left was superior to the one they encountered in exile. In a similar manner, the experience with liberalism and other ideological traits may have been one of gradual influence and where the actual implications became evident only back in Germany. However, the great change that took place, that of the transition to a new country, to take up a new language and to write for a new audience, was one of great success. Whatever traumas they had they kept to themselves, in a manner typical of men of their age.

Conclusion

The issue of observing change in scholarship, the adoption of new ideas and perceptions is difficult in and of itself, but these difficulties are compounded by the fact that even the persons themselves were not aware of these changes. Many of the German scholars who ended up in Britain during the 1930s were people with a previous interest in British culture (if there may be said to exist such a thing) and a certain admiration towards Britain. Hermann Kantorowicz, one of the most famous of the Romanist emigrants, was a long-time anglophile, who admired British humanism and individualism (Ibbetson 2004: 276).

It is hard to estimate the impact that Britain, its strange ways and its liberal democracy, had on the exiles. It is evident that for them the British scientific world was very much lacking compared to the one that they had left behind in Germany. However, the same German scientific world had rejected them on grounds that they must have considered barbaric (not to mention the deprivations by the Nazis they endured). In Britain, they were helped by the peculiar British idealism. The British exile was, if nothing else, a mixed bag of traumatic experiences and human kindness.

The relationship with Britain and its influence on scholarship was thus mostly one of unintended consequences. Firstly, the need to explain things to a new audience forced all of them to open up their writing and to say out loud much that was considered self-evident in Germany. Secondly, the fact that they were speaking to a new audience meant that much had to be presented through a new vocabulary, in a language and terminology that the new audience would understand. Thirdly, within this process of opening up, there was perhaps an unintentional way of dealing with the negation of law that Germany had turned into. Thus, the classicism and the rather preachy tone of some of the writings, the reference to a rule of law and rather anachronistic liberal political references can be seen not only as appealing to the audience but also as the working through of the trauma at home. This applied almost exclusively to Pringsheim and Schulz, as Daube would escape much the trauma of the exiles and the need to work through them.

Notes

1 This research has made been possible by the European Research Council under the European Union's Seventh Framework Programme (FP7/2007-2013)/ERC grant agreement n°313100 (Reinventing the Foundations of European Legal Culture 1934–1964).

2 Fermi 1968; Ash and Söllner 1996; Rösch 2014. On exiled lawyers, see also Graham 2002: 777; Lutter, Stiefel and Hoeflich 1993; Breunung and Walther 2012; Breunung and Walther, forthcoming.

3 In the case of Schulz, the main work is still Ernst 2004, but future work by Jacob Giltaij will shed new light on his career. Pringsheim has been studied by Honoré (2004), while Daube is covered by Rodger 2004 and Carmichael 2004. While these studies all have their deficiencies, they all discuss at length the exile experience. What they do not discuss, however, is the impact of that exile on their scholarship.

4 While there were Jewish legal scholars of German background in the United States, they were also greatly affected by the Nazi takeover due to what happened to their friends and relatives in Germany.

5 Issues of temperament are notoriously hard to verify; thus we are here reliant on Honoré's statement. Similar statements do pop up regularly, even late in his stay in Britain. Oxford University Press Archives, Oxford, Schulz CP GE 000345, 23, Warden of Merton College to Sisam (13.1.1944) about Pringsheim, who has 'prickly sensitiveness about his own resultant position'. He states that 'I think the College has treated him very handsomely, and am surprised that he shouldn't recognize it', concluding that he is a 'very difficult case'.

6 Breunung and Walther 2012: 409. There were two articles in the *JRS* in 1933, one in *Law Quarterly Review* in 1933 and one in *Cambridge Law Journal* in 1935.

7 Pringsheim's main works are collected in *Gesammelte Abhandlungen*, showing his combative and assertive style of scholarly debate.

8 Paragraph 19 of the NSDAP party programme from 24 February 1920: 'We demand that Roman Law, which serves a materialistic world order, be replaced by a German common law.' The debate between Pringsheim and Schmitt is now reproduced in Pringsheim 1960: 532–8. On Schmitt's position, see Mehring 2009; Cumin 2005; Balakrishnan 2000; Koenen 1995.

9 This is based on the works in the *Gesammelte Werke*. On the practical effects of the ban on publishing, see the article by Finkenauer and Herrmann 2017 which traces the references in the *Savigny Zeitschrift* and the downturn in the citations of Jewish authors.

10 Pringsheim's *Greek Law of Sale* (1950), his main occupation during the war, was ultimately published in East Germany. There is no indication in the archives on why this happened, because the book had been prepared for OUP.

11 Pringsheim 1944: 62: 'Compared with Roman classical law all other laws were unscientific.'

12 We have one of the letters Pringsheim wrote for Wieacker, dated 12 May 1947, for the use of the committees examining former Nazis. On Pringsheim's travel to Germany in the post-war period, see the letters in the Bodleian Library, Oxford, Archives of the Society for the Protection of Science and Learning, MS. SPSL. 272.1, 233 on his schedule; 190, Pringsheim to Ursell (3 April 1946), on his intent to go to Freiburg and need of a certificate of identity from the HO and a return visa; 272.1, 191 Skemp to Under Secretary of State (5 April 1946), application for travelling papers for Pringsheim, who is willing to assist in the educational reconstruction of Germany, short-term, children remain in Great Britain. Letters 192–206 about the arrangements for travel to Germany show how difficult movement was at the time.

13 Humboldt-Universität zu Berlin, Universitätsarchiv zu Berlin, UK Personalia Sch 303, Personal-Akten des Prof Dr Schulz, Band 2, letters nos. 86, 88–91; The correspondence around Schulz's move to Britain and his funding are at the SPSL archives (Bodleian Library, Oxford, Archives of the Society for the Protection of Science and Learning, MS. SPSL. 274.2). The collection consists of 183 pages between 1933 and 1948 about the conditions of his move, the potential locations and the funding available. Ernst 2004: 126–30; Breunung and Walther 2012: 432–59.

14 The index was the crowning achievement of the interpolationist movement, but its origins are in the works of Gradenwitz and Lenel. One of Schulz's main contributions was his article 'Überlieferungsgeschichte der Responsa des Cervidius Scaevola' (Schulz 1931).

15 On Daube's career, see also Rodger 2001 (his *Nachruf* in the Savigny *Zeitschrift*).

16 Carmichael 2004: 55–6, 69–71. He reproduces Lenel's letter from 7 July 1933.

17 The facts of Daube's early life are from his own recollections collected by Rodger 2004 and Carmichael 2004: 11–28, and thus to be taken with a grain of salt.

18 In fact, one of his best friends from high school would join the Nazis. Carmichael 2004: 22, 63.

19 Carmichael 2004: 63–5; Rodger 2004: 234 only glosses over this episode.

References

Arendt, H. (1951), *The Origins of Totalitarianism*, New York: Henry Holt.

Ash, M. G. and Söllner, A., eds. (1996), *Forced Migration and Scientific Change: Émigré German-Speaking Scientists and Scholars after 1933*, Cambridge and New York: Cambridge University Press.

Balakrishnan, G. (2000), *The Enemy: An Intellectual Portrait of Carl Schmitt*, London: Verso.

Breunung, L. and Walther, M. (2012), *Die Emigration deutschsprachiger Rechtswissenschaftler ab 1933. Ein bio-bibliographisches Handbuch*, vol. 1, Göttingen: De Gruyter.

Breunung, L. and Walther, M. (forthcoming), *Die Emigration deutscher Rechtswissenschaftler ab 1933*, vol. 2, Göttingen: De Gruyter.

Carmichael, C. (2004), *Ideas and the Man: Remembering David Daube*, Frankfurt: Vittorio Klostermann Verlag.

Cumin, D. (2005), *Carl Schmitt*, Paris: Cerf.

Daube, D. (1965), *Collaboration with Tyranny in Rabbinic Law*, Oxford: Oxford University Press.

Daube, D. (1987), *Appeasement or Resistance and Other Essays on New Testament Judaism*, Berkeley, Los Angeles, London: University of California Press.

Edgcomb, G. S. (1993), *From Swastika to Jim Crow: Refugee Scholars in Black Colleges*, Malabar: Krieger.

Ernst, W. (2004), 'Fritz Schulz (1879-1957)', in J. Beatson and R. Zimmermann (eds), *Jurists Uprooted*, 105–203, Oxford: Oxford University Press.

Fermi, L. (1968), *Illustrious Immigrants: The Intellectual Migration from Europe 1930–1941*, Chicago: University of Chicago Press.

Finkenauer, T. and Herrmann, A. (2017), 'Die Romanistische Abteilung der Savigny-Zeitschrift im Nationalsozialismus', *Zeitschrift der Savigny-Stiftung für Rechtsgeschichte. Romanistische Abteilung*, 134: 1–48.

Graham, K. (2002), 'The Refugee Jurist and American Law Schools, 1933-1941', *American Journal of Comparative Law*, 50: 777–818.

Honoré, T. (2004), 'Fritz Pringsheim (1882-1967)', in J. Beatson and R. Zimmermann (eds), *Jurists Uprooted*, 205–32, Oxford: Oxford University Press.

Ibbetson, D. (2004), 'Hermann Kantorowicz (1877-1940) and Walter Ullman (1910-1983)', in J. Beatson and R. Zimmermann (eds), *Jurists Uprooted*, 269–98, Oxford: Oxford University Press.

Koenen, A. (1995), *Der Fall Carl Schmitt*, Darmstatt: Wissenschaftliche Buchhandlung.

Koontz, C. (2003), *The Nazi Conscience*, London and Cambridge, MA: The Belknap Press.

Lepsius, O. (2003), 'The Problem of Perceptions of National Socialist Law or: Was there a Constitutional Theory of National Socialism?', in C. Joerges and N. S. Ghaleigh (eds), *Darker Legacies of Law in Europe*, 19–41, Oxford and Portland, OR: Hart Publishing.

Lutter, M., Stiefel, E. C. and Hoeflich, M. H., eds. (1993), *Der Einfluß deutscher Emigranten auf die Rechtsentwicklung in den USA und in Deutschland*, Tübingen: Mohr Siebeck.

Mehring, R. (2009), *Carl Schmitt: Aufstieg und Fall*, München: Beck.

Neumann, F. (1944), *Behemoth: The Structure and Practice of National Socialism 1933–1944*, New York: Harper & Row.

Pringsheim, F. (1930, repr. 1961), 'Aequitas und bona fides', in *Gesammelte Abhandlungen* 1, 154–72, Heidelberg: Carl Winter & Universitätsverlag.

Pringsheim, F. (1934), 'The Legal Policy and Reforms of Hadrian', *Journal of Roman Studies*, 24: 141–53.

Pringsheim, F. (1944), 'The Unique Character of Classical Roman Law', *Journal of Roman Studies*, 34: 60–4.

Pringsheim, F. (1950), *The Greek Law of Sale*, Weimar: Böhlau.

Pringsheim, F. (1960), 'Die Haltung der Freiburger Studenten in den Jahren 1933-1935', *Die Sammlung*, 15: 532–8.

Riccobono, S. (1925-1926), 'Outlines of the Evolution of Roman Law', *University of Pennsylvania Law Review*, 74: 1–19.

Rodger, A. (2001), 'David Daube (8.2.1909-24.2.1999)', *Zeitschrift der Savigny-Stiftung für Rechtsgeschichte. Romanistische Abteilung*, 118: XIV–LII.

Rodger, A. (2004), 'David Daube (1909-1999)', in J. Beatson and R. Zimmermann (eds), *Jurists Uprooted*, 233–48, Oxford: Oxford University Press.

Rösch, F. (2014), *Émigré Scholars and the Genesis of International Relations. A European Discipline in America?*, Basingstoke: Palgrave Macmillan.

Schönbauer, E. (1939), 'Zur "Krise des römischen Rechts"', in *Festschrift Paul Koschaker II*, 390–1, Weimar: Böhlau.

Schulz, F. (1931), 'Überlieferungsgeschichte der Responsa des Cervidius Scaevola', in *Symbolae friburgenses in honorem Ottonis Lenel*, 143, Leipzig: B. Tauchnitz.
Schulz, F. (1934), *Prinzipien des römischen Rechts*, Berlin: Duncker & Humblot.
Schulz, F. (1946), *History of Roman Legal Science*, Oxford: Clarendon Press.
Schulz, F. (1951), *Classical Roman Law*, Oxford: Clarendon Press.
Stolleis, M. (1998), *The Law Under the Swastika: Studies on Legal History in Nazi Germany*, Chicago: University of Chicago Press.
Urbanik, J. (2016), 'Husband and Wife', in P. J. du Plessis, C. Ando, and K. Tuori (eds), *The Oxford Handbook of Roman Law and Society*, 473–86, Oxford: Oxford University Press.

3

Francis de Zulueta (1878–1958): An Oxford Roman Lawyer between Totalitarianisms

Lorena Atzeri

Introduction

Reading about the lives of 'German-speaking émigré lawyers in twentieth-century Britain', to quote the subtitle of the absorbing book *Jurists Uprooted* (Beatson and Zimmermann 2004), there is, even if not immediately visible, a red thread that links the lives and destinies of many of the jurists of Jewish origin – in particular Roman lawyers – who sought refuge in Oxford during the Nazi regime. This thread is constituted by one man, Francis de Zulueta, Regius professor of civil law in Oxford between 1919 and 1948.[1] Together with William W. Buckland, who held the corresponding chair in Cambridge, de Zulueta was the most important Roman lawyer in Great Britain in the first half of the twentieth century.

Although of vital importance, the role played by de Zulueta in helping German scholars of Jewish origin has, it seems to me, never received adequate recognition. This is all the more striking because it was precisely three of the most famous of these refugees, Fritz Schulz,[2] Fritz Pringsheim[3] and Hermann Kantorowicz,[4] who received fundamental support from de Zulueta, both in their private lives and in their academic activity. Even David Daube,[5] although based in Cambridge in the same years and linked rather to Buckland,[6] enjoyed his help and support. It is no coincidence that in 1952 the private library of de Zulueta came to reside, at the instigation of T. B. Smith, in the University of Aberdeen,[7] where the previous year Daube had been offered the newly established (and his first) chair in jurisprudence.[8] Nor is it widely known that it was on de Zulueta's recommendation that Daube became his successor in Oxford just a few years later (Carmichael 2004: 94), in 1955, after the short tenure of Herbert F. Jolowicz.[9]

The personal engagement of de Zulueta in supporting the lives of these scholars kept alive an important nucleus of Roman law scholarship, when the world seemed to be consumed in flames and the subject – at least in Nazi Germany – was in danger of annihilation:[10] a nucleus which was going to bring important fruits.

This vital moment in intellectual history has never been sufficiently highlighted or properly investigated. The reason for this may lie, at least in part, in a more general negative attitude towards de Zulueta, an attitude largely stemming from the sympathy and support expressed by him towards General Franco and his rise to power in Spain in the 1930s. This sympathy, shared by very few in the British academic elite, has certainly cast a shadow not only over de Zulueta's crucial role towards the émigrés, but even – I would argue – on his contribution as a scholar. Indeed, it has led to the simplistic syllogism, that de Zulueta must himself have been a fascist, a sympathizer of totalitarian regimes: a syllogism, as I would like to show, based on false premises, which misses the real reasons for his support for the Spanish insurgents.

It is therefore the purpose of the present chapter to dispel some false myths, first by briefly outlining the scholarly contribution of Francis de Zulueta, and then by investigating more closely his attitude towards the totalitarian regimes established in Europe in the 1930s, with a closer focus on *Franquismo* in Spain. I will try to highlight the deeper reasons which motivated him to support the Spanish *Generalissimo*, in marked contrast to the position taken by the vast majority of his scholarly colleagues at the time.

Francis de Zulueta: Myth and Reality

Among Romanists the name of Francis de Zulueta is mainly associated with the *Institutes of Gaius*, of which he produced a new edition with an English translation and commentary (de Zulueta 1946, 1953). Among legal historians he is known for his critical edition of the *Liber Pauperum* of Vacarius (de Zulueta 1927). It is probable that the association of his name with the didactical works of Gaius and Vacarius has contributed to creating his own reputation as primarily a 'teacher', who dedicated his life and work almost entirely to undergraduates and to the teaching of Roman law, and who addressed almost all his research effort towards didactical works. This reputation has been accompanied by another myth, namely that of being a rather 'unproductive' scholar, a notion which was first set down on paper immediately following de Zulueta's death, which occurred on 16 January 1958. In the anonymous obituary published two days later (*The Times*, 18 January 1958), almost certainly written by an Oxford colleague, his achievements are described as follows: 'Like many other learned men who set themselves a high standard, he did not publish much ... . What remains are chiefly pamphlets and articles in learned periodicals.' This rather negative judgement, which spread around quickly, reaching even South Africa and the United States,[11] seemed to be confirmed a year later by the list of de Zulueta's publications (fifty items in all) given in the book *Studies in the Roman law of sale*, edited by David Daube in 1959,[12] which was originally intended to celebrate de Zulueta's eightieth birthday.

This reputation for unproductiveness was again reinforced in the biography published in the *Dictionary of National Biography* in 1971 by his friend and colleague, F. H. Lawson (Lawson 1971). According to Lawson, de Zulueta 'published much less than his contemporaries desired and expected'. In speaking of a 'relative unproductiveness' Lawson does add, significantly, that 'he became in truth too learned to see opportunities in a well-tilled field' (Lawson 1971: 1098). This judgement has been echoed in more recent years by Alan Rodger, who again stresses de Zulueta's 'unproductiveness', describing him in addition as someone who 'seemed to lack the necessary confidence to advance his own views', concluding that 'rather than put forward fresh ideas on his own, he was content to survey the work of others'.[13]

On a more personal level, this negative opinion of de Zulueta is reinforced by more recent scholars: Calum Carmichael, in his memoirs of David Daube, also published in 2004, leaves us with a picture of de Zulueta as someone who 'from his home in a castle near the sea, well away from Oxford[14] … regarded his Oxford colleagues as plebeians' (Carmichael 2004: 95). The clue to this negative judgement can be found in Daube's view, reported by Carmichael, that 'de Zulueta's Oxford colleagues disdained him … because he was a supporter of Franco'. According to Carmichael himself, de Zulueta 'was a fascist but not a socialist', to which he adds that he 'was not the first or last fascist (or anti-Semite) that Daube got along with'.[15] This process of denigration reaches its apogee when H. L. MacQueen, misinterpreting those words, finally arrives at the (absurd) conclusion, certainly not intended by Carmichael, that de Zulueta had 'anti-Semitic attitudes'.[16]

The overall picture which emerges from these views is of an unproductive scholar lacking in original opinions or ideas, an upper-class snob looking with contempt on his Oxford colleagues, a fascist 'with repugnant views' and 'anti-Semitic attitudes'. What I wish to demonstrate is that not only is this *leyenda negra* a distorted image and an unjust assessment; it is also partly based on false premises. In particular, it completely ignores de Zulueta's incredibly generous engagement for colleagues and others in need, and his fundamental role in supporting the lives and the scholarly work of German émigré Roman lawyers of Jewish origin in Oxford: hardly the engagement of a fascist and anti-Semite.

As regards the charge of 'unproductiveness', it should be noted that the list of de Zulueta's publications produced by Daube in 1959, which is still the only one in existence, in the first place reveals a far from negligible literary production and secondly is by no means complete. A letter written by Daube and kept in the Oxford University Press Archives indicates that the basis of the list was an elementary and very incomplete record given to him by de Zulueta's widow,[17] which in the end Daube could only partially supplement.[18] After some research, I have been able to identify at least forty-five further contributions. These are, to be sure, mainly shorter articles, reviews, obituaries, contributions to encyclopaedias and the like: but it nevertheless almost doubles the number of items recorded by Daube. When the list of de Zulueta's publications is set out in full (almost 100 items),[19] his scholarly production seems to me one of which any scholar could justly be proud, and, although this new material will not change the substance of his contribution to Roman law, it should at least help to dispel the myth of 'unproductiveness'.

The opinion expressed by Alan Rodger (which in fact goes back to the biography of Lawson) that de Zulueta was a scholar lacking in original thought, who was content to 'survey the work of others', is surely excessive. Leaving aside his numerous book reviews and bibliographical overviews, which in many cases go beyond a simple report, from the beginning of his career de Zulueta had shown an independent and critical attitude towards the various streams of Roman law studies pursued in the rest of Europe. He was, for example, very sceptical about the value of the reigning interpolationist approach, which, to an Oxford – or, thinking of Buckland, we should rather say Oxbridge – mindset, was lacking in any solid foundation and often led to questionable conclusions. Open criticism of the almost universally accepted approach to Roman law at the time was already expressed by de Zulueta in his inaugural lecture, delivered in Oxford in 1919 (de Zulueta 1920). He also followed closely the evolution of Wenger's idea of an *Antike Rechtsgeschichte*, contributing an article to the debate (de Zulueta 1929) and exchanging opinions with Paul Koschaker on the subject (Atzeri 2010) – but here too, he had his doubts.

In short, de Zulueta was well aware of the contemporary streams in Roman law studies on the Continent, not just taking note of the discussions but actively participating in them and manifesting an open but above all critical mind to these currents. Not only was he in close touch with the new discoveries and directions in Roman law studies in his time, he was also in direct contact and correspondence with a constellation of major Continental Romanists – among the Italians, Riccobono, Arangio-Ruiz and Albertario; among the Germans, Wenger, Koschaker, Rabel, Schulz, Conrat, Kantorowicz; and with the Frenchmen Fournier, Collinet and Le Bras.[20] This is revealed by the letters found among his papers and books, together with the dedications written in the books and offprints of his personal library, which has survived intact in Aberdeen University.[21] In short, his books and papers reflect the image of a Roman law scholar fully the equal of his European colleagues, while the latter, for their part, clearly considered him as a scholar of the highest repute.

Despite all this, it cannot be denied that in the field of Roman law scholarship the name and fame of de Zulueta, which certainly also suffers from being overshadowed by his Cambridge contemporary W. W. Buckland, is fading, and he has never really been fully admitted into the pantheon of Roman law scholars. Moreover, de Zulueta's role in opening up the Oxford (indeed English) Roman law world to international scholarship through his contacts with the Romanistic scene in Continental Europe is still underestimated. For it was these contacts, which had long been established, which form the background to the pre-eminent role he played from 1933 onwards in giving aid and support to the German Roman lawyers of Jewish origin who sought refuge in Oxford.

Opening Up Oxford

One of de Zulueta's most important contributions was the internationalization of Roman law studies in Great Britain,[22] opening up Oxford to European scholars on Roman law.[23] It all started in April 1913, when the third International Congress of Historical Studies took place in London, a section (presided over by Vinogradoff) being dedicated to 'Legal History'.[24] Here de Zulueta, who had just become the All Souls Reader in Roman law, served as secretary. Some of the leading European scholars in the field of ancient law participated: from Germany there came Wenger, Seeck, Lenel, von Gierke, Hübner, E. Mayer and Koschaker; from France Caillemer, Esmein, Huvelin;

from Italy Arnò and Riccobono; as well as other scholars from many other countries, including some from outside Europe. The Congress gave de Zulueta the opportunity to make the acquaintance of some of the most important Continental Roman law scholars.[25] Indeed, in some cases, such as those of Riccobono and Koschaker, it proved to be the beginning of a lifelong friendship.

Following in the footsteps of his teacher, Paul Vinogradoff,[26] occupying the Regius Chair, to which he was appointed in 1919, de Zulueta was always keen to encourage contacts with international scholars and exchanges between Britain and Continental Europe. When he started his career, apart from a few isolated contacts, British Roman law scholarship was still not playing a full part in Continental academia. On more than one occasion de Zulueta lamented the fact that the participation of British Roman lawyers on the European scene was too limited, sometimes indeed non-existent. There were only very few or no British contributions at all in the contemporary *Festschriften* or *Atti di Congressi*. In a review of *The Girard Testimonial Essays*, de Zulueta expresses his regret: 'It is disappointing to find no English names in the list of forty-eight collaborators in these volumes, since his English colleagues are certainly not less in debt to him than those of other countries, and they would be the first to do him every honour in their power' (de Zulueta 1914: 215). And even at the important Conferenze per il XIV centenario delle Pandette held in 1930, as he pointed out later, no English scholars participated.[27] Even at that date, despite the efforts of de Zulueta and Buckland in surveying most of the Continental production, Roman law in Britain was rather isolated from the rest of Europe, where Roman law studies were flourishing and the connections between the various schools growing.

De Zulueta in particular made every effort to change this situation. Thanks to his exceptional knowledge of several foreign languages, he established and maintained contacts with many leading Roman law scholars throughout Europe. It is a highly learned correspondence,[28] where technical and philological questions were discussed at length. These contacts were also maintained at a personal level, in an era when international travel was much more limited. Thus he opened the doors of Oxford to guest lecturers like Pringsheim, Koschaker, Collinet and Fournier.[29] And, although not clearly stated in the accessible documents, we can be fairly sure that behind the honorary degrees in civil law conferred by the University of Oxford on Riccobono (in 1924),[30] Buckland (in 1932) and Koschaker (in 1934) lay the recommendation of de Zulueta.[31]

Helping the Refugees

When the Nazi regime came to power in Germany in 1933, Oxford was for many Roman law scholars their first place of refuge, and it was the name of Francis de Zulueta that naturally came to their minds in their moment of need. He did not fail them. One of the most moving aspects of investigating the life of Francis de Zulueta is following his engagement for the émigrés in Oxford.

As regards Fritz Schulz, Fritz Pringsheim and, above all, Hermann Kantorowicz, de Zulueta sought out financial support and at the same time provided them with

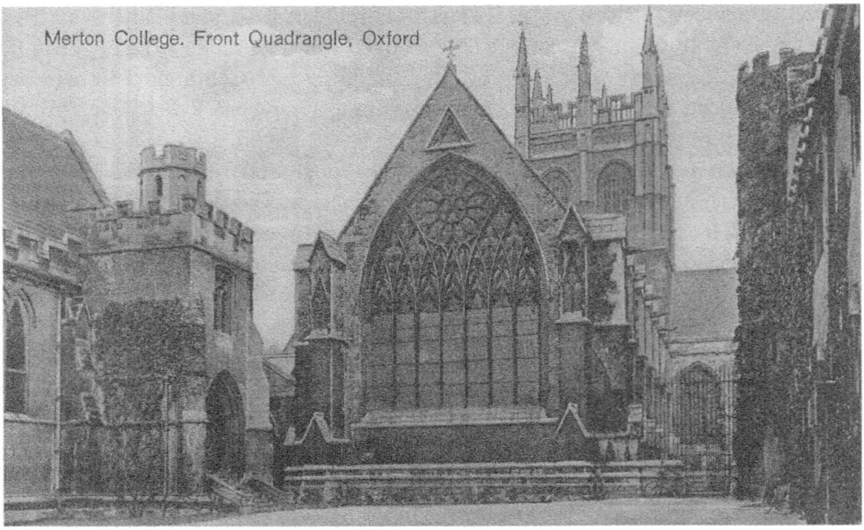

Figure 3 Merton College (Front Quadrangle, Oxford). Postcard from the 1900s. Photo by Culture Club via Getty Images.

the possibility of holding lectures and seminars,[32] playing also a personal role in their organization. He sent students to them for private tuition.[33] He asked the Oxford University Press for funding for projects.[34] Although he was already working on his own edition of the *Institutes of Gaius*, he even offered to give this up in favour of Schulz, if it would help him to receive some payment from Oxford University Press, as emerges from the correspondence with its editor, Kenneth Sisam.[35] When de Zulueta was planning an *Oxford History of Legal Science* together with Kantorowicz, whom he wanted to be the co-editor,[36] a project 'of a then unprecedented international character' (Ernst 2004: 171) (even if it was not fully realized), he also asked Schulz for a contribution to replace that of de Francisci,[37] not least in order to allow Schulz to receive a small income. This contribution was eventually to become the seminal work *History of Roman Legal Science*, and it was again de Zulueta who personally translated the whole book into English, at the same time doing a great deal of editorial work (Ernst 2004: 173).

As for Kantorowicz, the help provided went even further: After Kantorowicz's death, de Zulueta obtained from All Souls College a grant for the education of his children.[38] Touchingly, Kantorowicz's wife Hilda wrote in a letter to him: 'Lucky the man who has won in life such a friend.'[39] Finally – surely an act of great self-sacrifice for any scholar – while still working on his commentary on Gaius, he gave away his own extraordinary private collection of Roman law and legal history books to the University of Aberdeen, which otherwise would have lacked the requisite library to enable David Daube – another German Jewish émigré – effectively to take up the newly established chair of jurisprudence.[40]

In these years his personal engagement was not restricted solely to scholars. On the occasion of the conferment on de Zulueta of an honorary degree by the University of

Aberdeen, in 1953, the *laudator* T. B. Smith gives full recognition to this aspect of de Zulueta's character:[41]

> His generosity is well known, despite his efforts to conceal it. Few people can have extended so much unselfish help to refugees of various creeds and races – from Spain, Germany, Poland. Entire books written by exiled scholars have been translated or revised by him, and during the recent war he was instrumental in establishing and maintaining the Polish University in Oxford.[42]

All this should be sufficient to dispel the notion that de Zulueta was in any sense an anti-Semite. One further detail can be added: In the letter to Riccobono already mentioned,[43] in which de Zulueta expressed his appreciation of Daube, although he considered him as a suitable candidate for the vacant chair in Roman law in London, he seemed to think an appointment problematical. His remark is revealing: 'But he [Daube] seems to have made enemies, or possibly it is just anti-Semitism which makes his appointment doubtful (as I am told it is)': a comment which should dispel any doubt about de Zulueta's own position.

In his Introduction to the *Studies in the Roman Law of Sale*, David Daube could pronounce it to be 'the first collection of essays on Roman law produced exclusively by scholars from United Kingdom universities'. This flourishing of Roman law scholarship in Britain is surely also attributable in some measure to the lifetime dedication of Francis de Zulueta. So much is clear. However, much more than this, de Zulueta's quiet, unsung dedication behind the scenes also made a significant contribution to ensuring that the same could also be said about the flourishing of a pluralistic post-war Roman law scholarship in Continental Europe, where the discipline was able to rise again from the ashes of Nazi persecution.

Living his Catholic faith

But it was religion which played the crucial and defining role in de Zulueta's life. Francis de Zulueta belonged to an aristocratic Spanish family of diplomats, businessmen and bankers,[44] not only of the Catholic faith, but also deeply involved with the Roman Catholic Church: An uncle was a Jesuit father;[45] one of his mother's brothers – whose family was of Irish origins – was a priest;[46] a nephew, don Alfonso Manuel de Zulueta, became chaplain at the University of Oxford;[47] finally, a more famous cousin, Rafael Merry del Val, belonged to the upper echelons of the Church hierarchy, rising to be a cardinal and, in the years 1903–14, the secretary of state of Pope Pius X. Like other male members of his family on both sides, de Zulueta began his education at Beaumont College, a Jesuit boarding school situated in Berkshire.[48] He then went on to the Oratory School at Edgbaston, Birmingham.[49]

De Zulueta was well known among his contemporaries as a devout Roman Catholic. His obituary published in *The Times* points out that 'his most outstanding characteristic was a burning religious zeal, which guided his conduct throughout life'.[50] When de Zulueta came up to Oxford, in 1897, religion was still an important issue.[51] Catholic students had been readmitted to the University only a few decades before, and they were given official permission by their bishops to attend the (Protestant) University only two years before, in 1895. In 1912 there were only two Catholic dons in Oxford: Francis de Zulueta and Francis Urquhart.[52] When de Zulueta filled the Regius chair of civil law in 1919, he was the first Roman Catholic professor to hold the position since the Reformation, as was pointed out in an article in *The Times*.[53] In 1920, the year after, only six members of the teaching staff were Catholics.[54] In 1939, almost twenty years later, there were still only four Catholic professors in the whole of the University of Oxford, one being de Zulueta himself, another the famous writer J. R. R. Tolkien. With Tolkien, indeed, de Zulueta developed a deep friendship[55] and became godfather to his daughter, Priscilla (Ferrández Bru 2008; Stark 2014).

De Zulueta lived his religious life with great personal conviction and engagement. He was the secretary and an active member of the Oxford University Catholic Association,[56] and was close to the Oxford University Newman Society[57] (named after the famous English Catholic convert Cardinal J. H. Newman). He was also a member of the Universities' Catholic Education Board (*The Tablet* 23 April 1921, 18) and was more generally engaged in questions relating to the participation of Catholic students at universities.[58] He was a member of the local branch of the Society of St. Vincent de Paul,[59] of which he became president, and was part of the circle which included such eminent English Catholics[60] as Ronald Knox, Martin D'Arcy, Evelyn Waugh, G. K. Chesterton and the aforementioned Tolkien.

Francis de Zulueta actively participated in Roman Catholic ceremonies in Oxford, such as the one held on the occasion of the visit of the Archbishop of Birmingham, commemorating the death of the Franciscan monk sent to England to found a province of his religious order;[61] or the visit of Cardinal Bourne on the occasion of the ceremony of the stone laying of the new Dominican Priory.[62] During the Festival of Corpus Christi he used to carry the Baldacchino of the Blessed Sacrament in St Giles.[63] De Zulueta was not simply a very welcome guest, nor was he just playing a role: He was and felt himself to be fully part of that world. The importance of his contribution to the religious life in Oxford was fully acknowledged after his death by the master of Campion Hall, Father Thomas Corbishley S. J.[64]

This deep religious faith[65] and his personal involvement with Catholic institutions led him on various occasions to intervene publicly on the pages of the leading British newspaper, *The Times*, defending the religious orders and the position of the Church,[66] especially when this came to collide with that of the 'State'. One example is given by his letters to the editor of *The Times* on what had been considered, by general public opinion, unwarranted papal interference with domestic political affairs in Malta, at that time part of the British Empire. In the summer of 1930, most probably following higher dispositions, Maltese bishops had denied absolution and administration of the sacraments to – and even menaced with excommunication – those Catholics who, at the coming political elections, intended to cast their vote for Lord Strickland, then prime minister of Malta, who had clashed in the past with the ecclesiastical authorities and was therefore considered by them to be anticlerical. Critical voices and protests were heard in Britain. De Zulueta wrote to *The Times* fully justifying the Church's intervention: 'In the judgment of the Maltese Bishops, the continuance of Lord

Strickland's Government would have been a serious injury to religion … . Their right so to act is a fundamental Catholic position.'[67] De Zulueta's letter provoked a series of irritated replies, among them one of Isaac Foot, a Member of Parliament for the Liberal Party.[68] In a further letter,[69] de Zulueta clearly called the administration of Lord Strickland 'inimical to the Church', renewing his support for the Church and linking it this time to the defence of the democracy and the right of self-government of the Maltese people.[70]

De Zulueta's public intervention on such a minor political dispute perhaps gives us a fundamental insight into his motivations and attitude in a much more serious conflict, which has done so much to colour his reputation. This is the savage and highly divisive Spanish Civil War, in which he had of course a special interest. His decision openly and vociferously to take the side of Franco in the pages of *The Times* (5 October 1936, 13; 7 November 1936, 8; 7 December 1936, 15; 18 March 1937, 17) certainly made him unpopular, not least among his Oxford colleagues (*The Times*, 8 October 1936, 10). But they were hardly political reasons of Left or Right which lay behind his sympathies. The main reason for de Zulueta's position is succinctly described in his obituary published in *The Times*: 'in later years devotion to the Church underlay his passionate support of the cause of General Franco' (*The Times*, 18 January 1958, 8).

The gravity and complexity of the situation in Spain was well known to de Zulueta: Not only could he follow the events day by day in England in the columns of *The Times*, he also had an insider's view of Spanish affairs, since his cousin, Alfonso Merry del Val, was the Spanish ambassador in London, and his brother Pedro Juan was also working in the embassy as attaché. Moreover, the family had, as we have seen, direct links to the Vatican. Francis de Zulueta, Spaniard by birth, nobleman, conservative, educated in Catholic schools and, as we have seen, devotee of the Catholic Church, could not remain indifferent to the terrible events which were taking place in Spain.

Conclusion

Where should Francis de Zulueta be located in his attitude to the totalitarian regimes of the twentieth century? He was a Catholic conservative, without any doubt firmly against communism,[71] and was wholly on the side of Franco from the beginning of the insurrection, making no attempt to hide his sympathy and support. Fritz Schulz, the Jewish refugee given so much help by de Zulueta, could nevertheless describe him as 'a Spanish fascist' (Ernst 2004: 169 and note 503). It is true that British newspapers at the time tended to call the 'Falangists' (the supporters of Franco in Spain) 'Fascists'. Yet this identity had already been criticized at the time[72] as a possible cause of misunderstanding. De Zulueta's support for Franco was motivated by his religious convictions and was deeply rooted in his reaction to the oppression of the Church in Spain under the Republican government. Such a reaction in the particular circumstances of the Spanish struggle cannot be equated with support for the other totalitarian regimes – Italian fascism and German Nazism (which were helping the Spanish insurgents) – or with support for totalitarian ideology in general. On the contrary, de Zulueta's 'unselfish help' (in the words of T. B. Smith) to German refugees who had to flee their country, and to Polish soldiers who were fighting against the Germans, together with his deep friendship with Kantorowicz, reveals just how much he detested Nazism.

Of course, de Zulueta was living in a Europe deeply marked by totalitarian regimes, whose influence extended also to academic enterprises, and this aspect could simply not be ignored. A remarkable example is de Zulueta and Kantorowicz's famous project of an *Oxford History of Legal Science*.[73] As a letter of de Zulueta to Kenneth Sisam, editor of the Oxford University Press, shows, the choice of the contributors inevitably had to be carefully weighed on the basis of political affiliations.[74] What emerges, for example, is the need to counterbalance the presence of Kantorowicz, who was 'persona ingratissima' to the Nazis; otherwise someone like Koschaker – who had been preferred to a 'strong Nazi' like San Nicolò for the part on oriental laws – could 'harm himself by contributing to a work part-edited by Kantorowicz'. In a pragmatic attempt to find a balance and avoid complications, de Zulueta suggested involving the Italian Romanist Pietro de Francisci, partly for his political position: 'this whole trouble … will be cured if the most important contribution to Vol. 1 [i.e. the one on Roman legal science] comes from the pen of a prominent, though not a violent, fascist'. This compromise would avoid involving an outright Nazi, as he considered Kunkel (the other candidate for that section). The letter clearly shows him seeking the lesser of two evils. No adhesion can be seen here to totalitarian ideologies: just an attempt to secure the success of an important project without having to renounce the best scholars in their respective fields.

Finally, very few know of the adhesion of de Zulueta to the originally ecumenical movement known as the 'Sword of the Spirit'.[75] This was a lay organization founded in 1940 by the Archbishop of Westminster, Cardinal Hinsley,[76] after the fall of France and Italy's entry into the war. It was intended to contribute to the defeat of totalitarian regimes of both Left and Right (especially Nazism) and to the promotion of higher religious and spiritual principles. The first two points of its programme significantly read as follows: '(1) The movement stands for the principles of Christianity and the Natural Law; (2) Our opposition to Nazism and other totalitarianisms is the result of their denial of these principles.' Pamphlets were to be issued 'to make clear the principles of Christianity and of the Natural Law'.[77] It was intended that Francis de Zulueta should contribute with a pamphlet on 'The Natural Law'.[78] This single detail encapsulates very clearly de Zulueta's moral position.

The conclusion is clear: de Zulueta was a devout Catholic, who oriented his opinions, acts and deeds according to the values of his religion. Defending the Church and its institutions, rejecting who and what was against it, giving his help and support to people in need: All these are different facets of one and the same individual. Well informed on Spanish atrocities, from an insider's point of view, he inevitably chose to support the side which was acting in defence of the Church. This was the motivation that informed his actions, as was clearly discerned by Peter Stein, who had known de Zulueta personally. In his obituary he writes:

> De Zulueta was fearless in his advocacy of policies in which he believed and was unconcerned by the unpopularity which they sometimes gained him. He was criticised for his strong support of the cause of General Franco during the Spanish Civil War. This was certainly due to his zeal for the Catholic Church, to which he was passionately devoted. (Stein 1958: 240)

The same conclusion was drawn by another of his colleagues, F. H. Lawson, in his biography of 1971. Nevertheless, the shadow of fascism cast on de Zulueta because of his support for Franco has never wholly abandoned him. Interestingly, a similar fate befell J. R. R. Tolkien, de Zulueta's fellow Catholic at Oxford, who shared with him the ignominy of being labelled a fascist for his 'discreet moral support' of the insurgents led by Franco.[79] What has been written on Tolkien (Ferrández Bru 2011) in precisely this context can equally be applied to de Zulueta:

> When historical events are analysed from a distance and evaluated according to contemporary parameters and not according to the circumstances when they developed, it is easy to attain wrong conclusions, or at least get a distorted view of the different attitudes of the participants and witnesses of those events.

In reading his obituary published in *The Times*,[80] one cannot help but already detect a certain tendency to diminish de Zulueta's achievements as a scholar. There seems to be a vein of criticism and dislike which the anonymous author cannot completely conceal. One wonders how much this was due to a lingering distaste for this outspoken supporter of Franco and his brutal regime, which is hard enough for us to overlook even today, and must have been all but impossible for contemporaries who had lived through this deeply polarizing struggle.[81]

This impression is confirmed by a very revealing reaction which came two weeks after the publication of the obituary. In a letter to *The Times* H. G. Hanbury, the famous legal author of one of the most important manuals of English law, submitted a supplement to the obituary which was clearly meant as a protest, to re-establish the truth and to give the deceased his due.[82] It begins with the ringing affirmation:

> De Zulueta was one of the most brilliant and learned jurists who ever lived. His obituary notice really does him less than justice in saying that he published little .... No one who attended his classes could bear to miss a moment of his exposition and his textual criticism.

The original obituary had clearly been read by Hanbury as an attempt to 'damn with faint praise'. Yet, in the judgement of history, this intervention did not succeed in repairing the damage which had been done. To be Spanish (although naturalized British), a devout Catholic and a supporter of Franco in Oxford: This was an explosive mixture which has left a permanent mark. A 'black legend' has enveloped the reputation of de Zulueta, projecting its long shadow up to the present day.[83]

Notes

1 The main surveys of de Zulueta's life are *The Times* 18 January 1958, 8 ('Prof. Francis de Zulueta. The Teaching of Civil Law'); *The Catholic Herald* 4 June 1948, 4 ('Catholic profiles: 159'); Stein 1958; Nicholas 1958; Lawson 1971; Ferrández Bru 2008, unfortunately without any indication of sources.

2 On Schulz, see the excellent biography of Ernst 2004.
3 On Pringsheim, see Honoré 2004.
4 On Kantorowicz, see Ibbetson 2004.
5 On Daube, see Rodger 2004; Carmichael 2004.
6 On the relationship between Daube and Buckland, see Rodger 2010.
7 Sold by de Zulueta at a low price, as reported in the *Minutes of the University Court of the University of Aberdeen*, vol. XVII. *Meetings*, MXI–MLIV (10 October 1950 to 6 July 1954), p. 401 (*Meeting of the University Court of the University of Aberdeen*: 11 November 1952): '(c) A letter was submitted from the Librarian intimating that Professor F. de Zulueta, Banbury, Oxon., had given his valuable books on Jurisprudence and Roman Law to the University for the nominal sum of £ 300 plus carriage'. In a letter to the editor of the Oxford University Press, P. J. Spicer, de Zulueta manifested his satisfaction for having taken that decision: 'The price was reasonable, and it is a satisfaction that the collection has gone where it will be appreciated and used' (OUP Archives: PB/ED/017846 Box OP 2442, letter of 20 November 1952). The generosity of de Zulueta was also stressed in the *laudatio* given by T. B. Smith, the promoter of the initiative, on the occasion of the conferment upon de Zulueta of an honorary degree by the University of Aberdeen on 10 July 1953, an account of which was published in *The Aberdeen University Review* 1953–1954: 295: 'only last year he most generously made over to this University his excellent library of Roman and Canon Law, which contains works not available in any other Law Faculty in Britain.' The importance of de Zulueta's library for the teaching of Roman law under Daube in Aberdeen, indeed for the revival of the Civilian tradition there, was again stressed by the same T. B. Smith in an article dedicated to the memory of the Oxford professor: 'It was appropriate … that while Professor Daube … was still at Aberdeen, the law library there should have received a most generous benefaction of the de Zulueta collection of Civil and Canon Law works' (Smith 1958–1959: 629). See also Stein 2001: 434 ('de Zulueta had generously transferred his private collection of Roman law books to Aberdeen to help David's work'); Carmichael 2004: 94; MacQueen 2013: 827–8.
8 This designation, peculiar to Aberdeen University, effectively means the chair in Roman law.
9 In an unpublished letter to Riccobono dated 19 December 1948, written by de Zulueta soon after the appointment of Jolowicz (formerly professor of Roman law in London), he comments that, in his opinion, the best choice for the now vacant London chair would be Daube ('I do not know who will succeed him at London. The best scholar is Daube, and I myself find him a very agreeable person'). A copy of this and of other letters (twelve in total), which are kept in Palermo and form part of the correspondence between the two scholars, has been kindly put at my disposal by Riccobono's heirs Lilia and Mariella through the courtesy of Professor Mario Varvaro (University of Palermo). To all of them I would like to express my gratitude. De Zulueta's great admiration for Daube, his work and the depth of his erudition we find expressed again a few years later in various unpublished letters addressed to Peter Stein (de Zulueta to Stein, 8 July 1956: 'David's work on Legislative Forms seems to me a brilliant performance. What a man!'; 28 January 1957: 'I was very glad too to get first-hand news of Daube. It does me good to hear what a success he is') and to Eleanor Rathbone ('Stein is asking Daube who is almost omniscient'). These letters are preserved among the papers of Peter Stein, which have been entrusted by his daughter, Barbara Judkins, to Douglas J. Osler (MPIeR, Frankfurt a.M.), a pupil of Peter Stein. I am very grateful to them for putting the letters at my disposal.

10 It is well known that, from the very beginning (1920), clause 19 of the *Parteiprogramm* of the NSDAP foresaw the substitution of the subject 'Roman Law' by 'German Common Law' (*deutsches Gemeinrecht*) in the curriculum of law faculties: on this, see Landau 1989.

11 Harding-Barlow 1958 (in fact an obituary of Francis de Zulueta); Beck 1959. In the former the very same words used by *The Times* and reported above are repeated, but without acknowledgement of the source. Other obituaries also seem to have been inspired by it: Stein 1958: 240 ('he set himself a very high standard and was reluctant to publish much'); Nicholas 1958: 138 ('he allowed himself perhaps to be too restricted by his own very high standards … he published relatively little').

12 Daube 1959; the list is found at pp. ix–xi.

13 Rodger 2004: 238. According to him, 'de Zulueta was, in many ways, like an old-fashioned war correspondent, not embedded with any of the fighting forces, but watching and reporting the battle from a safe vantage point': an opinion not entirely justified.

14 The author means here Oxburgh Hall, a country house in Norfolk which was in fact owned by the family of his wife.

15 Carmichael 2004: 96. It continues: 'Stressing their humanity, Daube put much emphasis on forgiving people with repugnant views', associating de Zulueta with the latter.

16 MacQueen 2013: 827–8: 'They [Daube and de Zulueta] first met in Oxford in the 1930s, when Daube discovered that de Zulueta's Spanish origins led him to sympathize with Franco's brand of fascism. But some anti-Semitic attitudes did not prevent him [de Zulueta] rendering much support to Jewish refugees from Nazi Germany and, subsequently, to Polish exiles as well.'

17 OUP: PB/ED/001310: Daube to Sutcliff, letter of 12 February 1958: 'My dear Sutcliff, this morning I received from de Zulueta's widow a list of his publications … It is not long, 27 items …'.

18 OUP: PB/ED/001310: Daube to Sutcliff, letter of 20 August (?) 1958: 'I am glad you agreed to the list of de Z's publications. I am just verifying it.'

19 I am currently working on a biographical and academic profile of Francis de Zulueta, which will provide a new and more complete list of his publications.

20 As for the correspondence with Riccobono, on the letters in Palermo see note 9. An earlier letter, sent by Riccobono to de Zulueta in 1921, I found in the Law Library of Aberdeen inside the offprint of an article by the same Riccobono (Riccobono 1921) presented by him to de Zulueta (AUL, Taylor Library, p. 34089.25/4 [olim ZU 34089.25/4]).

21 Respectively kept in the University Archives (Francis de Zulueta: Papers and Notes, Aberdeen University Library - Special Collections, MS 2785 [3 Boxes]) and in the Taylor Library.

22 A role often anachronistically assigned to Daube: see, for example, MacQueen 2005: 336.

23 On the teaching of law in Oxford, see Lawson 1968.

24 The papers given within this section were collected and published the same year by Vinogradoff (Vinogradoff 1913).

25 His first encounter with Riccobono in 1913 was recollected by de Zulueta in a letter written 19 December 1948 to the Italian scholar (see note 9).

26 In his obituary of Vinogradoff, de Zulueta describes himself as 'one who had the privilege of being among Vinogradoff's first Oxford pupils, and later his colleague' (de Zulueta 1926: 206).

27 de Zulueta 1932: 272: 'The lecturers were seven Italians, three Germans, one Frenchman and one Belgian. Why no Englishman, when we possess so eminent an exponent [meaning Buckland]?'.

28 See notes 20 and 21.
29 Collinet had been invited to give a series of lectures in March 1922; Pringsheim in October 1930; Fournier in November 1931; Koschaker in February 1934.
30 During his stay in England for the occasion, Riccobono also gave two lectures on 'The formation of Roman Law' at the University College in London: de Zulueta was in the chair (*The Times* 29 May 1924, 13).
31 Officially the conferment was recommended by the Board of the Faculty of Law. In the case of Riccobono, we know that the qualifications for the degree were stated by the Warden of All Souls: see the *Hebdomadal Council Papers* No. 128 [April 22–July 19, 1924], xxxi.
32 As for Kantorowicz, in the *Oxford University Gazette* (OUG) seminars were advertised on 'Mediaeval Legal Manuscripts' (for 1936: OUG 20 March 1936), 'Roman and Canon Law in Bracton' (for 1937: OUG 11 December 1936), 'Latin Textual Criticism, with special regard to Mommsen's Praefatio to his edition of the Digest' (for 1938. OUG 10 December 1937); 'The nature of Law and Legal science' (for 1939), the last of which he had the intention to repeat the subsequent year (OUG 15 December 1939). Some seminars were held in the rooms of All Souls. Pringsheim, on the other end, supported also by H. Lawson and other scholars, was giving lectures at Merton College on 'The general character of Justinian's legislation' (1939: OUG 17 March 1939), 'Classical and Post-classical law' (1939: OUG 23 June 1939) and 'Greek private law (guarantee and sale)' (1940). On the offer made by Merton, see Honoré 2004: 220.
33 As was the case with Pringsheim, 'rescued' by de Zulueta after the grant from Merton had run out. He recommended him among his law colleagues to offer coaching work for the students coming to Oxford after the war, as emerges from a letter written by de Zulueta to Kenneth Sisam, the editor of the Oxford University Press (OUP Archives: PB/ED/010382 Box OP 1390: letter of 31 May 1948). The recommendation was successful: see Honoré 2004: 224.
34 Like the *Manual of Roman Law*, to be written by Schulz in order to provide him with financial support (Ernst 2004: 147).
35 OUP Archives, PB/ED/010382 Box 1390: Sisam to Schulz, letter of the 15 February 1939.
36 More details on this enterprise in Ernst 2004: 171-9.
37 One of the original contributors: Ernst 2004: 172.
38 The decision had been taken already in March at a general meeting of the Finance and Research Fellowships Committee of All Souls, where it was decided to assign a sum not exceeding 200 pounds for the education of Kantorowicz's children 'in the event of an application being received'. A colleague informed de Zulueta with an informal note of the successful meeting (Aberdeen University Library - Special Collections, MS 2785/2/2).
39 Aberdeen University Library - Special Collections, MS 2785/2/2, Hilda Kantorowicz to de Zulueta, letter of 3 March 1940.
40 See note 7.
41 The *laudatio* was reported in *The Aberdeen University Review*, 35 (1953-1954): 296.
42 The Polish Faculty of Law at Oxford was created in March 1944 after an agreement between the Polish Government in exile and the British authorities. (Other Polish universities abroad had already been established in Britain in the previous years.) Inaugurated at the end of April of the same year, this university was to help young Polish soldiers and airmen to keep up their university studies while they were serving in the Armed Forces in Britain during the Second World War. Part of the teaching staff

was made up of professors and teachers from the University of Oxford: de Zulueta was among them. On the Oxford Polish Faculty of Law, which was to remain active, according to its statute, until the conclusion of an armistice with Germany, see the *Oxford University Gazette* 16 March 1944, 350; *The Oxford Magazine* 4 May 1944, 1.

43 See note 9.

44 On his family background, see Lawson 1971.

45 Francis M. de Zulueta, S.J.

46 Father Denis F. Sheil, who became Superior of the Oratory in Birmingham. He was the last novice received by Cardinal John Henry Newman, founder of the Oratory. Other members of his mother's family also entered religious orders.

47 As the successor of Monsignor Ronald Knox.

48 On the Spanish students at Beaumont College from its foundation (in 1861) up to 1892 see Rodríguez Caparrini 2007, 2011 and esp. (on the members of de Zulueta's family) 2012, 2014 and 2016.

49 Both boarding schools had been founded with the aim of constituting a Roman Catholic alternative to Eton, the most famous public school in England: see Rodríguez Caparrini 2003 (on Beaumont College); Shrimpton 2005.

50 See note 1.

51 On the presence of Catholics in Oxford, see Martindale 1925.

52 Sire 1997: 33. Urquhart was lecturer in History and Fellow at Balliol College, later becoming its Dean.

53 *The Times* 10 November 1919, 15 ('New professor of Civil Law at Oxford').

54 *The Tablet. The International Catholic News Weekly* 7 February 1920, 5 ('Catholics at the universities').

55 In February 1930 we find Tolkien attending a dinner at All Souls College, given by de Zulueta in honour of the Archbishop of Birmingham, who the previous day had held an ordination at the Dominican Priory. The dinner was attended by the superiors of the Congregations in Oxford, by the Senior Fellow of Balliol College Francis Urquhart, and 'one or two others': *The Tablet* 12 April 1930, 488 ('University Notes').

56 *The Tablet* 31 December 1927, 24 ('University Notes. Oxford'). Sometimes meetings were held in All Souls.

57 As was Tolkien.

58 On this issue he gave various papers: *The Tablet* 6 August 1927, 20 ('Catholic education notes'); 5 November 1927, 19.

59 *The Catholic Herald* 4 June 1948: see note 1.

60 Most of them converts: see Allit 1997.

61 *The Times* 31 October 1924, 7 ('Franciscans at Oxford. 700th Anniversary'): de Zulueta figures among the guests invited at luncheon afterwards. Again, on the 4 October 1931, de Zulueta (together with Tolkien, Ronald Knox and other guests) attends the formal opening of the new Franciscan friary at Oxford: *The Tablet*, 10 October 1931, 478 ('The New Franciscan Friary at Oxford'). See also *The Times* 19 May 1936, 28 ('Roman Catholic ceremony at Oxford').

62 *The Times* 16 August 1921, 5 ('Dominicans at Oxford. Stone-laying of new Priory'); *The Tablet* 20 August 1921, 20–5 ('The Dominicans at Oxford. Foundation-stone of new Priory'): de Zulueta figures again, representing the University, among the guests invited at luncheon afterwards. See also note 54.

63 *The Catholic Herald* 4 June 1948 (see note 1).

64 *The Tablet* 1 February 1958, 19 ('Professor de Zulueta'): 'In more tangible ways … he contributed to the building of a strong Catholic life there [i.e. Oxford] … so modest

and unostentatious was he that few can do more than guess at the range of his charities.'

65 Not without prejudice are the recollections of Rowse, who describes de Zulueta as 'not only an ardent Catholic but an ultramontane, a real reactionary': Rowse 1993: 96.

66 In 1928 he made a public intervention with a letter to the editor (*The Times* 15 June 1928, 12 'The Jesuits'), entering into the heated debate around the 'Prayer-book Measure', which had just been defeated in the House of Commons, when Roman Catholic members had abstained from voting. The intervention – a passionate defence of the Jesuits – was a reply to the letter of Sir Frederick Milner (former Member of Parliament for the Conservative Party), published on the same newspaper a few days before (*The Times*, 13 June 1928, 17). Milner had expressed his criticism in a negative way, describing certain tactics used by the Catholics to influence the vote as typical 'of the Jesuits'.

67 *The Times* 1 July 1930, 12 ('The dispute in Malta. Suspension of the Constitution').

68 *The Times* 2 July 1930, 10 ('The dispute in Malta. Right of electoral freedom'): 'While Parliamentary Roman Catholic members ... walk delicately [referring to a recent debate within the British Parliament], Professor de Zulueta marches into the controversy with a challenging stride … it is at least difficult to reconcile his soft sentences [on the Maltese bishops] with the hard facts.' 'If England becomes predominantly Roman Catholic – Foot polemicized – are we to expect these methods of political persuasion whenever they are deemed to be appropriate by the clerical hierarchy of the day?' Ironically regretting the 'disapproval of the learned Professor', Foot claimed that the opposite position represented that of 'the overwhelming majority of the English people'.

69 *The Times* 4 July 1930, 12 ('The dispute in Malta. Episcopal authority').

70 The exchange between de Zulueta and Foot on the dispute in Malta went on for weeks (*The Times* 8 July 1930, 12; 15 July 1930, 10; 17 July 1930, 10), with de Zulueta on the one side rhetorically and repeatedly appealing to the liberty of the Maltese people to choose their own representatives – the elections having been cancelled in the meantime and their Constitution suspended – while on the other side there were accusations that this was minimizing the gravity of the interference of the bishops and of their threats towards the Maltese electors.

71 On more than one occasion in his letters to *The Times* he criticizes the 'left [or 'Red'] propaganda'.

72 By Douglas Jerrold, for example, the editor of the *Catholic English Review* and an active supporter of Franco: see his letter in *The Times* 24 April 1937, 8.

73 On the project in general, see Ernst 2004: 171–9.

74 An extract of this letter is published by Ernst 2004: 172.

75 Walsh 1980; Walsh 1982; Mews 1983. The movement was subsumed, in 1965, into the 'Catholic Institute for International Relations', which then became 'Progressio'. It also involved friends of de Zulueta, like M. D'Arcy.

76 It would go beyond the limits of this contribution to analyse the profile of Cardinal Hinsley, but it is noticeable that, unlike some members of the Catholic hierarchy, he was openly against all forms of totalitarianism and absolutism, viewing both communism and fascism (or Nazism) equally as enemies.

77 The programme and more information on the planned activities were published in *The Catholic Herald* 30 August 1940, 8.

78 Ibid. It is therefore all the more perplexing when Lawson 1971: 1098 observes in his biography of de Zulueta: 'His scepticism in matters of legal scholarship … led him …

to entertain a radical and very un-Catholic disbelief in natural law.' So far I have been unable to find any trace of such a pamphlet.

79 Ferrández Bru 2011. The text is also available at http://www.josemanuel ferrandez.com/ENguerra.html (unpaginated, accessed on 17 January 2017). Like de Zulueta, Tolkien too was driven by personal motives: his guardian, Father Francis Xavier Morgan, whom he regarded with much affection, was a Catholic priest of Spanish origins, who had also studied at the Oratory School in Birmingham. And, again like de Zulueta, 'Tolkien's support to the Franco movement rests precisely on his perception of him as the champion of the Catholic Church against communist menace' (Ferrández Bru 2011).

80 See note 1.

81 Especially in Oxford, where even in 1939, when the final victory of Franco was evident, many academics still took a public position against the official recognition of Franco's administration 'so long as the Spanish Government holds territory and Italian or German troops remain in Spain'. A telegram urging this position and signed by forty-two professors and tutors was sent to the chancellor of the University, Lord Halifax, and published in *The Times* 17 February 1939, 16 ('Oxford professors and General Franco'). This is all the more striking, considering that the general opinion by that time, shared even by a liberal like Salvador de Madariaga, considered such a recognition as the only means to put an end to the bloodshed which was still continuing in Spain.

82 *The Times* 10 February 1958, 14 ('Professors R. W. Lee and F. de Zulueta').

83 Only very recently the World Wide Web (the authors hidden behind its anonymity) is starting to restore a fairer picture. Thus the German version of the website dedicated to Francis de Zulueta in Wikipedia added the following note to the existing entry in April 2015: 'Obwohl er kein Faschist war, unterstützte Zulueta, wie viele katholische Spanier seiner Zeit, Franco im Spanischen Bürgerkrieg. Diese Unterstützung brachte dem hoch angesehenen Juristen einen schlechten Ruf in Oxford ein, wo er als faschistischer Aristokrat dargestellt wurde. Dieser Darstellung widerspricht allerdings seine Unterstützung prominenter deutscher Juden wie Fritz Schulz und David Daube, der eine tiefe Freundschaft zu Zulueta entwickelte' (trans.: Although he was not a fascist, like many other Catholic Spaniards in his time Zulueta supported Franco in the Spanish Civil War. This support gave to this highly regarded jurist a bad reputation in Oxford, where he was depicted as a fascist aristocrat. This picture contrasts with his support to prominent German Jews like Fritz Schulz and David Daube, who developed a deep friendship with Zulueta).

References

Allit, P. (1997), *Catholic Converts: British and American Intellectuals Turn to Rome*, Ithaca, NY: Cornell University Press.

Atzeri, L. (2010), 'La "storia del diritto antico" e una lettera inedita di Paul Koschaker', *Iuris Antiqui Historia*, 2: 191–222.

Beatson, J. and Zimmermann, R., eds. (2004), *Jurists Uprooted: German-speaking émigré lawyers in twentieth-century Britain*, Oxford and New York: Oxford University Press.

Beck, W. H. (1959), 'Francis de Zulueta', *Tulane Law Review*, 33 (3): 451.

Carmichael, C. (2004), *Ideas and the Man: Remembering David Daube*, Frankfurt am Main: Vittorio Klostermann.

Daube, D., ed. (1959, repr. 1977), *Studies in the Roman Law of Sale: Dedicated to the Memory of Francis de Zulueta*, Oxford: Clarendon Press (repr. Aalen: Scientia Verlag).

Ernst, W. (2004), 'Fritz Schulz (1879–1957)', in J. Beatson and R. Zimmermann (eds), *Jurists Uprooted: German-speaking Émigré Lawyers in Twentieth-century Britain*, 105–203, Oxford and New York: Oxford University Press.

Ferrández Bru, J. M. (2008), 'Junio 1929. Oxford'. Online: https://jmferrandezbru.wordpress.com/2008/12/02/junio-1929-oxford/ (posted 2 December 2008, accessed 17 January 2017).

Ferrández Bru, J. M. (2011), 'J. R. R. Tolkien and the Spanish Civil War', *Mallorn: The Journal of the Tolkien Society*, 51: 16–19.

Harding-Barlow, M. (1958), 'De Zulueta of Oxford University and his Teaching of the Study of Roman Law', *South African Law Journal*, 75: 418–27.

Honoré, T. (2004), 'Fritz Pringsheim (1882–1967)', in J. Beatson and R. Zimmermann (eds), *Jurists Uprooted: German-speaking Émigré Lawyers in Twentieth-century Britain*, 205–32, Oxford and New York: Oxford University Press.

Ibbetson, D. (2004), 'Hermann Kantorowicz (1877–1940) and Walter Ullmann (1910–1983)', in J. Beatson and R. Zimmermann (eds), *Jurists Uprooted: German-speaking Émigré Lawyers in Twentieth-century Britain*, 269–98, Oxford and New York: Oxford University Press.

Landau, P. (1989), 'Römisches Recht und deutsches Gemeinrecht. Zur rechtspolitischen Zielsetzung im nationalistischen Parteiprogramm', in M. Stolleis and D. Simon (eds), *Rechtsgeschichte im Nationalsozialismus. Beiträge zur Geschichte einer Disziplin*, 11–24, Tübingen: J. C. B. Mohr (Paul Siebeck).

Lawson, F. H. (1968), *The Oxford Law School 1850–1965*, Oxford: Clarendon Press.

Lawson, F. H. (1971), 'Zulueta, Francis de (Francisco María José)', in E. T. Williams and H. M. Palmer (eds), *The Dictionary of National Biography 1951–1960*, 1097–9, Oxford: Oxford University Press. Reprinted (with minor changes and additions) in Lawson, F. H. (2004), 'Zulueta, Francis de (Francisco María José)', in H. C. G Matthew and B. Harrison (eds), *Oxford Dictionary of National Biographies, from the Earliest Times to the Year 2000*, vol. 60, 1021–3, Oxford: Oxford University Press.

MacQueen, H. L. (2005), 'Rev. of Carmichael, Ideas and the Man', *The Edinburgh Law Review*, 9: 335–8.

MacQueen, H. L. (2013), 'A Friendship in the Law: David Daube and T. B. Smith', *Tulane Law Review*, 87 (4): 811–65.

Martindale, C. C. S. J. (1925), *Catholics in Oxford*, Oxford: Blackwell.

Mews, S. (1983), 'The Sword of the Spirit: A Catholic Cultural Crusade of 1940', *Studies in Church History*, 20: 409–30.

Nicholas, B. (1958), 'Francis de Zulueta (12-9-1878 – 16-1-1958)', *IVRA*, 9: 138.

Riccobono, S. (1921), 'La forma della *stipulatio*. A proposito del fr. 35 § 2 D. 45,1', *Bullettino dell'Istituto di Diritto Romano*, 31: 29–39.

Rodger, A. (2004), 'David Daube (1909–1999)', in J. Beatson and R. Zimmermann (eds), *Jurists Uprooted: German-speaking Émigré Lawyers in Twentieth-century Britain*, 233–48, Oxford and New York: Oxford University Press.

Rodger, A. (2010), 'Buckland and Daube: A Cambridge Friendship', *Zeitschrift der Savigny-Stiftung für Rechtsgeschichte. Romanistische Abteilung*, 127: 245–54.

Rodríguez Caparrini, B. (2003), *"El Eton católico": el internado jesuita de Beaumont (Old Windsor, Inglaterra) durante el rectorado del Padre Joseph M. Bampton, S.J. (1901–1908)*, PhD diss., Universidad de Cádiz. Published online: http://rodin.uca.es/xmlui/handle/10498/14827 (accessed 23 April 2017).

Rodríguez Caparrini, B. (2007), 'Alumnos españoles en el internado jesuita de Beaumont (Old Windsor, Inglaterra) 1861–1868', *Archivum Historicum Societatis Iesu*, 76: 3–37.

Rodríguez Caparrini, B. (2011), 'Alumnos españoles en el internado jesuita de Beaumont (Old Windsor, Inglaterra) 1869–1874', *Archivum Historicum Societatis Iesu*, 80: 151–250.

Rodríguez Caparrini, B. (2012), 'Alumnos españoles en el internado jesuita de Beaumont (Old Windsor, Inglaterra) 1874–1880', *Miscelánea Comillas*, 70 (136): 241–64.

Rodríguez Caparrini, B. (2014), 'Alumnos españoles en el internado jesuita de Beaumont (Old Windsor, Inglaterra) 1880–1886', *Hispania Sacra* 66, Extra I: 403–52.

Rodríguez Caparrini, B. (2016), 'Alumnos españoles en el internado jesuita de Beaumont (Old Windsor, Inglaterra) 1886–1892', *Miscelánea Comillas*, 74 (145): 371–442.

Rowse, A. L. (1993), *All Souls in My Time*, London: Duckworth.

Shrimpton, P. (2005), *A Catholic Eton? Newman's Oratory School*, Leominster: Gracewing.

Sire, H. J. A. (1997), *Father Martin D'Arcy: Philosopher of Christian Love*, Leominster: Gracewing.

Smith, T. B. (1953–1954), '[*laudatio* of F. de Zulueta]', *The Aberdeen University Review*, 35: 292–6.

Smith, T. B. (1958–1959), 'A Meditation on Scottish Universities and the Civil Law', *Tulane Law Review*, 33: 621–30.

Stark, E. (2014), 'A vida de Priscilla Tolkien. Parte 1', *Tolkien Brasil*, 2014. Online: http://tolkienbrasil.com/categoria/artigos/colunas/eduardostark/page/4/ (posted 28 June 2014, accessed 23 April 2017).

Stein, P. (1958), 'Ricordo di Francis de Zulueta', *Labeo*, 4: 238–41.

Stein, P. (2001), 'David Daube 1909–1999', *Proceedings of the British Academy*, 111: 429–44.

Vinogradoff, P., ed. (1913), *Essays in Legal History Read Before the International Congress of Historical Studies Held in London in 1913*, London: Oxford University Press.

Walsh, M. J. (1980), *From Sword to Ploughshare: Sword of the Spirit to Catholic Institute for International Relations 1940–80*, London: Catholic Institute for International Relations.

Walsh, M. J. (1982), 'Ecumenism in War-Time Britain: The Sword of the Spirit and Religion and Life, 1940–1945', *The Heythrop Journal*, 23 (3–4): 243–58 (part 1); 377–94 (part 2).

de Zulueta, F. (1914), 'The Girard Testimonial Essays', *Law Quarterly Review*, 30: 216–17.

de Zulueta, F. (1920), *The Study of Roman Law To-Day: Inaugural Lecture Delivered May 12th, 1920, Before the University of Oxford*, Oxford: Clarendon Press.

de Zulueta, F. (1926), 'Paul Vinogradoff 1854–1925', *Law Quarterly Review*, 42: 202–11.

de Zulueta, F., ed. (1927, repr. 1972), *The Liber Pauperum of Vacarius*, London: Selden Society.

de Zulueta, F. (1929), 'L'histoire du droit de l'antiquité', in *Mélanges Paul Fournier*, 787–805, Paris: Sirey.

de Zulueta, F. (1932), 'Rev. of Conferenze per il XIV Centenario delle Pandette', *Law Quarterly Review*, 48: 272–4.

de Zulueta, F. (1946), *The Institutes of Gaius, I: Text with Critical Notes and Translation*, Oxford: Clarendon Press.

de Zulueta, F. (1953), *The Institutes of Gaius, II. Commentary*, Oxford: Clarendon Press.

4

Autonomy and Authority: The Image of the Roman Jurists in Schulz and Wieacker

Jacob Giltaij[1]

Introduction

The idea of a common European legal past can be traced back to two sets of scholars working between the 1930s and the 1960s in the field of Roman law and its reception. The first set of these scholars was exiled from Germany at the advent of the Second World War, necessitating a formulation of their theories to a new audience that lacked the Roman legal tradition that had been present in Germany. Among this group, Fritz Pringsheim (Honoré 2004: 206–32) and Fritz Schulz (Ernst 2004: 106–204) (along with, for example, Hermann Kantorowicz, David Daube and Ernst Levy) continued their scientific endeavours in the Anglophone academic world. The second set of scholars working on the notion of a common European legal past had remained in Germany during this period. Of this set of scholars, Paul Koschaker was effectively ousted from his office in Berlin,[2] Helmut Coing was, in 1940, established as a professor of Roman law in Frankfurt am Main (Luig 2002: 663) and Franz Wieacker, a pupil of Pringsheim, may have been a Nazi sympathizer (Behrends 1995: XXV–XXXIX; Winkel 2010: 213–21). These five professors of Roman law from both sets of scholars contributed profoundly to the development of the idea of a common European past as it is still employed, for example, in modern discussions on the legislation of a European private law.[3] Elements of this common European past, then, should be understood to be the result of an accumulative process of reception of Roman law from the eleventh century on, as discussed by Koschaker (Koschaker 1947: 124–64; Van Caenegem 2002: 22–37, 89–90), Wieacker (see, for example, Wieacker 1967, 1995) and Coing (see, for example, Coing 1985), and the notion of classical Roman jurisprudence as a legal science functioning independently from and even in antithesis to the political sphere. The latter notion is central to the works of Schulz and Pringsheim.[4]

This chapter aims to problematize the wartime and post-war manufacturing of a common European legal history around a single subject: that of the historical image of the Roman jurists. That is to say, the major works of these creators of a common European legal history are somehow linked together fundamentally by the creators' appreciation for the texts of the Roman jurists, be those in their classical,

Byzantine or otherwise received form. To investigate this relationship, I shall first determine the defining characteristics of Roman jurisprudence as understood by some or all of these scholars. For this, the works of Fritz Schulz are paramount, as they deal almost exclusively with Roman law in its Classical period.[5] Secondly, I shall compare the defining characteristics of Roman jurisprudence as understood by these scholars with their own study of the reception of Roman law, primarily Wieacker's *Privatrechtsgeschichte der Neuzeit* (1952). Even though similar ideas can certainly be found in the works of Pringsheim (Pringsheim 1921: 391–449; Pringsheim 1961) and Koschaker (Koschaker 1947: 166–7, 191–2), there are various reasons to single out Wieacker in this respect, primarily because he composed major works on both Roman law in Antiquity and its reception in the Middle Ages. In tracing the defining characteristics of the Roman legal science according to Schulz and Wieacker, I shall focus primarily on similarities between and direct citations in and among these scholars as well as the political context of Roman jurisprudence as an autonomous legal science - that is, as functioning independently from or even in antithesis to the political sphere.

The image of the Roman jurists in Schulz

The Roman jurists as a concept

For the sake of clarity, by *the Roman jurists*, I am referring specifically to the jurists that were active during the Roman Republic and subsequently the Roman Empire, from around the first century BCE up to the early third century CE. Already in many ancient legal and non-legal sources, these jurists are referred to as a relatively closed group of legal practitioners.[6] Some individuals belonging to this group can be identified primarily from the inclusion of their names in our main source for Roman legal texts, the sixth century CE compilation by Emperor Justinian known as the *Corpus iuris civilis*.

As a notion, *the Roman jurists* were rediscovered during the sixteenth century,[7] mainly with the goal of summarizing the works of the jurists in the late Republic and early Empire from the texts referred to in the *Corpus juris civilis*. It was also in the sixteenth century that the timeframe in which this group of jurists lived was given the title of the 'classical period', on the one hand to distinguish it from the later period of 'vulgarized law' (Wieacker and Wolf 2006: 207–18. Compare Levy 1956: 1–5 and Kop 1980), on the other to connect the work of the jurists to that of other classical sources, primarily Cicero.[8] In many ways, following the legal humanists, this distinction has echoed through the ages, for example, when, in the nineteenth century, the Historical School and their successors the Pandect scientists made it one of their goals to strive for a 'pure Roman law', one in any case made by individual jurists or legal scientists, not by the legislator (Stein 2004: 120–1). In the early twentieth century, the categorization of classical Roman jurists resulted in a large-scale hunt for so-called interpolations - that is, elements introduced to classical Roman legal texts by Justinian in his sixth century compilation (Stein 2004: 128–9).

As was the case in the sixteenth century (Stein 2004: 128), an emphasis on the content of Roman law in the Classical period arguably created the need for closer examination of the biographical details of the Roman jurists of the Classical period. The most important and influential work in this respect is Wolfgang Kunkel's *Herkunft und soziale Stellung der römischen Juristen*, first published in 1952, by which time the hunt for interpolation had already fallen out of fashion.[9] There were also several earlier incarnations of this endeavour, most notably the references to sources for individual jurists in Otto Lenel's *Palingenesia iuris civilis*, a nineteenth-century reconstruction of the works of the jurists of the Classical period, as well as Schulz's 'trilogy' (Ernst 2004: 185) on classical Roman law: the *Principles of Roman Law* (1934, 1936), *History of Roman Legal Science* (1946)[10] and *Classical Roman Law* (1951). Some years before publishing these, Schulz had already co-edited with Hermann Kantorowicz a sixteenth-century volume on the individual Roman jurists originally composed by a Byzantine scholar working in Italy.[11] However, Schulz had first set out his own views on the Roman jurists in what he presented as a series of lectures held at the University of Berlin, published in 1934 under the title *Prinzipien des römischen Rechts* (hereafter: 'the *Prinzipien*'), a noteworthy and peculiar work that discusses in each of its chapters a single 'principle' of predominantly classical Roman law.[12] While the content may be historical, it is interesting to note that recent scholarship has questioned whether or not a political agenda motivated the work, namely to employ principles derived from the ancient texts as a political attack against Nazi law and ideology.[13]

The Roman jurists according to Schulz

Since the work as a whole may have had a political character, it would stand to reason that the image of the Roman jurists detailed in the *Prinzipien* has perhaps also been informed by contemporary circumstances. To test this hypothesis, the hallmarks of the image of the Roman jurists as a category need first to be discussed. Famously, and perhaps apparently somewhat contrary to what one would expect, Schulz concurs with Savigny in his assessment of Roman jurists as 'fungibele Personen' ('interchangeable people').[14] Not only is it impossible to divide the history of Roman legal science into various distinctive periods, it even appears difficult to attribute specific legal scientific peculiarities to individual Roman jurists.[15] According to Schulz, no jurist had taught one thing fundamentally different from his predecessors or successors, nor had there been any fundamental changes in method or jurisprudence (Schulz 1934: 73). Even in his own time, this was something of a minority view,[16] and he has been roundly criticized for this assumption by later Roman legal scholars.[17] Moreover, the assumption appears to be somewhat at odds with the fundamental emphasis on classical Roman law, the relatively minimal usage of interpolations as arguments[18] and various other aspects of his work.[19] Two 'external' political motives could have been at play here: for one, the criticism the Nazis levelled at Roman law, evidenced by the infamous Article 19 of the party programme of the *Nationalsozialistische Deutsche Arbeiterpartei* (NSDAP) – that is, its perceived 'individualism' over against the collectivism championed in Germanic law.[20] Not without purpose, Schulz refutes this individualism extensively throughout the *Prinzipien*.[21] Similarly, regarding the Roman jurists as 'fungibele Personen',

Schulz refers to the tendencies towards the individual in nineteenth-century Roman legal scholarship.[22]

The second possibly politically inspired theme in Schulz relates to the first in that the lack of fundamental changes in the legal method of the Romans, according to Schulz, may have been partly due to the isolated position of Roman legal science, particularly from Greek law and philosophy. Schulz suggests this somewhat implicitly by referring to the two schools of jurists in the early Empire known as the *Sabiniani* and *Proculiani* without noting any distinctive features in method,[23] whereas there now exists some scholarly consensus that the use of Greek philosophy may have divided these two schools.[24] The political undertones of Roman law as a legal order free from 'foreign' influences are made explicit in the discussion on the principles of isolation and 'nation,' especially in the latter discussion.[25] Yet, interestingly, the isolated development of Roman legal science did not, according to Schulz, give way to political independence.

From his discussion of the principle of 'authority', we perhaps get the clearest vision of Schulz's image of the Roman jurists as a group. In Schulz, 'authority' is both a fundamental feature of the jurists externally speaking (i.e. with regard to non-jurists) and among the jurists themselves.[26] However, this authority is in a sense curtailed following the collapse of the Republic and the subsequent rise of the Empire. The impact affected Roman jurists to the extent that both the ancient legal and historical sources indicate that Augustus allowed several jurists to 'respond based on his authority' (Schulz 1934: 127, n. 112; *Dig.* 1.2.2.49) - granted, the exact meaning of this notion is unclear and still heavily debated in modern literature.[27] Given the potential political motivations behind the book, however, it is worth noting that, in Schulz's earlier writings, he had already referred to Augustus as a 'Führer'[28] who founded the 'third Reich',[29] possessed with a Weberian 'charismatic authority' (Schulz 1934: 123) and enacted racial legislation.[30]

The social background of the Roman jurists was also important in Schulz's assessment of the image of the Roman jurists. Based on the available sources, jurists seem to have been drawn from the upper echelons of Roman society - for example, *nobiles, honestiores* and *equites*.[31] As such, they are generally referred to as belonging to the aristocracy, not only in Schulz[32] but also, for instance, in Pringsheim[33] and Kunkel.[34] The hallmark of the image of the Roman jurists as necessarily aristocratic in background is further elaborated on in Schulz's *History of Roman Legal Science*. In this regard, it should first be noted that Schulz divides Roman legal science in the whole of its development into four distinct periods,[35] a division only implied in the *Prinzipien*.[36] There are perhaps two reasons why Schulz outlines these time periods in his *History*: firstly, the chapter on the Hellenistic period contains a large section on the influence of Greek dialectic on Roman law,[37] whereas in the Classical period juristic interest in dialectic according to Schulz had declined severely.[38] If Greek influences can be detected in the Classical period, they would be (p. 137) 'of some interest to the sociologist, ... of no value to the jurist' and generally to be found in the works of 'academic jurists', such as Pomponius and Gaius (Schulz 1946: 137). The second reason for Schulz distinguishing between a Hellenistic and a Classical period in Roman legal science is the lack of individual traits and differences in method among the jurists of the Classical period (Schulz 1946: 125). Here, the lack of individual traits is placed in a similar historical and social framework as in the *Prinzipien*,[39] placing it in the context of aristocracy,[40] tradition and authority and defining it as an (essentially still republican) 'esprit de corps'.[41] In my view, there can be little doubt that the differences between the Hellenistic and Classical periods in Schulz are closely linked to the idealization of several Republican jurists as the 'founding fathers' of legal science, Quintus Mucius Scævola *pontifex* in particular.[42]

The ideal type of jurist in Wieacker

The Roman jurist in Wieacker's works on Roman law and two letters to Carl Schmitt

Schulz's observations are largely founded on ancient sources and earlier research, a research practice closely followed by other well-regarded Roman legal scholars - chief among them Franz Wieacker (1908–94),[43] one of the most famous legal historians of the twentieth century. Unlike Koschaker and Coing, Wieacker composed large studies on both ancient and medieval Roman law, which allows for a more thorough comparison of a single author's vision on the ideal type of jurist in both time periods. Some similarities between Schulz's conception of the Roman jurists and that of Wieacker are immediately apparent: for instance, with regard to the jurists' independence and autonomy from the Roman government,[44] their position in Roman aristocracy[45] and the relatively minimal role played by Greek philosophy and culture in their works.[46] An interesting case in point as regards the political function of jurists was their relationship with the government and with the emperor in particular: For instance, the relationship between the Roman jurists and the early emperors receives a separate section in *Römische Rechtsgeschichte* II.[47] Here, a narrative similar to that in Schulz emerges in Wieacker: One the one hand, the Roman jurists as a professional class remained autonomous from state power and emperor;[48] on the other, they no longer issued their juristic opinions on the basis of their own authority but rather by that of Augustus and his successors (Wieacker and Wolf 2006: 31). Nowhere in presenting this paradoxical argument does Wieacker refer to Schulz directly; then again, Schulz was not the first or the only scholar to make this claim.[49] However, the political relationship between state and jurist did play a role in Wieacker's 'Vom römischen Juristen',[50] an article published around the same time as Schulz's *Prinzipien*. This article is noteworthy for several reasons: Firstly, the dichotomy between autonomy and authority is not yet present here, at least not to the extent that it is in Wieacker's later monograph; and, secondly, the degradation of the professional class of jurists into an office in the imperial bureaucracy is only roughly sketched out.[51]

The references to 'bureaucratization' are not, at any rate, the only aspects of Wieacker's writings reminiscent of Schulz: Also striking is Wieacker's description of the role of Greek philosophy during the formation of Roman jurisprudence as a scientific endeavour. In 'Vom römischen Juristen', we come across a peculiar distinction that Schulz would later discuss in much more detail (Schulz 1946: 62–9) - namely the assertion of a large-scale systematizing influence of Greek philosophy on

Roman jurisprudence as a science in the late Republic (Tuori 2007: 80–4), followed by what is merely lip service to more ethically charged Greek philosophical notions in later periods as a sign of the degradation of legal science.[52] This same distinction is also still clearly visible in Wieacker's monograph on Roman legal history[53] and resurfaces in a work published even more proximately to the *Prinzipien* than 'Vom römischen Juristen': a letter from Wieacker to the famous legal philosopher Carl Schmitt dated July 1935.[54] In the letter, Johannes Stroux and Bernhard Kübler are particularly singled out as *bêtes noires* for their emphasis of the influence on the Roman jurists by other Greek philosophies than those considered in the late Republic to pertain to considerations of system and logic.[55] Again, this criticism is very similar to that of Schulz.[56] Furthermore, as Schulz did before him, Wieacker explicitly contrasts ethical 'considerations of equity' (*Billigkeitserwägungen*), those being of a later date and probably all interpolated[57] with the use of Greek philosophy as a model for juristic technique and system. In this context, the relevant paragraph is worth quoting in full:[58]

> As one can see, Stroux emphasizes the direct influence of the Hellenistic speculations on the legal science of the early Classical period. My own preliminary view is something along the lines of the following: the Hellenistic theory of science had a deep impact on the jurists of the late Republic (particularly on Mucius Scævola maior, who lived ca. 100 BC). While the theoretical divisions had previously been employed in empirical – sometimes quite poignant, sometimes rather overcooked but still logically grounded – standards (they are closer to a German legal proverb than an Enneccerus teaching maxim), the attempt toward a systematic subdivision began only then (the distinctive animosity towards systems in Roman legal thinking stood in the way of the success of these efforts, as the living Edict already had); for once, this system led to a legal theory of Greek pedigree which proved to be somewhat [insignificant] to Classical Roman law on the relationship between the natural law and the law proper to Roman citizens.

Here, Wieacker does employ a similar narrative to that of Schulz in the *Prinzipien*: an initial influence of Greek dialectic on legal system building in the late Republic spearheaded by Mucius Scaevola, followed by what amounts to lip service to this theory through the division between *ius naturale* and *ius civile* in the subsequent Classical period.[59] Moreover, concepts presented as principles of Roman law by Schulz – like 'authority', 'tradition', 'isolation', 'fidelity' and 'humanity' – play a significant role in Wieacker's later works.[60] Thus, in his consideration of the methods of the Roman jurists, it appears that Wieacker was possibly influenced by Schulz's *Prinzipien*.

What primarily connects Schulz and Wieacker (and certainly also Pringsheim[61] and Koschaker)[62] is that they both seem to imagine a pre-existing ideal type of the Roman jurist. That Wieacker does not seem to have any ideal type of 'the jurist' based on the Roman jurists is confirmed not by his academic writings[63] but by another personal letter written by him to Carl Schmitt several years later, in 1942.[64] The context of the letter seems to be a comparison between Schmitt's 1934 work on the three types of legal scientific thinking and Wieacker's 'Vom römischen Juristen'.[65] The relevant passage reads as follows:[66]

> On the matter, I cannot provide you with a [judgement], even though the proof in the account is [enthralling]. Your claim of reifying general [aspects] of the French spirit or character by employing the specific [professional] image is well-founded; [the same] goes for the starting point that there is no such thing as a legal talent proper only to some persons but not [to others]. Nor do I see the talent of the Roman jurists as 'the' single possible type of legal talent, solely for that which comes closest to a possible phenomenal type of 'the' jurist. When you take heed of the particular English, French and German [modes] of [applying] the law, one may wish that we also learn from this.

The letter is all the more interesting not only because it refers to the Roman jurists (much more than Schulz) but because Wieacker appears to explicitly extend the ideal notion of a 'jurist' beyond Roman law as such and into later historical periods. To test whether this is indeed the case, I turn now to the search for hallmarks of the ideal type in Wieacker's main work, the *Privatrechtsgeschichte der Neuzeit*.[67]

The ideal type of the jurist in *Privatrechtsgeschichte der Neuzeit*

The employment of 'the jurist' as an ideal type by both Schmitt and Wieacker seems to fit into a more general trend in Germany during the 1930s to recalibrate the position of legal science to the new political atmosphere. The field of Roman legal scholarship was not the only one to be made redundant in a system that emphasized the administrative application of largely unwritten ideological norms; so, too, were the law faculties as a whole forced to rethink their function under a new German legal order (Stolleis 2004: 332–40). The notion of 'the jurist' as a legislative organ under an authoritarian state framework found expression in the attempts to create a *Volksgesetzbuch*, per Article 19 of the NSDAP programme by the Academy of German Law, which would host many of such figureheads of the 'new legal science' as Schmitt himself (Stolleis 2004: 340–3). Any potential role for Roman legal science prior to 1942 was complicated by the existence of this article (Koschaker 1947: 311–36; Stolleis 1989: 183). With respect to both Roman law in the Classical period and its later history of reception from the eleventh century CE onwards, new arguments had to be made to justify the continued study of Roman law under a fascist regime.[68] The exact function of the *Prinzipien* in this context is debatable: According to Stolleis, Schulz attempted to support the study of Roman law in the new political landscape by emphasizing its authoritarian (*imperiale*) aspects and communal values (*Gemeinschaftswerte*).[69] Against this, Wolfgang Ernst, highlighting the reaction of Lange and the great personal and professional risk Schulz took in writing the work in the first place, has criticized this argument as 'off the mark' (Ernst 2004: 125, n. 160). It thus remains to be seen whether or not certain notions pertaining to Roman law as formulated in the *Prinzipien* can also be found in the *Privatrechtsgeschichte der Neuzeit.*

Already in the second paragraph of the first section of the latter work dealing with the Medieval Roman origins of European legal culture, we encounter the themes also present in Schulz: the vulgarization and bureaucratization of Roman law and the separation of imperial legislation from juridical legal science (Wieacker 1967: 27). Moreover, Wieacker explicitly states that the 'deeper and more difficult form' resurged in the later Middle Ages (Wieacker 1967: 27, that is, 55, 69, 81–2). In this context, there are other familiar tropes to be found, such as the application of Greek philosophical thought in legal thought.[70] Wieacker elaborates on the equal social standing and level of expertise among the German learned lawyers from the fifteenth century on: *Doctores iuris* were also able to reach a status similar to the rank of *Ritter*,[71] whereas non-educated practitioners formed a type of proletariat class of jurists (Wieacker 1967: 160). As in Schulz, the only good jurist is a noble jurist. Closely related to Schulz's concept of nobility are his notions of autonomy and authority, most clearly in the context of the imperial *ius respondendi*, a discussion which Wieacker would later take up.[72] Certainly, *autonomy*[73] and *authority*[74] are the two central terms of the *Privatrechtsgeschichte der Neuzeit* – autonomy relating specifically to the reinvention of legal science in the west, authority not to that of the (Holy Roman) emperor but rather to that of Roman law as *ratio scripta* itself, from which the authority of the Medieval learned lawyers is derived.[75]

Without doubt, an ongoing theme in the *Privatrechtsgeschichte* is the relationship between an autonomous legal science and centralized state power in its various forms, specifically as a reflection of the original Roman situation. The following passage is worth quoting in full:[76]

> He [the lawyer] started out by marshalling ideological and jurisprudential arguments mined from the texts of the absolutist Justinian in support of the prince's claim to sovereignty and then, more importantly, used his superior techniques of documentation and astute negotiation to help make the principality more powerful than the old estates.

As is evident from this quotation, even in a work on Medieval learned law, Wieacker decries Justinian and his code as absolutist and despotic.[77] In spite of their reliance on the authority of the *Corpus iuris civilis*, according to Wieacker the glossators of the twelfth century were the first to reinvent legal science in the Middle Ages. Still, it was the subsequent generation of jurists, known as the commentators or conciliators, who put the legal notions developed by their predecessors into Europe-wide practice.[78] This is relevant primarily because of the possible analogy with the Roman practice of *responsa* and the juristic image it carries.[79] The relationship between legal science and autonomy from state power is then made explicit on various occasions. Most poignantly, Wieacker compares the 'scientific authority' of the conciliators to that of the professors in the German law faculties,[80] the point being that, regardless of whether or not it reflects historical reality,[81] this is very similar to the image Schulz had presented us with in the *Prinzipien* regarding the position of 'the jurists' vis-à-vis the emperor in Roman Antiquity. German law professors like Roman jurists to a large extent are autonomous law makers, independent from central state power.

Another link to the *Prinzipien* seems to be Wieacker's discussion of the natural-law-inspired legal books of the eighteenth and nineteenth centuries.[82] Wieacker states:[83]

> But when these tenets hardened into recipes for legislators determined to lay down rules of eternal validity, they became something of a straightjacket, for different historical situations call for different legal rules, lest justice should die.

Similarly, Schulz before him states the following:[84]

> Codification is apt to lead to literal translation and to deflect attention from the nature of the matter itself; a code purports to be a complete and finished whole, which it is not; it demands abstract formulation of legal rules, a process which seems full of danger to the Roman mind and is too rigid of a system to be capable of adaptation.

Both Schulz and Wieacker present an argument against the codification of law very much in the vein of Savigny: General, abstract rules laid down by a concrete centralized state divorced from the nature of the individual legal case and real-life justice are to be avoided at all costs. Thus, according to both Wieacker and Schulz, individual judges and jurists not only have been but should be understood as authoritative law makers.[85] Furthermore, the only proper legal orders are casuistic and legal-remedy-based ones, such as the legal orders in (Classical)[86] ancient Rome, Medieval Germany, and common law.[87] We may therefore make the following conclusion: Although Wieacker and Schulz wrote about two historically different epochs, the images of 'the jurist' Schulz and Wieacker present us with are similar if not the same. This seems to be the case regardless of whether or not such an image reflects historical reality, whether by coincidence or through a wider conscious scholarly tradition.

Conclusion

To be clear, I do not doubt either the veracity of what Schulz and Wieacker claim or the scientific vigour with which they pursue their sources. However, there also seem to have been selective processes of source selection in both Schulz and Wieacker, leading to several idiosyncratic similarities that suggest either that they were participating in a more generally held set of pre-conceived notions in the Romanist field at the time or that one was heavily inspired by the other. Particularly the projection of ancient concepts on later periods in the works of both scholars suggests this conclusion. This conclusion is not surprising considering that neither Schulz nor Wieacker has ever been really shy about working with anachronistic notions and concepts or investigating particular historical or sometimes modern developments, of which various instances have been given in this chapter. However, the possible presence of more contemporary considerations also leads to the question of the veracity of what might be deemed the more idiosyncratic aspects of their works: the Roman jurists as 'fungibele Personen', the autonomous position of the role of jurists vis-à-vis the government and legislator and the otherwise still troublesome relationship between (Greek) philosophy and (Roman) law. In my view, the veracity of these claims is worth considering but only when done alongside contemporary considerations that go beyond the mere reflection of historical sources as such.

If their ideas were at least influenced by the contemporary political circumstances, it is all the more peculiar that Schulz and Wieacker were on fairly opposite ends of the political spectrum before and during the Second World War. Congruence in their scholarship may have been the result of a post-war turn to one another, something that happened more generally upon the return of refugee scholars to Germany. However, the wartime publication 'Vom römischen Juristen' as well and the letters of Wieacker to Schmitt suggest that this is not the case, since similarities in thought were already present in these documents. One explanation for this fact might be that Schulz was simply authoritative and widely circulated to the degree that even scholars who may have had political differences adopted the book's ideas, at least initially. As such, despite their political differences, there seem to be strong links and similarities between the scientific thought of Schulz and Wieacker, particularly in their image of the Roman jurists.

Another possibility may simply have been that this line of thought was generally present at the time, shared, for example, with Pringsheim and Koschaker, and that both Schulz and Wieacker, being a part of that close-knit group of academics, adopted this line of thought for their respective areas of research. In this case, the historical image of the juristic profession as an authoritative and autonomous group with respect to the political sphere would have been developed by a group of professional jurists who perceived themselves as autonomous and authoritative vis-à-vis the political sphere, a notion that lives on in the idea of a common European legal culture.

Notes

1 This research has made been possible by the European Research Council under the European Union's Seventh Framework Programme (FP7/2007-2013) / ERC grant agreement n°313100 (Reinventing the Foundations of European Legal Culture 1934–1964). He wishes to thank the Landesarchiv Nordrhein-Westfalen at Duisburg for their permission to publish the archival material cited in the chapter, Saara Uvanto for the transcripts (any mistakes in which are the responsibility of the author and the author alone) of these archival sources, Dr Andreas Kulick (University of Tübingen) for his corrections and comments and Kenneth Lai for proofreading the text.

2 Somewhat implicitly, Ries 1979: 608–9.

3 The veracity of this claim will not be treated in this chapter, but see Van Caenegem 2002.

4 Cf., for instance, Schulz 1951: 17 (on the *lex–iurisdictio* relationship and the minimal role of *lex*): 'It is a true Roman principle revealing the whole attitude of Roman jurists towards law-creating acts of State, viz. their unconcealed distaste for legislation.' For Pringsheim, see Honoré 2004: 214–16.

5 Meaning the early empire, up to about 250 CE, corresponding roughly to the death of the late Classical Roman jurist Ulpian and the heyday of his pupil Modestinus; Schulz 1946: 99–261 (as opposed to the Hellenistic and bureaucratic periods), perhaps even more so than Schulz 1951.

6 The main source is the work of a later Roman jurist himself, Pomponius's *Enchiridium* in *Dig.* 1.2.2, with the group being referred to as *jurisconsulti, juris prudentes*, and so forth, already by Cicero: Wieacker 1988: 531–2.
7 See, for instance, the list of works in Tuori 2007: 56–7.
8 Stein 2004: 77.
9 Due to Kaser 1972: 94–102, in particular. For the roles of Schulz and Wieacker, see Liebs 2010: 42–4.
10 Referred to by Kunkel 1952: 3, n. 1, noting 'Die obige Abhandlung war Sch. bei der Abfassung seines Werkes noch nicht zugänglich', seemingly referring to Jörs 1888.
11 Diplovatatius 1919, as well as fragments of Sabinus in Schulz 1906.
12 The chapters are named as follows: *Gesetz und Recht, Isolierung, Abstraktion, Einfachkeit, Tradition, Nation, Freiheit, Autorität, Humanität, Treue and Sicherkeit.*
13 Cf. Stolleis 1989: 184–6, Ernst 2004: 123–5 and Schermaier 2010: 691–2. The political background can be deduced from Schulz's dedication of the book to his wife, who was of Jewish descent. Moreover, the *Schlußwort* states (Schulz 1934: 172): 'Neues staatlich-politisches Erleben läßt uns auch das römische Reich und sein Recht neu erleben und zeigt uns vieles in neuem und klarerem Lichte.' See the review of Lange 1934: 1493–500 as referred to by Stolleis 1989: 185; Ernst 2004: 124–5 and Schermaier 2010: 699.
14 For the context of the principle of 'tradition', see Schulz 1934: 72, who refers to Savigny 1828: 28, 157.
15 Schulz 1934: 72–3, contrary to later times, as is the case with jurists such as Cujacius, Donellus, Grotius and Savigny himself. It should be noted of the 'scientific personalities' Schulz mentions, at least three (viz., Donellus, Grotius and Thomasius) were exiled during their lifetime due to politico-religious circumstances.
16 See the literature in Schulz 1936: 72, n. 90 and n. 91, mainly Kübler's lecture at the celebration of the fourteenth centenary of the *Digest* in 1931, at which Schulz was also present. Schulz does acknowledge some changes in style between the jurists (72) but suggests that these may have been the result of later alterations to the texts (73, n. 90).
17 Interesting in this respect is Winkel 2005: 425, who cites Schulz 1946 (and Wieacker 1969) against this theory, suggesting the anomalous character of the idea in the works of Schulz in general.
18 Schermaier 2010: 682: 'Mit Interpolationsvermutungen geht Schulz- gemessen an der Mode der Zeit- recht Vorsichtig um.'
19 For example, Tuori presents Schulz as claiming the late Republican jurist Quintus Mucius Scævola *pontifex* as the 'founding father' of Roman legal science; Tuori 2007: 64 referring to Schulz 1934: 33 and 36–7. Furthermore, pride of place is given to Papinianus, *Quaestiones* and other specific works of classical Roman jurists in Schulz 1946; Ernst 2004: 175–7.
20 For instance, Van Caenegem 2002: 95–7; Schermaier 2010: 696–7.
21 See, for example, Schulz 1934: 107 (liberalism, capitalism). Other examples in Schermaier 2010: 696–7.
22 Schulz 1934: 73: 'Das individualistische neunzehnte Jahrhundert hat diesen Mangel an Individualität als Mangel der römischen Jurisprudenz empfunden und – natürlich Vergebens- versucht, die so heiß verehrten römischen Meister von diesem Mangel zu reinigen' as well as quoting (n. 84) Nietzsche's *Wille zur Macht*, nr. 783: 'Hier will der einzelne in einem großen Typus untertauchen.' Schulz 1934: 120: Mommsen's *Liberalismus*.
23 Schulz 1934: 73: 'like Oxford and Cambridge'. Again, against Kübler: n. 91.

24 See the discussions in Liebs 1976: 198–286 and Leesen 2010.
25 Schulz 1934: 13–44 (for moral considerations, see 15: 'Auch schließt das feine römische Gefühl für die Grenzen des Rechtes Gebiete wie das persönliche Familienrecht von der rechtlichen Regelung aus (...)'), 84–91; Schermaier 2010: 693, 698; on Jewish law, see 89.
26 Schulz 1934: 125, where Schulz contrasts Cicero's conception of authority to that of the Greeks, stating that even the latter do not blindly follow authority; this remains an important argument in regards to accepting legal opinion.
27 The *ius publice respondendi ex auctoritate.* See Tuori 2007: 104–20 for an overview of the discussion.
28 Schulz 1934: 123–4. The English edition gives the more neutral 'leader': Schulz 1936: 181.
29 Schulz 1934: 62, n. 30, 'Noch Justinian ist überzeugt, im ‚dritten Reich' zu leben, das von Augustus an kontinuierlich bestanden hat (…).' The English edition is again more neutral (Schulz 1936: 91, n. 5): 'Justinian was still convinced he was living in the "Third Empire" which had existed without a break from the time of Augustus.' The reference here is to the *tertia principia* of Justinianus, *Novellae* 47.
30 Schulz 1934: 82; Schulz 1936: 120; Schermaier 2010: 698. According to Schulz, such legislation was doomed to fail.
31 Schulz 1934: 125: 'Angehörige der vornehmste Geschlechter.'
32 On nobility as a prerequisite to hold office and the aristocratic and timocratic character of the state, see Schulz 1934: 115–16.
33 Pringsheim 1961: 53–62, 54 in particular.
34 For example, Kunkel 1952: 42. Both Schulz 1946: XV and Kunkel 1952: 4 refer to Münzer 1920.
35 That is, Archaic (pp. 5–37), Hellenistic (pp. 38–98), Classical (pp. 99–277) and Bureaucratic (pp. 278–329).
36 Schulz 1934: 3; contra, for example, Pringsheim 1961: 54: 'Das ist in ersten Zeit des Prinzipates, also bis zum Jahre 150 etwa, nicht anders geworden.'
37 Schulz 1946: 60–9 and the introduction on pp. 38–9; on the exclusion of other branches of philosophy, see pp. 69–75.
38 Schulz 1946: 129–32, 130; Greek philosophy, in general, was (135) 'taken no more seriously by them than by their predecessors', in spite of 'observations of a philosophical nature' on justice and jurisprudence (*Dig.* 1.1.10), (136) law (*Dig.* 1.1.1pr.) and natural law (*Dig.* 1.1.1.3).
39 Schulz 1946: 125, n. 3 referring to Schulz 1936: 106 (= Schulz 1934: 72), Savigny's theory of 'fungibele Personen'.
40 Schulz 1946: 125: 'This aristocratic atmosphere gave little scope for scientific individuality.' However, (102) instead of the aristocracy the jurists of the Classical period rather stem from 'urban Roman families that had come to the front only in the last decades of the Republic'. 'The old families were extinct or worn out.'
41 Schulz 1946: 125: 'The old republican *esprit de corps* was kept alive by the sturdy professional tradition of the small select band of leading jurists.'
42 Cf. Schulz 1946: 62–9 and e.g. Tuori 2007: 64.
43 Particularly in the field of 'Textstufenforschung'; Ernst 2004: 177–8, n. 552; Winkler 2014: 231. Babusiaux indicates many similarities between Schulz 1934: 234 and Wieacker 1960: 336–40, particularly regarding their views on Papinianus's *Quaestiones;* Babusiaux 2011: 10–12.
44 Wieacker 1988: I, 553: 'Unparteilichkeit und Unentgeltlichkeit bestimmen auch das Leitbilt juristischer Berufsmoral', etc.; Wieacker and Wolf 2006: 90, 99.

45 See, for instance, Wieacker 1939: 446–7: 'regierenden Geschlechter', 'adelige Rechtskenner wie die Scævola', etc., and, later, Wieacker 1988: 528–31; Wieacker and Wolf 2006: 30.

46 Cf. Winkler 2014: 235–6 on Wieacker's works in the 1950s. Highly telling is Wieacker 1965: 27 (with reference to Schulz 1946: 66): 'vor allem aber eben der demagogische und advokatorische Geist der öffentliche Rede- zuletzt also die maßlose Leidenschaft für das schöne Wort: trug all dies Schuld daran, daß dieses begabteste Volk nicht nur des Altertums eine seiner würdige Fachjurisprudenz so wenig hervorgebracht hat wie ein dauerndes Reich.' Despite his criticism of Schulz, Wieacker refers only indirectly to Greek philosophical influences - contrary to Wieacker 1988 but much like in Schulz 1946 and Wieacker and Wolf 2006 - via, for example, the notions of *ius naturale*, *ius gentium*: 87–90.

47 *Der frühe Prinzipat und die Juristen*: Wieacker and Wolf 2006: 28–35.

48 Wieacker and Wolf 2006: 28: 'In der Tat hat er sich offenbar bewußt um der Kräftigung des Ansehens der Juristen bemüht. Es gibt keinen Anhalt dafür, daß er dieses Ziel im Prinzip digiristisch, durch Auslese, Einflußnahme oder Mißbrauch der Juristen für seine politischen Zwecke verfolgte.' Reluctance of Augustus to take sides: 29, referring to Justinianus, *Institutiones* 2.25pr., describing Augustus requesting advice for judging on the application of codicils.

49 Schulz 1934: 127 refers to Wlassak 1924. Tuori 2007 has compiled a bibliography on the relevant text in Pomponius (*Dig.* 1.2.2.48–50) at 107, n. 15, that goes back to Zasius in 1541 but starts the modern works with De Visscher 1936: 615–50 rather than with Schulz 1934. Schulz 1946 calls the text 'post-classical' and 'corrupted': Tuori 2007: 109.

50 Wieacker 1939: 440–63. Other articles Wieacker published on the topics mentioned include Wieacker 1969: 331–49 and Wieacker 1985: 71–94.

51 Wieacker 1939: 444: 'In der *Kaiserzeit* wird die freie Jurisprudenz freilich mehr und mehr Amtsjurisprudenz … Diese Verlagerung der Rechtsbildung wirkte auch auf die Jurisprudenz zurück, die vom Prinzipat in seinen Dienst gestellt wird und dadurch aus der alten Amtlosen Autorität zu glänzender bürokratischer Wirksamkeit aufsteigt. Schon Augustus legitimiert, seinem Konservatismus getreu, die alter Gutachtung aus seiner *auctoritas principis* und bringt sie damit wie zu gesteigerter Geltung so auch in seinen Bereich. Wenige Generationen später beginnt die Eingliederung in die kaiserliche Bürokratie.' The term *bureaucracy*, however, is not used in Schulz 1934; cf. the introduction: 3 ('nachklassisch'); nevertheless, the idea is present: 164.

52 Wieacker 1939: 449–60, 'pedantische Abstraktionswahn', 'Orientalisierung'.

53 Wieacker 1988: 522 criticizes Schulz for overestimating the role of Mucius Scævola ('folglich die (vorausgehende) „archaische" Periode bis zum Ende des 2. Jhs. erstrecken müßte'), and underestimating his influence on the jurists of the Classical period ('den fortdauernden Einfluß der griechischen wissenschaftlichen Kultur auf die klassischen Juristen außer acht').

54 On the relationship between Wieacker and Schmitt, see Winkler 2014: 316–17. For a recent biography of Schmitt see Mehring 2009, which discusses their relationship on pp. 365 ('Auffällig ist Schmitts Neigung zu adeliger Herkunft') and 434. Schulz is also described as a colleague of Schmitt both in Bonn: 141, and Berlin: 332, Schulz being quoted to him on p. 356.

55 LAV NRW R, RW 265 Nr. 17971 (letter from Franz Wieacker to Carl Schmitt (13 July 1935), p. 1: 'Die Schrift ist für uns Romanisten umso eindrucksvoller gewesen, als man hierorts jeder fachmännisch-philologischen Äusseru[n]g als besonderer

Erleuchtung unbeschränkte Autorität zumisst (was der glänzende Strouxche Aufsatz eher verdient als andere) und weil sie mitten in die modernste Fragestellung der Disziplin einschlägt. Streitig ist nämlich das Ausmass in dem die grosse hellenistische Kulturrezeption seit Begin des 2. Jhs. v. Chr. auf die zünftlerische Sonderwelt der älteren römischen Rechtslehre, einer artistisch-pontifikalen Kunstlehre kasuistisch-empirischer Art, gewirkt hat. Einige (eine italienische Schule, die sich um Riccobono nicht ohne Einfluss des neuen Imperiumsgefühls gruppiert, bei uns etwa Wenger-München, Schönbauer-Wien, auch Kübler-Erlangen glaubt [corrected to glauben] mit Stroux dass die hellenistische, insbesondere stoische Gerechtigkeitsphilosophie schon damals für immer in die römische Fachjurisprudenz eingebrochen und den naturrechtlichen Kontrollen der aequitas usw. schon in der klassischen Jurisprudenz Raum gegeben hat.'

56 Schulz 1934: 88–9 (n. 109 and 114 in particular).

57 LAV NRW R, RW 265 Nr. 17971 (letter from Franz Wieacker to Carl Schmitt (13 July 1935), p. 1: 'Vorwiegend nimmt man jedoch in Deutschland an, dass die etwas verwaschenen und abstrakt-humanitären Billigkeitserwägungen, die die Digestentexte beherrschen, erst seit Konstantin (die formale Substanz des römischen Rechtsdenkens zerfressen haben, in den Digesten (aequitas, humanitas usw.) also in aller Regel interpoliert sind; man führt dann diese mittelbar natürlich gleichfalls hellenistischen, besser nachsokratischen, selbst schon sophistischen Theorema auf den Einbruch des Christentums, des Neuplatonismus und auf das obrigkeitsstaatliche Gefüge des frühbyzantinischen Dominats zurück; an die Stelle der nach Papinian überreifen spätklassischen Theorie, die gegen 230 zusammenbrach, tritt seit dem 4 Jh und vor allem im 5.Jh. in den östlichen Rechtsschulen ein „pneumatisches" Denken, dessen Stilfremdheit deutlich nachweisbar, dessen Herkunft noch ziemlich ungewiss ist; ich persönlich bin von einem entscheidenden Einfluss der antiochenischen und anderer Rechts[corrected to Theologen]schulen überzeugt. Der äussere Wendepunkt ist Konstantin: die noch männlich klaren Reskripte Diokletians und den wüsten Prunkstil Konstantins trennen Welten.' Wieacker seems to change his opinion on this later on: see Wieacker 1977: 5–6, 33–4; Wieacker and Wolf 2006: 89–90. See Schulz 1934: 129–30 on such interpolated terms as *humanitas*. Several passages in the manuscript of the letter have been underlined and corrected, possibly by Schmitt himself, but the underlines have been left out of the transcription here and those cited later in this chapter.

58 LAV NRW R, RW 265 Nr. 17971 (letter from Franz Wieacker to Carl Schmitt (13 July 1935), p. 2: 'Stroux, wie man sieht, misst der unmittelbaren Einwirkung der hellenistischen Spekulation auf die frühklassische Jurisprudenz ein ziemlich grosses Feld zu. Meine unvorgreifliche Ansicht ist etwa: die hellenistische Wissenschaftstheorie hat einen tiefen Einfluss auf die spätrepublikanischen Juristen (besonders den älteren Mucius Scaevola, um 100 a.Chr.) gehabt. Während sich bisher die theoretische Stoffgliederung mehr in empirischen, teilweise wirklich kernigen, teilweise etwas überspitzten aber logisch noch ungefügen Kunstregeln niederschlug (sie stehen einem deutsche Rechtssprichwort noch näher als etwa einem allgemeinen Lehrsatz des Enneccerus), beginnt jetzt der Versuch zu systematischer Durchgliederung (die ausgeprägte Systemfeindlichkeit römischen Rechtsdenkens hat einen Erfolg dieser Bemühungen verhindert, dem schon das lebende Edikt im Wege stand); dies System bringt einmal ei[n]e für das klassische römische Recht ziemlich [unerhebliche] Rechtstheorie griechischen Musters über das Verhältnis von natürlichem und bürgereigenem Recht hervor.'

59 Schulz 1934: 33–44.

60 For instance, in Wieacker 1961: 14–17: *fides* is defined in Schulz 1934: 15 as 'sittliche Bindung an eigenes Wort und Verhalten'. On *humanitas*, see Wieacker 1961: 14 and Wieacker and Wolf 2006: 89–90. On isolation, see Wieacker 1961: 1, 9: 'Er ist berechtigt, wenn F. Schulz in seinen „Prinzipien des römischen Rechts" ein ganzes Kapitel der „Isolierung" widmet' and Wieacker 1977: 2, n. 3 and 15, n. 54.

61 Winkler 2014: 59–134 emphasizes an early influence of Pringsheim on Wieacker, as well as of Andreas Bertalan Schwarz, Hermann Kantorowicz and Max Weber. On Pringsheim's conception of the relationship between Greek philosophy and Roman law, see Giltaij and Erkkilä 2015: 47–53.

62 The notion of 'authority' is paramount in Koschaker; see Koschaker 1947: 48, in particular. For the Wieacker–Koschaker relationship, see Winkler 2014: 174–6 and 239–43.

63 Wieacker 1939: 462, 'Was sagt am Ende das Bild des römischen Juristen über Recht und Richter unseres eigenen Volkes?', but: 'Ich glaube, er ist vielmehr die reinste Verwirklichung schöpferischer Rechtskunde in einem großen fremden Volk: als solcher nicht wiederholbar und als er selbst auch nicht wiederholenswert.'

64 On the influence of Weber and Schmitt (2004 in particular) on the ideal type of the jurist in Wieacker, see Winkler 2014: 318–20.

65 For Schmitt's take on Wieacker's chapter on legal thinking in France (and England), see Schmitt 2004: 85–8.

66 LAV NRW R, RW 265 Nr. 17976 (letter from Franz Wieacker to Carl Schmitt (25 August 1942), p. 2: 'Zur Sache darf ich mir, auch wo man durch den Evidenz der Darstellung mitge[zogen] wird, ein [Urteil] nicht zusprechen. Ihre Förderung, durch Herausarbeitung eines besonderen [Berufs]bildes die allgemeinen [Aufstellungen] über den französischen Geist oder Charakter erst konkret zu machen, ist sehr berechtigt; [ebenso] der Grundsatz, daß es nicht eine juristische Begabung gibt, die einigen Völkern zukommt, [anderen] nicht. Ich halte auch den römischen Juristen nicht für den einzigen denkbaren Typus „der" juristischen Begabung, freilich für einen, der einem etwa denkbaren phänomenalen Typs „des" Juristen am nächsten kommt. Wenn Sie die Aufmerksamkeit auf die spezifisch englische, französische und deutsche [Weise] der Ausf[..]ung des Rechts lenken, so möchte man wünschen, daß bei uns auch die Lehre daraus gezogen werde.'

67 On the work, see Landau 2010: 49–74.

68 See, for example, Kreller writing in 1936 as referred to by Simon 1989: 166–7 for the dichotomy between jurists as a true '*Rechtswahrer*' as opposed to a positivist '*Paragraphenkenner*'.

69 Stolleis 1989: 186. Also, Schermaier 2010: 696–7, with reference to Stolleis.

70 Meaning the method of the Roman jurists: Wieacker 1967: 53, 92–3, 163–5. Particularly in the period of 'Vernunftrecht'; Winkler 2014: 36–7.

71 Wieacker 1967: 159. Cf. 93: 'Das Ansehen der neuen Rechtswissenschaft teilte sich überall der Erziehungs- und Standesgemeinschaft der Juristen mit' and Wieacker 1964: 19: 'Ritterideal Europas'. See also Lange 1980: 279–94.

72 Tuori 2007: 131–44; Wieacker 1985: 336–40, citing Schulz on several instances.

73 Wieacker 1967: 69: 'autonomen juristischen Sachproblems'. Compare Winkler 2014: 28, 34, 37, 39, 49 and 50.

74 Wieacker 1967: 55. Compare Winkler 2014: 27, 28 and 31.

75 Wieacker 1967: 69: 'Kult der Autorität'. See also, Winkler 2014: 53 and Haferkamp 2016: 794–5.

76 'Gab er dem Souveränitätsanspruch des Fürsten erst die ideologische und juristische Begründung aus den Quellen des justinianischen Absolutismus, so hob er praktisch vor allem durch die überlegene Technik der Aktenführung und der sachlichen Verhandlung den Fürstenstaat über die altständischen Gewalten hinweg in den Sattel.' Wieacker 1967: 94. Translation by T. Weir in Wieacker 1995: 66.

77 See also Winkler 2014: 76–82 and 180–4 for legal science in Byzantium under Justinian in particular.

78 Wieacker 1967: 81–8; 88, 'Auch die „Rezeption" des römischen Rechts in Deutschland ist in ihrer reifsten Form nichts anderes als ein Sonderfall dieser Wirkung.' The categories and starting points were derived from Kantorowicz: Landau 2010: 54. On the term *conciliators*, see Landau 2010: 59. See also Winkler 2014: 27–9 and, more specifically, the *Usus modernus*; Winkler 2014: 35.

79 Wieacker 1967: 82: 'Konsultationspraxis'. See also Wieacker 1964: 27, 'Als die Europäer im Hochmittelalter durch die Digesten mit dieser großen Kunst der römischen Juristen bekannt wurden, entwickelte sich daraus für alle Zeiten eine sachlich und technisch bestimmte Rechtswissenschaft. Diese Herrschaft des gelehrten Juristen hat Europa nicht nur Segen gebracht; aber sie schuf eine neue öffentliche Macht, die über Interessen und Emotionen der Einzelnen wie der Völker hinweg eine von der Sache her begründete objective Entscheidung der soziale Konflikte durchsetzte, und die bis in unsere Zeit maßgebend geblieben ist.'

80 Wieacker 1967: 181–2. Also see 184: 'Bindung an die Wissenschaft.'

81 See, for example, the discussion between Whitman 1990 and Nörr 1992 (and Tuori 2007: 122–6) regarding the 'later history' of *ius respondendi*, for which the lack of sources both in Antiquity and the Early Modern period is extremely problematic.

82 Winkler 2014: 39 on the ALR (1798). See Wieacker 1967: 334: 'Dem Selbstgefühl des Gesetzgebers entsprach eine Skepsis gegen die wissenschaftliche Jurisprudenz, die nicht nur in den persönlichen Meinungen des alternden Herrschers und in ihrem Zurückbleiben hinter den besten Geistern der Zeit.' Wieacker does not so much criticize the law books as he does the legal positivism they inspired in the nineteenth and twentieth centuries; Winkler 2014: 46 and 55–7.

83 'Erstarrt zu Rezepten einer Gesetzgebung, die sich anmaßte, für einen konkreten Staat das ein für allemal richtigen Recht zu finden, wurden sie eher zum Hemmschuh lebendiger Gerechtigkeit, die ja gerade als unveränderliche Richtschnur verschiedenen geschichtlichen Lagen je verschiedenes positives Recht abfordert.' Wieacker 1967: 349, translated by T. Weir in Wieacker 1995: 280. On the link between natural law and the law books, see Landau 2010: 67. On Wieacker's conception of the role of Roman *leges* and the Law of the XII Tables in particular, see Wieacker 1944: 38–85, where Wieacker contrasts the case-based Republican legislation with the general imperial 'Reformgesetze' (80–5).

84 '(D)ie Kodifikation verleitet zur Wortinterpretation und lenkt ab von der Natur der Sache: sie täuscht eine Geschlossenheit und Vollständigkeit vor, die sie nicht hat: sie fordert eine den Römern gefährlich dünkende abstrakte Formulierung der Rechtssätze, legt auch die Rechtsordnung zu stark für die Zukunft fest.' Schulz 1934: 9; Schulz 1936: 13.

85 Wieacker 1967: 190: '[D]och gelingen vor allem bei Beteiligung bedeutender Juristen auch wohlüberlegte und glückliche Neuschöpfungen.' Cf. Van Caenegem 2002: 44–8.

86 Wieacker 1967: 186. On the idealization of the (Republican) Roman jurists in his works on Roman law, set against Hellenistic theories of state and the law and statutory abstractions, see Winkler 2014: 248–9.

87 Wieacker 1967: 186–9, 187, n. 48, in particular. Cf. Schulz 1934: 9–11 and Winkler 2014: 32.

References

Babusiaux, U. (2011), *Papinians Quaestiones: Zur rhetorischen Methode eines spätklassischen Juristen*, München: Beck.

Behrends, O. (1995), 'Franz Wieacker 5.8.1908–17.2.1994', *Zeitschrift der Savigny-Stiftung für Rechtsgeschichte. Romanistische Abteilung*, 112: XIII–LXII.

van Caenegem, R. C. (2002), *European Law in the Past and the Future: Unity and Diversity over Two Millennia*, Cambridge: Cambridge University Press.

Coing, H. (1985), *Europäisches Privatrecht Band I. Älteres gemeines Recht (1500 bis 1800)*, München: Beck.

Diplovatatius, T. (1919), *De claris iuris consultis*, F. Schulz and H. Kantorowicz, (eds), Berlin and Leipzig: de Gruyter.

Ernst, W. (2004), 'Fritz Schulz 1879–1957', in J. Beatson and R. Zimmermann (eds), *Jurists Uprooted: German-speaking Émigré Lawyers in Twentieth-century Britain*, 106–204, Oxford: Oxford University Press.

Giltaij, J. and Erkkilä, V. (2015), 'An Interview with Tony Honoré', *Forum Historiae Iuris* (15 February 2015).

Haferkamp, H.-P. (2016), 'Review of Winkler 2014', *Savigny Zeitschrift für Rechtsgeschichte. Germanistische Abteilung*, 133: 794–7.

Honoré, A. M. (2004), 'Fritz Pringsheim (1882–1967)', in J. Beatson and R. Zimmermann (eds), *Jurists Uprooted: German-Speaking Émigré Lawyers in Twentieth-century Britain*, 206–32, Oxford: Oxford University Press.

Kaser, M. (1972), *Zur Methodologie der römischen Rechtsquellenforschung*, Wien: Österreichische Akademie der Wissenschaften.

Kop, P. C. (1980), *Beschouwingen over het zogenaamde 'vulgaire' Romeinse recht*, Den Haag: Universitaire Pers Leiden/Zwolle: Tjeenk Willink.

Koschaker, P. (1947), *Europa und das römische Recht*, München and Berlin: Beck.

Kunkel, W. (1952), *Herkunft und soziale Stellung der römischen Juristen*, Weimar: Böhlau.

Landau, P. (2010), 'Wieackers Konzept einer neueren Privatrechtsgeschichte: eine Bilanz nach 40 Jahren', in O. Behrends and E. Schumann (eds), *Franz Wieacker. Historiker des modernen Privatrechts*, 49–74, Göttingen: Wallstein.

Lange, H. (1934), 'Deutsche Romanistik? Grundsätzliche Bemerkungen zu Fritz Schulz, "Prinzipien des römischen Rechts"', *Deutsche Juristen-Zeitung*, 1493–1500.

Lange, H. (1980), 'Vom Adel des Doctor', in K. Luig and D. Liebs (eds), *Das Profil des Juristen in der europäischen Tradition. Symposium aus Anlaß des 70. Geburtstages von Franz Wieacker*, 279–94, Edelsbach: Gremer.

Leesen, T. (2010), *Gaius Meets Cicero: Law and Rhetoric in the School Controversies*, Leiden: Brill.

Levy, E. (1956), *Weströmisches Vulgarrecht: das Obligationenrecht*, Weimar: Böhlau.

Liebs, D. (1976), 'Rechtsschulen und Rechtsunterricht im Prinzipat', *Aufstieg und Niedergang der römischen Welt*, II.15: 198–286.

Liebs, D. (2010), 'Franz Wieacker (1908 bis 1994)- Leben und Werk', in O. Behrends and E. Schumann (eds), *Franz Wieacker. Historiker des modernen Privatrechts*, 23–48, Göttingen: Wallstein, 2010.

Luig, K. (2002), 'In memoriam Helmut Coing (28.2.1912-15.8.2000)', *Zeitschrift der Savigny-Stiftung für Rechtsgeschichte. Romanistische Abteilung*, 119: 662–77.

Mehring, R. (2009), *Carl Schmitt. Aufstieg und Fall*, München: Beck.

Münzer, F. (1920), *Römische Adelsparteien und Adelsfamilien*, Stuttgart: J. B. Metzler.

Nörr, D. (1992), 'Romanistische Phantasien (Review of Whitman 1990)', *Rechtshistorisches Journal*, 11: 163–75.
Pringsheim, F. (1921), 'Beryt und Bologna', in *Festschrift Lenel*, vol. 1, 391–449, Leipzig: Rechts- und Staatswissenschaftlichen Fakultät der Universität Freiburg i. Br.
Pringsheim, F. (1961), 'Höhe und Ende der römischen Jurisprudenz', in *Gesammelte Abhandlungen*, vol. 1, 53--62, Heidelberg: C. Winter.
Ries, G. (1979), 'Paul Koschaker', *Neue Deutsche Biographie*, 12: 608–9.
von Savigny, F. C. (1828), *Vom Beruf unserer Zeit für Gesetzgebung und Rechtswissenschaft*, 3rd edn, Heidelberg: Mohr und Zimmer.
Schermaier, M. J. (2010), 'Fritz Schulz' Prinzipien. Das Ende einer deutschen Universitätslaufbahn im Berlin der Dreißigerjahre', in S. Grundmann et al. (eds), *Festschrift 200 Jahre Juristische Fakultät der Humboldt-Universität zu Berlin*, 683–700, Berlin: Humboldt-Universität zu Berlin.
Schmitt, C. (2004), *On the Three Types of Juristic Thought*, trans. J. W. Bendersky, Westport, CO and London: Verso.
Schulz, F. (1906), *Sabinus-fragmente in Ulpians Sabins-commentar*, Halle: M. Niemeyer.
Schulz, F. (1934, repr. 1954), *Prinzipien des römischen Rechts. Vorlesungen gehalten an der Universität Berlin von Fritz Schulz*, München and Leipzig: Duncker & Humblot.
Schulz, F. (1936), *Principles of Roman Law*, Oxford: Clarendon Press.
Schulz, F. (1946, repr. 1953, 1963), *History of Roman Legal Science*, Oxford: Oxford University Press.
Schulz, F. (1951, repr. 1954, 1961), *Classical Roman Law*, Oxford: Oxford University Press.
Simon, D. (1989), 'Die deutsche Rechtswissenschaft vom römischen Recht nach 1933', in M. Stolleis and D. Simon (eds), *Rechtsgeschichte im Nationalsozialismus. Beiträge zur Geschichte einer Disziplin*, 161–76, Tübingen: Mohr Siebeck.
Stein, P. (2004), *Roman Law in European History*, Cambridge: Cambridge University Press.
Stolleis, M. (1989), '"Fortschritte der Rechtsgeschichte" in der Zeit des Nationalsozialismus?', in *Geschichte einer Disziplin*, 177–97, Tübingen: Mohr Siebeck.
Stolleis, M. (2004), *A History of Public Law in Germany 1914–1945*, trans. T. Dunlap, Oxford: Oxford University Press.
Tuori, K. (2007), *Ancient Roman Lawyers and Modern Legal Ideals*, Frankfurt am Main: Klostermann.
De Visscher, F. (1936), 'Le "ius publice respondendi"', *Nouvelle Revue Historique de Droit francais et etranger*, 15: 615–60.
Whitman, J. Q. (1990), *The Legacy of Roman Law in the German Romantic Era*, Princeton, NJ: Princeton University Press.
Wieacker, F. (1939), 'Vom römischen Juristen', *Zeitschrift für die gesamte Staatswissenschaft*, 99: 440–63.
Wieacker, F. (1944), 'Lex publica. Privatrechtsgesetzgebung und politische Grundordnung im römischen Freistaat', in *Vom römischen Recht. Wirklichkeit und Überlieferung*, 38–85, Leipzig: Koehler & Amelang.
Wieacker, F. (1960), *Textstufen klassischer Juristen*, Göttingen: Vandenhoeck & Ruprecht.
Wieacker, F. (1961), 'Römertum und römisches Recht', in *Vom römischen Recht*, 1–17, Stuttgart: Koehler.
Wieacker, F. (1965), *Cicero als Advokat: Vortrag gehalten vor der Berliner Juristischen Gesellschaft am 29. April 1964*, Berlin: De Gruyter.
Wieacker, F. (1967), *Privatrechtsgeschichte der Neuzeit*, Göttingen: Vandenhoeck & Ruprecht.
Wieacker, F. (1969), 'Über das Verhältnis der römischen Fachjurisprudenz zur griechisch-hellenistischen Theorie', *IURA*, 20: 448–77.

Wieacker, F. (1977), 'Offene Wertungen bei den römischen Juristen', *Zeitschrift der Savigny-Stiftung für Rechtsgeschichte. Romanistische Abteilung*, 94: 1–42.
Wieacker, F. (1985), 'Respondere ex auctoritate principis', in J. A. Ankum et al. (eds), *Satura Robert Feenstra oblata*, 71–94, Fribourg: Editions Universitaires Fribourg Suisse.
Wieacker, F. (1988), *Römische Rechtsgeschichte* I, München: Beck.
Wieacker, F. (1995), *A History of Private Law in Europe*, trans. T. Weir, Oxford: Oxford University Press.
Wieacker, F. and Wolf, J. G. (2006), *Römische Rechtsgeschichte* II, München: Beck.
Winkel, L. C. (2005), 'Quintus Mucius Scævola once again', *Fundamina*, 11: 425–33.
Winkel, L. C. (2010), 'Franz Wieacker. Romanist und Rechtshistoriker, zwei Seelen in einer Brust?', in O. Behrends and E. Schumann (eds), *Franz Wieacker. Historiker des modernen Privatrechts*, 213–21, Göttingen: Wallstein.
Winkler, V. (2014), *Der Kampf gegen die Rechtswissenschaft. Franz Wieacker "Privatrechtsgeschichte der Neuzeit" und die deutsche Rechtswissenschaft des 20. Jahrhunderts*, Hamburg: Verlag Dr. Kovac.
Wlassak, M. (1924), *Die klassische Prozeßformel mit Beiträgen zur Kenntnis des Juristenberufes*, Wien: A. Steinwenter.

5

Roman Law after 1917: Exile, Statelessness and the Search for Byzantium in the Work of Mikhail von Taube

Dina Gusejnova

Introduction

The modern history of Roman law has been frequently associated with Western European political integration. Legal and intellectual historians have repeatedly looked at the geographical spread and intellectual lineages of Roman law to assess the degree of Westernization in different polities, from the Russian Empire to the British Isles.[1] By discussing the reception of Roman law as an aspect of the political thought of an exile from Bolshevik Russia, I hope to flesh out one of its less prominent uptakes in the intellectual culture of Europe, as a source of inspiration for Russian international law and what remained of it after the demise of the Russian empire.[2] While the broader framework of this story reaches from the last decade of Europe's Continental empires to the start of the Cold War, I am particularly interested in the way elements of Roman law were invoked in intellectual debates around the First World War and in the interwar period. At this time, revolutions shook not just particular empires, such as the Russian, but the legitimacy of imperial rule as such.

My main case study is the intellectual biography of Baron Mikhail von Taube (1869–1961). In some ways, this is a history of an intellectual cul-de-sac. Born in the imperial residence of Pavlovsk near St. Petersburg, Mikhail von Taube, or Michel de Taube, as he was known in France, was a Russian subject, of Swedish extraction, German-speaking yet, unlike most Baltic Barons, neither Protestant nor Orthodox but of Catholic faith. By the age of thirty-five, he could already look back on a stellar career: He was professor of international law, succeeding his renowned teacher Fyodor Martens in this post; he worked in the Russian foreign office on highly visible cases of international dispute, including the so-called Hull Incident when a ship of the Russian Navy had accidentally fired on private fishermen off the British coast, and several other major naval incidents involving conflicts with Venezuela, France and Italy. By the second year of the Great War, he had become senator, and a year later, he was promoted to the role of deputy minister for education and a member of the State Council of

Figure 4 Aerial photograph of the Peace Palace in The Hague (opened in 1913, photo from 1920–40). Wikimedia Commons.

the Russian Empire. His international career was no less outstanding. In 1913, he was among the dignitaries who inaugurated the Hague Peace Palace, a crowning achievement of the field of legal scholarship he and his teachers had represented, and served as a judge in major disputes before the First World War broke out.[3]

In 1917, however, Taube's career as a public civil servant, like that of many leading Russian intellectuals of his time, ended abruptly, as the Russian Empire disintegrated during a decade of civil war, during which the Soviet Union emerged as a new type of republican federation in 1922. In 1918, Taube was briefly asked to serve as foreign minister of the Russian government in exile in Finland, a post which soon evaporated, leaving him with a modest academic career and the prospect of working as a private lawyer for other exiled aristocratic families.

The ruptures to his personal intellectual trajectory reveal new aspects of Europe's political transformation. As the Bolsheviks declared a war on legal systems resting on private property, there was no longer a place in Russia for lawyers of Taube's bent. Later, the Soviet authorities developed new understandings of sovereignty and international law.[4] As Lenin had put it, just as 'capitalism' was only permitted at state level in the Soviet state, it would admit no 'private law' and repeal the old form of 'private contract', which he called a '*corpus juris romani*' (Lenin 1924). Instead, Lenin demanded the introduction of a 'revolutionary legal consciousness'. In assaulting earlier publications on Roman law, Marxist legal theorists like Evgeny Pashukanis believed that it would eventually be possible to develop an alternative legal system not resting on private property.[5] German communists like Alfons Paquet also argued that 'war should be declared on the contemporary civilization which rests on Roman foundations'. He also blamed Roman law for the heightened struggle between nations which led to the collapse of all morality (Paquet 1923: 872–3). At around the same time, in Germany, the notorious Article 19 of the NSDAP called to replace the 'materialist' ideas of Roman law with old 'German common law' (*ein deutsches Gemeinrecht*), an idea which the Nazis began to put into practice partially, but particularly, in the context of the recolonization of Eastern Europe (cf. Landau 1989: 11–24). For all their ideological differences, both new regimes, the Soviet Union and later the Third Reich, made their hostility towards Roman law into a cornerstone of their respective legal policies.

Among lawyers of different political orientation, these juridical as well as political upheavals associated with the Soviet and the Nazi regimes elicited a widespread search for new foundations of European legal culture. Roman law and its reception served as a key intellectual resource for exiled lawyers of a wide range of political orientations, and Mikhail von Taube was one of many contemporary lawyers who contributed actively to this search. A biographical perspective can shed light on the divergent agendas which governed ideas of Roman law in its twentieth-century contexts and the adaptability of concepts to situational needs.[6] In the mid-twentieth century, references to Roman law can be used as a litmus test for understanding intellectual developments in the face of new quasi-imperial ideologies which grew in eastern and central Europe.[7] Legal scholars whose careers have been described as interrupted or uprooted mostly hailed from parts of Europe occupied by Nazi Germany.[8] However, most historians examine the trajectories of lawyers in exile in twentieth-century Europe through the eyes of refugees from Nazi Germany and adjacent territories. Taube represents a different group of exiles, one for whom Nazi-occupied France and Germany under Nazi rule functioned as a place of refuge from the Soviet regime. One of the consequences of his situation was that his legal thought was not absorbed into the canon of Anglo-American thought on international law, which is associated with other émigré figures such as Hans Kelsen and Hersch Lauterpacht.[9] Though he was no committed Nazi, Taube was loyal to the regime. Arguably, this makes his case all the more fascinating among the more familiar examples of 'uprooted' jurists.

In the next section of this chapter, I will provide an outline of the relationship between ideas of Roman law and notions of the frontier between East and West, before placing Taube in this context. The final section focuses on Taube's changing ideas of legal international order after 1917, and analyses in what way it presented as a turning point for his political thought.

Roman law as a Russian concept of Western civilization

By the end of the nineteenth century, the legal profession in the Russian Empire was dominated by the German historical school, which envisaged the geographic spread of 'civilizing ideas' from west to east.[10] Liberal intellectuals in Russia idealized the Western tradition, and many had studied at German universities. In Russia, Roman law was embedded in the legal curriculum of the universities of Moscow, Kiev, Yur'ev and Yaroslavl', where this legal heritage of ancient Rome was used to identify gaps in

Russia's own legal landscape. Rome, argued Vladimir Guerrier, a Russian constitutional monarchist, 'having lost a world', came to 'rule in the sphere of ideals'. The original, ancient Rome lost its empire, restored it in Constantinople as the 'second' Rome before remaining instead purely as an 'empire in the realm of spirit'.[11]

The idea of Roman law has been used to define concepts of the West both in Western and in Eastern European scholarship, but the precise nature of their relationship has been conceptualized in very different ways.[12] For German and French jurists and historians of the early modern and modern era, lineages of Roman law allowed them to demarcate a *longue durée* transformation of ancient empires into the civil societies of modern imperial nations and then nation states in Continental Europe, a transformation which evolves around the codification of a *Corpus juris civilis*. After the demise of the last European empire presumed to have been built on its foundation, the Holy Roman Empire of the German Nation, the French and the German civil codes were treated by scholars as the closest incarnation of Roman law in the modern era. Thus by 1900, it was the German cultural sphere, which Tacitus had once so influentially defined as 'barbarian', that came to epitomize the most effective application of Roman law to a modern civil code, leading, as one textbook has put it, from 'Justinian to the BGB [*Bürgerliches Gesetzbuch*]' (Rainer 2012).

Russian admirers of Roman law presented it as an essential element for enabling the transformation of empires into modern nations. In its function as a force of integration for civil society, Roman law was also seen as a repository of regulating civil relations. As such, Roman law outlasted not just the Roman empire and its successors, but also numerous other states which had embedded it in their jurisdictions. However, this wide range of applications also meant that 'too much' civil law had the potential of rendering powerful governments superfluous. In Russia, the infamous ideologue of Russian autocracy, Konstantin Pobedonoscev, had written an influential set of monographs on the history of civil law, in which he explained the necessary limits for the application of Western models to Russia (Pobedonoscev 1871, 1873, 1880). By contrast, his liberal critics such as Vladimir Nechaev and Iosif Pokrovsky did not miss an opportunity to point out that the future of Russia's constitutional development depended on the availability of legal knowledge in its Western European form, some of whose proponents, such as Konstantin Nevolin, had been exiled for much of the nineteenth century.[13] The fact that Rome and Roman law were hotly contested concepts in late imperial Russia can be seen in various entries of the renowned *Encyclopaedia Brockhaus and Efron* (1896–1907), including 'Rome', 'Roman law', '*Corpus juris civilis*', 'Codification' (*Kodifikatsia*) and 'civil law' (*grazhdanskoe parvo*). These entries not only represented a wide range of disciplinary perspectives, from archaeology to jurisprudence, but also served as a foil for laying out a range of political agendas, from constitutional monarchism to Marxism (ESBE 1890–1907). Roman law was also placed in relation to European political thought on international relations, particularly starting in the early modern era, epitomized in the work of Hugo Grotius and others (cf. Gordley 1991; Mälksoo 2012a, 2015).

Perhaps the least contested sphere of Roman law in Russia was international law. Scholars in Russian intellectual circles beyond the legal profession were influenced by the arguments of authors such as Rudolf Sohm and Rudolf von Ihering. Elements of

Roman law had permeated particularly in the domain of inheritance law not only in the Baltic region but also in parts of what is now Ukraine and Poland, which might explain the high number of civil lawyers from this region. But upon closer look, there were significant differences both in their intellectual trajectories and in their understanding of law. For instance, one lawyer who specialized early in the Baltic region's legal exceptionalism was Axel Freytag-Loringhoven; his interest in the Germanic roots of some Baltic legal systems eventually encouraged him to seek a career in Germany, where he became a high-flying publicist of Nazi ideas of Lebensraum.[14]

Scholars of German–Baltic background were prominent among the administrative elite of the Russian Empire (cf. Holquist 2006). Sociologically speaking, many teachers of civil law were intellectuals of non-Slavic background. Many of them had a complex relationship to the anti-Western and Pan-Slavic elements of Russian society as well as to German intellectuals in Prussia (Mälksoo 2015: 42–7). During the revolution of 1905, driven by nationalist and socialist movements in the Baltic region many representatives of this region's elite articulated their commitment to Roman law as a civilizing force in this area, which was threatened by the revolutions.[15] Against the tendencies of Russification at the level of education and civil administration, they were intent on maintaining their own ideas of sovereignty against rival claims to power from Russia's autocrats, on the one hand, and from its peasant or vernacular populations, on the other.

Russia was, of course, still an autocratic state, but one with a newly found outward ambition to shape soft power discourses alongside wars and conquests. In 1898, Tsar Nicholas II invited fifty-nine sovereign states to the Hague International Conference of 1899. Even as late as 1914, 'Russia's proposals for the next peace conference' continued to be discussed in the British liberal press.[16] For all their differences, the last Tsars, the two Alexanders and Nicholas II, sought to increase Russia's international standing as a beacon of international law, not only through wars with the Ottoman Empire in defence of 'Christendom' but also by laying institutional foundations of a certain type of peacemaking which could be useful as means for regulating property and the control over territory in wartime.

The leading names in the emerging Russian tradition of international thought – Friedrikh Martens, Baron Boris Nolde and Mikhail von Taube – were of Baltic background (Martens 1883; Mälksoo 2014). Taube belonged to the establishment of an international community of lawyers who had been intent to devise new, positive foundations for a civilizing European international law that transcended even Europe's Roman legal past, as Martti Koskenniemi has argued (see Koskenniemi 2001). Taube's widely used textbook on international law examined its key principles and historical foundations from the second century CE to the Reformation.[17] His wide chronological framework and the focus on Eastern Europe challenged the conventional narrative of the origins of European international law with its emphasis on Hugo Grotius and the Westphalian order of seventeenth-century Western Europe.[18]

In this work, Taube developed the conjecture that even though the concept of *jus gentium* originated in Justinian's code, there was no ancient or medieval international law as such. Nonetheless, the history of legal practices in some places resembled modern international law. These examples of good practice were more likely to be found in empires than in unitary states. Taube emphasized that it was the papacy, with its use of canon law designed to uphold imperial power in Byzantium, which saved Roman law for subsequent uses in international law. Christianity, in his view, had rendered Roman law more universal in aspiration than it had been when the Roman Empire itself was in existence. In the light of Taube's conception of empire and hegemony as a benign force in international law, the year 1917 signalled profound crisis to his political thought.

'*Pacta sunt servanda*' and the interwar crisis of international law

The 'twenty-year crisis' famously identified by E. H. Carr was particularly visible in the European legal tradition, where new sources for realist responses to the challenges of the day were not self-evident.[19] For many scholars of law from areas such as Eastern Europe and the Baltic, the crisis not just was intellectual but also affected their livelihood, as they experienced various tectonic shifts in their professional lives (Mälksoo 2015). The uncertain nature of their social and political contexts makes many individual cases appear isolated. They resist any 'emplotment' in terms of either normative or deviant paths of intellectual development in relation to the Nazi or Soviet ideologues or their overt critics.

Just as for these other lawyers, his preoccupation with Roman law served Taube as a source of continuity amidst a changing, post-imperial legal landscape. The nineteenth-century German Romanists like Rudolf Sohm had suggested that already in Antiquity, Roman law had evolved from a city law of the republican era (*Stadtrecht*) into a global civil law (*Weltrecht*) under the empire's universal aspirations.[20] For Ihering, similarly, the essence of Roman law remained its spirit and its codifications rather than the institutions it served (von Ihering 1852, 1854, 1858). This notion that Roman law could be applied on a modest, pragmatic scale, as well as being open to claims to global or at least universal power, provided an opportunity to legal internationalists of different political orientation, but as we shall see below, it was particularly appealing to Mikhail von Taube.

Taube's key contribution to the interwar crisis of the law was an attempt to revisit the concept of the *inviolability of treaties*, which is embedded in the Roman concept *pacta sunt servanda*. In the absence of any stable authority or fixed notions of sovereignty, these notions of trust had to be relied upon in order for society to move forward. As Taube put it, 'Pacta sunt servanda, tel est, de temps immémorial, l´axiome, le postulat, l´impératif catégorique de la science du droit de gens.'[21] In his view, the sanctity of pacts derived from their original, religious function as covenants in ancient societies, rather than from the practice or codified norms of contractual exchange. The phrase, in this sense, was not a norm but a kind of golden rule, which suggested that rules be followed. Unlike Hersch Lauterpacht, who alluded to John Milton's critique of the Presbyterians in the English Civil War, when he suggested that international law was often 'but private law "writ large"', Taube placed this phrase from canon law in a different genealogy, to describe treaties between unequal partners and in the absence of a common civilizational core.

As in earlier work, Taube now demanded that a 'minimum of juridical relations' – the existence of a kind of informal civil society, a common sense – was necessary in order to make agreements possible. He had developed this concept in a revised version of his work on the Christian and medieval foundations of international relations, now called *Perpetual Peace or War Everlasting?*[22] He believed that this juridical minimum could only stem from spiritual, not from purely economic forms of intercourse – an idea which gained further weight in the publication thanks to a facsimile of a letter of support he had received from Leo Tolstoy in 1902 (Taube 1905). The central author for Taube was Thomas Aquinas, not Hugo Grotius.

However, precisely to what end Taube may have wanted to put his theory – in other words, in the hands of which governments or which organizations – was not immediately apparent from his written work. He presented it to the legal community at the Hague; yet Taube's own political affiliations had gone through various permutations by the time this article appeared and were not easily accommodated within the largely Protestant-influenced Hague Academy and its partner, the Carnegie Foundation. The initial picture of Mikhail von Taube's situation after the October Revolution of 1917 is one of multiple alienation. After a brief spell as the appointed minister of foreign affairs of the Russian government in exile in Finland, headed by Alexander Trepov, he went on to teach briefly at Uppsala University in Sweden, before moving to Germany and then France.[23] In contrast to the liberal language of the Hague Academy of International Law, Taube's golden age was the pre-Mongolian period of Russian–Western approximation (see Taube 1926a,b). Here, he differed from the other Western-oriented European jurists like Charles Lyon-Caen, Nicholas Politis and James Scott.

In 1921, in addition to his lecturing commitments, Taube had joined informal associations committed to the reinstatement of monarchy in Russia. These included the Munich-based *Wirtschaftliche Aufbau-Vereinigung*, which was an association of German Nazis and Russian Monarchists, and included Alfred Rosenberg, who would later become one of the most influential ideologues of the Third Reich and Reich minister for the occupied territories in the East.[24] 'White' Russians from the Baltic region were particularly prominent there. In 1931, he was invited to teach at the University of Münster in Westphalia, a job he carried out until 1939, lecturing on international law.[25] In 1937, like most other professors, he made an oath of allegiance to Hitler, having reassured the rector in a note that he believed this oath of a 'former Russian subject of German extraction and State Minister would not be in contradiction to an earlier pledge of honour made to the Imperial House of the Romanoffs'.[26] At a time when most prominent exiled lawyers of his generation were in exile *from* the Nazis, Taube chose Paris under Nazi occupation as his destination.

In the 1930s, Taube became affiliated with the initiative of another exile from Bolshevik Russia, the artist and guru Nikolai Roerich, who used to be identified as a Catholic before discovering a blend of oriental religions later in life.[27] He was one of the initiators of a movement to protect cultural heritage in times of war. The Roerich Pact was based on the encouragement extended to governments to sign agreements for the mutual protection of cultural heritage sites. Between 1929 and 1933, according to Roerich, more than thirty national societies for the protection of cultural heritage had been set up (Andreyev 2014: 340–1). The organization was also linked to the League of

Nations, the Carnegie Foundation and to US President Roosevelt personally. Roerich believed that the symbols of his flag, three red dots on white background, would function like the Red Cross and indicate neutral territory over cultural goods. Taube ran the French society, together with a French admirer of Roerich, Marie de Vaux Philipau, and another Russian émigré, George Shkliaver, out of Shkliaver's apartment. Both Catholics, Philipau and Taube were especially active in establishing ties between Roerich's organization and the Catholic institutions both in France and in the United States.[28] Taube's collaboration with Roerich's 'pact' – a soft power organization, as it would be called to day – was the closest practical application of his interpretation of *pacta sunt servanda* that I have been able to find.

In sum, during the interwar crisis of European politics, Taube is particularly difficult to pin onto clear ideological patterns such as 'progressive' and 'reactionary', 'white Russian' or 'anti-Nazi'. Yet, it is the difficulty of making sense of his ideas in context that is illuminating. Unlike other émigrés from Russia flirting with the Western European right, Taube remained detached from the Eurasianists, whose image of Byzantium was that of an anti-Western cultural polity.[29] Russian thinkers traditionally preferred an 'eastern' perspective on the Roman Empire, focusing on the Byzantine Empire as an antidote to the Roman path of Western European development.[30] Taube fit neither the German historical school's vision of Roman law nor the 'Byzantinism' of his fellow Russian thinkers like the philosopher Vladimir Soloviev or the linguist Nikolai Troubetskoi, who emphasized Russia's historical distance from the West (Wiederkehr 2007).

The interwar years were also a time when Taube became concerned with the question when Russia had entered its deviant path towards what he called the 'great catastrophe' (Taube 1928; Taube 1929). At this point, he had crossed a wide range of social and political worlds, which many of us today tend to think of as politically and conceptually separate. He was fiercely loyal to Europe's most autocratic regime associated with the Romanoff family, until their execution in 1918 in the wake of the revolution. Yet, he upheld a strong belief in the importance of what we might call the horizontal fabric of power, rooted in the notion of the sanctity of treaties. The ideology of the empire he served was entailed in triad, formulated by Sergei Uvarov, of 'Autocracy – Orthodoxy – Folk spirit'.[31] He saw his work at the Hague as continuing in the spirit of the Holy Alliance. His main opposition was to the Protestant internationalism of the territorial nation states of Western Europe, a consequence of the great schism of 1045. The latter, in his view, affected the Western world more than of the East, where a new state, the union between the Grand Duchy of Lithuania and Catholic Poland, as well as further pacts in the Baltic region, promised a rapprochement with the Catholic west. By contrast, the period of the high Middle Ages – before the invasion of the Tatars – was, for him, the closest Europe had come to a 'Respublica Christiana'. Unlike his contemporary 'Byzantinists' such as Konstantin Leont'ev, who insisted on irreconcilable differences between Orthodoxy and the West, he thought that Russia's recovery would come from a reunification with Catholicism under a strong emperor. Even in the twentieth century, he thought, the cities of Central and Eastern Europe, like Vilnius, Warsaw and Lemberg, remained important religious and cultural centres. He liked to contrast them with Muscovy, which, with its false pretences of being a 'third Rome', had become a sort of dystopian capital of the 'Third international' (Taube 1938: 46).

Like other displaced legal scholars from Central and Eastern Europe, including Hersch Lauterpacht, Raphael Lemkin and Vladimir Hrabar, Taube turned to international law and its sources in Roman juridical concepts as a source of orientation.[32] Taube's professional training in international civil law enabled him to maintain a professional career even after the empire whose 'indestructible historical foundations' he had announced in late 1915 had collapsed in 1917 (Taube 1915: 60). Yet, the points of orientation for his work had fundamentally changed. For another four decades, he continued practicing international law by teaching at the universities of Uppsala, Louvain, the Russian university in exile in Berlin, the Hague Academy of International Law, and the University of Münster, as well as making a living as a private genealogist in Paris. However, as I want to show in the next section, to analyse Taube's turn to Roman law solely as a reaction to the events involving the Soviet and Nazi regime would leave us with an incomplete picture of his interpretation of Roman law's relevance for international law.

Two views of 1917: Sovereignty without territory

If the collapse of his empire following the year 1917 inspired Taube's work on 'pacta sunt servanda' as the juridical minimum of international relations, another concept of Roman law was inspired by a more 'intellectual' set of events of that year. In 1904, Pope Benedict XV had commissioned Cardinal Gaspari to produce what is a new Code of Canon Law, a compilation which some have compared in significance to *Justinian's Digest*. (Whether or not this is an exaggeration only the future can tell.) This was finally completed in 1917. (In fact, it is now known as the 1917 Code of Canon Law.) The Canon enabled the Vatican to sign a record number of agreements with new post-imperial governments in Central and Eastern Europe, including Lithuania, Poland, Czechoslovakia, as well as to work in a clandestine manner within the Soviet Union as well. Special funds were used via the papal legate Eugenio Pacelli to bring together émigrés from Russia, Ukraine, Poland and other Eastern European countries in a common struggle against Soviet communism.[33] Taube belonged to this group informally but also published an historical essay in a volume edited by Ludwig Berg, an aide of Pacelli's.[34]

As a Catholic, Taube had an additional reason to develop an historical sense of distance from the – already conflicting – historical teleologies upheld, respectively, by the Baltic German elite, the Panslavists, as well as by the liberal Westernizers.[35] Taube reverted this genealogy, which was widely promoted particularly by institutions such as the League of Nations, according to which we progress from the law of the medieval Italian municipal communities, to the law of peoples of the time around the Thirty Years' War, to the Enlightenment models of Vattel, Kant, and so forth, and eventually, the Geneva conventions and the United Nations (and in the present day, authors like Rawls).[36] But the other notion that Taube sought to revive in this context was *ius interpotestates*. The background to his interest in this concept was Taube's renewed engagement with Catholicism, this time, as a political movement of resistance to Soviet expansion.

In doing so, he pointed to the centrality of Roman and canon law as the moments in European history when the connection between church and empire was at its strongest. He championed Byzantium not because it was eastern but because it was the main source of civil – Roman and canonical – law. Having been the architect of the Russian Tsar's peace and education projects whose Catholic faith had been a private affair, he now turned into a more active theorist of Eastern and Western European Catholic unity. As a Catholic, Taube had belonged to a minority in the Russian Empire, but during his exile in Western Europe, his Catholic faith and the experience of interfaith communication proved to be a point of connection. In 1936, in Warsaw, Taube additionally published a collection titled *Agrafa*, a compilation of the uncodified sayings of Jesus geared to contribute to a consolidation of Christian faiths in the twentieth century (Taube 1936).

Taube's political loyalty belonged to the autocratic and Orthodox dynasty of the Romanoffs, but as a legal historian and theorist, even in this period of his life, he produced influential accounts on the transmission of Roman law through canon law, particularly, in treaties and relations between the early princes of medieval Rus' and their Western contemporaries (Taube 1933). He rejected the post-Westphalian teleologies of international law which other international jurists such as his teacher Martens subscribed to, and which he associated with Protestantism, believing instead that the Pope possessed a form of sovereignty which enabled the emergence of a type of legal regime which was different from *ius interstatum* or *ius gentium* because it implied the possibility of a potential global sovereignty without territorial control. As Taube put it, in fact the role of the Catholic Church in the modern world calls for a 'juridical category of its own', which he proposed to call *droit entre pouvoirs* or *jus inter potestates*, specifying that by 'potestas' he meant not only a Hobbesian territorial state but also a non-territorial form of sovereignty. This non-territorial form of sovereignty, in his view, preceded the Westphalian political order of the seventeenth century. Its provenance was what he called '*deux sciences fondamentales de la jurisprudence d'autrefois*' – '*du droit canonique et du droit romain*'.[37]

In Taube's view, the Western Europeans were mistaken in seeing the power of Roman law in territorial forms of sovereignty. He believed that the classical expression of sovereignty, the notion of non-recognition of a superior power [*superiorem non riconoscere*], which began to proliferate in the early modern period, was mistakenly only applied to territorial power. In the interwar period, a group of Russian émigrés in Germany had formed an intellectual community whose aim was fostering ties between Catholic and Orthodox faiths. Taube contributed a book to a series in their publishing house, in which he argued that any territorial power was ultimately more 'ephemeral' than spiritual power. The aspirations of Constantinople to become the Second Rome, or of Moscow to serve as the Third, were therefore mere hubris (Taube 1927). Moscow's attempt to defeat the other imperial powers in the Crimean war had failed in 1853. But Taube was optimistic about the prospects of a united Church. In his view, the task was to recall the survival of the 'first' (and timeless) Rome of the 'Respublica Christiana', therefore, which would outlast 'Nero and Attila, the Saracenes and Normans, the Byzantine kings and German emperors, Luther and Voltaire, Napoleon and Garibaldi, the empire of Protestant Berlin and the empire of Orthodox Petersburg'. In what was an unusual intellectual move, Taube looked East and not West to recover unity among the Christian churches, at Russia from the period before the Mongol invasion.

Conclusion

Taube's work as a jurist in the interwar period did not have even a fraction of the impact of other international lawyers who were displaced or uprooted in the twentieth century. Hersch Lauterpacht's conception of international law, and his reading of Roman law in this context, with the centrality of the individual, prevailed as the more influential engagement with this heritage.[38] Some of Taube's model of a benign imperial hegemony was out of sync with his time. But even those activities which could have had more resonance, such as the Roerich Pact, the organization for the protection of cultural heritage in wartime, ultimately remained little known, since this organization was absorbed by UNESCO after the Second World War. Nonetheless, his work, the way he adapted to the uncertainties of political exile and the social process by which his career was ultimately disrupted, are emblematic of a wider cultural history. The fading empires of his present provided Taube with a foil for recalling how Roman law had been used to consolidate the Byzantine Empire.[39]

It was somewhat ironic that the tenure of this professor who specialized in the sanctity of treaties ended in the year of the Hitler–Stalin pact – an agreement which, apart from being unjust in its treatment of peoples to be subject to a shared Nazi–Soviet hegemony, was soon broken. The case of this twentieth-century *peregrinus* with his experiences of statelessness and shifting allegiances provides a fascinating window on this period in European social and cultural history.

Yet, alongside imperial dissolution and catastrophe, the year 1917 had also ushered in a new codification of canon law which held the promise of a future union of Christians. Had he lived until the 1990s, Taube might well have concluded that the idea of breaking down communism under the umbrella of the Catholic Church through separate pacts with nation states and subnational groups was ultimately successful, considering the rise of civil society in Eastern Europe from the 1970s onwards and the role of the Church in this context.

In 1929, the Russian medievalist Pavel Vinogradoff in Oxford called the medieval history of Roman law a 'ghost story' set in dark times, when the demise of the Western Roman Empire coincided with an era of legal decay across all of Europe, having to wait a long time to return to earth (Vinogradoff 1929: 4). A similar spirit prevailed among lawyers who found themselves displaced or, indeed, uprooted in the mid-twentieth century. In practice, it was not at all clear to what extent the ideal of Roman law as civil law could still be upheld in the age of new rising empires which constantly broke the norms of international pacts, from Brest-Litovsk to Molotov–Ribbentrop (Anzilotti 1902). The example of the princes of early medieval Rus' served him as a repository of historical experience for uncertain times. But, set against the youthful imperialism and internationalism of the Nazi and Soviet anti-Romanists, this 'Byzantium' was emphatically a country for old men.

Notes

1 Most influentially, of von Savigny 1840; Pokrovsky 1917; followed by Levy 1929; Vinogradoff 1929; Koschaker 1947, and most recently, Avenarius 2004 and 2014. See also Caenegem 1991.
2 For an outline of this perspective from the modern point of view, see, for example, Bunce 2000.
3 See Taube 1929, 2007. See also a review of Taube's reflections on Russian politics before the revolution by Hans Wehberg (Wehberg 1931).
4 On Soviet international law, see Grabar 1927.
5 Cf. Pashukanis 1924 (repr. 1980). On Soviet legal exceptionalism, see also Tarakouzio 1935.
6 For reference, see, for example, Zimmermann 2015: 452–80.
7 Cf. Lieven 1995; Stolleis and Simon 1989; Joerges and Galeigh 2003.
8 Beatson and Zimmermann 2004; Palmier 2006; contrast with Koskenniemi 2004. On Raphael Lemkin's intellectual response to the condition of statelessness, see Moyn 2014; and on Lemkin, see Siegelberg 2013.
9 For overviews, see Butler 1980; Bernhard 1984; Bull and Watson 1984; Koskenniemi 2004, 2012; Fassbender 2012; Fassbender, et al. 2012. See also Schiavone 2012; Schulz 2007; and Scobbie 2012.
10 For the most recent overview, see Avenarius 2014. For a more historical overview, see Grabar 1901; Martens 1883; Martens 1874–1909; 'Das römische Recht in Russland' (1906); Nippold 1924.
11 ESBE *sv*. 'Rim' (Guerrier).
12 As defined prominently by the school of von Savigny 1840. See also Maine 1875; Pobedonoscev 1873, 1871, 1880; Sohm 1908; Pokrovsky 1917; Koschaker 1947; Halecki 1957; Lemberg 2000. For recent scholarly perspectives on Roman law, see Johnston 2015.
13 ESBE *sv*. 'Grazhdanskoe pravo' (Vladimir Nechaev). The names of exiled civil law experts are Nevolin, Redkin, Kalmykov, Kunitsyn, Krylov and others. See also ESBE *sv*. 'Rimskoe pravo' (Pokrovskii).
14 Cf. von Freytag-Loringhoven 1905. Loringhoven had begun his career with an analysis of this special status at Tartu university (then renamed Yur'ev), but eventually fled Russia and had a high-flying career as a publicist in Nazi Germany, where he edited the journals *Völkerrecht und Völkerbund* and subsequently *Europäische Revue*. See also Freytag-Loringhoven 1919; Freytag-Loringhoven 1936. For the context of Baltic legal exceptionalism, see Fassbender, et al. 2012, especially Mälksoo 2012b; and Lieven 2006. On National Socialist law, see Stolleis 1989.
15 'Das römische Recht in Russland' (1906); von Transehe-Roseneck 1906–1907. See also Pokrovac 2007; Rudokvas and Kartsov 2007; Kartsov 2007; Luts-Sootak 2007.
16 'Russia's proposals for next Peace conference', 7 April 1914, *The Manchester Guardian*. For an historical overview, see Mälksoo 2015. See also Taube 1929 and Rybachenok 2005; Roshchin 2017.
17 Taube 1894, 1899, 1902. See also the excerpts in Gorovcev 1909.
18 For an overview, see Koskenniemi 2012.
19 Carr 1939. On crisis and the law, see Joerges and Galeigh 2003.
20 Sohm 1908: 52ff. For a new view of Roman law as a source of global law, see Domingo 2010.

21 Taube 1930: 291, 295ff. See also discussion in Wehberg 1959; and *passim* in Kōnstantopoulos and Wehberg 1953.
22 Taube 1922; see also discussion in Starodubtsev 2000 and Paramuzova 2008.
23 On Taube's role in the government in exile, see Elenevskaia 1968: 152–3.
24 For more details on this organization, see Kellogg 2005.
25 On the end of his career in 1939, and his inconclusive attempts to return to it in 1941, see Steveling 1999: 460, n. 317. For his publications from this period, see Taube 1933; Taube 1935.
26 Taube to the Rector of Münster University, 19 December 1937. Cited in Steveling 1999: 368, n. 435.
27 On Roerich's Catholicism, see Elenevskaia 1968: 69.
28 Andreyev 2014: 341. See also the letter from Taube to Roerich, 10 August 1932. International Roerich Centre, Moscow, Fond 1. № 8075, pp. 39–40 (http://lib.icr.su/node/1320, seen on 28 August 2017).
29 On Taube's view of Byzantium, see Taube 1939. On the Eurasian connections with the right, see 'Delegation in Germany', in Russisches Wissenschaftliches Institut: Various Correspondence, Financial Statements, Press Cuttings, etc., 1922–1932, C1255/151/170.1, UNOG Records and Archives Unit, Nansen Fonds, Refugees Mixed Archival Group, 1919–1947. On the connections between the Russian expatriate universities and the old imperial elites, see the papers of Mikhail Nikolaevich de Giers, the last Russian ambassador in Rome during the First World War. Mikhail de Giers papers, Box 21, Folder 1, Hoover Institution Archives, Stanford, California. See also Browder and Kerensky 1961.
30 Soloviev 1896; Troubetskoi 1925; Mitteis 1963. On Byzantinism, see Cameron 1992; Marciniak and Smythe 2015.
31 For a biography of Taube in his Russian context, see Mälksoo 2015; Mälksoo 2008. For Taube among the white Russians form an archival perspective, see the discussion of the Bakhmeteff archive in Raeff 1990. On the Russian diaspora and its politics, see Fassbender 2012.
32 For a good indication of his reputation in later years, see the oblique references to Taube's political views in Wehberg 1959/1960. For the broader context of central European lawyers' orientation towards international law, see Sands 2016. See also Lesaffer 2016. See also Fassbender, et al. 2012. For more precise examples, see Grabar 1893; Grabar 1901; Grabar 1912; Grabar 1990; and Lauterpacht 1927.
33 Weir 2015. On the Soviet Union as an empire, see Keep 2002.
34 Berg 1927. More on Catholicism in the Russian émigré community, see Golovanov 2015. On Russians in interwar Germany, see Casteel 2008.
35 For the various debates about longue durée history in Russian imperial discourse, see Etkind 2011. On Catholicism as a minority religion in late imperial and early Soviet Russia, see Solchanyk and Hvat 1990. Taube himself recommended this source for a history of Catholicism in Russia: Tolstoj 1863/1864. For the perspective of the Baltic genealogists, see Dellinghausen 1928; Stackelberg 1930; Stavenhagen 1939.
36 Cf. Jellinek 1914: 337. See also Jellinek 1892.
37 Taube 1907/1908. On the history of Catholicism in the Cold War, especially in Eastern Europe, see Ramet 1990.
38 Scobbie 2012. On the German concept of the subject of international law in the 1930s, see Steck 2003.
39 On ideas of Europe in imperial contexts, see Osterhammel 2004.

References

Unpublished

'Delegation in Germany', in Russisches Wissenschaftliches Institut: Various Correspondence, Financial Statements, Press Cuttings, etc., 1922–1932, C1255/151/170.1, UNOG Records and Archives Unit, Nansen Fonds, Refugees Mixed Archival Group, 1919–47.

Mikhail de Giers papers, Box 21, Folder 1, Hoover Institution Archives, Stanford, California.

Mikhail Taube to Nikolai Roerich, 10 August 1932. International Roerich Centre, Moscow, Fond 1. № 8075, pp. 39–40. http://lib.icr.su/node/1320, seen on 28 August 2017.

Published

Andreyev, A. (2014), *The Myth of the Masters Revived: The Occult Lives of Nikolai and Elena Roerich*, Leiden: Brill.

Anzilotti, D. (1902), *Teoria generale della responsibilitá dello stato nel diritto internazionale*, Florence: F. Lumachi.

Avenarius, M. (2004), *Rezeption des römischen Rechts in Russland: Dmitrij Mejer, Nikolaj Djuvernua und Iosif Pokrovskij*, Göttingen: Wallstein.

Avenarius, M. (2014), *Fremde Traditionen des römischen Rechts. Einfluß, Wahrnehmung und Argument des »rimskoe pravo« im russischen Zarenreich des 19. Jahrhunderts*, Göttingen: Wallstein.

Beatson, J. and Zimmermann, R., eds. (2004), *Jurists Uprooted: German-Speaking Emigré Lawyers in Twentieth Century Britain*, Oxford: Oxford University Press.

Bernhard, R., ed. (1984), *Encyclopaedia of Public International Law*, North-Holland: Elsevier.

Browder, R. P. and Kerensky, A., eds. (1961), *The Russian Provisional Government 1917 Documents*, vol. 1, Stanford: Stanford University Press.

Bull, H. and Watson, A., eds. (1984), *The Expansion of International Society*, Oxford: Oxford University Press.

Bunce, V. (2000), 'The Historical Origins of the East-West Divide: Civil Society, Political Science, and Democracy in Europe', in N. Bermeo and P. Nord (eds), *Civil Society before Democracy: Lessons from Nineteenth Century Europe*, 209–36, London: Rowman & Littlefield.

Butler, William E., ed. (1980), *International Law in Comparative Perspective*, Alpen aan den Rijn: Sijthoff.

van Caenegem, Raoul C. (1991), *Legal History: A European Perspective*, London: Hambledon.

Cameron, A. (1992), *The Use and Abuse of Byzantium*, Cambridge: Cambridge University Press.

Carr, E. H. (1939), *The Twenty Years' Crisis: 1919–1939: An Introduction to the Study of International Relations*, London: Macmillan.

Casteel, J. (2008), 'The Politics of Diaspora: Russian German Émigré Activists in Interwar Germany', in Matthias Schulz, James M. Skidmore, and David G. John (eds), *German Diasporic Experiences: Identity, Migration, and Loss*, 117–30, Waterloo: Wilfrid Laurier University Press.

'Das römische Recht in Russland' (1906), in R. Leonhard(ed.), *Stimmen des Auslands über die Zukunft der Rechtswissenschaft*, 105–6, Breslau: M&H Marcus.
von Dellinghausen, E. (1928), *Die Entstehung, Entwicklung und Aufbauende Tätigkeit der Baltischen Ritterschaften*, Langensalza: H. Beyer.
Domingo, R. (2010), *The New Global Law*, Cambridge: Cambridge University Press.
Elenevskaia, I. (1968), *Vospominaniya* [Memoirs], Stockholm: no publisher known,
Encyclopedicheskiy slovar' Brokgauza i Efrona [ESBE], 86 vols. (1890-1907), St. Petersburg and Leipzig: Efron.
Etkind, A. (2011), *Internal Colonization: Russia's Imperial Experience*, Cambridge: Polity.
Fassbender, B. (2012), 'Hans Kelsen', in B. Fassbender, A. Peters, S. Peter and D. Högger (eds), *The Oxford Handbook of the History of International Law*, 1167–73, Oxford: Oxford University Press.
Fassbender, B., Peters, A., Peter, S. and Högger, D., eds. (2012), *The Oxford Handbook of the History of International Law*, Oxford: Oxford University Press.
von Freytag-Loringhoven, A. (1905), *Vstuplenie naslednika v obiazatel'stva i prava trebovania nasledovatelia po ostzeiskomu pravu do kodifikatsii 1864 g.*, Yur'ev: K. Matthiessen.
von Freytag-Loringhoven, A. (1919), *Russland*, Halle: Max Niemeyer.
von Freytag-Loringhoven, F. (1936), 'Rechtfertigung des Völkerrechts', *Völkerbund und Völkerrecht*, 3: 161–6.
Golovanov, S. (2015), *Russkoe katolicheskoe delo. Rimsko-katolucheskaia tserkov' i russkaia emigratsia*, Omsk: Amfora.
Gordley, J. (1991), *Philosophical Origins of Modern Contract Doctrine*, Oxford: Oxford University Press.
Gorovcev, A. (1909), *Mezhdunarodnoe pravo. Izbrannaia literatura. Kratkaia Encyclopedia*, St. Petersburg: Trenke and Fusno.
Grabar, V. (1893), 'Voina i mezhdunarodnoe pravo', *Uchenye zapiski imperatorskago Iur'evskago universiteta*, 4: 23–45.
Grabar, V. (1901), *Rimskoe pravo v istorii mezhdunarodno-pravovykh uchenii: elementy mezhdunarodnogo prava v trudakh legistov XII–XIII vv.* [Roman law in the history of international doctrine: elements of international law in the works of the 12th and 13th-century jurists], Yur'ev: Matthiesen.
Grabar, V. (1912), *Nachalo ravenstva gosudarstv v sovremennom mezhdunarodnom prave*, St. Petersburg: Kirschbaum.
Grabar, V. (1927), 'Das heutige Völkerrecht vom Standpunkte eines Sowjetjuristen', *Zeitschrift für Völkerrecht*, 9: 188–214.
Grabar, V. (1990), *The History of International Law in Russia, 1647–1917: A Bio-bibliographical Study*, ed. and transl. William E. Butler, Oxford: Oxford University Press.
Halecki, O. (1957), *Europa. Grenzen und Gliederung seiner Geschichte*, Darmstadt: Herman Gertner.
Holquist, P. (2006), 'Dilemmas of a Progressive Administrator. Baron Boris Nolde', *Kritika: Explorations in Russian and Eurasian History*, 7 (2): 241–73.
Jellinek, G. (1892), *System der subjektiven öffentlichen Rechte*, Freiburg: Mohr.
Jellinek, G. (1914), *Allgemeine Staatslehre*, Berlin: Haering.
von Ihering, R. (1852, 1854, 1858), *Der Geist des römischen Rechts auf den verschiedenen Stufen seiner Entwicklung*, 3 vols, Leipzig: Breitkopf & Härtel.
Joerges, C. and Galeigh, N. S., eds. (2003), *Darker Legacies of Law in Europe: The Shadow of National Socialism and Fascism over Europe and its Legal Traditions*, Oxford: Hart.

Johnston, D., ed. (2015), *The Cambridge Companion to Roman Law*, Cambridge: Cambridge University Press.

Kartsov, A. (2007), 'Das Russische Seminar für Römisches Recht an der juristischen Fakultät der Friedrich-Wilhelms-Universität zu Berlin', in Z. Pokrovac (ed.), *Juristenausbildung in Osteuropa bis zum Ersten Weltkrieg. Rechtskulturen des modernen Osteuropa. Traditionen und Transfers*, 317–53, Frankfurt: Klostermann.

Keep, John L. H. (2002), *A History of the Soviet Union 1945–1991: Last of the Empires*, Oxford: Oxford University Press.

Kellogg, M. (2005), *The Russian Roots of Nazism: White Émigrés and the Making of National Socialism 1917–1945*, Cambridge: Cambridge University Press.

Kōnstantopoulos, Dēmētrios S. and Wehberg, H., eds. (1953), *Gegenwartsprobleme des internationalen Rechtes und der Rechtsphilosophie. Festschrift für Rudolf Laun für seinem siebzigsten Geburtstag*, Hamburg: Girardet.

Koschaker, P. (1947), *Europa und das römische Recht*, Munich: C. H. Beck.

Koskenniemi, M. (2001), *The Gentle Civilizer of Nations: the Rise and Fall of International Law, 1870–1960*, Cambridge: Cambridge University Press.

Koskenniemi, M. (2004), 'Hersch Lauterpacht and the Development of International Criminal Law', *Journal of International Criminal Justice*, 2: 810–25.

Koskenniemi, M. (2012), 'International Law in the World of Ideas', in J. Crawford, M Koskenniemi and S. Ranganathan (eds),*The Cambridge Companion to International Law*, 47–64, Cambridge: Cambridge University Press.

Landau, P. (1989), 'Römisches Recht und Deutsches Gemeinrecht', in M. Stolleis and D. Simon (eds), *Rechtsgeschichte im Nationalsozialismus*, 11–24, Tübingen: Mohr.

Lauterpacht, H. (1927), *Private Law Sources and Analogies of International Law: With Special Reference to International Arbitration*, London: Longmans, Green and Co. Ltd..

Lemberg, H., ed. (2000), *Grenzen in Ostmitteleuropa im 19. und 20. Jahrhundert. Aktuelle Forschungsprobleme*, Marburg: Herder-Institut.

Lenin, V. (1924), 'O zadachakh Narkomyusta v usloviyakh novoi ekonomichesoi politiki' (On the tasks of the Narkomyust under the conditions of the New Economic Policy), Letter to Dmitry Kursky (20 February 1922), in A. Fradkin (ed.), *V Vserossiiskii s'ezd deiatelei sovetskoi yustitsii. Stenograficheskii otchet*, Moscow: Yuridicheskoe izd. Narkomyusta RSFSR.

Lesaffer, R. (2016), 'Roman Law and the Intellectual History of International Law', in A. Orford and F. Hoffmann (eds), *The Oxford Handbook of the Theory of International Law*, 38–59, Oxford: Oxford University Press.

Levy, E. (1929), 'Westen und Osten in der nachklassischen Entwicklung des römischen Rechts', *Zeitschrift der Savigny-Stiftung*, 49: 230–59.

Lieven, D. (1995), 'The Russian Empire and the Soviet Union as Imperial Polities', *Journal of Contemporary History*, 30: 607–36.

Lieven, D., ed. (2006), *The Cambridge History of Russia. Vol. II: Imperial Russia 1689–1917*, Cambridge: Cambridge University Press.

Luts-Sootak, M. (2007), 'Der lange Beginn einer geordneten Juristenausbildung an der deutschen Universität zu Dorpat (1802–1893)', in Z. Pokrovac (ed.), *Juristenausbildung in Osteuropa bis zum Ersten Weltkrieg. Rechtskulturen des modernen Osteuropa. Traditionen und Transfers*, 357–91, Frankfurt: Klostermann.

Maine, H. S. (1875), *Lectures in the Early History of Institutions*, New York: Henry Holt & Co.

Mälksoo, L. (2008), 'The History of International Legal Theory in Russia: A Civilizational Dialogue with Europe', *The European Journal of International Law*, 19 (1): 211–32.

Mälksoo, L. (2012a), 'Encounters "Russia-Europe"', in B. Fassbender, A. Peters, S. Peter and D. Högger (eds), *The Oxford Handbook of the History of International Law*, 764–87, Oxford: Oxford University Press.
Mälksoo, L. (2012b), 'Friedrikh von Martens', in B. Fassbender, A. Peters, S. Peter and D. Högger (eds), *The Oxford Handbook of the History of International Law*, 1147–52, Oxford: Oxford University Press.
Mälksoo, L. (2014), 'F. F. Martens in His Time', *The European Journal of International Law*, 25 (3): 811–29.
Mälksoo, L. (2015), *Russian Approaches to International Law*, Oxford: Oxford University Press.
Marciniak, P. and Smythe, Dion C., eds. (2015), *The Reception of Byzantium in European Culture since 1500*, London: Routledge.
Martens, F. (1883), *Sovremennoe mezhdunarodnoe pravo civilisovannykh narodov*, 2 vols [Modern International Law of Civilized Peoples], St. Petersburg: Benke.
Martens, F. (1874-1909), *Receuils des traités et Conventions Conclus par la Russie avec les puissances étrangères*, St. Petersburg: Imprimerie du Ministère de Voies de Communication.
Mitteis, L. (1963), *Reichsrecht und Volksrecht in den östlichen Provinzen des Römischen Kaiserreichs: Mit beiträgen zur Kenntniss des griechischen Rechts und der spätrömischen Rechtsentwicklung*, Hildesheim: Olms.
Moyn, S. (2014), *Human Rights and the Uses of History*, New York: Verso.
Nippold, O. (1924), '"Les conférences de La Haye et la Société des Nations". Le développement historique du droit international depuis le Congrès de Vienne', in Hague Academy of International Law (ed.), *Collected Courses of The Hague Academy of International Law*, vol. 2, 1–99, The Hague: Martinus Nijhoff Publishers.
Osterhammel, J. (2004), 'Europamodelle und imperiale Kontexte', *Journal of Modern European History*, 2: 157–81.
Palmier, J.-M. (2006), *Weimar in Exile: The Antifascist Emigration in Europe and America*, London: Verso.
Paquet, A. (1923), *Rom oder Moskau*, Berlin: Drei Masken.
Paramuzova, O. (2008), 'Sovremennye tendencii recepcii rimskogo prava v svete reshenia problem konceptual'nogo pereosmyslenia mezhdunarodno-pravovoi nauki', *Vestnik Sankt-Peterburgskogo Universiteta*, 6 (3): 152–67.
Pashukanis, E. (1924), *General Theory of Law and Marxism Obshchaia teoriia prava i marksizm: Opyt kritiki osnovnykh iuridicheskikh poniatii*, reprinted in Evgeny Pashukanis (1980), *Selected Writings on Marxism and Law*, ed. Piers Beirne and Robert Sharlet, 32–131, London: Academic Press.
Pobedonoscev, K. (1873, 1871, 1880), *Kurs grazhdanskogo prava*, 3 vols [Course in civil law], St. Petersburg: V. I. Golovine.
Pokrovac, Z., ed. (2007), *Juristenausbildung in Osteuropa bis zum Ersten Weltkrieg. Rechtskulturen des modernen Osteuropa. Traditionen und Transfers*, Frankfurt: Klostermann.
Pokrovsky, I. (1917), *Istoria rimskogo prava* [History of Roman Law], 3rd edn, Petrograd: Pravo.
Rudokvas, Anton D. and Kartsov, A. (2007), 'Der Rechtsunterricht und die juristische Ausbildung im kaiserlichen Russland', in Zoran Pokrovac (ed.), *Juristenausbildung in Osteuropa bis zum Ersten Weltkrieg. Rechtskulturen des modernen Osteuropa. Traditionen und Transfers*, 273–317, Frankfurt: Klostermann.
'Russia's proposals for next Peace conference', 7 April 1914, *The Manchester Guardian*.

Raeff, M. (1990), *Russia Abroad: A Cultural History of the Russian Emigration, 1919–1939*, New York: Oxford University Press.

Rainer, J. M. (2012), *Das römische Recht in Europa: von Justinian zum BGB*, Vienna: Manz.

Ramet, P., ed. (1990), *Catholicism and Politics in Communist Societies*, Durham, NC: Duke University Press.

Roshchin, E. (2017), 'The Hague Conferences and "International Community": A Politics of Conceptual Innovation', *Review of International Studies*, 43 (1): 177–98.

Rybachenok, I. (2005), *Rossiya i Pervaya konferenciya mira 1899 v Gaage*, Moscow: Institut rossiiskoi istorii.

Sands, P. (2016), *East West Street. On the Origins of "Genocide" and "Crimes Against Humanity"*, London: Weidenfeld & Nicolson.

Savigny, F. C. von (1840), *System des heutigen Römischen Rechts*, 3 vols, Berlin: Veit und Comp.

Schiavone, A. (2012), *The Invention of Law in the West*, trans. J. Carden and A. Shugaar, Cambridge, MA: Belknap Press.

Schulz, M. (2007), 'Vom Direktorialsystem zum Multilateralismus: Die Haager Friedenskonferenz von 1907 in der Entwicklung des internationalen Staatensystems bis zum Ersten Weltkrieg', *Die Friedens-Warte*, 82 (4): 31–50.

Scobbie, I. (2012), 'Hersch Lauterpacht', in B. Fassbender, A. Peters, S. Peter and D. Högger (eds), *The Oxford Handbook of the History of International Law*, 1179–85, Oxford: Oxford University Press.

Siegelberg, Mira L. (2013), 'Unofficial Men, Efficient Civil Servants: Raphael Lemkin in the History of International Law', *Journal of Genocide Research*, 15 (3): 297–316.

Solchanyk, R. and Hvat, I. (1990), 'The Catholic Church in the Soviet Union', in P. Ramet (ed.), *Catholicism and Politics in Communist Societies*, 49–93, Durham, NH: Duke University Press.

Sohm, R. (1908), *Institutionen. Ein Lehrbuch der Geschichte und des Systems des römischen Privatrechts*, 13th edn, Leipzig: Duncker & Humblot.

Soloviev, V. (1896), *Vizantizm I Rossia*.

Stackelberg, O. M. von (1930), *Genealogisches Handbuch Der Estländischen Ritterschaft*, Görlitz: Verl. für Sippenforschung und Wappenkunde Starke.

Starodubtsev, G. (2000), *Mezhdunarodno-pravovaya nauka rossiiskoi emigratsii* (1918–1939), Moscow: Kniga i biznes.

Stavenhagen, O. (1939), *Genealogisches Handbuch der Kurländischen Ritterschaft*, Görlitz: Verl. für Sippenforschung und Wappenkunde Starke.

Steck, Peter K. (2003), *Zwischen Volk und Staat. Das Völkerrechtssubjekt in der deutschen Völkerrechtslehre (1933–1941)*, Baden-Baden: Nomos.

Steveling, L. (1999), *Juristen in Münster: Ein Beitrag zur Geschichte der Rechts- und Staatswissenschaftlichen Fakultät der Westfälischen Wilhelms-Universität Münster*, Münster: LIT-Verlag.

Stolleis, M. (1989), 'Introduction', in M. Stolleis and D. Simon (eds), *Rechtsgeschichte im Nationalsozialismus*, 1–11, Tübingen: Mohr.

Stolleis, M. and Simon, D., eds. (1989), *Rechtsgeschichte im Nationalsozialismus*, Tübingen: Mohr.

Tarakouzio, T. (1935), *The Soviet Union and International Law*, New York: Macmillan.

von Taube, M. (1894, 1899, 1902), *Istoria zarozhdenia sovremennogo mezhdunarodnogo prava*, 3 vols [The history of the genesis of modern international law], St. Petersburg: P.I. Schmidt.

von Taube, M. (1905), *Khristianstvo I mezhdunarodnyi mir*, 2nd edn, Moscow: Posrednik.

von Taube, M. (1907/1908), 'La situation internationale actuelle du Pape et l'idée d'un "droit entre pouvoirs" (jus interpotestates)', *Archiv für Rechts- und Wirtschaftsphilosophie*, 1 (3): 360–8; and no. 4 (1907/08): 510–18.
von Taube, M. (1915), 'Istoricheskie korni tepereshnei voinny v epokhu imperatorov Aleksandra i Nikolaia I', in A. Shemansky (ed.), *Istoria Velikoi Voiny*, vol. 1, 20–60, Moscow: Vasil'yev.
von Taube, M. (1922), *Vechnyi mir ili vechnaia voina? Mysli o Ligi Natsii*, rev. edn, Berlin: Detinets.
von Taube, M. (1926a), 'Études sur le développement historique du droit international dans l'Europe orientale', *Collected Courses of The Hague Academy of International Law*, 11 (1): 341–525.
von Taube, M. (1926b), *La Russie et l'Europe Occidentale à travers dix siècles*, in *Etudes d'histoire internationale et de psychologie ethnique*, Bruxelles: La Lecture au Foyer, Librairie Albert Dewit.
von Taube, M. (1927), 'Rom und Rußland m der vormongolischen Zeit, Kap. V: Altrußlands religiöse Verbindungen mit der katholischen Welt in der vortatarischen Periode', in L. Berg (ed.), *'Ex Oriente'. Religiöse und philosophische Probleme des Ostens und des Westens- Beiträge orthodoxer, unierter und katholischer Schriftsteller in russischer, französischer und deutscher Sprache*, Mainz: Matthias Grünewald. Russian text available at http://www.unavoce.ru/library/taube_premongol.html, accessed 13 January 2017.
von Taube, M. (1928), *Rußland und Westeuropa: Rußlands historische Sonderentwicklung in der europäischen Völkergemeinschaft*, Berlin: Georg Stilke.
von Taube, M. (1929), *Der Großen Katastrophe Entgegen. Die russische Politik der Vorkriegszeit und das Ende des Zarenreiches (1904–1917)*, Berlin: Neuner.
von Taube, M. (1930), 'L'inviolabilité des traités', *Collected Courses of The Hague Academy of International Law*, 32: 295–389.
de Taube, M. (1933), *Les origines de l'arbitrage international. Antiquité et Moyen Age*, Paris: Sirey.
von Taube, M. (1935), 'Le statut juridique de la mer Baltique jusqu'au début du xixe siècle', *Collected Courses of The Hague Academy of International Law*, 53: 462.
von Taube M. (1936), *Agrafa. O nezapisannykh v Evangelii Izrecheniakh Iisusa Khrista*, Warsaw: Biblioteka bratstva pravoslavnykh bogoslovov v Pol'she.
von Taube, M. (1938), 'Internationale und Kirchenpolitische Wandlungen im Ostbaltikum und Russland zuz Zeit der deutschen Eroberung Livlands (12. und 13. Jahrhundert)', *Jahrbücher für Geschichte Osteuropas*, 3 (1): 11–46.
von Taube M. (1939), 'De l'apport de Byzance au développement du droit international occidental', *Collected Courses of The Hague Academy of International Law*, 67: 233–9.
von Taube, M. (2007), *'Zarnitsy'. Vospominaniya o tragicheskoi sud'be predrevoliutsionnoi Rossii*, Moscow: ROSSPEN.
Tolstoj, Comte D. A. (1863/1864), *Le Catholicisme romain en Russie*, Paris: Dentu.
von Transehe-Roseneck, A. (1906), *Die lettische Revolution, with an Introduction by Theodor Schiemann*, vol. 1, Berlin: G. Reimer (vol. 2, Berlin: G. Reimer, 1907).
Troubetskoi, N. (1925), 'Evraziistvo I beloe dvizhenie', in Trobetskoi, N (2015), *Sbornik Rabot* (Moscow: Direkt-Media), 5-26.
Vinogradoff, P. (1929), *Roman Law in Medieval Europe*, Cambridge and New York: Cambridge University Press.
Wehberg, H. (1931), 'Review of *La Politique russe d'avant guerre et la Fin de l'Empire des Tsars(1904—1917)* by Baron M. de Taube', *Die Friedens-Warte*, 31 (5): 159–60.

Wehberg, H. (1959), 'Pacta Sunt Servanda', *The American Journal of International Law*, 53 (4): 775–86.

Wehberg, H. (1959/1960), 'Zum 90. Geburtstag von Prof. Michael v. Taube', *Die Friedens-Warte*, 55: 56–8.

Weir, T. (2015), 'A European Culture War in the Twentieth Century? Anti-Catholicism and Anti-Bolshevism between Moscow, Berlin, and the Vatican 1922 to 1933', *Journal of Religious History*, 39 (2): 280–306.

Wiederkehr, S. (2007), *Die eurasische Bewegung. Wissenschaft und Politik in der russischen Emigration der Zwischenkriegszeit und im postsowjetischen Russland*, Cologne: Beiträge zur Geschichte Osteuropas.

Zimmermann, R. (2015), 'Roman Law in the Modern World', in D. Johnston (ed.), *The Cambridge Companion to Roman Law*, 452–80, Cambridge: Cambridge University Press.

6

The Denaturalization of Nordic Law: Germanic Law and the Reception of Roman Law

Johann Chapoutot[1]

Introduction

In a novella taking place during the Second World War, Louis Aragon has one of his characters, a military judge, say:

> I was a professor of Roman law. But to give priority to Germanic law, it is my point of view one has to erase all traces of Roman law from the modern world. Roman law as a basis for modern laws is a disgusting absurdity and contrary to the German spirit.

He adds:

> In these times, our courts are still infested with Roman law, the Napoleonic code, Jewish laws … . Today, we would have never let off Dimitrov; he would have been found guilty … according to Germanic law.[2]

This novella, entitled *Roman Law Is No More*, suggests a profound knowledge on the part of Louis Aragon of the debates, developments and in-fighting in the world of Nazi jurists. Let's pause straight away for a moment on the term *jurist*: The sources I have looked at are as much writings and reflections of academic experts on the matter as they are of the lawyers and vulgarizers of the party. These texts were as much composed by the intellectual elite of the academic body as they were by the functional elite of the regime's technocratic lawyer class, endeavouring to put their theory into practice, to formulate a new German law, which demanded from the outset a confrontation with 'Roman law' as it had been received in Germany in the course of the fifteenth century. Other sources, produced by educators charged with drafting vulgarizing contributions, in the press, or the ideological publications of the Party (NSDAP) and its sub-organizations (SA, SS, HJ etc.), are similarly invaluable. Most often legal teachers, their authors, were brought up in the culture, if not the cult, of Roman law, model and birth mother to national law: It was from these chains they wanted to liberate German law.

Roman law according to the Nazis: Article 19 of the NSDAP programme

The positions, stances and arguments of the opponents of Roman law under the Third Reich were not conceived within a single generation, but they emanated from a long and age-old dialectic, the debate between Germanists and Romanists, on which Olivier Jouanjan in his *Histoire de la pensée juridique en Allemagne* (Jouanjan 2005) has delivered the best French interpretation. In this debate, the National Socialist movement at its inception took its position in the context of a document that would mark its birth and its constitution. In the Nazi programme of February 1920, one comes across a slightly surprising article, which, by virtue of its theoretical nature, sits almost incongruously in between the catalogue of political and economic entitlements. Article 19 of the NSDAP programme effectively proclaims, 'We demand the substitution of a German common law for Roman law. Roman law serves a materialistic world order.' As one is at pains to believe this clause enlivened the debate and raised the spirits of the audience in the *Bierkeller*, its presence in such a document requires scrutiny. What are we to make of it?

Firstly, one can read in Article 19 the concurring echoes of the 'Germanist' jurists, according to whom there existed a Germanic law from the outset, already visible in Tacitus' *Germania*, and more explicitly present in the *Sachsenspiegel*.[3] Hence, if a Germanic law existed then, it suffices to invoke that law to substitute it for Roman law. In the context of 1920, greatly enhanced by feelings of national humiliation after Versailles, in its Article 19 the NSDAP programme reinvigorated an old theme of German nationalism: the dichotomy between Germanity and Latinity. This dichotomy, this struggle, is a fundamental aspect of a specific 'Germanic' identity, for lack of a better term, during the Middle Ages: After the confrontation between the (Germanic) Holy Roman Empire and the (Roman) Holy See crystallized in the Canossa humiliation, Luther took up the fight against Rome again, while the German Protestant princes defied Vienna, Madrid and Catholicism, from the Schmalkaldic League up until the Thirty Years' War. The dialectic between Germanity and Romanity subsequently took the form of a war between the Germans and revolutionary and imperial France, between Ludwig of Prussia, where Fichte defended German freedoms, and the Gallo-Romanic tyrant Napoleon. The war continued with Bismarck, who in his *Kulturkampf* confronted papists, *ultramontani* and other political Catholics. In this period, humanists, writers, historians and poets worked on the reception, backed by German nationalism, of Tacitus's Germania, and exalted Arminius-Hermann, the free and rebellious Cherusc, conqueror of Varus, his legions and Augustus.

For others, the text of Article 19 provided a link between Roman law and a 'materialist' vision of the world. What does 'materialist' signify here? For this, we have to look at the context of the article, or, in other words, we have to read the rest of the text. Moreover, the term *materialist* appears in another article from the programme, Article 24, which stipulates that the NSDAP 'opposes the Jewish materialistic spirit within and around us and is convinced that a lasting recovery of our people can only come about by an effort from within based on the principle: the common good before the individual good'. The key is in the wording 'Judeo-materialist': Roman law should be seen as materialist, because it is Jewish, and the other way around. Here we touch on a *topos* reiterated over and over again in Nazi discourse: Only the Nordic spirit can reach the ideas as expounded in the immortal and sublime works of Plato, Bach and Kant. As pure representatives of the Nordic race, the Nazis are idealists in the face of the contemporary 'mammonism' of the Industrial Revolution, of liberalism, and of Marxism, as well as the other cultural avatars of the Jewish race pre-occupied with collecting material goods and realizing profits. Individualistic, egoistic and nomadic, the Jew as presented by the Nazis is incapable of conceiving of any interest other than the private one, of thinking about and valuing the common good. The last part of Article 24 as cited previously refers, among other things, to a supposed fundamental maxim of Germanic law, turned into a Nazi slogan repeated *ad nauseam*: *Gemeinnutz geht vor Eigennutz*, the common good before the individual good, the community before the individual.

From this point forward, the theoretical aspects of Article 19 are less surprising once one sees them from the Nazi standpoint that law is a culture, and it contains a conception of the world, of mankind and of the relations between members of the human race. Upon reading the NSDAP programme, one may wish that jurists had lent a helping hand in expounding the primary doctrinal corpus of the Nazi party. The German legal historian Peter Landau (Landau 1989: 10–22) has actually discovered conduits between the reflections of nineteenth-century German jurists and the NSDAP, singling out the notable figures of Johannes Lehmann-Hohenberg and Arnold Wagemann, two intellectuals, a professional jurist and a jurophile of sorts, who were precocious members of the young party.[4] These two incense bearers of Germanic law inspired the programme of the *Deutschsozialistische Partei*,[5] published on 31 May 1919, which states that the question of land and the ownership of land carries a fundamental importance. Among other things, it is land ownership which is the dividing line between Roman law and 'Germanic law' – the Nazi jurists did not cease to revisit this before crying victory over the enactment of the *Erbhofgesetz* in September of 1933:

> The premier cause of our distress lies with our right of ownership over the earth .... Therefore, we demand:
>
> 1. The free disposition of earth and land ....
> 2. The abolition of Roman law, dominant up until now, which is to be replaced by a German common law [*Deutsches Gemeinrecht*]. Our right of ownership of the earth rests within Roman law .... Roman law was introduced in Germany 400 years ago by the princes and the high members of the clergy; the people opposed it, without success. The people know well that this foreign law estranges them from their land and their other possessions. The Peasants' War,[6] the first uprising from the community, was a bloody war against Roman law. Relentlessly the farmers demanded reinstatement of ancient Germanic law. Today, we state the same demand. It is only due to you, the people of Germany, that it does not remain ignored. This question is more important than anyone can fathom: it is the cornerstone of our future way of living and our existence [*Bestehen*]. Roman law was conceived in an era when

> Rome, in all her decadence, was flooded with Jews. It is antisocial and protects private profit at the cost of the community. It is a law for knaves and the ill-willed. On that legal foundation, Germany always loses faced with the Jew. The facts confirm what we are claiming. This is the way the German people need to be provided with a law that corresponds to their race and their culture that respects the old principle: the common good takes precedence over the individual good. The profound greed, dishonesty and immorality that manifests itself in our market place, this Judaification of our people, is the fault of Roman law, just as our economy is transformed into an economy of pure interest – which has imparted its evil to the world in recent decades, and finally resulted in the war.

It is worth citing this text at length, just to show how much it inspired Article 19 of the NSDAP programme. Merely viewing this article shows that it contains several themes and structural obsessions of the German extreme right with respect to the law. In this text, one finds that the question of Roman law is connected to that of the land and its ownership. It is Roman law that, by introducing the principle of individual property, had separated the blood from the soil, and by doing so alienated land previously owned by the racial community. Like innumerable jurists, the authors of the text interpret the Peasants' War, a large-scale *Jacquerie* at once societal and eschatological with Thuringia as its epicentre, as an insurrection against Roman law and the introduction of its principles and categories.[7] Thus, Roman law is presented as a war against the people, not only in the biological sense (the race) but also in a sociological sense (the community, the common people): Its extreme sophistication renders it inaccessible to the common people, who, instead of being protected by it, to the contrary turns them into its victims. Only the Jews are able to manipulate Roman law, by virtue of their well-known intellectual and moral degeneracy.

Roman law and the Nazi *Rechtswahrer*

The discourse of the Nazi *Rechtswahrer*[8] is utterly replete with these themes, which I will now proceed to discuss. The first attack the Nazi jurists addressed to Roman law concerns the transformation of traditional Germanic law, with Roman law considered an alienation of this law, the cultural alienation of a race that does not recognize itself in the legal formulations it imposes. Nazi party lawyer Hans Frank, doctor of laws, *Reichrechtsführer* (overseer of the Reich's legal corps), minister without portfolio and later in 1940 governor-general of occupied Poland, writes, 'Popular Germanic law has become alien to us in the course of recent centuries. One has to conclude that the reception of Roman law has exerted an overall malicious influence over the development of Germanic law.' In effect, Roman law, in its principles and method, is 'incompatible with the feelings of how life should be led among the Germans. It is not true that what was good for ancient peoples remains good for the German people. We should be proud of ourselves in the field of law as well' (Frank 1935). Frank suggests here that, with life being in a constant state of flux, popular law (*Volksrecht*) has to be as lively as the life of the people itself. One cannot impose on a living organism the mummified corset of a dead law, like Roman law, formulated in other times, in other circumstances, for other peoples. However, Frank concedes, 'Roman law was a remarkable law and [in it] one can see one of the major cultural monuments of mankind.' Academic and practising jurist alike pay tribute to Roman law for this, inasmuch as they offer it a first-class burial: the law is a monument to the human spirit, which without doubt has its place in a museum of the humanities.

Frank also maintains that the German people should be proud of their Germanic past instead of giving credence to the *Greuelpropaganda* making the Germanists into brute savages. The Nazi discourse aims to soothe: for a nation humiliated by the peace of 1919, its purpose is to reinstate the reasons for it to idealize itself and its history. Just as the Germans are not caricature barbarians, homage needs to be paid to Germanic law, desired as the foundation for the new law and as a substitute for Roman law. The alienation of the German peoples by Roman law has its historical causes. The Nazi jurists became its etiologists and diagnosed Roman imperialism to a greater degree than it had been. Roland Freisler, delegate secretary of state at the Reich's Ministry of Justice, later president of the *Volksgerichtshof*, certainly treats not only the Roman Empire in this sense in one of his many texts (Freisler 1938: 23–4) but also the Catholicization of the German realm, the French Revolution and Napoleon's Empire as some of the many avatars of this eternal imperialism.

The pillars and cornerstones of this Romanization of Germanic legal culture, if one wants to believe someone responsible for the ideology at the core of the Nazi party such as Alfred Rosenberg, were primarily the Church and the State (Rosenberg 1937: 567–8). Rosenberg incriminates those 'imperial doctors foreign to the people' (Rosenberg 1937: 567–8) (*kaiserliche volksfremde Doktoren*) who, educated *in utroque jure*, introduced the Roman law of suzerainty and individuality to Germanic legal culture. Rosenberg merely repeats the claims of anti-Romanist legal historians who exposed gaps in the process of reception of Roman law in the fifteenth century: To enrich themselves with the ownership of land, the Church and the State privatized what had been communal before, if not the land in general, at least that of the communities. The introduction of legal individuality (it is the individual who is the holder of rights, not the community, the *Gemeinschaft*) and private property had transformed the land, birth mother and property of the race, from its pure form: an immovable good quickly changed to a movable one through the demonic mechanism of sureties. The practice of mortgage had made the land into a pure paper title (*Wertpapier*) that usurers, bankers and other parasites had quickly turned into an object of speculation. Thus the injection of Roman law and its categories not only removed the *Volk* from its land, and separated *Blut* from *Boden*, but at the same time turned the soil into an abstract value, given over to commerce. As a jurist contemptuous of Roman law and its reception holds, one had in this manner 'replaced slavery to a master with slavery to the Jew and the usurer' (Jung 1934: 186).

The holy alliance between the usurer, the prince and the doctor of laws left Germans in the net of an intellectual construction from which they could no longer find their way out. This thesis became the creed for the National Socialist jurists, of whom the lawyer Hermann Schroer testifies in his famous 1936 colloquium on the de-judification of the law:[9] 'It's remarkable that, in German legal life, the creation of the law was passed from a man of the people to professional jurists, to scholars, in the middle of the 16th century, that is to say in an era where one can feel the direct influence of Roman law coming from the East (*oströmisches Recht*) and from the '*Schulchan Aruch*'[10] of the Jews. The presence of these considerations in the works of Rosenberg nonetheless well shows that they were not limited to the legal profession but were made into the object of a larger campaign. If Rosenberg overall passes quickly over the law of land ownership and its alienation by Roman law, it is further developed by *Das Schwarze Korps*, the first weekly, then daily, journal of the SS, in an article entitled 'Two Types of Law' (*Zweierlei Recht*) (Petersen 1935). In this heavily circulated and widely read daily, the quoted article respectively (and supposedly) compares the laws of land ownership of the Romans and the Germans: The private property of the land with the Romans is juxtaposed to the communal ownership of the Germans, where the farmer is no more than the operator and the usufruct, because the actual owner is the community of the people. In Germanic legal culture, the farmer is thus subordinated to the *Gemeinschaft*. Roman law turned not only land into a good but also the land's inhabitants, which it turned into serfs, chained to masters and later to banks. The conclusion of Rosenberg and in the SS journal is the same: the 'Peasants' War' of 1525 was lawful, provoked by the malicious doctors of laws and strangers to their own race.

One may comprehend that, beyond even this question of the law of land ownership, the explicit juxtaposition between Roman and Germanic laws is one of two ways in which to view the world, where confrontation offers vast pedagogical perspectives. Moreover, one may conclude that the question is nothing but a scholarly matter, and that it acquired a didactic function important enough to figure in a teaching manual for SS officers:

> Let us oppose again and again some maxims of our ancestors from Roman-Byzantine law that they have imposed upon us over recent centuries so that it became alien to our race, to demonstrate to what degree these foreign legal conceptions were – and it cannot be any other way – devastating to our thinking and our racial will: Roman-Byzantine law says: 'The owner may use his good according to his good judgment'. On this, Saxon law lays down: 'The common good goes before the individual good'. Roman law proclaims: 'The land is prone to cession on the same title as that for slaves or animals'. On this, Saxon law lays down: 'One cannot cede the land without the permission of the heirs' .... Or even: 'The law is codified in fifty books for all eternity'. Saxon law says: 'Written law cannot supersede the law of nature.'[11]

What is noteworthy about the text, apart from the audience it addresses, is that it summarizes the essential features of the attacks that Nazi jurists addressed to Roman law. This entails, according to them, rendering a good as an absolute, conceived as a good in itself, an absolute good, that is to say not relative to its utility for the community, making it flawed. Roland Freisler, for instance, had long before conceived this argument in several of his texts:[12] Should the same legal regime be applied to a ballpoint pen, a car and the land? The abstraction is only suited for tired brains, corsets for the imagination in a stifling schematic nature! Roman law is subjected to criticism for its abstraction, its schematic nature, its separation from daily life, and on the basis of the *gesunder Menschenverstand*,[13] in the same vein that 'positivism', 'normativism' and all these legal theories are the product of the Jewish tendency towards abstraction, the basis for which had been Roman law. Mixed in with his critical reproof of individualism and critique of the notion of a good, Hans Frank moreover takes up torts in Roman law: 'Roman law handed down to us the concept of legal personality as the titular of subjective and objective rights, much like the notion of a good' (Frank 1934a: 8).

On top of this abstraction foreign to daily life, Roman law is effectively at fault for its individualism, and these two aspects are connected, as the example of the law of land ownership shows. Roman law reasons from the individual, instead of the community, which is the principle and end of Germanic law. This fundamental difference is at its core the result of a difference in terms of the racial structure of the 'Roman' and Germanic peoples. This is the notion defended in 1933 by Rudolf Bechert of the University of Munich at a conference pertaining to commercial law and necessary reform of that law. Why were the Romans so prone to abstractions? The Roman Empire was 'international' (Bechert 1933: 81–2): It was applicable to all the races and cultures it absorbed on the basis of a legal discourse that all could comprehend. The Roman people were also a minority in this Empire, and since 'they were flooded with foreigners' (Bechert 1933: 82), it would not have been feasible to regulate the Empire by means of a '*völkisch*' (Bechert 1933: 82) law, but instead it was reigned over by a law that was '*individualistisch*' (Bechert 1933: 82): As the *Volk* could not have been the foundation and point of reference for the law, the individual became the smallest common denominator in what Rosenberg termed *racial chaos* when he speaks of Rome in late Antiquity.

The author maintains that he does not aim to 'underestimate the value of Roman legal thinking': The problem is not to establish a dichotomy between values (*Wertunterschied*), but to reiterate a difference of essence (*Wesensunterschied*) (Bechert 1933: 82), in the instance of racial make-up. The Germanic people, identical to one another and racially coherent, could conceive of a law that was the reflection of this purity and this coherence, a communal law, since this biological community existed, contrary to the Roman case.

Foreign to the Germanic–Nordic race and culture, Roman law could not purport to impose itself on them and mutilate them, like a normative bed of Procrustes. To German ears the adjective 'Roman' carried with it immutable connotations of polemic, imperialism and universalism. And it is precisely this claim that the Nazis were not willing to accept. Alfred Rosenberg then writes, 'We have constantly contested with Roman law its claim of universality; in the same vein, it is impossible to consider that that which was conceived there, in a village, can establish a rule for all states and all peoples' (Rosenberg 1936: 226). Like all laws, Roman law is particular, and not universal. Apart from being a cultural phenomenon, it is the creation, the outcome of a specific race and blood-line and cannot, on that basis, offer any kind of universal pretence. The Nazis assumed and argued for their own particularity: German (or Germanic) law is a creation of the German (or Germanic–Nordic) race. It has no validity outside of the boundaries of that race. The law, like language, art and culture, is radically and irrevocably ethno-centric and as such non-transferable. The feeble attempts by the Romanists to save their discipline on the basis of Roman law providing access to a universal juristic language are ill-advised.[14]

Saving Roman law from itself

However, the Nazis did not all identically challenge the prestige of Roman law, and we will see that it is exactly this analysis in terms of race that rescues it from definitive downfall, making it possible, through their eyes, to save it *in fine*. In every text one can read the reluctance and the shame that overcomes the jurists in repudiating a Roman law with which they are familiar and which they were otherwise impressed with. Moreover, the existence or non-existence of Germanic law was evident for many jurists, who could do nothing but acquiesce in the statement by Houston Stewart Chamberlain, generally a convinced Germanophile, related to Wagner, and torch-bearer for nationalist–racist Germanic thought: 'Roman law is as peerless and inimitable as Greek art. This teutomaniacal ridicule does not change that. We hear jokes about a "Germanic law" that we have been deprived of by the introduction of Roman law: there never has been a "Germanic law", only a chaos of brutal and contradictory laws, one for each people.'[15]

Therefore, *in petto*, the notion subsisted that Germanic law may have been nothing more than a vain fantasy, as persistent as the Romanist image of a profession intimidated by the *maiestas* of the *Corpus Iuris*. Instead of repudiating Roman law wholesale, the Nazi jurists, except only for the most radical, wanted to find common ground with Roman law, in the form of its annexation by the Germanic–Nordic race and its culture. A small text composed in 1937 (most likely) by the association of National Socialist jurists, *Die Paragraphensklaverei und ihr Ende* ('Slavery to the paragraph and its purpose'), explicitly shows the nuances. Certainly, the text concerns the 'Roman law' of 'debt' (*Schuldenmasse*) necessary for a bankruptcy. But how does it understand Roman law? The text takes pains to determine and distinguish it:

> The ancient Romans were a juristically gifted people. They created a highly developed legal technique. But none of the ancient Romans were any longer around when it was attempted, in the 15th century, to replace the diversity of Germanic laws by a general legal system. In this era, there was nothing left but decadent late-Roman legal science, and it is this foreign legal science that became law in Germany .... The spirit of a decadent science from late Antiquity reigned intact for centuries.[16]

This passage suggests that Roman law was foreign not only to Germanic culture but without a doubt also to Roman culture itself, since the 'Roman law' inherited by Germany in the fifteenth century did not have anything in common with the 'ancient Romans' of its origins. This later law, formulated later on, is a 'decadent' law. A foreign principle had effectively been interjected between the Romans of its origins and the

Roman law inherited by the East, a racial principle that was foreign to Romanity itself: the law that it passed on to the Germans is a 'Judaified law'[17] (*verjudetes Recht*).

Inherited Roman law is therefore a later law, passed on by an era of (cultural) decadence and (racial) degeneracy. In an ideological SS teaching pamphlet one can read that the mixing of the races, in Rome, had the effect of diluting the racist and elitist culture of the ancient Romans and replaced it with an ideology of the melting pot.[18] For example, the Roman conception of citizenship had radically changed: the perversion of the legal tradition of the Romans through racial mixture succeeded in establishing that 'ink is thicker than water',[19] that is to say that it became the stroke of genius, henceforth, that decided the status of a person, no longer his blood. By virtue of the Edict of Caracalla, the simple artifice of agreement and a decision made by free will from then on took over from the simple biological necessity that one could be born, but never become, a Roman: Selling citizenship cheaply at the auction of law had been a crime against the blood – naturalization as opposed to nature. The historians of Roman Antiquity were not only to be found among the jurists. Professor Fritz Schachermeyr specifically incriminated two jurists from the later Empire, Ulpian[20] and Papinian,[21] two North Africans from the Levant, who had Orientalized and judaified Roman law (Schachermeyr 1944: 467). In this he was followed by Ferdinand Fried, who scolded the 'Phoenician-Jewish' (Fried 1937: 125) Ulpian, the 'Syrian' (Fried 1937: 125) Papinian, as much as Salvius Julian, of 'African' (Fried 1937: 125) descent and Julius Paulus, 'the most important of them all, who was also of true Semitic origin' (Fried 1937: 125). The historian referred to did not turn to racial expertise for fun or out of taxonomical pathology: All discourse has to be related to the race it emanates from. A political philosophy and a legal system are much like a work of figurative art or a musical genre, the expression of a world view dictated by race.[22]

The Roman law inherited by Germany in the fifteenth century is therefore intellectually decadent, because it is biologically degenerate. This Roman law is effectively in essence, that is to say, by its essence, in itself, a 'Judaeo-Roman law' (*römisch-jüdisches Recht*) (Gundelach and Volkmann 1933: 80), as the SA publication confirms. This 'Judaeo-Roman' or 'Roman-Byzantine' law, as it is designated earlier on, is contagious, in the very medical sense of the word. The pamphlet title *Slavery to the Paragraph* effectively reveals the author and the beneficiary of this legal contamination, in posing the question *cui bono*:

> Who profits from the law? Roman law, in its decadent form, as it was introduced in Germany, was auxiliary to a materialist perspective on the world. Disconnected from any and all relation to the race and the fatherland, from blood and from soil, it encouraged bourgeois-liberal as much as proletarian-Marxist materialism, which led to disastrous consequences, devastating for the race.[23]

Individualist and materialist, Roman law had metastasized in contemporary legal constructions that the Reds (Marxists), like the Blacks (Conservatives), had employed to further their own interests. It is a constant of Nazi legal discourse that affirms the partisan character of the law and states that the law of the past, hostile to the *Volk* but expedient for left and right-wing factions, is no more. For the first time, Reinhard

Heydrich, head of the Security Service of the SS, congratulated himself that the outlaws, the enemies of the state (*Staatsfeinde*), were also the enemies of the people (*Volksfeinde*) (Heydrich 1936: 121–3). This dichotomy between Roman law at its origin and the crossbred law of Jewish thought is well-suited to distinguishing the good racial wheat from the degenerate chaff and allows for partial salvation of the Roman monument, free from external sediment and stratification.

Hans Frank himself, who we have read at the opening of this chapter as being frankly more binary and more clear-cut, often took a more conciliatory position in distinguishing between good and bad Roman law:

> The battle that we are waging against Roman law does not concern the law of the original state of Rome. It addresses the falsification of Roman law we inherited several centuries ago in the guise of Roman-Byzantine law. (Frank 1934b: 3)

One can see all of the beneficence that he has in him joining 'Roman' with the epithets 'Byzantine', 'Jewish', 'liberal' or 'late-' to avoid demonizing a whole intellectual tradition to which the Nazi jurists were themselves attached. Basically, if Roman law at its origins is commendable, it is because of its racial tenets. Roman law is racially related to Germanic law, since it is a Germanic–Nordic law. What is confirmed by numerous historians of ancient Rome is projected here on the level of law: the original Romans were the Nordic populations that immigrated to the Mediterranean. Their cultural creations (law, State, Empire, military legions) are therefore to the credit of the Germanic race, where their creative genius is celebrated and their prestige enhanced. To demonstrate this, the work of German jurist Burkhard von Bonin is used in the programmatically entitled book *Vom nordischen Blut im römischen Recht* (1935), where one can read:

> We have to consider Nordic biological strength as predominant in the most ancient elaborations of Roman law. This should not surprise us: once again, the Nordic armies and masses had emigrated to the south - which took place in the prehistoric era or later. (Von Bonin 1935: 4)

This original law, what is it? By a stroke of good fortune, little if anything of it is known, and the author, like so many others, can conveniently hide behind the Law of the XII Tables, from which by endless glossing one can retrieve the anthropological characteristics of Germanic law, from the superiority of the *paterfamilias* to the primacy of the common good, to the pre-eminence of the community, as well as from its military-like ethic of devotion to the city.

Conclusion

This easy annexation of Roman law at its origins, otherwise made easier since it is so poorly transmitted, did not force the Nazi jurists to reconcile themselves with the 'Roman law', which remained, due to its clerical, revolutionary, liberal aspects, the antithesis of the principles and purposes of Nazi political action. The term *Roman law*, never clearly and seriously defined in the texts I have presented in this chapter, is nothing but a straw man set up for purposes of political condemnation and created, by means of which a sentimental connotation could be inferred with respect to all things Roman and the 1,000-year-long struggle between eternal Rome – in all its guises, Augustan, Catholic, Napoleonic – and 'eternal' Germany, that which the Nazis renounced under the terms of a liberal law, 'bourgeois-liberal' or 'Judaeo-liberal': a normative system that, in their eyes, presented all of the evils of the post-revolutionary age, that is to say, individualistic, and as such the destroyer of the organic community of the *Volkstum*; abstract and therefore absurd; universalist and therefore ignorant of the essential particularity of all cultural creations. The *Kampf um das Recht*, the 'battle for the law' that the Nazi jurists aimed to take up, reveals something of fundamental importance from their perspective: In substituting one normative system for the other, they fulfilled the necessary conditions for a successful acculturation and the communal–biological new foundation of the Nordic race. Its purpose was to end the alienation of the German people done by the destruction of the grand normative systems that had violated and harmed it, international law post-Versailles certainly, but also liberal, positivist, normative post-Roman law, the law of the codification imported from revolutionary and imperialist France, as well as, in the greater scheme of things, the whole of Judaeo–Christian ethics.

Notes

1 A first version of this contribution was published as a chapter in Chapoutot 2017.
2 Major Von Lüttwitz-Randau, a military judge and character in Aragon 1980: 366, 373.
3 The *Sachsenspiegel* (Saxon Mirror) is one of the first written codes recording customary law in German. It was formulated in the first half of the thirteenth century.
4 Johannes Lehmann-Hohenberg (1851–1925): professor of minerology at Kiel, and an amateur jurist, fought the codification of the Bürgerliches Gesetzbuch (BGB) and created the journal *Der Volksanwalt* (People's Lawyer). This violation of the duty to remain neutral led to a disciplinary procedure, and he was barred from public service in the imperial administration. Heavily in debt due to some disastrous speculations on the housing market, he acquired a strong resentment against legislation on ownership and mortgages, evils he attributed to the bad influence of Roman law. Unlike him, Arnold Wagemann was a professional jurist. An administrative judge (*Amtsgerichtsrat*) in Bochum, he founded the *Bund für Deutsches Recht* and became close to the NSDAP in 1920. It was he who took up the debate on Germanic law at the time of the first NSDAP congress in Munich, on 31 January 1922. Already an author before the war (of *Unser Bodenrecht* (Jena, 1912) and *Geist des deutschen Rechts* (Jena, 1913), he denied the existence of private property, which he considered a Roman perversion, as he did with the concept of subjective rights and legal personality. The sole legal entities (*Rechtsträger*) are communities (*Volk, Familie, Schulen, Universitäten, Bauernhof*). Author of numerous essays on Germanic law and the need to reform the law (among others, *Deutsche Rechtsvergangenheit als Wegweiser in eine deutsche Zukunft* in 1922 and *Schafft Deutsches Recht!* in 1921), he

lived long enough to become a member of the *Akademie für Deutsches Recht*, created after the Nazis took power.

5 The German Socialist Party was formed in May 1919 by sympathizers of the anti-Semitic, nationalist and anticapitalistic far right. Many of the members of that party, dissolved in 1922, quickly joined the ranks of the NSDAP, which inherited its channel of publication, the *Völkischer Beobachter*, and some of its cadres, such as Julius Streicher, editor-in-chief and owner of the violently anti-Semitic journal *Der Stürmer*. Before 1922, dual membership was not uncommon.

6 The *Bauernkrieg*, 1524–25.

7 Cf., for example, Jung 1934: 183–7, 213–16: (184). 'In the course of the Peasants' War …, they aimed to sideline the Doctors, jurists trained in Roman law. The struggle primarily concerned the laws of the community over land and soil that the Roman principle of individual ownership then threatened.'

8 The term *Rechtswahrer* ('guardian of the law') is a Germanism forged to contradict employment of the Latinism *Jurist(en)*.

9 On 3 and 4 October 1936 a colloquium entitled 'The Jew in the Legal Sciences' organized by the Association of National Socialist Jurists (NSRWB), under the presidency of Carl Schmitt, was held in Berlin. After a first session dedicated to the 'struggle against the Jewish spirit in the legal sciences', every half-day session involved examining Jewish influence and the means of eradicating it from different fields. The colloquium has become notorious in recent years, as an element of the indictment in the debate surrounding the role of Carl Schmitt in the Third Reich. Despite all of the well-intentioned anti-Semitism that it may have produced, Carl Schmitt was intellectually and political marginalized by the jurists of the SS (Reinhard Höhn above all), who inferred that Schmitt's *totaler Staat* was contradictory to the essence and purpose of the Nazi *völkischer Staat*.

10 Schroer 1936: 19. Hermann Schroer was a *Gauführer* in the *Nationalsozialistische Rechtswahrerbund* (NSRB).

11 *Schulungs-Leitheft für SS-Führeranwärter des Sicherheitspolizei und des SD* (likely 1941), BABL/ RD 19/11: 106.

12 Cf. notably Freisler 1938: 18–19.

13 Literally 'man's rational feeling', in the sense of 'the people's good judgment'.

14 Cf. notably the courageous and brilliant essay by the jurist Paul Koschaker, who defended Roman law on the basis of a European cultural community of which it was the foundation. This argument was a non-starter for the Nazis; if Europe existed, it is only founded on the racial unity of the Germanic–Nordic race: Koschaker 1938.

15 Chamberlain 1899: 194. Here, Chamberlain argues in the context of the debates surrounding the codification and redaction of the BGB.

16 *Die Paragraphensklaverei und ihr Ende* (1937): 8.

17 *Die Paragraphensklaverei und ihr Ende* (1937): 9.

18 Cf. Chapoutot 2008, particularly part III.

19 Chef der Ordnungspolizei – SS-Hauptamt (ed.). 1942. *Deutschland ordnet Europa neu* Heft 4 (Berlin), BABL / RD18/16: 17.

20 Domitius Ulpian was a Roman jurist who died in 228 AD. We do not know his exact place of birth nor Papinian's for that matter.

21 Aemilius Papinianus was a Roman jurist who died in 212 AD during the reign of Caracalla. He was a Praetorian Prefect under Septimius Severus.

22 Cf. Chapoutot 2017, chapter 1 in particular.

23 *Die Paragraphensklaverei und ihr Ende* (1937): 9.

References

Aragon, L. (1980), 'Le droit romain n'est plus', in *Le mentir-vrai*, 366–73, Paris: Gallimard.

Bechert, R. (1933), 'Der Geist des deutschen und des römischen Rechts in der Wirtschaft', *Deutsches Recht – Zeitschrift des Bundes National-Sozialistischer Deutscher Juristen*, 1933: 81–2.

Von Bonin, B. (1935), *Vom nordischen Blut im römischen Recht*, Leipzig: Klein.

Chamberlain, H. (1899), *Die Grundlagen des Neunzehnten Jahrhunderts*, Munich: F. Bruckmann A.-G.

Chapoutot, J. (2008), *Le national-socialisme et l'antiquité*, Paris: PUF.

Chapoutot, J. (2017), *La révolution culturelle nazie*, Paris: Gallimard.

Die Paragraphensklaverei und ihr Ende (1937), Berlin: Nationalsozialistischer Rechtswahrerbund.

Frank, H. (1934a), 'Nationalsozialismus im Recht', *Zeitschrift der Akademie für Deutsches Recht*, 1: 3.

Frank, H. (1934b), *Neues Deutsches Recht – Rede vor dem diplomatischen Korps und der ausländischen Presse am 30. Januar 1934 bei einem Empfangsabend des aussenpolitischen Amtes der NSDAP*, Munich: Franz Eher Verlag, Zentralverlag der NSDAP.

Frank, H., ed. (1935), *Nationalsozialistisches Handbuch für Recht und Gesetzgebung*, Munich: Franz Eher Verlag, Zentralverlag der NSDAP.

Freisler, R. (1938), *Nationalsozialistisches Recht und Rechtsdenken*, Berlin: Spaeth und Linde.

Fried, F. (1937), *Der Aufstieg der Juden*, Reichsbauernstadt Goslar: Verlag Blut und Boden, Die Goslarer Volksbücherei.

Gundelach K., Von Volkmann, L. et al. (1933), *Vom Kampf und Sieg der schlesischen SA. Ein Ehrenbuch*, Breslau: SA-Gruppe Schlesien.

Heydrich, R. (1936), 'Die Bekämpfung der Staatsfeinde', *Deutsches Recht*, 6 (1936): 121–3.

Jouanjan, O. (2005), *Une histoire de la pensée juridique en Allemagne (1800–1918). Idéalisme et conceptualisme chez les juristes allemands du XIXème siècle*, Paris: PUF.

Jung, E. (1934), 'Deutschrechtliches und Römischrechtliches zur Reform des Bürgerlichen Rechts', *Zeitschrift der Akademie für deutsches Recht*, 1 (1934): 181–216.

Koschaker, P. (1938), *Die Krise des römischen Rechts und die romanistische Rechtswissenschaft*, Munich: Beck.

Landau, P. (1989), 'Römisches Recht und deutsches Gemeinschaftsrecht. Zur rechtspolitischen Zielsetzung im nationalsozialistischen Parteiprogramm', in M. Stolleis (ed.), *Rechtsgeschichte im Nationalsozialismus: Beiträge zur Geschichte einer Disziplin*, 10–22, Tübingen: Mohr Siebeck.

Petersen, W. (1935), 'Der nordische Mensch – Zweierlei Recht', *Das Schwarze Korps* (17 April 1935).

Rosenberg, A. (1936), 'Deutsches Recht', in *Gestaltung der Idee (Blut und Ehre II) – Reden und Aufsätze der Jahre 1933–1935*, 222–34, Munich: Franz Eher Verlag.

Rosenberg, A. (1937), *Der Mythus des 20. Jahrhunderts*, Munich: Hoheneichen-Verlag.

Schachermeyr, F. (1944), *Indogermanen und Orient. Ihre kulturelle und machtpolitische Auseinandersetzung im Altertum*, Stuttgart: W. Kohlhammer Verlag.

Schroer, H. (1936), 'Das Verhältnis des Juden zum Gesetz', in *Das Judentum in der Rechtswissenschaft. Ansprachen, Vorträge und Ergebnisse der Tagung der Reichsgruppe Hochschullehrer des NSRB am 3. Und 4. Oktober 1936 – 1 – Die deutsche Rechtswissenschaft im Kampf gegen den jüdischen Geist*, 18–26, Berlin: Deutscher Rechtsverlag.

References

7

The Idea of Rome: Political Fascism and Fascist (Roman) Law

Cosimo Cascione

Introduction

Studies on the relationship between fascism and law have multiplied in recent years (Lacchè 2015; Birocchi and Loschiavo 2015; Stolzi 2014; Montagnani 2012).[1] Yet the specific relationship between the policies of the fascist regime and Roman law (more in general the history of law) still appears only partially explored.[2] The point is that this is a multiform matter. It clearly touches the adherence to fascism by individual professors of the discipline, as well as a series of links that during two decades of totalitarian power emerged between Roman law (a legal system which carries the motives of tradition and order) and the ideology of the dominant policy at the time. The laws of the ancient Romans were proposed as an ideal, a model for the present (not a new idea, indeed, but in a new context). Here I would like to put in evidence at least one of these links, that is, the widespread influence of the idea of ancient Rome on the regime's political rhetoric and how that idea also played a role in reconstructing a connection with Roman law considered as a genetic factor of the fascist legal order.

An encyclopaedia entry: The idea of Rome

A useful observation point from which to regard the idea of Rome during the fascist era could be one of the most important cultural enterprises of the regime, namely the *Enciclopedia Italiana di Scienze, Lettere ed Arti*, better known as *Enciclopedia Treccani*, after the name of its initiator, Giovanni Treccani (1877–1961), a businessman and patron of many significant intellectual initiatives in those days. It is the *Enciclopedia* and two of its entries, 'Rome' and 'Fascism' (in this perspective 'law' is of lesser importance),[3] which form the starting points of this brief reflection on fascist Roman law.

The director of *Enciclopedia Treccani* was the neo-Hegelian idealist philosopher and politician Giovanni Gentile (1875–1944), who is usually called the 'philosopher of fascism' (Gregor 2001). This major work was first published between 1929 and 1936 in thirty-five volumes (plus one index volume). In this *magnum opus* great importance is dedicated to classical antiquity (Cagnetta 1990). Roman history forms the very centre, the core, of the *Enciclopedia*, and of course Roman law (with its tradition in the Middle Ages and in the modern era) has its proper place. This is not unusual, considering that, from the beginning of his political movement, Mussolini had stressed the common Roman heritage of Italians, and he fervently wished to restore the former glory of the Romans in Italy and indeed the world (Giardina 2008; cf. Giardina and Vouchez 2000: 212–86).

The strategic choices made by Gentile in assigning roles of direction within the enterprise and the individual entries were clearly generally, though not always, aligned with the policy of the regime. Gentile was inspired by what has been called 'lucky double dealing' (Cagnetta 1990: 11): He attracted not only fascist intellectuals. In the section dedicated to classics, former neutralists and Germanophiles, such as the great historian Gaetano De Sanctis (1870–1957), well known as an anti-fascist,[4] and the authoritative philologist Giorgio Pasquali (1885–1952), very close to German culture since his studies at Göttingen, were involved, and the direction of the section on law was given to the Romanist Pietro Bonfante (1864–1932),[5] who some years earlier had engaged in a fierce polemic against the same Gentile and the other great representative of Italian idealist philosophy, Benedetto Croce (1866–1954), which ended up almost in mutual insult.[6]

In the *Enciclopedia Italiana*, the entry 'Roma' was particularly significant.[7] The part devoted to the 'idea of Rome'[8] – assigned to Pasquali – shows two perspectives in the history of the classical tradition: the idea as contained in ancient writings and a matching construction of the myth of Rome. These perceptions are intertwined, but the myth is clearly more useful to politics than an erudite scholarly historical treatment of sources and related bibliography. The use (or abuse) of Roman-ness (Italian *Romanità*) (cf. Arthurs 2012, with Chiari 2013: 1; Nelis 2013) had been a typical political tool of trends in Italian nationalism since the Middle Ages.[9] Rome was one of the principal aims of the Italian Risorgimento: the political unification of the Italian peninsula took on a new meaning with the seizure of the city in 1870, a sense of continuity with ancient *grandeur* (cf. Gramsci 1975a: 971).

An anecdote, a *dictum* of the great German historian and jurist Theodor Mommsen (1818–1903), reveals a common feeling among European intellectuals. Mommsen once asked Quintino Sella, Italian minister of finance (1827–84), a 'spirited' (Chabod 1996: 155) question: 'What do you intend to do in Rome? This is worrying all of us: it is impossible to stay in Rome without cosmopolitan purposes' (Sella 1887: 292).[10] Mommsen's view was, of course, influenced by his evaluation of the universal role of Roman law as well as by consideration of the millenarian mission of the Roman Catholic Church, whose temporal power had just been abolished by the Italian government. The universal idea of Rome existed over and above its mere existence as an Italian city (and the new capital of the realm, after Turin and Florence).

The great innovation of fascist attitudes towards this myth was its diffusion in a global dimension (not only among the educated classes), which led to the rhetorically simple equation of Italians as contemporary Romans: a significant new political implication of the masses. Anyone could understand the meaning of the Roman military force (especially the veterans of the First World War), even without being able to understand a poem by Ovid or Catullus, to discuss a passage from Tacitus or to interpret a fragment of Roman law.

Indeed the 'fascist sense of roman-ness could do without books' (as it was written) (Giardina 2008: 63). However, books were aimed at nurturing a culture of glorification of the past and constantly setting connections with contemporary Italian life. Books offered, among other things, a messianic vision of Italy's imperialist commitment in the Mediterranean (the ancient *Mare nostrum*) and especially in Africa. Fascist culture is not only 'printed' but also expressed in rituals, celebrations, images, art and architecture (spread across the media: radio, newspapers and cinema), constantly referring to the myth of Rome. This is not always the historic Rome: Sometimes it is only a shadow or a distorted projection of that reality.

The Roman model was immediately clear in the symbolism of fascism: the very name of the party has Roman roots (Giardina and Vouchez 2000: 224ff). *Fascism* derives from the *fasces*, rod-bundles used by the *lictores* (auxiliaries preceding magistrates) to drive away the masses and able to carry out violent coercion against those who disobeyed the orders of their superiors (cf. Mommsen 1887: 373): *Fasces* were weaponized with an axe when the magistrate was holder of the power of life and death. Thus the name recalls at the same time violence, unity of force and, according to Mussolini, even justice.[11] Besides, the fascist salute (right arm raised with outstretched palm)[12] corresponded to the Roman (also Greek) iconographic repertory (cf. Hug 1920: col. 2065), but in more recent times was used by the 'legionnaires' (another Roman retrieval) of the poet and military leader Gabriele D'Annunzio (1863–1938) (cf. Falasca Zamponi 2003: 231ff), who occupied the Istrian city of Fiume in 1919–21 to protest the results of the Versailles peace treaty (corresponding to his idea of a 'wingless victory', which deprived Italy of the hope of acquiring territories formerly belonging to the Austro-Hungarian Empire).[13]

The myth of the good old Roman (between citizenship and imperialism)

Mussolini strongly emphasized tradition and typical Roman features, such as military strength, courage, order and discipline, and glorified himself as the *duce* (Italian for the Latin *dux*), the leader. This identification of modern times with ancient models, based on a naive hereditary theory, was obsessively repeated and easily made extensible among the simplest people through mass communication. This revival of Roman greatness increased enthusiasm and interest not only in Italy but also abroad: It was a comforting model, made of order and composure (the Roman *disciplina*) in the agitated era after the First World War, when traditional societies (both conservative and liberal) felt threatened by the eastern monster of Bolshevism. The exaltation of this myth enabled the joinder of fascism with traditional conservative and nationalist political forces.

'The myth of Rome was used by Mussolini, with a multiplicity of positive references, even before the fascist movement became a party' (Giardina 2008: 55; cf. Giardina and Vouchez 2000: 238ff, and also Nelis 2012). Very soon he drew the relationship between fascism and Rome in a line that took the political centre of the movement along the two decades of its power, although there were not insignificant subsequent deviations. In fact, he said in a speech in 1922, some months before the March on Rome, on the occasion of Rome's birthday (21 April,[14] which for fascists and then for the 'new' fascist Italy replaced the celebrations for 1 May, socialist workers' day):

> As a matter of fact, Rome and Italy are two inseparable terms .... The Rome we honour is certainly not the Rome of the monuments and ruins, the Rome of the glorious ruins among which no civilized man walks without feeling a thrilling shiver of veneration .... The Rome we honour, but primarily the Rome we are longing for and planning is another one: it is not about honourable stones, but living souls: it is not the nostalgic contemplation of the past, but the hard preparation of the future. Rome is our starting point and reference; it is our symbol, or, if you will, our myth. We dream about a Roman Italy, that is, wise, strong, disciplined, imperial Italy. Much of what was the immortal spirit of Rome is reborn in fascism: the *lictor* is Roman, our organization of combat is Roman, our pride and our courage is Roman: *Civis Romanus sum*. (Mussolini 1956: 160f [1922: ix]; cf. Giardina and Vouchez 2000: 241ff)

Several political aspects of this discourse are relevant: the different aspects of the Roman tradition, the explicit reference to the lictors, especially the rhetorical affirmation of Roman citizenship in its Latin wording *civis Romanus sum*, stressing the identity-making representation.[15]

To a certain extent the statement was prophetic: After seizing power in 1924, in a solemn ceremony held in Campidoglio (in the *Sala degli Orazi e Curiazi*), again on 21 April, Mussolini obtained (modern) Roman citizenship. He could now also formally proclaim himself a Roman citizen (Mussolini 1956: 234–6 [1924: xi]), and he again used the Latin words. On that day ancient fascist Rome was born, and the project of the new fascist Rome proclaimed.

Mussolini declared the impenetrability of the Roman phenomenon merely by historical research. The actual fascist interpretation of the past rejects the slow elegance of philology: It could simply be action and intuition, also violence against the historical truth. The return to Roman-ness was a sort of 'back to the future' (Giardina and Vouchez 2000: 212f),[16] a pompous time-machine bringing the past into the present and connecting the future to the glory of the past with a political purpose that would be realized with the return of the Empire. Even though based on the past, this ideology was completely modern. It was of course a rhetorical exercise, but, at the same time, *Realpolitik*, practical politics.

As the years passed, Italians and the world perceived the stabilization of the tenth anniversary of the March on Rome (the powerful demonstration by which Mussolini came to power in October 1922). The revolutionary idea that had characterized the early days of the regime in 1932 was changed. It became more an imperial idea and took up the theme of the eternal destiny of Rome and its military power. In Italy, the war against Ethiopia (1935–6), the enemy that had blocked Italian colonial enterprises in Eastern Africa at the end of the nineteenth century, and its subsequent conquest represented the moment of the greatest *consensus* for Mussolini and the regime. Many

Figure 5 Benito Mussolini touring ancient ruins with Achille Starace (left) and Italo Balbo (right). Photo by Time Life Pictures/Pix Inc./The LIFE Picture Collection/Getty Images.

opponents aligned themselves with the expansionist policy that realized the old dream of an African Empire, reacting to the sanctions imposed by the League of Nations.[17] On 9 May 1936, the Duce triumphantly proclaimed from the balcony of Palazzo Venezia 'the reappearance of the empire over the fatal hills of Rome' (Giardina and Vouchez 2000: 250ff).[18] The highest point of political support for Mussolini corresponded to the climax of the rhetoric of the myth of Rome. While Vittorio Emanuele, the King of Italy, also became emperor of Ethiopia, Mussolini reserved for himself the more expressive title of 'founder of the Empire' (cf. Calamandrei 2014: 93).

The asserted continuity was celebrated through a symbolic discontinuity: the transition in fascist rhetoric from the centrality of the character of Julius Caesar (the revolutionary dictator) to Augustus (the warrior but also the peacemaker and very Father of the Nation) (cf. Schieder 2016: 130ff):[19] both powerful ancient images that aimed to reflect (and enhance) the figure of the Duce. The Caesarian idea of a perpetual dictatorship (cf. De Martino 1973: 239ff) enthused Mussolini, but he was a superstitious man: He feared the Ides of March (the notorious and symbolic date of the assassination of Julius Caesar in 44 BC). At this stage, the Augustan idea of Rome, imperialism and the empire are perfectly combined in military and political action in Eastern Africa, then in Spain (beside the nationalist forces of Francisco Franco, 1936–9) and in the Albanian enterprise (militarily occupied by Italian forces and annexed in 1939).

Abusing the past: Cosmopolitan empire and active racism

What the regime concealed was the fact that the idea of Rome as reconstructed in the sources and the myth of the strong Roman citizen, *rudis* and *pastorius* (Flor. 2.2.4), as a depository of all the qualities, was a Utopia even in ancient Rome. It was an ideal type forged by the conservative party in the Catonian era.[20]

Between the 1920s and 1930s, the idea of Rome, then of the Roman Empire, became a political catalyst activated to gain consent. This strategy resumed (with adaptations) the Risorgimento's themes of nationalism, irredentism (which had played a central role in Italy's siding in the First World War and then in subsequent events as above mentioned concerning the Fiume enterprise), the expansionist drive in Africa, as cultural, propagandistic (and also military) activity in Europe. This idea was treading in the footsteps of the mythical ancient Roman man depicted, the builder of an orderly cosmopolis, fascist and totalitarian, based on the principle of authority (and at this point emerges the ideological role of Romanistic legal and institutional tradition) turned into hierarchy. But the imperial cosmopolis in the ancient world was not the result of alleged Roman purity. Regardless of the significant role of the various Italic tribes, the *socii Italici* or allies in 'Roman' military and economic expansionism, the important flow of ideas from East to West, based on advanced Hellenistic culture, cannot be ignored.

Between 1934 and 1935, locked up in prison for anti-fascist activities, Antonio Gramsci (1891–1937) was able to develop a much deeper discourse that undermined the very idea of 'Roman man', showing how between the late Republic and early Principate, a kind of Roman arose, disconnected from the past:

> It does not seem to be understood that Caesar and Augustus radically changed the position of Rome and of the peninsula in the balance of the classical world, removing Italy's 'territorial' hegemony and transferring the function to a hegemonic imperial, i.e. supranational, class. If it is true that Caesar continues and concludes the democratic movement of the Gracchi, Marius, Catilina, it is also true that

> Caesar wins in the frame of the whole empire, while the problem for the Gracchi, for Marius, for Catilina arose so as to be solved in the peninsula, in Rome. This historical connection is of utmost importance for the history of the peninsula and of Rome, since it is the beginning of the process of 'de-nationalization' of Rome and of the peninsula and its becoming a 'cosmopolitan' territory. (Gramsci 1975b: 1959–60)

The fascist regime built its representation of the relationship between Caesarian and Augustan policy (and between the two historical characters) more on intuition than on scientific grounds based on a serious confrontation with classical culture and its tradition. Gramsci, on the other hand, goes deeply into the comparison with historiography: From his thinking emerges a central venture to reconsider the imperial transition from the Roman Republic to the Principate:

> The Roman aristocracy, which had, in the manner and by the means appropriate to the times, unified the peninsula and created a basis for national development, is overwhelmed by the imperial forces and the problems which it has raised: the historical-political knot is dissolved by Caesar with his sword and so a new era begins, in which the East has a weight so great that overcame the West and led to a rift between the two parts of the Empire. (Gramsci 1975b: 1959–60)

Augustus wanted to legitimate the new world, an issue of the civil wars. A successful way to achieve this aim could be to rebuild the tradition, the moral connection, already partially lost, with the past. The literature genre of imperial epic (firstly Virgilius, with his *Aeneid*) performed this fundamental task. In the fascist reading there was no break in tradition: Roman man was a steady positive image.

At the end of the 1930s, in a political phase when fascism was much closer to Nazism and had borrowed its racist ideology, turning it into law in 1938,[21] an extreme fascist fringe movement reused the mythical figure of the ideal Roman citizen to build the theory of 'active racism'. This theory sought to provide a non-biological basis and identity for the 'Italian race'. For Julius Evola (1898–1974), the anti-egalitarian, anti-liberal, anti-democratic philosopher and esotericist (cf. Ferraresi 1988: 84), the central point of racism was not the blood theory, but the spiritual construction of a new man, 'new' but at the same time old. He wrote in 1941 (Evola 1994 [1941]: 155ff) (on a theme already dealt by the author previously): 'What better ideal model than the Roman man – stern, sober, active, free of expressionism, measured, calmly aware of his dignity?' This model again retained from Roman times (or – better – from modern ideas of the ancient Roman) was to inspire the new Italian, but in an overall elitist vision of the fascist active man, remote from the masses: the multitasking abuse of the past.

Fascist law: Tradition and opportunism (An American point of view and another encyclopaedia entry)

In the phase of the *consensus* (1929–36),[22] fascism itself became a myth and (paradoxically in terms of logic) truth: the civilizing mission of Rome now stands alongside the ancient and the modern empire. The identification of past and present was seldom placed on a basis of serious historical analysis, as it was in the works of two fascist intellectuals, the historian Ettore Pais (1856–1939) and the Romanist Pietro de Francisci (1883–1971), who was rector of the University of Rome and then minister for justice. More often it was a superficial and ritual connection of past grandeur and (alleged) present glories. But the international context pushed the naive policy of Mussolini towards an unworthy and deadly embrace with Nazi Germany (which indeed had some anti-Roman founding traits, including in the field of law) (cf. Santucci 2009 and Vinci 2014).[23]

With respect to this vision of the idea of Rome, we should now look at the relationship between fascist policy and (Italian) law. In 1936 H. Arthur Steiner (1905–91), who was then teaching at UCLA as an associate professor, one of the sharpest Anglophone interpreters of Italian political totalitarianism, wrote a theoretical essay entitled *The Fascist Conception of Law*, in which he provided a useful explanation of the cultural arguments that sought to provide a philosophical basis for fascist law (cf. Skinner 2015: 74). Steiner sees fascist law as a *quid novi* compared to the earlier Italian legal system:

> Modern dictatorships, proceeding uniformly on the assumption that 'the regime is precarious which has not begun by transforming the law and by investing it with its principles', have sought to consolidate their positions behind a facade of distinctive legislation and juridical theory. Legal transformation not only insures the revolution, but actually makes it. (Steiner 1936: 1267)

His analysis highlights the transformations more than the continuity:

> But to one who is given an opportunity to absorb the spirit of Fascist literature and legislation and to observe the phenomena of Fascism at first hand, inevitably comes a … conclusion: that Fascism represents, fundamentally, an entirely different conception of Society, Law, and State, and that from its philosophical assumptions are derived some elements of a universal and permanent character. (Steiner 1936: 1267)

The American scholar remarks here on the importance of the phenomenon and its spread in Europe (see Albanese 2016). At the same time he emphasizes the incomplete and unsystematic nature of legal fascism, as a result of political opportunism:

> The striking expansion of Fascist thought in all of the countries of Western Europe suggests that its legal philosophy deserves careful study and analysis. It may be objected, at the outset, that Fascism should not be regarded as a complete philosophical system. For this doubt about its character, Fascists are themselves largely responsible. Fascist doctrine contains a substantial element of opportunism. (Steiner 1936: 1267)

This picture corresponds, to some extent, to the perspective that the Duce himself proposes in the entry on 'Fascism'[24] in the *Enciclopedia Italiana* (an article which owes much to the ideas of Giovanni Gentile). This, in 1932, was Mussolini's first formal and complete (although not extensive) exposition of fascist thinking. In this view, tradition (especially Roman tradition) is the touchstone of the future:

> 'Tradition is certainly one of the greatest spiritual forces of a people, inasmuch as it is a successive and constant creation of their soul.' Respect for tradition as the custodian of the national soul must, however, be confined simply to the observance of profitable examples; it must not restrict or confine future development. Political doctrine must retain dynamism and versatility. There is a dose of opportunism in this recipe: 'We do not believe in a single solution, be it economic, political or moral, a linear solution to the problems of life, because ... life is not linear and can never be reduced to a segment traced by primordial needs'.

Historical–legal studies taken seriously and the ornamental antiquity: Roman law between *Enciclopedia Italiana* and the Civil Code of 1942

Arriving at this point arouses the curiosity to fathom the reading of Roman law in Treccani's *Enciclopedia*. Only some mentions lie in the entry 'Law' (*Diritto*),[25] which, however, does not contain a section specifically devoted to 'Roman law': We must once again be directed to the entry on 'Rome'.

Anyone wishing to seek here explicit political traces and connections with the present would remain disappointed. This long essay is divided into four parts. The first – assigned to Emilio Albertario (1885–1948), a fascist scholar, at the time a full professor of Roman law in Rome – is dedicated to private law and consists of a long, detailed discussion of sources and doctrines (in various fields of law, such as subject, object, legal transaction, family, property rights, obligations, inheritance, gift), oriented to a search for classical law, clearly separated from that of Justinian, strongly affected, in Albertario's opinion, by interpolations and dogmatic errors (Albertario 1940).[26] Roman public and criminal law were the subjects treated by Vincenzo Arangio-Ruiz (1884–1964), an anti-fascist Romanist at that time teaching at the University of Naples, a signatory of the so-called Manifesto of anti-fascist intellectuals of 1925 (cf. Cascione 2009: 12ff). Hunting for signs of acquiescence to the regime in his pages is needless: Even the coercive powers of the magistrates and the emperors are treated according to the best scientific standards, without any concession to comparison with the contemporary situation. The fourth part, devoted to the *ius commune*, was committed to Francesco Calasso (1904–65), a historian of medieval (and modern) law. Despite emphatic expressions 'great historical fact' (*grandioso fatto storico*) and some abuse of superlatives[27] (but it could be a question of style), the preparation of the contribution does not appear in any way influenced by the political context.

Analogously, it must be said that the entry on *Fascismo* signed by Mussolini contains no reference to Roman law (with the exception of the above-quoted phrase on the *fasces*): It is much more a philosophical frame than a legal one.

Back to the fascist idea of law: It represents a crude, eclectic, revolutionary political perspective in which the myth of tradition emerges as an ideological trinket, an ornament, but an important one, especially with regard to codification. This observation does not mean that this particular aspect of the Roman heritage did not play an important role in fascist use of legitimating tradition. The image of Roman law is strongly linked with order. It was the legal system of the Empire which the subjects of all nations must obey. At the same time it is one of the most enduring traditions of ancient Rome in modern times.

Many perspectives exist in which the specific relationship between fascism and Roman law can be re-read (cf. Cascione 2009: 3ff): Three of these perspectives are – in my opinion – the most fruitful. They are strictly linked with three solid scientific personalities of Roman law scholarship of fascist times: the centrality of authority (*auctoritas*) in the Roman legal system (public and private) of de Francisci, put in parallel with the new fascist political constitution, the Romanism (the civilizing mission of Roman law in the ancient world as well as in later legal tradition) of Salvatore Riccobono (1864–1958) and the modernization of a renewed social law proposed by Emilio Betti (1890–1968) through dogmatics.[28] All these interpretations gain strength from the relationship between past and present and form part of a nexus of continuity of long duration, where the fracture is represented by liberal Italy, the historical period prior to fascism. Conservation, reaction and revolution can thus be welded together without apparent contradiction. Even corporatism is tied to Roman history (as well as that of medieval towns) and the Roman–Italic spirit.

But, on these issues, I have already expressed my point of view in the contribution published in 2009 (Cascione 2009: 12ff). Here I would like to look in a different direction, and that is the alleged continuity between Roman law (in particular classical Roman law) and the new codification of Italian civil and commercial law, that, after the preparatory works started in the 1920s (cf. Caprioli 2008: 131ff), was completed with the entry into force of the Civil Code on 21 April (once again that fateful date) 1942, in the middle of the war (at a not unfavourable moment for Italian and German troops).[29]

Rather than a comprehensive analysis of the Code (which would be a titanic work), I intend to restrict my observations to some points in the official 'Report' (*Relazione*)[30] which the minister of justice, the Bologna lawyer Dino Grandi (1895–1988), a former minister for foreign affairs and ambassador in London, formally presented to the king. I am not interested in highly specific technical passages but will recall some points where Grandi more openly (and strategically) quotes ancient Rome and Roman law (cf. Caprioli 2008: 200f).

Three points of the Report should be emphasized: the importance of the terminology, the inclusion of the new codification within the fold of the Roman tradition and the value of Roman law as a general principle for the interpretation of positive law.

The terminology, while modern and perfectly matching that of legislation of 1865, regains its full historical value acquiring new meaning with the attachment to tradition:

> When we say Civil Code, our thoughts go back to the notion of the Roman *civis*, the active member of the political community of Rome, with its well-defined position with respect to the family and *civitas*. This notion of *civis* has nothing in

> common with that of the *citoyen* of the French Revolution. The name of our code will not therefore mean that it is the code that governs the inherent rights of the citizen, as opposed to the rights of the State, much less does it mean the code of the bourgeoisie, that is, citizens of the middle classes (this concept also deriving from the French Revolution) as is sometimes called the French Code. (*Relazione*: 33ff, § 11)

The uncoupling of liberal values is made clear by the rejection of any connection with French revolutionary ideas: fascist revolution is another thing.

> *For us* – continues the Minister – *the Civil Code means only the code that includes the civil law, in the sense that it was originally in Rome, as defined by Gaius in his Institutions* (I.1): *ius proprium civitatis*. It is the proper law of the Roman *civitas*, like the walls and the gods born with it or received in it from the people who brought it into being, a law which cannot be confused with that of any other *civitas*. This original concept had necessarily become discoloured later, when what was once the exclusive law of Roman citizens, members of the *civitas*, became the general law of all subjects of the empire of Rome, whatever the race from which they derived. (*Relazione*: 34, § 11)[31]

Grandi here retrieves a great myth of Roman law: Gaius, the second-century author, the best-known Roman jurist thanks to the discovery (by Barthold Georg Niebuhr, in 1816) (cf. Vano 2000) of a manuscript containing the text of his *Commentarii Institutionum*, first represents the framework which will then be repeated by Emperor Justinian in the sixth century. The political breadth of the operation is clear in the insistent appeal to the constitutional pair *civis-civitas*: citizenship (belonging) as the heart of the system. We could not forget the Latin wording of Mussolini, *civis Romanus sum*.[32] The sense of the reference to tradition is already clear, but Grandi insists on the nationality of the Code:

> The name 'Civil Code' means, then, for us, *the own code of the Italian people*, and first of all denotes the purely national law of the Italian people. It is the law of our race: the law that arose in Rome, when it was still the *civitas*, and then ruled all the subjects of the Roman Empire and, through the centuries of the Middle Ages, carefully reworked by our thriving universities, bright headlights of science, and adapted by the practical experience of our jurists, could be adapted to the needs of new times, and come down to us still alive and active, able to regulate the relations of social life in countless conditions of time and civilization. (*Relazione*: 34, § 11; cf. also 35, § 13)[33]

This point is particularly interesting: It emphasizes the connection between national tradition and race and connects ancient Roman law with its medieval and modern continuation (through the work of lawyers and universities), declaring the timelessness, the everlasting value in the practice of Roman law. The theme is repeated, and again starting from the name of the new Code: formally the same as the previous codification of 1865 (*Codice civile*), but different in the sense that the lawmaker claims. The name issue is central to the building of the new legal ideology; it becomes the ideal (and rhetorical) bridge between past and present:

> The name given to the code then reaffirms our millennial unbroken tradition, Roman and Italian, and retrieves to its Roman origins the law of our people. The reaffirmation of our Roman law does not mean its immutability or crystallization. Roman law has proven over the centuries and through its application to many different countries such a force of adaptation that no progress in civil life was ever hindered by it. (*Relazione*: 24, § 12)

But here is a break: Grandi shows how tradition does not mean the stasis or immutability of Roman law. The observation could be historically founded, but in this part of the speech serves to justify the relationship of Roman law with the new regime's 'revolutionary' law and the necessary adjustment of old rules to something completely different from that in which they were developed. It is clear that the problem of the relationship between past and present is here in evidence and the minister again resolves it with a rhetorical exercise. He is, to a certain extent, contradictory:

> The sources of Roman law were the subject of processing for a secular time; the different generations have been able to interpret them according to their ideal needs, according to their own ideas and their own creative *genius*. The legal tradition was, and must be interpreted in the light of an idea. (*Relazione*: 34, § 12)

Even the execrable French Revolution had suited Roman law to its ideals! And, with regard to specific points of the Report in which the minister will summon Roman law as justification of a regulatory option, there are others in which he explicitly declares its uselessness. It is not a matter of opportunism with respect to the ideal declared (the perpetual importance of Roman law with a historical, genealogical connection with Italian fascist law). It is, rather, the simple revelation of the fact that that ideal reflected a political choice, very useful and strategic as a general statement, but impossible to follow when the needs of legislation (arising from economic and social links) imposed different options.

Fascinating fascism?

The third point refers to the part of the report dedicated to Article 12 of 'Rules on the law in general' (*Disposizioni sulla legge in generale*, commonly called '*Preleggi*'), a sort of preamble to the Civil Code (but of more general validity, not limited to private law), which contains the rules on interpretation. According to this Article, in the absence of a specific provision and the inability of analogical interpretation, judges have to use the 'general principles of the legal system of the State'. This is a typical way of integrating the provisions (necessarily limited) of a code. Even today, for example, in Austrian law (since the codification of private law of 1811), this is the way to enforce natural law in the presence of a gap in the Allgemeines Bürgerliches Gesetzbuch's rules.

In this perspective, the Italian formula of 1942 is new: It replaces the old wording of the Code of 1865, 'general principles of law', which is a widespread term in Romanistic codifications (Guzmán Brito 2011: *passim*).[34] The broadest sense includes all the rules and institutions of the State and also the national scientific tradition. Here Roman law reappears in the Report as a principle of existing law. In 1950, the Romanist Salvatore Di Marzo (1875–1954), writing a sort of historical commentary on the new Civil Code (Di Marzo 1950: 29ff),[35] attempted to re-read the latest wording as a result of a return to genuine Roman legal thought: 'To no Roman would it have come to mind that a case should be decided on the basis of abstract formulas and not according to the spirit of the legal system of the *civitas*.' The supposed *abstract formulas* are – here – the *general principles* of the natural law tradition, taken up again by nineteenth-century codifications.

Fascinating legal fascism for a Romanist today? Not at all: The interpretation of this Article in the *Relazione al Re* has to be considered, in that context, a rhetorical tribute to the tradition in which the lawmaker wants to route the interpretive activity of the fascist judge,[36] much more than the ultimate unveiling of the perennial actuality of Roman law. It is a rule that, as each rule (including meta-rules), has to be understood against their historical background.

Notes

1 Other bibliographical references can be found in Stolfi 2016: 63, n. 6. On the peculiar situation of Roman law in Italy during the fascist era, see Cascione 2009. Some relevant themes have already been briefly outlined by Casavola 1984: 4146–8. Important for the issues here discussed is the recent work of Marotta (2013).

2 In 2011, Tommaso Giaro wrote about my contribution (Cascione 2009): 'Unter dem Titel "Romanisti e fascismo" skizziert Cosimo Cascione … eigentlich zum ersten Mal in diesem Umfang die Geschichte der italienischen Romanistik während der Mussolini-Zeit' ('Under the title "Romanisti e fascismo" Cosimo Cascione outlines ... actually for the first time in this extension the history of Italian Romanistic in the Mussolini era') (Giaro 2011: 706).

3 *Roma* s.v. *Enciclopedia Italiana* XXIX (Roma 1936): 589–928; *Fascismo* s.v. *Enciclopedia Italiana* X (Roma 1932): 847–84; *Diritto* s.v. *Enciclopedia Italiana* XII (Roma 1931): 987–1007.

4 He was one of the very few Italian university professors who in 1931 refused to swear the legally required oath of allegiance to the fascist regime. As a result, his career was curtailed until after the Second World War. Cf. Goetz 2000: 62–75; Boatti 2001: 46–64.

5 On the political position of Bonfante, see Marotta 2015: 267–88.

6 For a short commentary on the polemic (with bibliography), see Cascione 2011.

7 It is, in fact, a monograph of 677 pages signed by several prestigious experts in different fields.

8 *Roma* s.v. *Enciclopedia Italiana* XXIX (Roma 1936): 589–928; I am specifically referring to the subentry 'L'idea di Roma – Antichità', pp. 906–16.

9 More widely, the reference to the Roman past as a model has for centuries been a central theme of European civilization: on Rome as generator of mythology and model for cultural choices, see Giardina and Vouchez 2000.
10 Sella'speech was on 14 March 1881; the fact dates back to 1871, some months after the Italian taking of Rome; cf. Marcone 2004: 220. Mommsen's words (through oral tradition) are also reported in Croce 1977: 3, where the opinion of the Italian philosopher is critical of the romantic idea of the 'missions' of the peoples.
11 *Fascismo* s.v. *Enciclopedia Italiana* X (Roma 1932): 843. Indeed the *praetores*, Roman magistrates who wielded jurisdiction were escorted by *lictores*.
12 On the assumption of the Roman salute as a social ritual in fascist Italy, see Turnaturi 2011: 120ff.
13 With the Rome Treaty (22 February 1924), Italy finally obtained Fiume plus a coastal corridor connecting the town with the Italian mainland.
14 The date that corresponds to the day on which Romulus, according to ancient tradition, founded the city in 754 or 753 BC was fateful in the fascist view of history. In ancient times it was a pastoral new year's day connected with spring rituals in ancient *Latium*, cf. Carafa 2006: 422ff. On fascist use, see Giardina and Vouchez 2000: 227ff.
15 The phrase used by Mussolini is a famous quotation from Cicero (*Verr.* II 5.147, II 5.162, II 5.168; cf. Quint. *Inst.* 9.4.102; Gell. *NA* 10.3.12). Pronouncing those words in the Roman world would, in a situation of danger, be an implement of protection directed to Roman magistrates or officers, a sort of appeal to a constitutional guarantee of personal inviolability for the Roman citizen (in the absence of a legal process), cf. Rodríguez-Ennes 1983: 110.
16 Chapter IV is entitled 'Ritorno al futuro: la romanità fascista'.
17 From a British point of view (highly critical of the Italian 'new Roman Empire'): Garratt 1938.
18 For the Roman law connections, see Marotta 2013: 425ff.
19 On the political aims of Augustus, see Licandro 2015.
20 On the stereotype and connected themes, see Labruna 1998.
21 For a brief introduction, Sarfatti 2002; more recently, from a specific historical–juridical point of view, Gentile 2011, with a huge bibliography. Cf. Giardina and Vouchez 2000: 258ff.
22 Following the well-known periodization proposed by De Felice 1974.
23 The problem of the relationship between Nazism and Roman law is complicated, see Mantello 1987; Giardina and Vouchez 2000: 268ff; Chapoutot 2012: *passim*.
24 *Fascismo* s.v. *Enciclopedia Italiana* X (Roma 1932): 847–84. In particular, see the subentry 'Political and Social Doctrine of Fascism', pp. 848–51.
25 See note 3.
26 The essay was published as number 3 of the series *Civiltà italiana*, edited by Istituto Nazionale di Cultura fascista. Cf. Cascione 2009.
27 See, for example, *Roma* s.v. *Enciclopedia Italiana* XXIX (Roma 1936): 695.
28 On these three capital representatives of Roman law scholarship involved with the regime, see the respective entries in the *Dizionario biografico dei giuristi italiani* I–II (Bologna 2013): for de Francisci, C. Lanza in *DBGI* vol. I: 675–8; for Riccobono, M. Varvaro in *DBGI* vol. II: 1685–8; for Betti, S. Tondo in *DBGI* vol. I: 243–5. Cf. also Mantello 2010; Marotta 2013; Bartocci 2012; Varvaro 2014; Brutti 2013: 85–190.
29 On the history of the Italian Civil code of 1942, Rondinone 2003 is now fundamental.
30 'Relazione alla Maestà del Re Imperatore del Ministro Guardasigilli (Grandi). Presentata nell'udienza del 16 marzo 1942-XX per l'approvazione del testo del Codice civile' (1943).

31 Italics in the original text.
32 See note 3.
33 Italics in the original text.
34 On the Italian experience of 1865, see especially Guzmán Brito 2011: 507ff.
35 On the position of Di Marzo towards the regime: Cascione 2009: 21ff.
36 On the formative role of judicial decisions in fascist law, see Abbamonte 2011.

References

Abbamonte, O. (2011), 'Fra tradizione ed autorità: la formazione giurisprudenziale del diritto durante il ventennio fascista', *Quaderni fiorentini*, 40 (2): 869–966.

Albanese, G. (2016), *Dittature mediterranee. Sovversioni fasciste e colpi di Stato in Italia, Spagna e Portogallo*, Roma and Bari: Laterza.

Albertario E. (1940), *Il diritto romano*, Milano: Giuffrè.

Arthurs, J. (2012), *Excavating Modernity: The Roman Past in Fascist Italy*, Ithaca: Cornell University Press.

Bartocci, U. (2012), *Salvatore Riccobono, il diritto romano e il valore politico degli Studia Humanitatis*, Torino: Giappichelli.

Birocchi, I. and Loschiavo, L., eds. (2015), *I giuristi e il fascino del regime (1918-1925)*, Roma: RomaTrE-Press.

Boatti, G. (2001), *Preferirei di no. Le storie dei dodici professori che si opposero a Mussolini*, Torino: Einaudi.

Brutti, M. (2013), *Vittorio Scialoja, Emilio Betti. Due visioni del diritto civile*, Torino: Giappichelli.

Cagnetta, M. (1990), *Antichità classiche nell'Enciclopedia italiana*, Roma and Bari: Laterza.

Calamandrei, P. (2014), *Il fascismo come regime della menzogna*, Roma and Bari: Laterza.

Caprioli, S. (2008), *Codice civile. Struttura e vicende*, Milano: Giuffrè.

Carafa, P. (2006), 'Introduzione', in A. Carandini (ed.), *La leggenda di Roma* I. *Dalla nascita dei gemelli alla fondazione della città*, xiii–lxxix, Milano: Monoladozi.

Casavola, F. P. (1984), 'Breve appunto ragionato su profili romanistici italiani', in V. Giuffrè (ed.), *Sodalitas. Scritti in onore di A. Guarino, vol. VIII*, 4133–48, Napoli: Jovene. Reprinted in (2001), *Sententia legum tra antico e moderno II. Metodologia e storia della storiografia*, 181-96, Napoli: Jovene.

Cascione, C. (2009), 'Romanisti e fascismo', in M. Miglietta and G. Santucci (eds), *Diritto romano e regimi totalitari nel '900 europeo. Atti del seminario internazionale (Trento 20-21 ottobre 2006)*, 3–51, Trento: Università degli Studi di Trento.

Cascione, C. (2011), '"Addendum" epistolare alla polemica Bonfante "versus" Croce (e Gentile)', in K. Muscheler (ed.), *Römische Jurisprudenz - Dogmatik, Überlieferung, Rezeption. Festschrift D. Liebs zum 75. Geburtstag*, 97–104, Berlin: Duncker & Humblot.

Chabod, F. (1996), *Italian Foreign Policy: The Statecraft of the Founders, 1870-1896*, Princeton, NJ: Princeton University Press.

Chapoutot, J. (2012), *Le Nazisme et l'antiquité*, Paris: Gallimard.

Chiari, E. (2013), 'Review of J. Arthurs, *Excavating Modernity. The Roman Past in Fascist Italy*', *H-SAE, H-Net Reviews*, June 2013: 1–3.

Croce, B. (1977), *Storia d'Italia dal 1871 al 1915*, Roma and Bari: Laterza.

De Felice, R. (1974), *Mussolini il Duce I. Gli anni del consenso*, Torino: Einaudi.

De Martino, F. (1973), *Storia della costituzione romana III*, 2nd edn, Napoli: Jovene.

Di Marzo, S. (1950), *Le basi romanistiche del Codice civile*, Torino: Utet.

Evola, J. (1994 [1941]), *Sintesi di dottrina della razza*, Milano: Edizioni di Ar.
Falasca Zamponi, S. (2003), *Lo spettacolo del fascismo*, Soveria Mannelli: Rubbettino.
Ferraresi, F. (1988), 'The Radical Right in Postwar Italy', *Politics & Society*, 16: 71–119.
Garratt, G. T. (1938), *Mussolini's Roman Empire*, Harmondsworth: Penguin.
Gentile, S. (2011), *La legalità del male. L'offensiva mussoliniana contro gli Ebrei nella prospettiva storico-giuridica (1938–1945)*, Torino: Giappichelli.
Giardina, A. (2008), 'The Fascist Myth of Romanity', *Estudos Avançados*, 22 (62): 55–76.
Giardina, A. and Vouchez, A. (2000), *Il mito di Roma. Da Carlo Magno a Mussolini*, Roma and Bari: Laterza.
Giaro, T. (2011), 'Review of Diritto romano e regimi totalitari nel '900 Europeo. Atti del seminario internazionale', *Zeitschrift der Savigny-Stiftung für Rechtsgeschichte. Romanistische Abteilung*, 128: 706–12.
Goetz, H. (2000), *Il giuramento rifiutato. I docenti universitari e il regime fascista*, Firenze: La Nuova Italia.
Gramsci, A. (1975a), *Quaderni del carcere II. Quaderni 6–11 (1930–1933)*, Torino: Einaudi.
Gramsci, A. (1975b), *Quaderni del carcere III. Quaderni 12–19 (1932–1935)*, Torino: Einaudi.
Gregor, A. J. (2001), *Giovanni Gentile: Philosopher of Fascism*, New Brunswick: Transaction.
Guzmán Brito, A. (2011), *Codificación del Derecho civil e interpretación de las leyes. Las normas sobre interpretación de las leyes en los principales Códigos civiles europeo-occidentales y americanos emitidos hasta fines del siglo XIX*, Madrid: Iustel.
Hug, A. (1920), 'Salutatio', in A. F. Pauly and G. Wissowa (eds), *Real-Encyclopädie, I A/2*, col. 2060–72, Stuttgart: J. B. Metzler Verlag.
Labruna, L. (1998), 'Il diritto mercantile dei Romani e l'espansionismo', in L. Labruna (ed.), *'Tradere' e altri studii*, 79–105, Napoli: Jovene.
Lacchè, L., ed. (2015), *Il diritto del Duce. Giustizia e repressione nell'Italia fascista*, Roma: Donzelli.
Licandro, O. (2015), "Restitutio rei publicae' tra teoria e prassi politica. Augusto e l'eredità di Cicerone', *AUPA*, 58: 57–130.
Mantello, A. (1987), 'La giurisprudenza romana fra Nazismo e fascismo', *Quaderni di storia* 13 (25): 23–71.
Mantello, A. (2010), 'A proposito di 'continuità' storiche', in C. Russo Ruggeri (ed.), *Studi in onore di A. Metro* IV, 33–58, Milano: Giuffrè.
Marcone, A. (2004), 'Collaboratori italiani di Mommsen', in *Theodor Mommsen e l'Italia*, 209–23, Roma: Atti dei Convegni Lincei.
Marotta, V. (2013), 'Roma, l'Impero e l'Italia nella letteratura romanistica degli anni trenta', in G. Cazzetta (ed.), *Retoriche dei giuristi e costruzione dell'identità nazionale*, 425–60, Bologna: Il Mulino.
Marotta, V. (2015), '"Mazziniano in politica estera e prussiano in interna". Note brevi sulle idee politiche di Pietro Bonfante', in I. Birocchi and L. Loschiavo (eds), *I giuristi e il fascino del regime (1918–1925)*, 267–88, Roma: RomaTrE-Press.
Mommsen, T. (1887), *Römisches Staatsrecht I*, 3rd edn, Leipzig: S. Hirzel.
Montagnani, C. (2012), *Il fascismo 'visibile'. Rileggendo Alberto Asquini*, Napoli: Editoriale scientifica.
Mussolini, B. (1956 [1922]), 'Passato e avvenire', *Il Popolo d'Italia*, 95 (21 April 1922): ix. Reprinted in Mussolini, B. (1956), *Opera omnia XVIII*, 160, Firenze: La Fenice.

Mussolini, B. (1956 [1924]), 'Per la cittadinanza romana', *Il Popolo d'Italia*, 97 (23 April 1924): xi. Reprinted in Mussolini, B. (1956), *Opera omnia XX*, 234-6, Firenze: La Fenice.

Nelis, J. (2012), 'Imperialismo e mito della romanità nella Terza Roma Mussoliniana', *Forum Romanum Belgicum*, 2: 1–11.

Nelis, J. (2013), 'The myth of "Romanità", "Antichistica" and the aesthetics in light of the fascist sacralization of politics, and modernism', *Mediterraneo Antico*, 16 (1): 259–74.

'Relazione alla Maestà del Re Imperatore del Ministro Guardasigilli (Grandi). Presentata nell'udienza del 16 marzo 1942-XX per l'approvazione del testo del Codice civile' (1943), in *Codice civile. Relazione del Ministro Guardasigilli preceduta dalla Relazione al Disegno di legge sul 'valore giuridico della carta del lavoro'*, Roma: Istituto Poligrafico dello Stato.

Rodríguez-Ennes, L. (1983), 'La 'provocatio ad populum' como garantia fundamental del ciudadano romano frente al poder coercitivo del magistrado en la epoca republicana', in *Studi in onore di A. Biscardi IV*, 73–114, Milano: Istituto Editoriale Cisalpino-La Goliardica.

Rondinone, N. (2003), *Storia inedita della codificazione civile*, Milano: Giuffrè.

Santucci, G. (2009), 'Diritto romano e Nazionalsocialismo: i dati fondamentali', in M. Miglietta and G. Santucci (eds), *Diritto romano e regimi totalitari nel '900 europeo. Atti del seminario internazionale (Trento 20-21 ottobre 2006)*, 53–82, Trento: Università degli Studi di Trento.

Sarfatti, M. (2002), *Le leggi antiebraiche spiegate agli italiani di oggi*, Torino: Einaudi.

Schieder, W. (2016), 'Romanità fascista – Kaiser Augustus in der geschichtspolitischen Konstruktion Benito Mussolinis', in E. Baltrusch and C. Wendt (eds), *Der Erste Augustus und der Beginn einer neuen Epoche*, Mainz: Philipp von Zabern.

Sella, Q. (1887), *Discorsi Parlamentari I*, Roma: Tipografia della Camera dei Deputati.

Skinner, S. (2015), 'Fascist by Name?, Fascist by Nature? The 1930 Italian Penal Code in Academic Commentary 1928-46', in S. Skinner (ed.), *Fascism and Criminal Law. History, Theory, Continuity*, 59–84, Oxford and Portland, OR: Bloomsbury.

Steiner, H. A. (1936), 'The Fascist Conception of Law', *Columbia Law Review*, 36 (8): 1267–83.

Stolfi, E. (2016), 'Ancora su Vittorio Scialoja (ed Emilio Betti)', in *Scritti per A. Corbino VII*, Tricase: Libellula.

Stolzi, I. (2014), 'Fascismo e cultura giuridica', *Studi storici*, 55 (1): 139–54.

Turnaturi, G. (2011), *Signore e signori d'Italia: Una storia delle buone maniere*, Milano: Feltrinelli.

Vano, C. (2000), *'Il nostro autentico Gaio'. Strategie della Scuola storica alle origini della romanistica moderna*, Napoli: Editoriale Scientifica.

Varvaro, M. (2014), 'Gli "studia humanitatis" e i "fata iuris Romani" tra fascio e croce uncinata', *Index*, 42: 643–61.

Vinci, S. (2014), "L'abominevole Babele del diritto'. Nazismo e fascismo fra diritto germanico e diritto romano-italico', in A. De Martino (ed.), *Saggi e ricerche sul Novecento giuridico*, 59–98, Torino: Giappichelli.

8

'Byzantium!' – *Bona fides* between Rome and Twentieth-Century Germany

Hans-Peter Haferkamp

Byzantium!

> The constant looming contradiction between the personal ethical standard expected from those party to a legal action and the general interest in the enforcement of the imperative legal order …, can only be solved in a satisfactory manner if the requirements of equity are not themselves regarded as changes to the objective law. If this necessary tension is simply removed, the result is a general equity that is at once mushy and totalitarian, as can be identified in Byzantine law, but also, in some respects, in the recent past. (Wieacker 1956a: 121)

In 1956, Franz Wieacker[1] drew a daring comparison between Byzantine law and National Socialism. This was in the context of a number of much-debated decisions of the *Bundesgerichtshof* in the years 1954 and 1955, in which the descendants of a farmer were awarded an inheritance against the express wishes of the deceased – by means of invoking *Treu und Glauben*[2] in Section 242 Bürgerliches Gesetzbuch (BGB). Wieacker highlighted the contradiction between 'objective law' and 'equity' and warned against a 'totalitarian general equity', which he delineated as a characteristic of both Byzantine and National Socialist law.

How did he arrive at this comparison between Byzantium and National Socialism, which seems somewhat puzzling today? Wieacker did not reference any sources at this stage, and thus seemed to expect that his contemporaries in 1956 remained as familiar with the idea of Byzantine equity as with the excessive application of general clauses within the 'völkische Rechtserneuerung'. And indeed, there is a long story behind this notion.

Fritz Pringsheim: *Ius aequum* and *ius strictum*, 1921

In 1921, Romanist Fritz Pringsheim[3] published a study on *ius aequum* and *ius strictum* in Roman law. He emphasized that classical jurists had not known this distinction and that it only began to emerge in the Byzantine period. According to him, this equalled an evolution, which resulted in '*aequitas* being the sole ruler, to which *ius* must bow down'.[4] In Pringsheim's view, *aequitas* prevailed over ancient Roman *ius*, which the Byzantines would from then on refer to as *ius strictum*. In this context, *ius strictum* would play the part of a narrow, limited, strict, grim, bitter and hair-splitting system of law, which had to be overcome (Pringsheim 1921a: 648).

At first glance, Pringsheim's study appears to form merely a part of a comprehensive reinterpretation of late Roman law. Pringsheim was a member of the circle around Ludwig Mitteis (Mitteis 1891; on this Zimmermann 2001: 14f; Winkler 2014: 63f). Along with other authors such as Eberhard Bruck, Joseph Partsch, Hans Lewald or Paul Koschaker, Pringsheim also endeavoured to distinguish Roman law from later influences. His focus on Byzantium emphasized the late victory of Greek philosophy: 'The great rivalry between Roman practical jurisprudence and Greek philosophy of law, which had waged for centuries, has been decided. The Romans' rough sense of reality yielded to the Greeks' theoretical speculation' (Pringsheim 1921a: 668).

Pringsheim was not alone in voicing the proposition that *aequitas* only assumed the Aristotelian function of correcting the written law in Byzantium. As early as 1898, Hugo Krüger had claimed that all prior mentions of *aequitas* in the *Corpus Juris* were interpolated.[5] Hence, three things stand out particularly from Pringsheim's treatise: Notable is firstly the underlying emotional tone of Pringsheim's writing: It is clear that Pringsheim was sympathetic towards *ius*, but not towards *aequitas*. For him, the Greek *aequitas* became an allegory for the decline of Roman Law, a symbol of a cultural war between Greece and Rome.[6]

What surprises further is the harshness of the criticism with which Pringsheim's treatise initially met among his contemporary Romanists. None other than Riccobono objected that such a methodology in the interpretation of sources could be used to prove anything, including ape's descent from man (Riccobono 1926: 300). Early on, Pringsheim was accused of equally misconstruing the legal thought of both classical[7] and post-classical Roman authors (Riccobono 1926: 286). Lastly, it is remarkable that Pringsheim's theories are today regarded as being largely incorrect.[8]

All this raises the suspicion that, like Wieacker in 1956, in 1921 Pringsheim construed his image of the contradiction between Byzantine and classical Roman Law with at least some regard to his present. His view on the ancient jurists was also a reflection of the judge in 1921. The last footnote of his article offered a hidden clue to such a backdrop. There, he referenced a 1911 article by Hungarian professor Géza Kiß titled 'The Interpretation of Statute Law and "Unwritten Law"'. In that article, Kiß drew a line from Roman jurists to the free law movement (*Freirecht*):

> The modern 'Free Law jurist' can feel right at home. Aequitas, as a basis for the application of law, precludes an adherence to the letter of the law in principle .... The Roman jurist is not satisfied with the outcome of a logical interpretation, merely because it is logical in itself, or because it corresponds to the original will of the legislator; all these circumstances must also withstand the test of aequitas. (Kiß 1911: 430f)

Pringsheim evidently did not share this view and countered that it seemed 'strange' that Kiß 'of all things chose to depict the Byzantine form of aequitas in his historic investigation into Free Law as intrinsically Roman'. *Aequitas* had indeed served classical jurists as a pressure relief valve of sorts, which yet had not stepped up 'to surmount and dominate the *ius*'. Jurists who thought this way were 'Greeks and Christians, and thus not authentic jurists in the Roman sense of the word' (Pringsheim 1921a: 668).

Indeed, by refusing to equate free law with his ideal of the Roman jurist, Pringsheim swam against the current of dominant views of Romanist scholars at the time. Traditionally, the Roman *interpretatio* was regarded as 'a mediator between the law and aequitas' (Kipp 1909: 9). Joseph Kohler had referred to his Theory of Objective Interpretation, which attempted to free itself from the will of the actual historical legislator, as 'in line with the Roman understanding' (Kohler 1886: 1, note 2).

Pringsheim's treatise does not lay out why, in 1921, he believed this to be taking things too far. The mood in 1921 was not consistent. After the debates between 1905 and 1909, which had regarded free law very favourably, the mood had shifted slowly until 1914, by which time the optimism towards the ability of the judiciary as a motor of modernization had received its first cracks. Then again, it was precisely the ultimately dysfunctional legislation during the First World War, which had undermined the faith in the ability of the legislator. One authority, however, Pringsheim referenced covertly: Max Weber. Already in 1921, Pringsheim read Weber's '*Wirtschaft und Gesellschaft*' and referenced Weber precisely with regard to the latter's typologization of Roman legal thought.[9] Weber had considered the role of the judge in relation to the written law since 1898 and his concept of rationalization without formalism sat quite comfortably with Pringsheim's ideal in 1921.[10]

Pringsheim: *Aequitas* and *bona fides*, 1930

In 1930, Pringsheim returned to the subject once again. Now however, he centred his discussion around one point in particular, which in 1921 had only formed one aspect of his consideration (Pringsheim 1921a: 651ff): the relationship between *aequitas* and *bona fides*. Now the contemporary dimension of his subject matter was evident. Pringsheim emphasized:

> Modern legal doctrine wrongfully categorises bona fides under the notion of equity; there is a danger in all modern laws that mere equity become the basis for a legal claim, instead of bona fides being used to determine the extent of liability, a danger to replace the law with *aequitas*. Equity alone cannot form the foundation for a legal order.

By referencing the legal philosophy of Julius Binder and the widely read treatise of Max Rümelin on justice and equity, Pringsheim made clear that he regarded his own work as a contribution to contemporary debates on legal theory. Binder's legal philosophy of 1925 now idealized the very idea which Pringsheim had criticized as Byzantine. Binder emphasized 'that equity, by struggling against that which is perceived as strict, outdated and ultimately unbearable, and by placing its own ideas in its place, thereby continually creates new law, which is law in itself, and falls under the idea of law'.[11] It was now Pringsheim's goal to clarify that equity, as it is understood in this context, had nothing to do with the ancient Roman concept of *bona fides*. *Bona fides* had, according to Pringsheim, never been a 'supra-legal authority', but a 'notion inherent in law', 'bridled' by the 'sober reasonableness; the practical rationality of the Romans' (Pringsheim 1961: 172). Pringsheim stuck with his ideal of Roman law: 'neither blurred equity, nor strict concepts, that is the Roman stance' (Pringsheim 1961: 162). And once again, Max Weber served as his authority. Pringsheim quoted Weber, 'The principles of fides, despite their informal character, by no means constitute vague products of emotion.'[12]

Why was it so important to differentiate between *aequitas* and *bona fides*? The reason was apparent. In the German Civil Code, the legislator had introduced the Roman concept of *bona fides* into Sections 242 and 157. Unlike *aequitas*, the concept of *bona fides* had thus been positively ratified by the legislator. If the concept of *bona fides* was now understood as equivalent to equity, the judge had consequently been authorized to openly use ideas of equity to sidestep the written law, namely *intra* rather than *contra legem*. All contemporaries in 1930 were very much aware of this danger.

In the 1920s, contemporaries observed that the number of cases in which courts based their verdicts on *bona fides* or good faith was increasing dramatically. The circumstances were the hyperinflation and the government's rigid position with regard to it, which caused a wave of litigation, the so-called revaluation decisions (*Aufwertungsrechtsprechung*) (see Nörr 1988: 55ff; Nörr 1996; Chlosta 2005: 42ff; Emmert 2001: 399ff), based on Section 242 BGB.[13] In the most spectacular revaluation verdict in 1923, the *Reichsgericht* justified the revaluation of mortgage claims on the basis 'of the dominant position of section 242 BGB in the German legal system.' Furthermore, the *Reichsgericht* refused to apply existing laws when determining face values, since they would lead to results which were 'irreconcilable with good faith and equity'.[14] When the government, which as a borrower benefitted from inflation (Geyer 1994), threatened to prohibit the practice of revaluation, the board of the Association of *Reichsgericht* Judges published a petition to the government (Vorstand des Richtervereins 1924: 90). The board of the Association referred to the 'great notion of good faith, which rules our legal system'. This notion was 'above any written law, above any express legal provision. No legal order, deserving of that honourable name, can exist without this concept. Consequently, the legislature cannot impede a result which is demanded by good faith.' The board of the Association had endowed Section 242 BGB with the power to bind the legislature against its will. Contemporaries perceived this notion as outrageous. It was a complete novelty.

Until 1933, however, it still remained merely an approach taken by only a number of judges who were members of the Association of *Reichsgericht* Judges. The president of the *Reichsgericht*, Walter Simons, clarified that, unlike the Association, the court officially rejected the idea that the judicature had the right to 'place itself above the sovereign legislator' (Simons 1924: 243). The idea that the notion of good faith could be expressed in a provision (Schröder 2012: 316), which could then enable the courts to control the legislator, remained a mere declaration.[15] However, it resulted in the emergence of an idea which, in 1925, caused Ernst Fuchs, himself an advocate of the free law school, to exult that 'good faith is the Archimedean point from which the ancient legal order has been lifted from its foundations' (Fuchs 1925/1926: 349).

Good faith began to be understood more and more as an intermediary between positive law on the one hand, and the deviating sense of justice on the other. In 1921, Max Rümelin described good faith as 'rules of conduct which are vivid in society. They are valid and fixed in common values, independent of any command of power by the state' (Rümelin 1921: 42). Thus, good faith was linked with the notion of a divided legal order: an antagonism between positive and sensed law. Ernst Heymann said (Heymann 1930: 132), 'The dark desire for a refined doctrine reveals itself through the strange emphasis on good faith and public policy in our jurisprudence. It is an unconscious and devastating appeal for a deeper philosophical understanding of law and justice.' Thus, a connection emerged between the notion of good faith and the rise of philosophical alternatives to positive law, which were characteristic of legal thought in Weimar (see Lepsius 1994).

In this sense, Pringsheim's fears appeared justified. There was a clear tendency to utilize *bona fides* as a supra-positive corrective, which replaced statute law with unconstrained assessments of equity. Yet it was precisely this, according to Pringsheim, which was at odds with Roman legal thought.[16] Pringsheim's ideal Roman jurist came to his decision rationally, but was at the same time pragmatic in his views. He remained close to life, thinking and deciding in concrete terms, not abstract ones, creating law, not reproducing it (Winkler 2014: 69). He was not a mere mechanic but a custodian of the law, aware of the great responsibility this task entailed. Pringsheim's Roman jurist was the trustee of due process as 'the twin of freedom' and at the same time, he played an essential part in the development and modernization of the law.

The warnings of Hedemann, 1932–3

As early as 1921, another aspect emerged from Pringsheim's writing, which is harder to place into the context of contemporary debates. Pringsheim accused the Byzantine emperors of purposefully changing ancient laws under the pretext of *aequitas*. The fact that the 'selective interpretation ranging between *ius* and *aequitas*' by Constantine was reserved for the emperor was characteristic of this (Pringsheim 1921a: 645). *Aequitas* and *bona fides* were not merely opportunities for judges to make equitable case-by-case decisions; they were a means for the emperor to demonstrate the extent of his power: 'The absolute empire and *aequitas* meant that the authority of the emperor's will was no longer confined by *ius*' (Pringsheim 1921a: 668).

His treatise developed the old word of caution, that judicial application of *aequitas* would lead to legal uncertainty and arbitrary decisions, into the accusation of deliberate manipulation: The judge is exploited by the sovereign for the purpose of bending positive law to the latter's will. The issue was not that the judge consequently possessed greater freedom in his rulings, but that, instead of being bound by written law, he was thus bound to the individually dictated will of the sovereign. Behind the deceptive appeal to individual justice was the will of the totalitarian ruler. This, interestingly, was not reflected in the situation in Weimar. Here, it was not primarily legislature which advocated an increased application of *aequitas* and *bona fides*, but the judiciary and legal academia. Nevertheless, this facet of Pringsheim's work was also picked up upon by his contemporaries.

In 1932, Justus Wilhelm Hedemann revisited the gloomy picture which Pringsheim had painted and transposed it into his contemporary reality: In his essay 'The Escape to General Principles', Hedemann stated that the relationship between *ius strictum* and *ius aequum*, or rather, *bona fides*, was 'the most important question for jurists in the 20th century' (Hedemann 1933: 3; see Wegerich 2004: 148f). Hedemann, a famous law professor from Jena, had worked on this topic for years and had, up to that point of time, been rather optimistic about the opportunities which general principles such as good faith would give to the judge (see Hedemann 1913: 40). But now, in 1932, and with reference to Pringsheim, he identified contemporary dangers: If the 'factor of flexibility' is merged with the 'factor of power', 'Byzantium will rise and decline will follow' (Hedemann 1933: 74).

Even if, in 1932, Hedemann did not yet write with reference to National Socialist Germany, he did nonetheless draw upon the example of another legislator who had sought to open up the formal law to unprecise general principles similar to *aequitas* or *bona fides*. His example was Russia: 'It is like the entire population of the country is torn in two. Classed, segregated by caste, religion, ideology, world-views – and one half states: We are the guardians of all matters moral and the rest of you are ignorant' (Hedemann 1933: 72). In Russia, he observed the use of 'general principles of law to an astonishing extent', with only 'the one (the ruling) class deciding upon the material content of those general principles' (Hedemann 1933: 73). Hedemann's words of warning regarding the political exploitation of general principles such as *aequitas* and good faith compounded into the prediction of a 'catastrophe for the legal order' (Hedemann 1933: 73). 'The cautionary tale of history' (Hedemann 1933: 76) that he identified in Pringsheim's work caused him to caution against a 'new kind of Byzantine equity' (Hedemann 1933: 75).

General principles as a political opportunity: National Socialism

When Hedemann's warnings from 1932 were published in 1933, the mood had shifted. An aspiring young professor and enthusiastic National Socialist by the name of Heinrich Lange now voiced his view on the matter. He, too, had read Pringsheim, but did not deem his analysis to be threatening at all. To Lange, Hedemann – as a 'dogmatist' – was still caught up in positivistic thinking, which was determined with regard to 'predictability, not by justice' (Lange 1933a: 2858; see Wolf 1998): 'The Byzantines are thus the object of contempt of legal scholarship; because they dared to nest in the temple of Roman law and yet displayed blatant disregard for its beauty through use of their blurred general principles' (Lange 1933a: 2858). Lange's own perspective on general principles was a lot more positive. To him, general principles were 'cuckoo's eggs within a liberal legal order' (Lange 1933b: 5), a kind of loophole within the positivist illusion of a binding body of law. Law itself instead consisted of 'one aspect of life's general moral order. The principle of equity and good faith must therefore be regarded as the fundamental law of life within a community, from which all other laws can be derived' (Lange 1933b: 7). Crucial to this concept was that the principle of equity and good faith did not become the 'fundamental law of communal order' merely because it provided a legal way to overcome the provisions of the BGB. Lange 'charged' equity and good faith with National Socialist content.

Carl Schmitt replied to Hedemann in his famous 1934 lecture '*Über die drei Arten des rechtswissenschaftlichen Denkens*'. Schmitt also regarded general principles such as good faith as opportunity rather than risk. He saw them as an indication of 'the extent to which the age of legal positivism is over'; as 'signs of a revolution' and the dawn of a 'new way of legal thinking'. His meaning was made perfectly clear when he stated, 'As soon as concepts such as good faith no longer refer to an individualistic and bourgeois society, but to the interests of the people as a whole, the entire existing body of law is modified, without the need to change even a single positive statute' (Schmitt 1993: 49). The principle of good faith became a methodological vehicle for Carl Schmitt's 'konkretes Ordnungsdenken' (Schmitt 1993: 48). Schmitt had already pointed out the consequences this would have for the work of judges. He emphasized that 'the decision of the judge' would 'not be affected' by the application of a general principle. Rather, the application of the principle was not to be left to individual judgement, but would much rather be directly and exclusively determined by the fundamental principles of National Socialist ideology (Schmitt 1933: 2793f). This also referenced an argument made by Karl Larenz when considering Hedemann's fear of the judge as sovereign: While an earlier judge –

> in times of ideological struggles – would constantly incense a part of the people against himself with every definitive statement made, he now can rely upon a … consistent understanding of the law and the state among the whole of the people. The threat of arbitrariness resolves itself as the convictions of the '*Volksgemeinschaft*', the foundation of any judge's rulings, grow stronger and stronger.

Carl Schmitt exposed this idealization, an alleged unity of the law, the state and the people, as a vehicle of political power: 'Convictions and opinions in general are not ruling, leading and binding, except those of a certain kind of people. The National Socialist movement dominates in the contemporary German state. The meaning of aequitas and good faith must therefore be determined according to its principles' (Schmitt 1933: 2794). This was precisely what Hedemann had warned about: If the terms and notions of *aequitas* and good faith are politicized in order to serve as instruments of governance to one group of people, they can be used against another group.

Thus, a new understanding of equity and good faith was established. The purpose of the principle of good faith had changed from a pressure relief valve for the sake of individual justice to a political tool, through which the state was able to reinterpret the BGB in line with its ideology, without having to alter its wording at all.

Wieacker and legal form in the year 1956

Now, what does Franz Wieacker have to do with this story? As a student of Pringsheim he had affiliated himself with his teacher's interpretation of late Roman history as a process of decline as early as the 1930s. From 1937 on, he had defended Pringsheim's narrative against attacks by Romanists such as Ernst Schönbauer, Hans Kreller and Max Kaser (on this, see Winkler 2014: 181ff). My opening quote from Wieacker's 1956 commentary proved itself to be merely one aspect of Wieacker's comprehensive re-evaluation of these questions in the 1950s. It reveals that Wieacker, more so even than Pringsheim himself, linked antiquity and modernity. The picture of antiquity which he painted in this context remained remarkably consistent and always in line with that of Pringsheim. When Wieacker, in 1955, turned his attention once again to the Roman jurists in his piece '*Vulgarismus und Klassizismus im römischen Recht der Spätantike Antike*', his fundamental ideas had not changed. Of the two Byzantine risks, he was now however less concerned with the danger of a purely logical jurisprudence of concepts. His discussion was now dominated by Pringsheim's warnings regarding emotive arguments of justice. This was, as Wieacker laid bare, first and foremost a reaction to their prevalence in National Socialism. According to Wieacker, one had, 'for the purpose of furthering short-term interests, abandoned the classical traditions of permanent manifestations in legal practice'. The characteristic 'appeal to manifest sentiment and popular affections' had served 'with notable prevalence as justification for the evil practices within the imperial administration' and 'the relentless plundering of the traditionally wealthy'. He concluded, 'The jurist knows that this alliance between political interest and what is purported to amount to healthy public opinion has not remained the last in human history.'

While, in this instance, he considered the present day from the point of view of antiquity, in another article he turned the perspective around and considered the past from the point of view of the present day. In '*Zur rechtstheoretischen Präzisierung des § 242 BGB*', which was also published in 1956, he described, with reference to then current case law, his concern that 'the law is softened through the careless, even demagogic use of equity' as a 'gateway for arbitrariness, especially for political interests and political coercion'.[17] He now openly attacked the age of National Socialism:

> At least under the extraordinary circumstances of totalitarianism, these predictions have been proven to be accurate, by the tendency of the legislator to utilise preferably vague and, where possible, emotive general principles ('honourable', 'special hardship', 'in accordance with healthy public opinion') to grant himself the greatest possible freedom. (Wieacker 1956b: 197 (reprint))

This text closed with a word of caution on 'equity as mushy as it is totalitarian', a perception of equity which was seen as a 'characteristic of Byzantine law'. Byzantium remained an exemplary lesson, now associated with National Socialism. Once again, present day and history appeared closely linked. By placing the Byzantine in parallel to the National Socialist legislator, Wieacker, as was highly typical of the time, shifted the legal profession from the role of the perpetrator into that of the victim. It had been the legislator, who had deprived the jurists of the rules which safeguarded stability. Thus, it was insinuated that the removal of the formal safeguards of private law had also resulted in the totalitarian submission of the legal profession. Wieacker thus adopted a particular version of the assertion initially formulated by Radbruch, that positivism had left the legal profession powerless after 1933.

The cautionary tale of Byzantium also served other functions, however, which point back to the contemporary discussions on methodology among legal scholars. Wieacker feared, much like Pringsheim back in 1930, the equating of good faith and equity.

> Namely, if one were to labour under the misapprehension that the place of justice would here be filled instead by another, extralegal quality such as caritas, social welfare, the greater good or the benefit to society, one would already have succumbed to the most arbitrary form of judicial discourse (*Kadijurisprudenz*). It is thus preferable to leave discussions of equity aside once and for all. (Wieacker 1956b: 196 (reprint))

Wieacker thus objected to any notion to the effect that the judge was entitled to enforce a certain concept of justice against the written law. 'In the process, it is easily forgotten that even after the triumph over positivism, the judiciary remains the servant of statute and the law' (Wieacker 1956b: 197 (reprint)). He thus opposed Christian natural law, to which the *Bundesgerichtshof* had subscribed under its president Weinkauff in the 1950s, with Kant's 'irreparable destruction of the dream of a law of reason'.[18] The same was true for the idea emphasized during National Socialism, namely that certain 'social norms', such as 'gesundes Volksempfinden', could be determined with certainty. Wieacker referred to such naiveties as 'the surrender of philosophical labour on an ethical problem' (Wieacker 1956b: 200 (reprint)). Wieacker thus suspected any appeal to the judicial sense of justice of being a disguised exercise of arbitrariness (cf. Wieacker 1958: 48 (reprint)).

On the other hand, Wieacker emphasized the 'voluntative elements' in every application of the law, which made 'every decision already an isolated element of creation of the law'. This applied particularly to *bona fides* in Section 242 German Civil Code:

> Thus the application of the general principle, and thereby every decision based on section 242 BGB, contributes to the creation of developing and emerging law. Like single needle-pricks on a piece of cloth, it actually carries forward a line of development, the direction of which is not yet pre-determined. (Wieacker 1956b: 201 (reprint))

Subsequently, Wieacker outlined the role of a judge, whose methodological proximity to the pre-Byzantine Roman model could not be missed.[19] Wieacker emphasized 'that consequently, the precepts governing the application of law (and thus its interpretation) are the object of a legal ethical art. The principles of this art are those of a practical form of conduct, of the art of decision-making; which preferably develop within the judicature itself' (Wieacker 1956b: 203 (reprint)).

Wieacker then secured the *officium judicis* within a web of technical orientation. In his treatise '*Gesetz und Richterkunst*', he listed the fundamental elements: 'the explicit value judgement of the constitution' (Wieacker 1958: 52 (reprint)), universally acknowledged 'realities of the time' of the *ordre public*, recognized principles of judicial equity, such as *ius commune* principles like *venire contra factum proprium*, *tu quoque* and others. A frame of reference was established through legal scholarship and recognized customs of the court as 'experience of the judiciary itself' (Wieacker 1958: 54 (reprint)). In addition, he adopted Hans Welzel's concept, which assumed the existence of 'prerequisite logical structures' within reality.

Seeking the contrast to Byzantine equity once again, Wieacker asked to 'keep the development of the law in accordance with the traditions of the judiciary and with the consensus among those concerned as well as among fellow experts'. Thus, he had arrived at the ancient Roman ideal, which he had previously outlined in his treatise '*Vom römischen Juristen*' in 1939. Following Pringsheim, he had described the Roman 'law of jurists'[20] as a continuous stream of communication among independent professionals and experts, which gave rise to the 'professional technique ... by means of routine and of continuous tradition' (Wieacker 1939: 14 (reprint)). The 'routine of decision-making' (Wieacker 1939: 19 (reprint)) was decisive, in contrast to a philosophically rooted jurisprudence of sentiment: 'It is un-Roman to ask whether a decision is just in itself, as it arises from a far more powerful force; the constans interpretatio iuris civilis' (Wieacker 1939: 23 (reprint)). Whereas in 1939 he had cautiously stressed that the ideal of the Roman judge was neither 'repeatable' nor 'worth repeating' (Wieacker 1939: 36 (reprint)), in 1957 he candidly raved over the 'glory of the great Roman practitioners' (Wieacker 1957: 62) as an inspiration for the art of judicial decision-making. Antiquity and modernity remained linked.

Notes

1 Regarding Wieacker, see Chapter 4 in this volume.
2 *Treu und Glauben* ('good faith') is the German term for the *bona fides* of ancient Roman law.
3 See Chapter 2 in this volume.
4 Pringsheim 1921a: 645. Page numbers refer to the original text, not the reprint (see bibliography).
5 Krüger 1898: 18f; for a critical discussion, see Kipp 1909: 9f, n. 27.
6 'It is Roman Law itself which is meant to be overcome' (Pringsheim 1921a: 668).
7 Cf. Stroux 1926: 60, n. 104 (page number refers to the 1949 reprint, see bibliography).
8 For a reconsideration of Byzantine jurisprudence see Liebs 1987; for contemporary influences of Pringsheim's interpretation of Byzantium see Winkler 2014.
9 Cf. the reference in Pringsheim 1921b: 207, n. I: 'During proofreading, I consulted Max Weber's "Rechtssoziologie...."'
10 For a clarification of false interpretations, see Winkler 2014: 120ff.
11 Binder 1925: 407; for a critical view, see Pringsheim 1961: 172, n. 104 (reprint of the 1930 original).
12 Pringsheim 1961: 165, n. 57 (referencing Weber, Wirtschaft und Gesellschaft, 436).

13 Cf. my analysis in Haferkamp 2007: 327, marginal no. 57.
14 Entscheidungen des Reichsgerichts in Zivilsachen 1924, 88 (decision of 28 November 1923).
15 For the same conclusion, see Nörr 1996: 30; Rückert 1994; Rückert 1997.
16 Pringsheim 1933: 54 (page number refers to the 1961 reprint; see bibliography).
17 Wieacker 1956b: 197 (page numbers refer to the 1983 reprint; see bibliography).
18 Wieacker 1956b: 199 (reprint); for a more careful wording of an essentially identical viewpoint, see Wieacker 1958: 49ff (page numbers refer to the 1983 reprint, see bibliography).
19 See Chapter 4 in this volume.
20 Wieacker 1939: 8 (page numbers refer to the 1944 reprint, see bibliography).

References

Binder, J. (1925), *Philosophie des Rechts*, Berlin: Georg Stilke.

Chlosta, C. (2005), *Nur dem Gesetz unterworfen?*, Frankfurt am Main: Peter Lang.

Emmert, J. (2001), *Auf der Suche nach den Grenzen vertraglicher Leistungspflichten*, Tübingen: Mohr Siebeck.

Fuchs, E. (1925/1926), 'Verhältnis der Freirechtslehre zum deutschen und ausländischen Rechtsdenken', *Die Justiz*, 1: 349–63.

Geyer, M. H. (1994), 'Recht, Gerechtigkeit und Gesetze: Reichsgerichtsrat Zeiler und die Inflation', *Zeitschrift für Neuere Rechtsgeschichte*, 16: 349–72.

Haferkamp, H.-P. (2007), '§ 242. Leistung nach Treu und Glauben. 20. Jahrhundert', in M. Schmoeckel, J. Rückert and R. Zimmermann (eds), *Historisch-kritischer Kommentar zum BGB*, vol. 2, 327–61, Tübingen: Mohr Siebeck.

Hedemann, J. W. (1913), *Werden und Wachsen im Bürgerlichen Recht*, Berlin: Heymanns.

Hedemann, J. W. (1933), *Die Flucht in die Generalklauseln. Eine Gefahr für Recht und Staat*, Tübingen: Mohr Siebeck.

Heymann, E. (1930), 'Rechtswissenschaft', in G. Abb (ed.), *Aus fünfzig Jahren Deutscher Wissenschaft. Festschrift Friedrich Schmidt-Ott*, 104–35, Berlin: de Gruyter.

Kipp, Th. (1909), *Geschichte der Quellen des Römischen Rechts*, 3rd edn, Leipzig: Deichert.

Kiß, G. (1911), 'Gesetzesauslegung und "ungeschriebenes" Recht. Kritische Beiträge zur Theorie der Rechtsquellen', *Jherings Jahrbücher*, 58: 413–86.

Kohler, J. (1886), 'Ueber die Interpretation von Gesetzen', *Grünhuts Zeitschrift für das Privat- und Öffentliche Recht der Gegenwart*, 13: 1–61.

Krüger, H. (1898), 'Die humanitas und die pietas nach den Quellen des römischen Rechtes', *Zeitschrift der Savigny-Stiftung für Rechtsgeschichte. Romanistische Abteilung*, 19: 6–57.

Lange, H. (1933a), 'Generalklauseln und neues Recht', *Juristische Wochenschrift*, 62 (3): 2858–9.

Lange, H. (1933b), *Liberalismus, Nationalsozialismus und Bürgerliches Recht*, Tübingen: Mohr Siebeck.

Lepsius, O. (1994), *Die gegensatzaufhebende Begriffsbildung*, München: C. H. Beck.

Liebs, D. (1987), *Die Jurisprudenz im spätantiken Italien (260-640 n. Chr.)*, Berlin: Duncker & Humblot.

Mitglieder des Gerichtshofes und der Reichsanwaltschaft, eds. (1924), *Entscheidungen des Reichsgerichts in Zivilsachen*, vol. 107, Berlin and Leipzig: de Gruyter.

Mitteis, L. (1891), *Reichsrecht und Volksrecht in den östlichen Provinzen des Römischen Kaiserreichs*, Leipzig: B. G. Teubner.

Nörr, K. W. (1988), *Zwischen den Mühlsteinen. Eine Privatrechtsgeschichte der Weimarer Republik*, Tübingen: Mohr Siebeck.

Nörr, K. W. (1996), *Der Richter zwischen Gesetz und Wirklichkeit. Die Reaktion des Reichsgerichts auf die Krisen von Weltkrieg und Inflation, und die Entfaltung eines neuen richterlichen Selbstverständnisses*, Heidelberg: Müller.

Pringsheim, F. (1921a), 'Jus aequum und jus strictum', *Zeitschrift der Savigny-Stiftung für Rechtsgeschichte. Romanistische Abteilung*, 42: 643–68. Reprinted in Pringsheim, F. (1961), *Gesammelte Abhandlungen*, vol. 1, 131–53, Heidelberg: Carl Winter Universitätsverlag.

Pringsheim, F. (1921b), 'Beryt und Bologna', in *Festschrift für Otto Lenel*, 204–85, Leipzig: Tauchnitz.

Pringsheim, F. (1933), 'Höhe und Ende der römischen Jurisprudenz', *Freiburger Wissenschaftliche Gesellschaft*, 22: 1–16. Reprinted in Pringsheim, F. (1961), *Gesammelte Abhandlungen*, vol. 1, 53–62, Heidelberg: Carl Winter Universitätsverlag.

Pringsheim, F. (1961), 'Aequitas und bona fides (1930)'. Reprinted in Pringsheim, F. (1961), *Gesammelte Abhandlungen*, vol. 1, 154–72, Heidelberg: Carl Winter Universitätsverlag.

Riccobono, S. (1926), 'Fasi e Fattori dell'evoluzione del diritto romano', in P. Collinet and F. de Visscher (eds), *Mélanges de droit romain dédiés à Georges Cornil*, vol. II, 235–309, Paris: Vanderpoorten.

Rückert, J. (1994), 'Richtertum als Organ des Rechtsgeistes: Die Weimarer Erfüllung einer alten Versuchung', in K. W. Nörr, B. Schefold and F. Tenbruck (eds), *Geisteswissenschaften zwischen Kaiserreich und Republik*, 267–313, Stuttgart: Franz Steiner.

Rückert, J. (1997), 'Der neue Richter: Weimar und die Folgen', *Kritische Justiz*, 30: 429–41.

Rümelin, M. (1921), *Die Billigkeit im Recht*, Tübingen: Mohr Siebeck.

Schmitt, C. (1933), 'Neue Leitsätze für die Rechtspraxis', *Juristische Wochenschrift*, 62 (3): 2793–4.

Schmitt, C. (1993), *Über die drei Arten des rechtswissenschaftlichen Denkens*, 2nd edn, Berlin: Duncker & Humblot.

Schröder, J. (2012), *Recht als Wissenschaft*, 2nd edn, München: C. H. Beck.

Simons, W. (1924), 'Das Reichsgericht in Gegenwart und Zukunft', *Deutsche Juristen-Zeitung*, 29: 241–6.

Stroux, J. (1926), *Summum ius summa iniuria: ein Kapitel aus der Geschichte der interpretatio iuris*, Leipzig: Teubner Verlag. Reprinted in Stroux, J. (1949), *Römische Rechtswissenschaft und Rhetorik*, 9–66, Potsdam: Eduard Stichnote.

Vorstand des Richtervereins (1924), 'Richterverein beim Reichsgericht', *Juristische Wochenschrift*, 53 (1): 90.

Wegerich, C. (2004), *Die Flucht in die Grenzenlosigkeit. Justus Wilhelm Hedemann (1878–1963)*, Tübingen: Mohr Siebeck.

Wieacker, F. (1939), 'Vom Römischen Juristen', *Zeitschrift für die gesamte Staatswissenschaft*, 99: 440–63. Reprinted in Wieacker, F. (1944), *Vom römischen Recht*, 7–37, Leipzig: Koehler & Amelang.

Wieacker, F. (1956a), 'Stillschweigende Hoferbenbestimmung?', *Deutsche Notar-Zeitschrift*, 115–25.

Wieacker, F. (1956b), *Zur rechtstheoretischen Präzisierung des § 242 BGB*, Tübingen: Mohr Siebeck. Reprinted in Simon, D., ed. (1983), *Franz Wieacker. Ausgewählte Schriften*, vol. 2, 195–227, Frankfurt am Main: Metzner.

Wieacker, F. (1957), 'Anmerkung zu BGH, Urteil vom 14.7.1956', *Juristenzeitung*, 12: 58–62.

Wieacker, F. (1958), *Gesetz und Richterkunst*, Karlsruhe: Müller. Reprinted in Simon, D., ed. (1983), *Franz Wieacker. Ausgewählte Schriften*, vol. 2, 41–58, Frankfurt am Main: Metzner.

Winkler, V. (2014), *Der Kampf gegen die Rechtswissenschaft. Franz Wieackers "Privatrechtsgeschichte der Neuzeit" und die deutsche Rechtswissenschaft des 20. Jahrhunderts*, Hamburg: Dr. Kovač.

Wolf, W. (1998), *Vom alten zum neuen Privatrecht. Das Konzept der normgestützten Kollektivierung in den zivilrechtlichen Arbeiten Heinrich Langes (1900–1977)*, Tübingen: Mohr Siebeck.

Zimmermann, R. (2001), '"In der Schule von Ludwig Mitteis". Ernst Rabels rechtshistorische Ursprünge', *Rabels Zeitschrift*, 65: 1–38.

9

The Arduous Path to Recover a Common European Legal Culture: Paul Koschaker, 1937–51

Tommaso Beggio[1]

Introduction

The aim of this chapter is to describe Paul Koschaker's effort to recognize and restore the idea of a European legal culture which had found its main foundation in Roman law, and how the conception of this scholar developed during the 1930s and 1940s.[2] Koschaker's main idea consists in stressing the role of Roman law – and, in particular, of Roman law as it emerges from *Justinian's Digest* – as the basis of European legal culture.

This is the *Leitmotiv* that distinguishes the book that has been considered Koschaker's masterpiece: *Europa und das römische Recht*, published for the first time in 1947.[3] We find, in any case, references to the topic of Europe and Roman law earlier in the long work that Koschaker published in 1938 under the title '*Die Krise des römischen Rechts und die romanistische Rechtswissenschaft*' (Koschaker 1938b), as well as in a few archival documents.[4]

This chapter will chronologically inspect the development of Koschaker's legal narrative on Europe and European legal culture, taking into account the different circumstances in which Koschaker explained his ideas, and what the aims of the author were. The starting point of the investigation will be *Die Krise des römischen Rechts und die romanistische Rechtswissenschaft*, which was the outcome of a long lecture held by Koschaker at the *Akademie für deutsches Recht* in December 1937, invited by the *Reichskommissar für die Gleichschaltung der Justiz* of the time, Hans Frank.[5] After this, I will discuss some archival documents from the 1940s, found mainly at the *Universitätsarchiv Tübingen* and at the archive of the *Humboldt-Universität zu Berlin*. One of the main features of these documents consists in offering us a more direct depiction of Koschaker's ideas during the years of the Nazi regime, as well as of his approach towards the regime.[6] Eventually, some aspects of his 'spiritual testament', *Europa und das römische Recht*, will be considered, together with a few passages from a letter that he sent, towards the end of his life, to his friend and colleague Salvatore Riccobono.[7]

Through a source-based reading of Koschaker's thought, this chapter will highlight the importance and influence of the ideas of the prominent scholar in the years to come, in order to recreate a common European legal space and identity based on the European tradition. In addition to this, it will be possible to take into consideration some striking inconsistencies which emerge from the documents from the time of the Second World War. These documents, in part still unpublished, are very significant because they reveal an idea of Europe sometimes likely to be too prone to indulge the ideology of the Nazi regime through a sort of adaptation of the role of Roman law.

Moreover, from a different perspective, the development of Koschaker's ideas on Roman law reconnects to a more general topic, namely the question of the 'use and re-use of Roman law'.[8] It is well known that Roman law has been used in different contexts and with different aims over the centuries, mainly as a foundation of the European legal culture but also sometimes as a source of historical legitimacy from a political point of view, as in the case of fascism.[9] Even if in many instances the study and use of Roman law has led to very significant goals, like in the case of the essential juridical contribution offered by the Pandect-science to the elaboration of a modern legal science (*Rechtswissenschaft*), nonetheless the extreme idealization of Roman law has sometimes provoked a misleading reinterpretation of Roman law itself. The result of this reinterpretation has thus been an excess of abstraction, an anachronistic understanding of Roman law, and the partial loss of its intrinsic historical–juridical meaning. The use of Roman law made by Koschaker under the Nazi regime can as well, even though only in part, be considered an example of this 're-use' of an idealized concept of Roman law.

Talking about Roman law at the *Akademie für Deutsches Recht*

In 1937, Koschaker had been invited to hold a conference at the *Akademie für deutsches Recht* in Berlin, an institution created in 1933 by the regime in order to promote 'German law' (a *deutsches Gemeinrecht*).[10] The president of the Academy was Hans Frank.[11] At the time, Koschaker was professor of Roman law and comparative legal history (*Römisches Recht und vergleichende Rechtsgeschichte*) at the University of Berlin, where he had taken the chair that had been Ernst Rabel's, a Jewish professor ousted by the regime.[12] He had become, in the meantime, a member of the *Preußische Akademie der Wissenschaften* as well as co-editor of the *Zeitschrift der Savigny-Stiftung*.[13] Without doubt, Koschaker was at the time one of the most prominent names in the field of Roman and ancient law, not only in Germany but also throughout Europe, and he could not be considered an opponent of the Nazis. In front of an auditorium composed of members and supporters of the regime (see Koschaker 1951: 105–25), he decided not to deal with Point 19 of the programme of the Nazi party, which directly attacked Roman law as the foundation of a materialistic and individualistic world order, and focused instead on other aspects of the crisis of Roman law that was at the time growing in Germany.[14]

The result of the conference was a long essay of almost ninety dense pages, in which Koschaker depicted the evolution of the European legal tradition, from the Middle Ages up to the 1930s. In the historical overview that he offered, the scholar constantly stressed the role of Roman law, trying to find the reasons for the crisis and some

Figure 6 Hans Frank (right, reading) with Heinrich Himmler, Joachim Von Ribbentrop and Rudolf Hess. Photo by Hugo Jaeger/Timepix/The LIFE Picture Collection/Getty Images.

solutions to the difficult situation that Roman law was facing in Germany at that time. As for the reasons of the crisis, it is important to underline that Koschaker found the causes of the decline of Roman law in the circumstances preceding the advent of the Nazi regime, and, in particular, in the so-called *Historisierung* of the study of Roman law. According to Koschaker, this trend was actually made up of two different sub-trends: the *Interpolationenforschung* developed during the nineteenth century by Gradenwitz, Lenel, Pernice and Eisele and the *antike Rechtsgeschichte* by Leopold Wenger.[15]

Koschaker's critique against these two trends was harsh and excessive, when compared, in particular, to the fact that Koschaker avoided ascribing any kind of responsibility for the crisis to the regime and to the new *Richtlinien für das Studium der Rechtswissenschaft*, developed in 1935 for the regime itself by Professor Eckhardt.[16] Considering instead the solutions suggested by Koschaker, they can be summed up by the motto '*Zurück zu Savigny*' – back to Savigny – and based on the idea of an *Aktualisierung* of the method of the Historical School. This kind of proposal and the persistent opinion that it was necessary to rebuild 'bridges' between Roman law and the current law was criticized not only by some contemporary scholars but also by scholars years later.[17] Recently, it has been argued that Koschaker was the representative of a so-called new (or second) Pandect-science.[18] Even though this remark would deserve deeper investigation, as already mentioned, in this chapter I would, however, prefer to focus on the connection between Europe and Roman law as a foundation of the European legal culture, rather than on Koschaker's proposal to try and solve the crisis of Roman law itself.

The first thing to notice is that the content of *Die Krise des römischen Rechts und die romanistische Rechtswissenschaft* actually consists of a clear-headed and technical analysis of the development of the Roman law tradition in European history up to the crisis of the 1930s. In the first chapter, Koschaker dealt with a historical overview of Europe in order to delineate the foundation of a common cultural conception; the second chapter is dedicated to Roman law in the Middle Ages and the following centuries, leading up to the Historical School of Savigny. Finally, in the two remaining chapters, Koschaker faced the problem of the crisis of Roman law and proposed thereupon the solution of the *Aktualisierung*. In this work, Koschaker officially debated for the first time in his career not only the problems that Roman law was facing but also more interestingly, the – in his eyes – indissoluble pairing of 'Roman law and Europe'. In order to stress the strong connections between these two terms, the author indulged in some imprecision in his historical depiction, which did not go unnoticed,[19] and tended to disregard any kinds of events that could instil doubts in his narrative. In some passages, after reading the text, the reader can affirm that European legal history had given in to the needs to defend the role of Roman law, and it is clear that its historical development has been idealized by Koschaker.

What emerges in the end is Koschaker's most important theoretical assumption: since Roman law is the main legal foundation of Europe and since Germany is one of the most important countries – or probably *the* most – in Europe and has to carry out a leading role in the continent, it is necessary that Roman law maintains a safe position in Germany and in German universities. Koschaker's reconstruction presents both sharable and not sharable points and mainly focuses on describing the role of Roman law; references to Europe and European history are above all used to defend his conception of Roman law, and this is probably the reason why he did not examine some problematic passages related to European history in depth.[20] Furthermore, the author stressed the necessity to consider Roman law as the main foundation of a new European private law system.

There were two essential consequences that came about as a result of this work by Koschaker. First, he helped to revive the academic debate on Roman law, the reasons for its crisis and its role in history and in the future of Europe.[21] Second, he presented in a nutshell the main argument of his conceptions, based on the idea of a tight historical connection between Roman law and European tradition. This assumption, which was the basis of his masterpiece, *Europa und das römische Recht*, gained huge success after the end of the Second World War.[22] But we will discover in the next paragraphs, how – sometimes differently bound to the political contingencies – this argument developed, after the publication of *Die Krise des römischen Rechts und die romanistische Rechtswissenschaft*, in other works and documents by Koschaker.

Which 'Roman law' for the '*Neuordnung Europas*'?

Koschaker dealt with the topic of Roman law as a foundation of Europe in other documents and letters after the above-cited work on the crisis of Roman law. The way in which he adapted the idea of Roman law and Europe to the newly changed –

political and cultural – circumstances sometimes appears really surprising. One of the main problems, with regard to Koschaker's approach, consists of his constant tendency to accommodate his ideas on Roman law and its role – that remain more or less always the same in the course of time – to different social, historical, and, more importantly, political contexts. Connected to these kinds of problems is a document Koschaker likely wrote in 1941 regarding the reform of Roman law studies in German universities.

This only recently published document (Beggio 2018b) document entitled *Die Reform des romanistischen Rechtsstudiums in Deutschland. Eine Denkschrift* ('The reform of Roman law study in Germany. A memorial') is preserved at least in the archive at the University of Tübingen and in the *Humboldt-Universität zu Berlin* archive.[23] The document was sent to the *Rektor* of the University of Tübingen, Hermann Hoffmann,[24] as well as to the *Reichsminister für Wissenschaft, Erziehung und Volksbildung* of the Nazi regime, Bernhard Rust.[25] In addition to the manuscript, the University of Tübingen archive also preserves a copy of the letter written by Rust's substitute, who sent Koschaker's document to the dean of the *Rechts- und Staatswissenschaftliche Fakultät* of the University of Berlin, Hans Weigmann,[26] on behalf of the minister. The University of Berlin dean had the duty of introducing the document and discussing it with the other deans of the German law faculties, during the forthcoming conference of the Law faculties deans in July 1942.

Once again, the declared aim of Koschaker was to secure the role and the teachings of Roman law in German universities; what was partially new, when compared to the content of *Die Krise des römischen Rechts und die romanistische Rechtswissenschaft*, was the way he used his arguments to always interpret facts, ideas and events in order not to make the regime responsible for the critical situation. If in *Die Krise* Koschaker's analysis remained at a more historical and scientific level, in *Die Reform des romanistischen Rechtsstudiums in Deutschland* the author introduced more than just a few arguments that could be used in a political way.

It is necessary to stress that the Nazi regime struck a blow against Roman law not only through Point 19 of the party's programme but also through the reform of the law faculties' course of study. The first step in this direction had been represented by the *Justizausbildungsordnung* of 1934, followed by the reform of the *Studienordnung* of 1935.[27]

Professor Eckhardt, the author of the reform and member of the Nazi party,[28] was a famous legal historian at the time and an open opponent of Roman law, in particular of Roman law as studied and retraced by Pandect-science, even if Koschaker seems to affirm the contrary in the document. In the *Grundgedanken* of the reform programme of 1935 Eckhardt wrote:

> Noch immer lebt die deutsche Rechtswissenschaft in den Gedankengängen des römisch-gemeinen Rechts …, die geistige Grundhaltung wird heute noch durch das Pandektensystem bestimmt. Diesem System gilt unser Kampf.[29]

The immediate result consisted in marginalizing the role of Roman law in German law faculties. The course on Roman law held since 1900, *Geschichte und System des römischen Privatrechts*, had been replaced with a new one, *Privatrechtsgeschichte der*

Neuzeit. Before the reform, in addition to the course on Roman private law, there was a course *Römische Rechtsgeschichte*, but after 1935 the students were given the possibility of choosing between the classes on Roman law history and the new course '*Antike Rechtsgeschichte*', inspired by the new research trend of the same name inaugurated in 1904 by Wenger at the University of Vienna.[30] Koschaker tried to react to this situation by writing *Die Reform des romanistischen Rechtsstudiums in Deutschland*. Exactly like in his work on the crisis of Roman law, the author insisted on associating the critical situation with the decadence of Pandect-science after the enactment of the *Bürgerliches Gesetzbuch* (BGB), on the one hand, and on the emergence of the above-mentioned trend of the so-called *Historisierung* of Roman law (that is to say, the *Interpolationenforschung* and the *antike Rechtsgeschichte*), on the other. The text at page one reads:

> Teils sind sie [Editor's note: the Roman law scholars in Germany] auf Grund einer noch zu erwähnenden Entwicklung reine Rechtsarchäologen geworden, die eine lebensfremde Wissenschaft vortragen, teils sind sie 'Auchromanisten', die römisches Recht im Nebenamte lesen, d. h. nicht aus eigenem Wissen und eigener Forschung, sondern auf Grund von Kompendien.[31]

Koschaker's critique was based on some scientific premises: Firstly, he considered the approach to Roman law of the *Historisierung* to be accountable for having destroyed the 'bridges' linking Roman law to the actual law in force in Germany. Secondly, and as a direct consequence of the first problem, this purely historical approach pushed away both the legal experts, who did not work at the University, as well as the students, who in the course of time lost their interest in studying a topic without any kind of connection to current legislation.[32] As we can read in Koschaker's writing, at page five:

> Die deutsche Romanistik aber – sie war um die Jahrhundertwende führend und ihr Beispiel hat die Entwicklung in anderen Ländern beeinflußt, flüchtete, um sich ein Feld ihrer Tätigkeit zu sichern, schon seit den letzten 20 Jahren des 19. Jahrhunderts in die reine Historie, die kein anderes Ziel kannte als das römische Recht als historisches Phänomen zu begreifen. … Die Romanistik wurde auf diesem Wege immer mehr zu einer Wissenschaft für Spezialisten, Professoren und immer weniger zu einer solchen für alle Juristen.[33]

And again, the text reads with regard to the law faculties' students:

> Ein Recht aber, das man den Rechtsstudenten ausschließlich als historisches Phänomen vorstellt, darf nicht erwarten, ein besonderes Interesse der Studenten zu finden.[34]

The way Koschaker tried to find and use arguments against the *Historisierung* in the document is very interesting. If it could be understandable to some extent to underline the risks connected to a study of Roman law being only of a historical nature, it is nonetheless not possible to accept the idea that almost the whole responsibility for the crisis of Roman law relapses only on the *Historisierung*.[35] It seems clear, while reading the text, that this was a technique to try to discredit the above-mentioned trend in the eyes of the regime, not only from a scientific point of view but also from a political point of view. Koschaker seemed to affirm that both the *Interpolationenforschung*, as well as the *antike Rechtsgeschichte*, could not be considered more than ancillary parts of Roman law study; they could not actually play any kind of role in the construction of a new European private law, but it did not mean that Roman law as a whole, if properly studied, could not do it either. What is more, with regard to the *antike Rechtsgeschichte* and the choice, made by Eckhardt, to make this course an alternative to *Römische Rechtsgeschichte*, Koschaker affirmed that the decision had been taken only for nominal reasons, because in the name *antike Rechtsgeschichte* there was no reference to the unbeloved adjective 'Roman'.[36] Koschaker wrote that Eckhardt could not be considered responsible for this choice, because he could not have known what the *antike Rechtsgeschichte* actually was, since this was still at the time a vague programme. Apart from the fact that Wenger presented his theories and programme already in 1904 in Vienna and these theories then developed through many works and publications and an intense debate among Roman law scholars,[37] Koschaker included, it is immediately clear that the author resorted to complex sophistry so as not to hold Eckhardt responsible for his conscious choice.

These considerations are strictly connected with the statements by Koschaker on Roman law and Europe, and therefore it is now necessary to move to these other questions. According to Koschaker, Roman law had to be one of the main foundations of a new common European legal culture – he talked of a '*neues gemeinsames Recht*' and of a '*neue europäische juristische Kultur*' on page three of the manuscript. The reason for this statement lay in the fact that all the systems of private law of Continental Europe have been deeply influenced by Roman law, wrote the author, and this is the reason why it is possible to talk of a European legal – and historical – tradition. At the same time, Roman law represents a unique patrimony from a juridical point of view, because it ruled the Roman Republic, then the Empire, and eventually the *Dominatus*.[38] It also developed through many different political and social circumstances and, even if it was perceived at the time in Germany as a 'foreign' law, it was the most significant 'foreign' law of European legal history. It is interesting to read the exact words that Koschaker wrote:

> Die Kenntnis keines anderen „fremden Rechts" ist in dieser Beziehung förderlicher als diejenige des römischen Rechts, weil es in seiner langen Entwicklung sich fast mit allen denkbaren sozialen und wirtschaftlichen Systemen auseinander zu setzen hatte: dem primitiven Agrar-, dem imperialen Handels- und Verkehrstaat, dem Staatssozialismus.[39]

Koschaker always referred mainly to private law, which he considered more important than public law, when he dealt with Roman law and the Roman law tradition.[40] However, private law in Europe could not (and still cannot) be thought of as separate from Roman law; it has been like this in the past, and it would be the same in the future. With regard to the situation in Germany, it was not correct to affirm that Roman law, inasmuch as it was individualistic and materialistic law, could not go along with a true national German law; the individualistic law which later merged into the BGB was not a Roman one, but rather Roman law as interpreted by the *Pandektenwissenschaft*. Therefore, if someone was guilty of having established an individualistic and materialistic order that was the Pandect-science, in particular with its radical tendencies over its last years. It is a noteworthy fact that in 1936 Frank, at the *Istituto fascista di cultura* in Rome, changed the target of the Nazi regime's hatred, which was actually no longer the so-called Roman law of the Romans, but rather the Roman law of the Pandectists.[41] Moreover, this stance on Pandect-science by Koschaker was partially contrary to the theory explained in *Die Krise* which was founded on the idea of the *Aktualisierung* of the method of the Historical School. We can notice, therefore, under this respect, a partial inconsistence in Koschaker's explanation under this respect.

In any case, since Germany was a leading country in Europe, it could not abandon Roman law and its teachings, because otherwise it would not have had the opportunity to exercise its power in the construction of a new common European law. Moreover, other countries where Roman law was still studied and highly considered, that is to say Italy, would have played the main role in this essential legal process. Koschaker was able in this way to bind Roman law not only to the legal tradition and to the history of Europe, which represented a less important aspect in the eyes of the regime, but also to the future of the new Europe. This is probably the most thorny and political argument in the whole narrative of Roman law and Europe depicted by Koschaker, not only in this document but also in all of his writings. Indeed, he did not hesitate to write on the sixth page of his document:

> Denn das römische Recht hat, wie schon ausgeführt, auch in der Zukunft Aufgaben zu erfüllen, heute, da es sich um die Neuordnung Europas handelt, vielleicht mehr als früher. Dann es handelt sich um nichts Geringeres, als um die Wiederbelebung einer europäischen Privatrechtswissenschaft, für die das durch die Geschichte gegebene Ferment das römische Recht ist.[42]

Furthermore, the text, on the same page, with regard to the question of the leading role of Germany in Europe, clearly reads:

> Heute muß sie [Editor's note: Koschaker referred to 'die Aufgabe' to create a European 'Privatrechtswissenschaft', a task already carried out during the nineteenth century by the Pandect-science] in zeitgemäßer Weise – nicht etwa durch Wiederbelebung des Pandektenrechts – Hand in Hand mit dem befreundeten Italien neu in Angriff genommen werden. … Die Deutschen werden zu den führenden Nationen des neuen Europa gehören und die deutsche Rechtswissenschaft wird zu sorgen haben, daß deutscher Geist bei dieser europäischen Privatrechtswissenschaft nicht zu kurz kommt. … eine Neuorientierung tritt, die das römische Recht für die Bedürfnisse der Gegenwart verwertet und so wieder die Brücke von der Rechtsgeschichte zur Dogmatik des geltenden Rechts schlägt, die heute abgebrochen ist.[43]

In order to secure a place for Roman law in German universities, Koschaker was even prepared to interpret Roman law and its teachings in accordance with the political programme of the *Neuordnung Europas*, conceived by Nazi Germany. It is at least surprising that Roman law, the bearer of legal principles and the representative of the European legal and cultural tradition, could be at the same time the foundation of a new common legal science and legal order in a new Europe, which, at the time Koschaker was writing this text, seemed to be doomed to be dominated by a totalitarian regime.

It is clear that Koschaker desired to offer a depiction of Roman law and Europe which could be accepted by the Nazi regime and by Nazi supporters who held important roles in German universities at the time. Nonetheless, it seems a paradox to tie Roman law and its survival not only to political power but also to a political power of this kind. It is almost a betrayal of Roman law itself. Does it really make sense to 'sell out' the valuable legal principles of Roman law and the tradition it represented just to have a few hours more of teaching at the university? Or could it be considered instead a way, the only way possible, to defend some cultural values in such dramatic circumstances?

On these problems, it has been argued that Koschaker tried to recover the references to Roman law in order to support the expansive tendencies of Germany (Giaro 2001b: 31–77; Somma 2005: 282). He would have therefore used Roman law for nationalistic purposes and to affirm the necessity of a reunified Western Europe, in which Germany should carry out its unquestionable supremacy.[44] Both these judgements seem to be extreme, but they likely contain some truth. For example, it is not possible to deny that Koschaker thought of Germany as the leading country in Europe. It is true, however, that such a feeling was common not only to Koschaker's ideas but also to the ideas of many other German scholars at that time. To complete the picture of Koschaker's position with regard to Roman law and to the regime, it is now appropriate to refer to a letter, found in the archives at the University of Tübingen.[45] This document – a *Bescheinigung* (certificate) – does not further illustrate Koshaker's ideas, but gives us nonetheless some very interesting information about his activities at the beginning of 1945. In the certificate written on 17 February 1945, we can read that Koschaker was at the time a collaborator at the *Gesellschaft für europäische Wirtschaftsplanung und Großraumforschung*, directed by the *Reichsamtleiter* of the regime, Werner Daitz, and was working on a project entitled *Untersuchung über europäisches Recht*. The task of this commission was the elaboration of a new common law, fitting in with the *Neuordnung Europas*. Once again, Koschaker was working to connect his ideas with a project of the Nazi regime and, very likely, these ideas again involved the study of Roman law. Furthermore, this document could be proof that some of the concepts he explained in the document on the reform of Roman law study in Germany could had been embraced by the regime, who invited him to collaborate with the committee directed by Daitz, or, at least, that Koschaker's ideas were not considered somehow risky by the Nazis. If Koschaker was a member of such a board in 1945, it means that the regime did not consider him a genuine or dangerous opponent.

After the Second World War and towards *Europa*

This section aims to describe the last step of the scientific and intellectual development of Paul Koschaker's *Leitmotiv* on Roman law and Europe. A necessary part of this description is the publication of his masterpiece, a sort of manifesto for a Europe in need of rebuilding: *Europa und das römische Recht*.[46] After the end of the Second World War, Koschaker became professor emeritus in 1946 and was invited as *Gastprofessor* to some German universities, as well as in Ankara.[47] While at his retreat in Walchensee, and despite being involved in the problems that the end of the war had brought about,[48] his train of thought returned to his previous reflections, expressed in *Die Krise des römischen Rechts und die romanistische Rechtswissenschaft*. Nonetheless, there is a big difference between the two works. In fact, *Europa und das römische Recht* was a cry of alarm in defence of Europe, of its cultural and legal tradition, that represented the outcome of the personal inner struggle felt by Koschaker, whereas in *Die Krise* he adopted a more technical and neutral approach to the topic. The brilliant narrative of his masterpiece leads the fascinated reader through an intense text of almost 400 pages, and it is easy to perceive the civil commitment of Koschaker, who tried to place the concept of Roman law at the centre of attention, in perfect harmony with the description of cultural and legal European history (Calasso 1962). From a scientific point of view, the work presents some stretches of interpretation, adequately underlined by Roman law scholars and legal historians.[49] In order to allow the description he had in mind, Koschaker was unable to leave the conception of 'continuity' in legal European history out of consideration. At the same time, the role of Roman law in this historical depiction changes unbearably easily from that of a *Kaiserrecht* during the Middle Ages to that of a *Professorenrecht* at the time of Savigny. In the first case, Roman law is closely connected with imperial and political power, whereas in the latter it survives thanks to its autonomy with respect to any sort of political power. Partially following Goethe's metaphor of the duck,[50] Koschaker described Roman law as a sort of monolithic system of rules and principles, never disappeared in European (i.e. in West European) history. The greatest value of the book does not lie in the solutions Koschaker suggested for restoring dignity to Roman law and its teachings, because they are the same as we can read in *Die Krise des römischen Rechts und die romanistische Rechtswissenschaft*.[51] In the eyes of Koschaker, the only way to give Roman law back its prominence consisted in a strong connection between Roman law and the needs of the current legislation. Inherent is the risk of tying Roman law only to passing necessities, which could change from time to time, leading to the role of Roman law changing as well, according to social needs or established power. That is exactly what happens in Koschaker's historical depiction of Roman law: it survives only inasmuch as it is connected to the needs of political power, as it has been described on the previous pages, when dealing with the documents on the reform of the teaching of Roman law in Germany.

Furthermore, Koschaker's idea presumes that European private law has remained in some way fixed and has crystallized over the centuries in the countries of the so-called tradition of Civil law. Of no less significance such a conception of Roman law reduces it and its study not only to private law, but only to those single topics whose influence is more evident in modern law. These few remarks highlight some of the most evident weakness of Koschaker's theory on Roman law as a foundation of European legal culture. Nonetheless, it is essential to introduce and acknowledge the value of such a work. First of all, it is a work that was able to attain a huge symbolic importance. It spread the idea that Europe, the same continent where the tragedy of totalitarianism had taken place, still nevertheless had solid and safe cultural and legal foundations.

Koschaker was able to give Roman law a symbolic value, as well as a very practical and operational one. After the tragic experience that Europe had gone through, the scholar succeeded in interpreting the deep need and desire to find once again robust and secure foundations for the future of the continent, to offer certainty and safety and to push away the threat of regimes and dictatorships. According to Koschaker, the only way to obtain this result consisted in looking at the historical roots of Europe and its juridical tradition. Quite paradoxically, Roman law seems to be partly unhooked from eternal legal values and principles in Koschaker's depiction, but at the same time this is the reason why it is possible to use it again as a foundation of Europe, after the Second World War. Of course, it sounds strange if we think that Koschaker suggested the very same Roman law as a basis of the new Nazi Europe just a few years before.

We can anyhow appreciate how the conception of Roman law went partially through a further development in Koschaker's thought by analysing the letter he sent to Salvatore Riccobono on 31 March 1951, just a few months before he died. The letter is three pages long, typewritten in Italian, sent from Koschaker's house in Walchensee. After the description of the situation in Ankara, where he had been *Gastprofessor* for two years, and the comparison between the situation in Turkey and in Germany, we can read a very critical statement against the historical positivism (that he called '*positivismo storico*') and, what is more interesting, a clear assertion on the so-called eternal values of Roman law. Even if the topic seems to be already present, but not in a clear-cut way, in some pages of *Europa und das römische Recht*, and we can recognize a hint of it already in a letter sent to Riccobono in 1949, the text of the letter of 1951 represents the 'last step' of the development of Koschaker's depiction of Roman law. I want therefore to reproduce here a few words of the text of the letter:

> La massima parte dei nostri romanisti sono aderenti ad un positivismo storico mentre si tratta di elaborare i valori eterni del diritto romano che consistono nei suoi concetti giuridici e la loro evoluzione che bisogna perseguire fin ai nostri tempi nei principali diritti positivi.[52]

Koschaker did not neglect to stress once again on one of his most important points about Roman law, namely the need to constantly link its study with the necessities of the current legislation. Nonetheless, he also affirmed that if we want to follow this path, we need to understand the eternal values and principles of Roman law. This is the last proof that we have of Koschaker's conception on Roman law, its study and its role as a foundation of historical, as well as future European legal culture. Koschaker died just two months later, on 1 June 1951, in Basel, after having held the last lecture of his life in Zurich two days before.

Conclusion

The first remark one can move after analysing Koschaker's works, documents and ideas is that the depiction of European legal history and culture offered by this scholar is highly idealized.

As already stressed, Koschaker tried to offer a monolithic description of this history, in such a way that it could fit the representation of Roman law that he desired to offer and defend.

With regard to this problem, it is nevertheless interesting to read what Genzmer wrote in his review of *Europa und das römische Recht*, where he affirmed that Koschaker tried to find a way towards a new historically based European natural law through the so-called *Rechtsvergleichung*.[53] Genzmer's interpretation is very interesting and broadly correct, even though in this respect Koschaker's aim seems to be more restricted to practical purposes and is essentially focused on the need to restore a link between Roman law itself and the law in force in a certain historical period. Koschaker actually talked of a 'relatives Naturrecht' (a relative natural law), which is not speculative, nor founded on reason, but rather on the historical comparison between the private law systems which have contributed to the *Aufbau Europas* ('the building of Europe') (Koschaker 1947: 345–6). This peculiar idea, truthfully not less vague than Koschaker's proposal of the *Aktualisierung* of the study of Roman law, had in any case a dogmatic foundation – following therefore the *Leitmotiv* of Koschaker's approach to Roman law, more generally. What is more, it represented an attempt to find a third way between natural law and positivism, as a new basis for the European legal culture that had to be rebuilt. It could therefore seem that he has sought, through the elaboration of this concept – the *relatives Naturrecht* – to sum up the main arguments and themes of his ideas on Roman law and Europe and to present them in a way which was suitable for the new European necessities.

Furthermore Koschaker, in particular in *Europa und das römische Recht*, constantly chose to underline the cultural, historical, legal – and sometimes political as well – foundations of Europe and their link to Roman law. For this effort, Paul Koschaker without any doubt deserves our gratitude.

It is nonetheless clear that such a depiction risks becoming eventually distant from the actual historical development of Roman law and its reception in Europe and to reveal itself partially as an abstraction. From a scientific point of view, Koschaker's stances therefore show some inconsistencies; they are not always clear and do not offer any new concrete solution to the crisis that Roman law had since the beginning of the twentieth century been through. If it can be said that Koschaker was able to underline some essential problems regarding the topic of the crisis of Roman law, at the same time he was unable to offer them concrete or convincing answers. Nonetheless it is not possible to share the idea that Koschaker just created a myth and invented the 'fairy tale' of the European legal tradition based on the reception of Roman law.[54] What Koschaker actually created was rather a new narrative for Roman law. After the crisis it went through in Germany in the first decades of the twentieth century, also because of the hatred of the Nazi regime, it was necessary to build new narratives and ways of thinking and studying Roman law in order to restore its role and its teaching. Koschaker was one of the protagonists of this process in Germany, together with, among others, Schulz, Wieacker, Kunkel and Kaser. Unlike other scholars, he opted for the underlining of the cultural and historical value of Roman law as a heritage for the new Europe that had to be built on the ruins that remained after the Second World War. In this way, Koschaker contributed substantially to return to and revive the debate on Roman law, and he influenced many future generations of scholars as well. Thanks to the publication of his masterpiece, *Europa und das römische Recht*, he provided a bridge between the pre-war European legal tradition that came from the previous centuries – which considered the role of Roman law in the history of the continent to be undisputed – and the scholars of a new Europe that had to be founded again. In Koschaker's eyes, all the values destroyed by totalitarianism could in this way be recovered.

It has nevertheless been correctly stressed that such a way of conceiving Roman law has to do with a conception of the topic *sub specie aeternitatis* (Mantello 1987: 53); in fact, if, on the one hand, Koschaker tried at times to underline the eternal value of Roman law, on the other hand, he somehow deprived it of content, and he simply linked it to the necessity of the law in force at the time. This is an evident limitation of Koschaker's stance on Roman law. Roman law thus becomes suitable for any kind of 'situation' and under any kind of conditions, including the foundation of the *Neuordnung Europas* as planned by the Nazi regime. This highly idealized – but at the same time partly empty – conception of Roman law is therefore ambivalent, just as Koschaker's approach to the regime could be considered ambivalent and opportunistic, as can be argued from the reading of the document written in 1942 on the *Reform des romanistischen Rechtsstudiums in Deutschland*. With regard to these ambiguities, it can be said that Paul Koschaker chose the only possible way he had to try to keep on dealing with Roman law under the Nazi regime. However, trying to bend Roman law to the necessity and the will of such a regime cannot be considered the best way to defend it.

It is in fact impossible to avoid asking how it could be possible that the kind of Roman law that in 1942 should represent a basis for the Nazi *Neuordnung Europas* could be the same Roman law that only five years later should again become a foundation for the new Europe freed from the fascist and Nazi regimes.

The transition from Koschaker's depiction of Roman law in 1942 and his ideas as presented in 1947, in *Europa und das römische Recht*, is probably the most evident case of the 'use and re-use of Roman law'[55] in his academic experience and works. It is clear that the depiction of Roman law that Koschaker proposed had to be very idealized in order to adapt it to two completely different contexts like these – the Nazi regime and the new Europe freed from totalitarianisms. This is probably the main weakness of Koschaker's approach; at the same time, however, this reconstruction of Roman law, this idea of its eternal linkage to the destiny of Europe, has influenced the studies of many scholars – not only in Germany – of the following generations.[56]

It is in any case true that, despite the fact that his behaviour was not exempt from the above-mentioned ambiguities, Koschaker was actually more or less coherent with regard to his ideas on Roman law, since in 1947 he suggested once again the *Aktualisierung* as a solution for the crisis of Roman law. In this sense, one could ask if Koschaker defended Roman law and its teaching for itself, falling thus his arguments in a '*petitio principii*', rather than for its principles or what it actually historically represented. However, Koschaker was able, thanks to the publication of *Europa und das römische Recht*, to leave his work as a heritage for future generations and to recover and reinforce the idea of a common European legal tradition. Even if Koschaker's depiction can in part be criticized, in 1947 he placed the focus of attention on the meaning and importance of this historical–legal tradition founded on Roman law. In this way, he was able to propose again solid cultural and legal roots for Europe after its collapse, the same roots that had been cut off by the Nazi regime.

Notes

1 This research has made been possible by the European Research Council under the European Union's Seventh Framework Programme (FP7/2007-2013) / ERC grant agreement n°313100 (Reinventing the Foundations of European Legal Culture 1934–1964).

2 Paul Koschaker was one of the most prominent scholars in the field of Roman law and Comparative legal history in the first half of the twentieth century. He was born in 1879, in Klagenfurt, and he died in 1951, in Basel. On his life and academic career, see Ries 1980: 608–9; Wesener 2004: 971–4. Further bibliography on Paul Koschaker can be found in Beggio 2017, 2018a.

3 Koschaker 1947. Noteworthy is the Italian translation of the book by Arnaldo Biscardi, enriched by a long introduction by Francesco Calasso; see Koschaker 1962.

4 Koschaker 1938b. With regard to the documents, I refer in particular to a letter and to a proposal of reform of Roman law study in German universities that I found at the *Universitätsarchiv Tübingen* and at the *Archiv der Humboldt-Universität zu Berlin* (see below, note 23, for more details on the documents).

5 On Hans Frank (*Karlsruhe, 1900 – †Nürnberg, 1946), see Willoweit 1989: 25ff. and Gruchmann 2001: 86–92, 434–48, 632–52 and *passim* with further literature.

6 It is not the aim of this chapter, however, to make a 'posthumous process', as we can find in works like, for example, Giaro 2000; Giaro 2001a: 159–87; Giaro 2001b: 31–76. On the sometimes harsh tones of these three works, see Sturm 2003: 352–62 and Guarino 2002: 10–17.

7 On Salvatore Riccobono (*San Giuseppe Jato, Palermo, 1864 – †Roma, 1958), see Varvaro 2013: 1685–8.

8 I'm here referring with this quotation to a recent work by Leo Peppe that offers a very interesting overview on the problem. See Peppe 2012.

9 On the use of Roman law under the Fascist regime, see Cascione in this volume.

10 The regime wanted to replace the German civil code – the *BGB* – with a new *Volksgesetzbuch*, only based on the 'true', national, German law. See Hattenhauer 1983: 255ff; Somma 2005: 222–40 (with further bibliographical references); Garofalo 2009: 177–213.

11 On Frank see note 5.

12 Koschaker was professor in Berlin from 1936 to 1941, when he decided to accept the call to the University of Tübingen. On Ernst Rabel (*Vienna, 1874 – †Zurich, 1955), see Hofer 2003.

13 He became a member of the editorial committee in 1936 and he took the place that from 1935 had been Wenger's.

14 This is the text from Point 19: '*Wir fordern Ersatz für das der materialistichen Weltordnung dienende römische Recht durch ein deutsches Gemeinrecht*' ('We demand substitution of a German common law in place of the Roman law serving a materialistic world-order'). The literature on Point 19 of the programme of the Nazi regime is vast, so it is enough to quote a couple of references here where other bibliographies can be found: Landau 1989: 10–24; Santucci 2009: 53–82.

15 In order to get an overview on the so-called *Interpolationenforschung*, see Santos 2011: 65–120.

16 The new guidelines written by Eckhardt, following the *Justizausbildungsordnung* of 1934 and preceding the reform of the *Studienordnung* of July 1935 (effective since October 1935), were openly directed against Roman law and, in particular, Pandect-science. See Frassek 2000: 294–361, 351–77; Mußgnug 2006: 300–2; Stolleis 1989: 177–97.

17 Levy 1939: 91–2; Grosso 1939: 505–20; Betti 1939: 120–8; Plachy 1939: 388–94. Although they are more than simply reviews of Koschaker's work, see Schönbauer 1939: 385–410; Pugliese 1941: 5–48; Guarino 1988: 43–4; Giaro 2001a: 159–87.

18 Giaro 2001c: 541 and 544–5. See also, more generally, Bretone 2004: 127–52. For a detailed analysis regarding these issues, see now Beggio 2018a: 191 ff. and 253 ff.

19 See note 17.

20 As we glean from Calasso, Koschaker's idea about the Middle Ages is unclear and unsatisfying, insomuch as his approach to this era and its legal developments often seem to remain superficial. The perception we get reading the text is one of a conception of law during the Middle Ages as a by-product of ancient Roman law, which only reappears in its full lustre in the nineteenth century, thanks to Savigny and his School. See Calasso 1985: 105 and ff.

21 But this kind of debate had already begun years before in Italy and also in some other European countries. In *Die Krise* Koschaker referred, in particular, to a work by Georgescu on which he wrote a review as well: see Koschaker 1938a: 425–27. For the state of the art in Italy, see a brief overview in Santucci 2016: 63–102.

22 The importance of Koschaker's assumption and Koschaker's work can also be gathered from the two volumes dedicated to him, after his death: *L'Europa e il diritto romano. Studi in memoria di Paolo Koschaker* (1954).

23 The signature of the document conserved in Tübingen is: UAT, *Personalakten Jur. Fak.* 601/42. The signature of the one found in Berlin is: *UA-HU: Jur. Fak. Bis 1945, Nr. 518, Bd. 2, 35.* There are some differences between the two documents: the one found in Berlin is eighteen pages long, whereas the one from Tübingen is only twelve pages long, but the content is the same. All the following quotations from the manuscript refer to the one from the University of Tübingen archive and all the English translations of the quotations are my own.

24 See the letter from the director of the *Rechtswissenschaftliche Abteilung* of the University of Tübingen, Merk, to the dean of the faculty, sent on 21 May 1942 (UAT, 126/346a).

25 On Rust (*Hannover, 1883 – † Berend/Nübel, 1945), see Kraus 2005: 301.

26 On the Law Faculty at the University of Berlin under the Nazi regime, see Jahr and Schaarmschmidt 2005 and von Lösch 1999.

27 Author of the reform was Karl August Eckhardt (*Witzenhausen, 1901 – †Witzenhausen, 1979), professor in Legal history; for him, see Frassek 2008b: 1179–80. On Eckhardt's reform of university studies, see note 15.

28 He was a *SS-Sturmbannführer.*

29 *Richtlinien für das Studium der Rechtswissenschaft*, 1935; on this point, see Mußgnug 2006: 301–2. The translation of the text is the following one: 'Still lives the German legal science in the way of thinking of the Roman common law …. The mental (spiritual) attitude is still nowadays determined through the *Pandektensystem*. Our fight against this system is necessary' (my translation). It is important to notice what Koschaker wrote in the document with regard to Eckhardt: *Prof. Eckhardt, ein*

Germanist von Namen, der Verfasser der Studienordnung, war und ist kein Feind des römischen Rechts. Er sah sich in der Frage des römischen Rechts einer schwierigeren Lage gegenüber als sie heute besteht ('Prof. Eckhardt, a renowned name in the field of German law, who was the author of the *Studienordnung*, was not and is not an enemy of Roman law. He found himself, with regard to the question of Roman law in a more difficult situation than the one which nowadays exists').

30 Wenger 1905. On Koschaker's position with regard to the *antike Rechtsgeschichte*, see Atzeri 2010: 191–222; Varvaro 2010–11: 303–15.

31 They [the Roman law scholars in Germany] have in part become pure 'Law archeologists' by reason of a development that has still to be mentioned, and they teach a science detached from the reality, in part they are 'Auchromanisten' ('also Romanists'), who read Roman law as a collateral job, that is, not on the basis of their own knowledge and research but rather on the basis of compendiums.

32 See Koschaker 1938b: 70–4 and the references in Guarino 1988: 43–4.

33 The German Romanistic – which was the leading one at the turn of the century and whose example has influenced the development [of Roman law study] in other countries – has however escaped into pure History to secure one branch of its study, since the last twenty years of the nineteenth century. But History did not know any other aim than the understanding of Roman law as a historical phenomenon. … So the Romanistic became, in this way, even more a science for specialists, professors and even less a kind of science for all jurists.

34 In any case, a law that is presented to the Law Faculty students exclusively as a historical phenomenon may not expect to find a particular interest among the students.

35 For an incisive critique of Koschaker's point of view on the so-called *Interpolationenforschung*, see De Martino 1979: XIV-V in particular.

36 Indeed, it was just a formal nominal question, according to Koschaker.

37 On the harsh discussion between Wenger and Ludwig Mitteis (Wenger was a Mitteis' pupil during his years at the University of Leipzig), see Höbenreich 1992: 547–62 and Varvaro 2010–11: 305–7.

38 For this aspect, see the essential article by Pugliese 1941: 5–48. Considering that the article has been written in 1941 and represented a sort of 'indirect answer' to Koschaker's *Die Krise des römischen Rechts und die romanistische Rechtswissenschaft*, it is not impossible to think that some suggestions and critiques by Pugliese influenced Koschaker's later point of view.

39 The knowledge of no other 'foreign law' in this respect is more useful than the knowledge of Roman law, because it had to do with all the conceivable social and economic systems during its long evolution: the primordial rural State, the imperial State based on commerce and trade, the socialist State (sic!).

40 On this point, see Pugliese 1941: 5–48.

41 Frank 1936: 1–3. On this point, see Somma 2005: 292–7.

42 Thus Roman law still has tasks to fulfil also in the future, as it already accomplished tasks (in the past), and today probably more than before, since nowadays the question concerns the *Neuordnung* of Europe. Furthermore, it is something that has to do with nothing less than the recovery of a European Private law legal science, and Roman law, throughout history, is the specific ferment of this European Private law legal science.

43 Nowadays the task (i.e. the creation of a renewed European private law legal science) has to be tackled in an up-to-date way – not somehow through the revival of Pandect-science – hand in hand with the friendly Italy.… Germans will belong to the leading nations of the new Europe and German legal science will have to take care

that the German *Geist* does not suffer a loss in (the building of) this European private law legal science. ... A new orientation emerges which aims to use Roman law for the needs of the present day and so lays again a bridge from the history of law to the dogmatics of the current law in force, a bridge that nowadays is broken.

44 Giaro 2001b: 31–77; the idea of German supremacy in Europe appears clearly in Koschaker 1940.

45 The document in question is a certificate attesting Koschaker's tasks at the beginning of 1945.

46 See note 3.

47 He obtained a *Gastprofessur* for Roman law in München (1946/1947), in Halle an der Saale (1948), in Ankara (1949/1950) and in Bonn (1951). See Müller 1982: 271–84. About the influence that Koschaker's teaching had in Ankara and in Turkish universities, see Apaydin and Franchi 2016: 277–300.

48 Problems regarding, for example, his apartment in Tübingen, his library and other matters, are well described in the correspondence with his pupil Guido Kisch. See Kisch 1970.

49 Calasso 1962; Wieacker 1949; Genzmer 1950: 595–611; Guarino 1955: 207–11.

50 The metaphor was used by Goethe on the 6 April 1829, during one of his many conversations with Johann Peter Eckermann, who later published the texts. Goethe actually compared Roman law to a duck: just as the duck dives in the water and seems to disappear for a while, but then re-emerges from the water, so Roman law seemed to have disappeared in Europe for a certain period of time, but actually it was still there and thanks to Savigny it appeared again in all its lustre. See Eckerman 1836.

51 Koschaker 1947: 337–54. I have found a different and partially inconsistent statement by Koschaker on the solution to adopt to fight the crisis of Roman law in a letter he wrote to his friend and colleague Salvatore Riccobono (I had access to this document, as well as to some other documents of Riccobono, thanks to the courtesy of Professor Mario Varvaro of the University of Palermo and of Riccobono's heirs that I desire in this occasion to gratefully thank). In this letter dated 31 December 1939, Koschaker wrote that he never affirmed the necessity of a revival of the methods of Pandect-science; rather, he suggested adopting an updated *mos italicus*. Koschaker's stance is actually no surprise, since he considered Salvatore Riccobono to be the most important proponent of this updated *mos italicus* against the new *mos gallicus*, that is to say the *neuhumanistische Richtung* (i.e. the *Interpolationenforschung* and the *antike Rechtsgeschichte*).

52 The majority of our Roman law scholars adhere to a historical positivism, whereas it is a question of elaborating the eternal values of Roman law, which consist in its juridical concepts and in the evolution of these juridical concepts. We have to pursue these concepts up to the present day in the most important positive current laws.

53 Genzmer 1950: 607–8. The author adds that Koschaker's programme was not actually new, because it returned to the ideas already suggested by Gustav Hugo (*Lörrach, 1764 – † Göttingen, 1844).

54 Such a critique is very clearly expressed in Giaro 2001b, c. Over the last few decades a critical trend on the role of Roman law and its reception in European history has developed; according to this view, it is necessary to reduce or deny the importance of a European legal tradition. Such kinds of stances provoked fierce reactions among scholars, and the Romanists in particular, to defend the idea of the European legal tradition and the role of Roman law. Examples of these reactions are the works of Knütel 1994 and Baldus and Wacke 1995. These kinds of debates demonstrate at the same time how the problems raised by Koschaker in *Europa und das römische Recht* seventy years ago are still present.

55 On this point, see *supra*, page 160 and note 8.
56 Just to make a couple of the many possible examples, see Hattenhauer 1992; Zimmermann, Knütel and Meincke 1999. It is proper to underline, in any case, that there are many nuances in the way Koschaker's heritage has been received and followed by the scholars.

References

Andrés Santos, F. J. (2011), 'Brevissima storia della critica interpolazionistica nelle fonti giuridiche romane', *Revista de estudios histórico-jurídicos*, 32: 65–120.

Apaydin, Ö. and Franchi, M. (2016), 'L'importanza e la metodologia del corso di diritto romano nella formazione del giurista dall'impero ottomano ad oggi', in I. Piro (ed.), *Scritti per Alessandro Corbino*, vol. V, 277–300, Lecce: Libellula.

Atzeri, L. (2010), 'La 'Storia del diritto antico' e una lettera inedita di Paul Koschaker', *Iuris Antiqui Historia*, 2: 191–222.

Baldus, Ch. and Wacke, A. (1995), 'Frankfurt locuta, Europa finita? Zur reinen Rechtsgeschichtslehre in Band 12, 1993, des Rechtshistorischen Journals (RJ) und zu anderen Zweifeln am Gegenwart des Römischen Rechts', *Zeitschrift für Neuere Rechtsgeschichte*, 17: 283–92.

Beggio, T. (2017), 'Paul Koschaker and the path to "Europa und das römische Recht" (1936–1947)', *European Legal Roots*, 6: 291–326.

Beggio, T. (2018a), *Paul Koschaker (1879-1951). Rediscovering the Roman Foundations of European Legal Tradition*, Heidelberg: Universitätsverlag WINTER.

Beggio, T. (2018b), 'Paul Koschaker und die Reform des romanistischen Rechtsstudiums in Deutschland. Ein unveröffentlichtes Dokument', *ZRG (RA)*, 135: 645–80.

Betti, E. (1939), 'La crisi odierna della scienza romanistica in Germania', *Rivista di diritto commerciale*, 37: 120–8.

Bretone, M. (2004), *Diritto e tempo nella tradizione europea*, 5th edn, Bari: Laterza.

Calasso, F. (1962), 'Introduzione', in P. Koschaker, *L'Europa e il diritto romano*, trans. A. Biscardi, ix–xxx, Firenze: Sansoni.

Calasso, F. (1985), *L'unità giuridica dell'Europa*, Soveria Mannelli: Rubbettino.

De Martino, F. (1979), *Diritto e società nell'antica Roma*, Napoli: Editori riuniti.

Eckermann, J. P. (1836), *Gespräche mit Goethe in den letzten Jahren seines Lebens*, vol. II, Leipzig.

Frank, H. (1936), 'Die Zeit des Rechts', *Deutsche Rechtswissenschaft*, 1: 1–3.

Frassek, R. (2000), 'Steter Tropfen höhlt den Stein – Juristenausbildung im Nationalsozialismus und danach', *ZRG (GA)*, 117: 294–361.

Frassek, R. (2008a), 'Wege zur nationalsozialistischen „Rechtserneuerung" – Wissenschaft zwischen „Gleichschaltung" und Konkurrenzkampf', in H.-G. Hermann, T. Gutmann, J. Rückert, M. Schmoeckel and H. Siems (eds), *Von den 'leges barbarorum' bis zum ‚ius barbarum' des Nationalsozialismus*, 351–77, Köln: Böhlau.

Frassek, R. (2008b), 'Eckhardt, Karl August', in A. Cordes, H. Lück, D. Werkmüler and R. Schmidt-Wiegand (eds), *Handwörterbuch zur deutschen Rechtsgeschichte*, vol. II, Band I, 1179–80, Berlin: Erich Schmidt.

Garofalo, L. (2009), 'Suggestioni per il giurista dai Quaderni e diari di Hannah Arendt', in *Studi in onore di Remo Martini*, vol. II, 177–213, Milano: Giuffrè.

Genzmer, E. (1950), 'Besprechung von P. Koschaker, Europa und das römische Recht, München und Berlin, Biederstein Verlag', *ZRG (RA)*, 68: 595–611.

Giaro, T. (2000), *Aktualisierung Europas. Gespräche mit Paul Koschaker*, Genova: Name.

Giaro, T. (2001a), 'Paul Koschaker sotto il Nazismo: un fiancheggiatore 'malgré soi'', in *Iuris Vincula. Studi in onore di Mario Talamanca*, vol. IV, 159–87, Napoli: Jovene.

Giaro, T. (2001b), 'Der Trobadour des Abendlandes. Paul Koschaker geistige Radiographie', in H. Schröder and D. Simon (eds), *Rechtsgeschichtswissenschaft in Deutschland 1945 bis 1952*, 31–76, Frankfurt: Vittorio Klostermann.

Giaro, T. (2001c), '"Comparemus!" Romanistica come fattore d'unificazione dei diritti europei', *Rivista critica del diritto privato*, 19 (4): 539–67.

Grosso, G. (1939), 'Recensione a P. Koschaker, *Die Krise des römischen Rechts und die romanistische Rechtswissenschaft*, München/Berlin, 1938', *SDHI*, 5 (2): 505–20. Reprinted in Grosso, G. (2001), *Scritti storico giuridici*, vol. IV, 101–16, Torino: Giappichelli.

Gruchmann, L. (2001), *Justiz im Dritten Reich 1933–1940: Anpassung und Unterwerfung in der Ära Gürtner*, 3rd edn, München: De Gruyter.

Guarino, A. (1955), 'L'Europa e il Diritto romano', *Labeo*, 1: 207–11. Reprinted in Guarino, A. (1993), *Pagine di Diritto romano*, vol. I, 295–9, Napoli: Jovene.

Guarino, A. (1988), 'Cinquant'anni dalla «Krise»', *Labeo*, 34: 43–55. Reprinted in Guarino, A. (1993), *Pagine di Diritto romano*, vol. I, 276–91, Napoli: Jovene.

Guarino, A. (2002), 'Sine ira et studio', in A. Guarino, *Trucioli di bottega*, vol. 3, 10–17, Napoli: A. de Frede.

Hattenhauer, H. (1983), 'Das NS-Volksgesetzbuch', in A. Buschmann, F.-L. Knemeyer, G. Otte and W. Schubert (eds), *Festschrift für Rudolf Gmür zum 70. Geburtstag*, 255–79, Bielefeld: Gieseking.

Hattenhauer, H. (1992 [4th edn 2004]), *Europäische Rechtsgeschichte*, Heidelberg: Müller.

Höbenreich, E. (1992), 'À propos „Antike Rechtsgeschichte": Einige Bemerkungen zur Polemik zwischen Ludwig Mitteis und Leopold Wenger', *ZRG (RA)*, 109: 547–62.

Hofer, S. (2003), *Neue Deutsche Biographie*, vol. XXI, 64–5, Berlin: Duncker & Humblot.

Jahr, C. and Schaarmschmidt, R. (2005), *Die Berliner Universität in der NS-Zeit. Band I: Strukturen und Personen*, Stuttgart: Franz Steiner.

Kisch, G., ed. (1970), *Paul Koschaker. Gelehrter, Mensch, Freund. Briefe aus den Jahren 1940 bis 1951*, Basel und Stuttgart: Helbing und Lichtenhahn.

Knütel, R. (1994), 'Rechtseinheit in Europa und römisches Recht', *Zeitschrift für Europäisches Privatrecht*, 2: 244–76.

Koschaker, P. (1938a), 'Besprechung von Georgescu, *Exista o criză a studilor de Drept Roman? (Gibt es eine Krise des Studiums des römischen Rechts?)*, Cernauti (Czernowitz), 1937', *ZRG (RA)*, 58: 425–27.

Koschaker, P. (1938b), *Die Krise des römischen Rechts und die romanistische Rechtswissenschaft*, München und Berlin: Beck.

Koschaker, P. (1940), 'Probleme der heutigen romanistischen Rechtswissenschaft', *Deutsche Rechtswissenschaft*, 5: 110–36.

Koschaker, P. (1947,[4th unmodified edn 1966]), *Europa und das römische Recht*, 1st edn, München und Berlin: Biederstein Verlag.

Koschaker, P. (1951), 'Selbstdarstellung', in N. Grass (ed.), *Österreichische Geschichtswissenschaft der Gegenwart in Selbstdarstellungen*, vol. II, 105–25, Innsbruck: Wagner.

Koschaker, P. (1962), *L'Europa e il diritto romano*, trans. A. Biscardi, Firenze: Sansoni.

Kraus, H.-C. (2005), 'Rust, Karl Josef Bernhard', in *Neue Deutsche Biographie*, vol. XXII, 301, Berlin: Duncker & Humblot.

Landau P. (1989), 'Römisches Recht und deutsches Gemeinrecht. Zur rechtspolitischen Zielsetzung im nationalsozialistischen Parteiprogramm', in M. Stolleis and D. Simon (eds), *Rechtsgeschichte im Nationalsozialismus: Beiträge zur Geschichte einer Disziplin*, 10–24, Tübingen: Mohr Siebeck.

L'Europa e il diritto romano. Studi in memoria di Paolo Koschaker (1954), vols I–II, Milano: Giuffré.

Levy, E. (1939), 'Review of *Die Krise des römischen Rechts und die romanistische Rechtswissenschaft* by Paul Koschaker, vi, 86 pages. Beck, Munich 1938', *The Classical Weekly*, 33 (8): 91–2.

von Lösch, A.-M. Gräfin (1999), *Der nackte Geist. Die juristische Fakultät der Berliner Universität im Umbruch von 1933*, Tübingen: Mohr Siebeck.

Mantello, A. (1987), 'La giurisprudenza romana fra Nazismo e Fascismo', *Quaderni di Storia*, 13, 25: 23–71.

Müller, M. (1982), 'Paul Koschaker (1879–1951). Zum 100. Geburtstag des Begründers der Keilschriftrechtsgeschichte', *Altorientalische Forschungen*, 9: 271–84.

Mußgnug, D. (2006), 'Die juristische Fakultät', in W. U. Eckart, V. Sellin and E. Wolgast (eds), *Die Universität Heidelberg im Nationalsozialismus*, 261–317, Heidelberg: Springer.

Peppe, L. (2012), *Uso e ri-uso del diritto romano*, Torino: Giappichelli.

Plachy, A. (1939), 'Recensione a P. Koschaker, *Die Krise des römischen Rechts und die romanistische Rechtswissenschaft*, München/Berlin, 1938', *Rivista di Storia del Diritto Italiano*, 12 (2): 388–94.

Pugliese G. (1941), 'Diritto romano e scienza del diritto', *Annali dell'Università di Macerata*, 15: 5–48. Reprinted in Pugliese, G. (1985), *Scritti giuridici scelti*, vol. III, 159–204, Napoli: Jovene.

Ries, G. (1980), 'Koschaker, Paul', in *Neue Deutsche Biographie*, vol. XII, 608–9, Berlin: Duncker & Humblot.

Santucci, G. (2009), 'Diritto romano e Nazionalsocialismo: i dati fondamentali', in M. Miglietta and G. Santucci (eds), *Diritto romano e regimi totalitari nel '900 europeo, Atti del seminario internazionale (Trento, 20–21 ottobre 2006)*, 53–82, Trento: Quaderni del Dipartimento di Scienze Giuridiche.

Santucci, G. (2016), '«Decifrando scritti che non hanno nessun potere». La crisi della romanistica fra le due guerre', in I. Birocchi and M. Brutti (eds), *Storia del diritto e identità disciplinari: tradizioni e prospettive*, 63–102, Torino: Giappichelli.

Schönbauer, E. (1939), 'Zur "Krise des römischen Rechts" in M. Kaser (ed.), *Festschrift Paul Koschaker*. Zum 60. Geburtstag überreicht von seinen Fachgenossen, vol. II, 385–410, Weimar: Böhlau.

Somma, A. (2005), *I giuristi e l'Asse culturale Roma-Berlino. Economia e politica nel diritto fascista e nazionalsocialista*, Frankfurt: Vittorio Klostermann.

Stolleis, M. (1989), '»Fortschritte der Rechtsgeschichte« in der Zeit des Nationalsozialismus?', in M. Stolleis and D. Simon (eds), *Rechtsgeschichte im Nationalsozialismus. Beiträge zur Geschichte einer Disziplin*, 177–97, Tübingen: Mohr Siebeck.

Sturm, F. (2003), 'Besprechung von T. Giaro, Aktualisierung Europas. Gespräche mit Paul Koschaker. Name, Genua, 2000', *ZRG (RA)*, 120: 352–62.

Varvaro, M. (2010–2011), 'La *antike Rechtsgeschichte*, la *Interpolationenforschung* e una lettera inedita di Koschaker a Riccobono', *Annali del Seminario giuridico dell'Università degli Studi di Palermo (AUPA)*, 54: 303–15.

Varvaro, M. (2013), 'Riccobono, Salvatore sr.', in I. Birocchi, E. Cortese, A. Mattone and M. N. Miletti (eds), *Dizionario biografico dei giuristi italiani (XII–XX secolo)*, vol. II, 1685–8, Bologna: Il Mulino.

Wenger, L. (1905), *Römische und antike Rechtsgeschichte. Akademische Antrittsvorlesung an der Universität Wien gehalten am 26. Oktober 1904*, Graz: Leuschner & Lubensky.

Wesener, G. (2004), 'Koschaker, Paul', in R. Domingo (ed.), *Juristas universales, vol. III, Juristas del siglo XIX. Da Savigny a Kelsen*, 971–4, Madrid-Barcelona: Marcial Pons Ediciones Jurídicas y Sociales.

Wieaker, F. (1949), 'Besprechung von P. Koschaker, Europa und das römische Recht, München und Berlin, Biederstein Verlag', *Gnomon*, 21: 187–94.

Willoweit, D. (1989), 'Deutsche Rechtsgeschichte und „nationalsozialistische Weltanschauung"', in M. Stolleis and D. Simon (eds), *Rechtsgeschichte im Nationalsozialismus. Beiträge zur Geschichte einer Disziplin*, 25–43, Tübingen: Mohr Siebeck.

Zimmermann, R., Knütel, R. and Meincke, J. P., eds. (1999), *Rechtsgeschichte und Privatrechtsdogmatik*, Heidelberg: Müller.

10

The Weakening of Judgement: Johan Huizinga (1872–1945) and the Crisis of the Western Legal Tradition

Diego Quaglioni

Introduction

Johan Huizinga's *In de schaduwen van morgen. Een diagnose van het geestelijk lijden van onzen tijd* (*In the Shadow of Tomorrow. A Diagnosis of the Spiritual Ills of Our Time*), together with his last work, *The World in Ruins*, written when he was already prisoner in an internment camp, can be placed, right from its title, among the works 'flowing from the gathering storm and its aftermath in Europe following the rise of the National Socialist Party in Germany' (Midglay 2012: 113). Huizinga's book was one of the best witnesses of the crisis of the Western legal tradition in the first half of the twentieth century, denouncing the ideological deformations of public law theories, instrumental to the construction of a simplified and authoritarian conception of sovereignty and power (see Colie 1964: 613; Kammen 1987: 255–80; Wesseling 2002: 485).

The book was published in October 1935. In his very short Preface, dated 30 July, the author says that it was an elaboration of an address delivered in Brussels on 8 March of the same year (Huizinga 1935a; Huizinga 1935b; Huizinga 1936a: 9). This means Huizinga probably wrote his book in a short period during the summer of 1935, which explains not only the discursive character and instant style of the text but also its indulgence on facts and reasons of the narrowest actuality.[1] The origins of the book can be traced to the conference on *L'avenir de l'esprit européen*, organized by the French Committee for European Cooperation and held in Paris in October 1933, in which Huizinga participated (Huizinga 1934: 64–5). 'The timing of this conference was pertinent', Anne-Isabelle Richard recently wrote:[2]

> The experience of the First World War had led to many works about the decline of European culture in the immediate aftermath of the War. The early 1930s saw a second wave of this type of work. By 1933 the Great Depression had been raging for a few years and had affected even the strongest economies. Hitler had come to power and was about to announce Germany's withdrawal from the League of Nations. The nations of Europe tended 'to retreat behind their borders'.

Huizinga was the first to take the floor, among the thirty intellectuals assembled in the conference and to answer the questions put by its chairman, Paul Valéry. Defending the role of history, '*tandis qu'il s'agit de l'avenir*', he said: '*L'histoire que j'aime, ce n'est pas cette histoire de parade qui sonne le clairon et qui prétend donner des leçons à l'humanité pour l'avenir. J'aime le passé pour lui-même et, au fond, je crois que le passé d'il y a mille ans n'est pas beaucoup plus loin de nous que le passé d'aujourd'hui, de l'heure où nous sommes entrés dans cette salle*'.[3] So, in the perspective of a socialist ideal, Huizinga evoked ancient, Medieval and modern roots of the European spirit, emphasizing the role of humanism and particularly of Grotius, the great Dutch jurist who gave the humanistic idea its best expression in legal and political terms, working for the incoming centuries and for the survival of fundamental principles. He also said that one had to first ask under which of the above forms the European spirit still existed, then if it had taken new forms previously unknown, and of what principles it lived, stressing that it seemed to him that none of its past forms had completely lost its meaning or force. The Christian ideal, the philosophical idea of a common humanity and of a law of nations, the ethical need for harmony and peace, the consciousness of a common civilization made of all the wonders of mind from poetry to political economy – all these concepts and these feelings – Huizinga said, were alive and contributed to make the Europeans desire the true unity of the old part of the world that was theirs (see Huizinga 1950: 265).

That was Huizinga's response to the crisis of the European spirit, against nationalism and its caricature of the true patriotism, in the anguishing year 1933, '*en cette année angoissante*'. Europe and, with it, European civilization were under threat, and only a reaffirmation of morality could save it from barbarity:[4]

> L'Europe d'aujourd'hui se trouve exposée à plus d'une force qui la menace d'un retour à la barbarie … . Le progrès technique a permis une rapidité et une solidité d'organisation des masses dont profitent la folie et le crime aussi bien ou mieux que la sagesse et le droit …. Un affaiblissement inquiétant des principes éthiques, dans la vie des nations comme dans celle des individus, n'a cessé de se faire jour. Quand on compare l'idéal professé par les nations de l'heure aux conceptions qui ont animé les grandes époques du passé, le contraste saute aux yeux. C'est le bien-être économique, la puissance politique, la pureté de race, qui ont pris la place des aspirations généreuses de liberté ou de vérité d'autrefois. Réalisme, dira-t-on, au lieu d'illusions et de fictions. Le fait reste que ces vieux concepts avaient une valeur éthique manifeste et générale. C'est la pratique de la morale, après tout, par les communautés comme par les individus, qui, seule, pourra guérir notre pauvre monde si riche et si infirme.

Two years later 'Huizinga's best-selling book, *In the Shadows of Tomorrow*, came out' (Richard 2012: 247). The great Dutch historian

> described what he saw as the ailments of contemporary society: moral decline, technocracy, 'heroism' and 'puerilism'. The 'door that gave access' to these weaknesses was nationalism. Although the book only claimed to be a diagnosis,

> Huizinga also indicated a (largely undefined) remedy: spiritual regeneration. This spiritual regeneration did not just apply to individuals but also to societies and states. As did many in the interwar period, Huizinga saw a special role for international law in preventing war. In line with Dutch views on international relations going back to Grotius …, Huizinga argued for an international moral standard. (Richard 2012: 247.)

The American reception of Huizinga's *In the Shadow of Tomorrow*

Translated into English by Huizinga's son, Jacob Herman, *In the Shadow of Tomorrow* received controversial judgements by the American readers. It was first reviewed by Lewis Mumford in *The New Republic*, the liberal magazine founded by Herbert Croly in 1914 (see Seideman 1986). Ironically entitled 'The Shadow of Yesterday', Mumford's review is highly symptomatic of the broad incomprehension with which the book was received in New Deal America, by both liberal and conservative writers. Mumford had already published several books of success like *The Story of Utopia* (1922), *Herman Melville* (1929) and *Technics and Civilization* (1934); he was one of the most influential writers on intellectual movements of the United States.[5] His review denounces a lack of serious consciousness of the author's intellectual and moral personality. After a brief introduction, devoted to sketching a profile of the book's content, Mumford underlines his 'dissatisfaction' for Huizinga's argument (Mumford 1936: 230):

> The first part of this pithily written book examines the nature of the present state of society, and distinguishes it from other periods of crisis in the past. Huizinga has no difficulty in showing that our culture is in a state of disequilibrium, that our superficial mass education, so far for enthroning reason, as the eighteenth century hoped, has only made larger collections of men a prey to irrational suggestion, and that there is a general decline of the critical spirit – a turning away from science and a recrudence of superstition, quite as marked among the intellectuals as among the submissive millions. On all these symptoms Huzinga has many just things to say …: he presents, on the whole, an equable exposure of the mental deterioration that has overtaken the modern world. Nevertheless, one follows Huizinga's argument with a growing sense of dissatisfaction: a dissatisfaction that grows out of the suspicion … that all his values lie in the past, and that he has no sense of fresh emergents in modern society, and no confidence in their capacity to alter our present situation.

Mumford's suspicion and dissatisfaction are clearly based on the fact that Huizinga 'does not trust the new sources of thought and creative power that are actually in existence', because, in his opinion, 'he either shrinks from embracing them or is unaware of their existence', he himself writing 'within the shadow of yesterday' (Mumford 1936: 230). Maybe one could attribute this criticism to that 'unperturbed optimism' that was only possible 'for those who in their social or political creed of salvation think to have the key to the hidden treasure-room of earthly weal from which to scatter on humanity the blessings of the civilization to come' (Huizinga 1936a: 19). Mumford's review leads to an ideological invective, in which the anti-intellectual dogmatism of his statement, like in some of his letters, 'is simply arrogant and silly', and in which Freud, Marx, Geddes and Wright are the champions of a new era (Mumford 1936: 230–1):

> To fail to recognize these forces and ideas, or to misappraise them, is to present a distorted picture of the modern world and to give a belittling view of its creative powers .... And it is here that Huizinga, despite his many excellent and endearing qualities of mind, fails us. Lacking faith in the forces that are symbolized by Marx, Freud, Geddes and Wright, forces that work toward a new integration of personality and community, the thinker is bound to accept either the brutal, irrational, unifying processes of fascism, or some form of disruptive dualism, which treats body and spirit as separate entities and attempts to cure one without altering the condition of the other .... The task of men of good will today is not to expose out weakness again .... The task of the philosopher is rather to fortify our virtues, by reaffirming the positive values of objective thought and rational cooperation: he must be aware of fascism in order that he may help create the dialectic antithesis to its organized tyranny, its mechanized ferocity, its glorified servility. The potential energy of civilization is still much greater than that of barbarism: but it must be released, directed, put to work in the active transformation of the social order. He who stops at a shorter goal is, despite himself, on the side of barbarism.

The philosopher Barbara Spofford Morgan reviewed Huizinga's book together with Hugo Ferdinand Simon's *Revolution. Whither Bound?* under the title *A Choice of Revolutions*. She was probably the only one, in comparing two books that dealt 'with the general malaise of civilization' (Spofford Morgan 1936: 16), Huizinga's anti-fascist work and the 'not unsympathetic to fascism' book of the former German consul general in Chicago (Berman 1936: 221), not to point out their lack of programmes of action, emphasizing instead 'the clarification of ideas, out of which, when they have sufficiently cleared, action will arise' (Spofford Morgan 1936: 16). After explaining that Huizinga 'considers the weakening of judgment ..., the misuse of science, the decline of the critical spirit, the deterioration of morals, and the decay of style', taking as a point of departure the defence of knowledge and understanding 'against "the worship of life"', that is against the general anti-rationalistic reaction of his time, Spofford Morgan wrote (Spofford Morgan 1936: 16):

> Huizinga is especially concerned with the effects of the anti-noetic principle in politics. The most effective chapter in the book, I think, is 'Life and Battle', in which he attacks the concept of the State as an absolute object on the same philosophical place as the concepts of truth and justice. Summarized all too briefly, his argument is that whereas all action is struggle, in order to be productive the struggle must be between real antitheses. The superstate, however, puts up the false antithesis friend-foe (taken from Carl Schmitt's *der Begriff des Politischen*), an opposition which is purely subjective and consequently anarchical.

She was right; but this clear and penetrating vision contradicts a notably trivial conclusive judgement, based on the supposed retrogressive character of Huizinga's whole argument: 'To demand a return to reason', she wrote, 'is like sighing for the Garden of Eden, although the Garden of Eden may have had more snakes and poisoned fruits than we are apt to think. To the real optimist the way out of the present morass of subjectivity is a disinfecting of the irrational with intellect – not a return to the extreme of rationality from which we are reacting' (Spofford Morgan 1936: 16).

Marvin McCord Lowes, reading the book for *The American Review* in December 1936, puts it among the 'works of a generally leftist and collectivist nature', emphasizing, however, that the 'earnest, wide-ranging, and somewhat overlong book' had been 'widely praised in the Catholic press' (McCord Lowes 1936: 251). After making good translations from Sheng-Cheng's *Ma mère* and *Ma mère et moi* (Sheng-Cheng 1930; see Messner 2015: 231–2 and 243), and from Paul Rival's *La reine Margot* (Rival 1930), Lowes (1903–60) became the managing editor of *The American Review*, the literary journal established in 1933 by the pro-fascist editor Seward Collins (1899–1952), who was the former editor of *The Bookman* (see Stone, Jr. 1960; Diggins 1972; Tucker 2006; Copsey 2011). Before starting his collaboration with *The American Review*, Lowes wrote several reviews for *The Bookman*, devoting himself both to a strong defence of anti-Soviet literature and to a sarcastic criticism of pro-socialist and anti-capitalist writers.

Lowes's writings in *The American Review* cover all the years of the journal's brief life, from June 1933 to January 1937, and show an exasperated attempt to satisfy Collins's desire for his chimeric support to fascist and authoritarian movements. One can find the same words in praise of authoritarian principles, and of course in blame of 'works of a generally leftist and collectivist nature', in almost all Lowes's contributions. One of the best examples is Lowes's review of a pro-fascist biography of Napoleon III, *Napoleon III. The Modern Emperor* (1933), written by the far-right polygraph Robert Sencourt (pen name of Robert Esmonde Gordon George, 1890–1969), a close friend of T. S. Eliot and a Catholic supporter of Franco during the Spanish Civil War. Talking of a man who was, in Sencourt's words, 'in every sense the modern man … the man of the present hour', Lowes agreed with the biographer in identifying the French emperor as 'a forerunner of our modern dictators' (McCord Lowes 1934: 620–1):

> 'Plebiscites, dictatorship founded on direct national choice without the intermediary of parliaments … are among the governing ideas of 1933, exactly a hundred years after Louis Napoléon wrote them down and published them in his little yellow pamphlets'. And in fact, until a few months before his reign ended in disaster, Napoleon III stood firmly upon the authoritarian principle. He believed in a central and absolute authority; he believed that the masses should not be allowed to 'dominate men of ideas'; he believed in 'the free instinct of a people accepting the guidance of authority'. He put these beliefs into action by abolishing the French parliament … and by reigning for sixteen years as an absolute monarch. In this, and in a particular sense, he was indeed modern.

The same spirit dominates other of Lowes's reviews, even when they were not devoted to defend the monarchic principle, or to condemn collectivism, but only to praise the modern colonialist conquerors, to introduce the biographies of political leaders such as the Irish Prime Minister De Valera, to flatter American writers such as Ford Madox Ford, to discuss the great pities of American education or to exalt the values of rural America. Among Lowes' polemically engaged writings we may remember especially a sarcastic review of Bertrand Russell's *In Praise of Idleness* (1935), whose title is the quintessence of a heavy polemics: *Pious Hopes and Drunken Assumptions* (McCord Lowes 1935), and another one against John Strachey's *The Menace of Fascism* (1933), judged by Lowes just as a book 'devoted to explaining to the British workman why he is putting himself at the mercy of "Fascism", and why "Fascism" is bad', a thing of 'little immediate interest for American readers'.[6]

One can understand what such a reviewer might say about Huizinga and his denounce of the decline of Western civilization. Lowes blames the lack of a specific prescription for a cure of the modern cultural crisis, and especially the 'conspicuous prejudice' arising 'from an insufficient consideration of the very various and conflicting elements in the modern Fascist movements' (McCord Lowes 1936: 252). Anyway, his ideological orientation did not prevent Lowes to sufficiently resume the content and the scope of *In the Shadow of Tomorrow*, even if the reviewer was evidently disagreeing with 'Dr. Huizinga's explanation of the modern crisis', which he saw as 'in essence a simple one', which is the dead-end of almost complete anti-intellectualism and anti-rationalism reached by the Romantic movement, 'with a consequent abolition of moral values which no civilization can withstand' (McCord Lowes 1936: 252).

The impact of Huizinga's book on European culture: The French translation and Gabriel Marcel

Not only in America but also in Europe the book received mixed reviews. A German translation, made by Werner Kaegi, was published in Switzerland in 1935 (Huizinga 1935b; Huizinga 1948: 7–149; see Kaegi 1946; Strupp 2000; Krumm 2011: 157–68), and a Spanish translation soon appeared in 1936, in the *Biblioteca de Revista de Occidente* edited by José Ortega y Gasset (Huizinga 1936b). A French translation (1939–46) was published with a Preface by Gabriel Marcel and with the title *Incertitudes. Essai de diagnostic du mal dont souffre notre temps* ('Uncertainties. A Diagnostic Essay on the Illness of Our Time') (Huizinga 1939–46; see Boone 2008: 32).

Marcel agreed with Huizinga, sharing his point of view on the decline of Western civilization and stressing that the first merit of his little book was the steadfast courage with which the author wondered in the presence of the great paradoxes of the modern world. Marcel had no doubt that Huizinga was perfectly right in thinking that the crisis from which humanity suffered in those days was without a precedent in the past (see Marcel 1939–46: 7–8). The crisis, in Marcel's opinion as well as in Huizinga's view, was due to a generalized lack of faith in timeless values and un-discussed principles. The gradual disappearance of these values and norms, of which in most cases nothing but a purely verbal residue survived any longer, had as a tragic consequence the fact that the historical development, considered as a whole, had lost all meaning and no longer had a direction. '*Cette époque*', Marcel wrote, '*apparaît aux jeunes générations, dans une très grande partie de l'Europe, comme un âge sénile, et je ne crois pas exagérer beaucoup en disant qu'elles tendent à soumettre le credo démocrate et scientiste du XIXe siècle au même verdict que portent les nazis sur la république de Weimar*'.[7] That's why Marcel put an emphasis on the need for a new universalism, writing a passage that had a strong prophetic significance:[8]

> Ce n'est, dit à peu près M. Huizinga, que sur la base d'une conception métaphysique de la vie qu'il sera possible d'édifier une notion de vérité d'où se laissent dériver des normes morales indiscutées. On ne saurait mieux dire. Mais le mot métaphysique n'a de sens qu'à condition de viser un enjeu intelligible de la vie et d'impliquer par conséquent la restauration de l'antique notion de salut, d'un salut qui ne saurait venir du progrès entendu à la façon du XIXe siècle .... En d'autres termes, c'est l'universalisme qu'il faut restaurer – non sans avoir réfléchi sur les raisons profondes pour lesquelles le XIXe siècle involontairement l'a trahi, pour lesquelles plus précisément le rationalisme véhiculé par la Révolution française a frayé la voie à des particularismes qui s'érigèrent en mystique et en fait se mirent au service de l'irrationnel le plus destructeur. Mon diagnostic de philosophie qui ne contredit au reste en rien celui de M. Huizinga consisterait à déceler au cœur même de l'idée d'universel une ambiguïté qui peut devenir mortelle tant que la réflexion ne l'a pas mise à nu. Le triomphe, momentané, nous en sommes sûrs, de l'entreprise hitlérienne, en refaisant dans le mensonge et dans le sang une Europe que l'idéologie démocratique et wilsonienne n'avait su que dissoudre, nous présente comme une anticipation caricaturale, inversée et hideuse, d'un impérium qui s'établirait non sur des abstractions où fermente l'hypocrisie, mais sur l'ardente unité d'une foi. L'Europe est à jamais perdue, et avec elle tout ce qui peut donner à la vie son sens, son contenu, sa plénitude, si la Chrétienté une ne ressuscite pas sous des espèces encore impensables – après quelles convulsions, quelles hécatombes, quels séismes?

Marcel's call for a new spiritual climate was combined with the dual belief that any return to the past was impossible and that the achievements of science were to be retained, provided that they could be justified and substantiated by a moral revolution. Failing that, humanity could not but flow back to a bestial condition, seconded by the use of new tools of destruction and extermination, '*des jouets de mort dont l'homme ne sait encore se servir que pour diffuser l'hébétude et pour perfectionner les techniques d'extermination*'.[9]

The Italian readers under fascism and after the Second World War

In Italy a translation from the English edition, later attributed to Barbara Allason (1877–1968), was published in 1937 by the young Giulio Einaudi.[10] It seems that the Italian translation has to be assigned, instead, to one of Huizinga's best friends, the anti-fascist economist Luigi Einaudi, who was the father of the publisher Giulio and became the first president of the Italian Republic after the Second World War, from 1948 to 1955. We owe this information to a letter of 6 December 1937, where Huizinga says to Luigi Einaudi: 'It is only now I learn that you did the translation yourself.'[11] It had been Einaudi, in fact, who previously had asked Huizinga for a French or English translation, in order to take it as a basis for the Italian edition, for which Huizinga adapted the Preface written for other translations from the Dutch original edition.[12]

The Italian edition appeared with the title *La crisi della civiltà*, expressly approved by Huizinga.[13] It was under this title that the work was reviewed by Delio Cantimori after the Second World War, once the publisher Einaudi issued in 1962 its first reprint. Cantimori had already reviewed the German translation in 1936,[14] defining Huizinga's book 'a pathetic *laudatio temporis acti*' and referring to its author with a mocking attitude: 'Nothing satisfies him: it is the fate of writers who want to be concerned with politics without thinking that this is a serious matter, which does not admit the beautiful spirits nor the beautiful souls.'[15] Nothing more and nothing better could we have expected from the fascist Cantimori, who in the same year 1936 translated, introduced and published an anthology of writings of the Nazi theorist Carl Schmitt (Cantimori 1936b). What one could have expected instead, after more than a quarter century and from the post-communist Cantimori, was a retraction. But this never came, not even in 1962, when Cantimori wrote the introduction to the reprint of Einaudi's 1937 edition. That essay is so reticent that even today one cannot read it without feeling a legitimate disdain, before the revival of the reviewer's 'intolerance' and 'impatience', only falsely attenuated, and instead still lingering in spite of repeated and reverent praise for the 'memory of the great and ingenious historian, the elegant scholar, the refined writer, the brave and firm man' (Cantimori 1962: VII). I think the following passage is proof enough:[16]

> La posizione dello Huizinga è chiara: il suo punto di vista si può paragonare a quello di chi stia in una garitta di guardia elevata su tre pilastri, composti di materiali eterogenei, ma concorrenti nel dar stabilità alla sua base. Fuor di metafora: 1) Valori etici fondamentali del cristianesimo, in un senso molto vicino a quello del celebre *Perché non possiamo non dirci cristiani* del Croce; che ad alcuni puritani la concezione di Huizinga possa sembrare poco moderna e cattolicheggiante, e ad alcuni cattolici romani in senso tradizionale possa sembrare un po' troppo puritana, è cosa secondaria. 2) Patriottismo civico olandese, fatto di gusto per la lingua, il sentimento, i costumi, e di senso della tradizione; è un 'patriottismo del piccolo Stato' che si identifica in sostanza con quell'altro 'patriottismo europeo', riducibili l'uno e l'altro a un legame saldissimo con quella patria ideale cosmopolitica e liberale, abitata da quella aristocrazia intellettuale nella quale e per la quale operò e scrisse tanto spesso Huizinga. 3) Fedeltà ai criteri e ai valori tradizionali della tradizione filosofica e storiografica positiva e razionale, il che non escludeva, se pur aliena da prese di posizione confessionali, senso del religioso e del trascendente; fedeltà ai canoni della ricerca attenta e precisa e della oggettività e imparzialità, come pure dell'esame sistematico e spregiudicato del materiale che si è impreso a studiare, e della narrazione suggestiva ed evocativa .... Certo, nel libro di Huizinga ci son tante righe che appaiono profetiche. Ma la catarsi non è

> venuta come l'aspettava Huizinga: anche perché catarsi non c'è, una sola e unica catarsi, come molta gente, compreso lo Huizinga stesso, sembra ritenere ovvio e accettato che ci possa essere; e non c'è neppure una serie di catastrofi e di catarsi, come sanno gli storici. Tuttavia, non è poco, ripetiamo, aver fatto sentire quanto fosse immane la barbarie razzista incombente, presentendo gli orrori di quel che era alle porte, avvertendo tutti il meglio che si poteva 'gridando sui tetti'.

Cantimori's double review represents and synthesizes a debate that in Italy, if we except the worst examples,[17] had many lukewarm readers of Huizinga's book and few who were capable of understanding and appreciating its stern warning. Among the first ones one may recall Mario Manlio Rossi (1895–1971) and Vittorio Foa (1910–2008) (Rossi 1939; Foa 1998: 442–27 and 776–9; see Endrizzi 2006: 206–7), and also Ranuccio Bianchi Bandinelli (1900–75), who shared Huizinga's diagnosis, while blaming him because he did not have towards the future a new faith, that could be only 'of social nature' (Bianchi Bandinelli 1976: 45); among the other ones not only the anti-fascist intellectuals assembled in the rising federalist movement (Carta 2006: 216) but also conservative Catholics such as the Jesuit father Angelo Brucculeri (1879–1969), who wrote a favourable review in the journal *La civiltà cattolica* (Brucculeri 1938; see Endrizzi 2006: 208).

Things changed very little after the Second World War. With few exceptions, ambiguity remained the main characteristic of the Italian readers of Huizinga's historical and philosophical writings. After Carlo Antoni (Antoni 1940: 191–210), Carlo Morandi especially gave room to criticism in his introduction to the Italian translation of *Der Mensch und die Kultur*, Huizinga's failed conference in 1938 Vienna (Huizinga 1938). Blaming Huizinga for his 'lack of a strong theoretical basis', for his 'simplistic philosophy' and for his supposed contradictions, he repeated an ambiguous judgement, midway between appreciation for the author's humanism and emphasis on the limits of Huizinga's denounce of the crisis of Western civilization.[18] It was a wrong, deeply superficial, unjust criticism, misguided by a total misunderstanding of the role of the 'aesthetic element' in Huizinga's historiography, and by the ignorance of what 'the value of the human being' meant for a man who had been able to perceive the inner aspects (both moral and intellectual) of the social crisis and who in 1933, as rector of the University of Leiden, challenged Nazism by denying the participation at an international conference to Johann von Leers, who was famous for his anti-Semite theses (see de Boer 1993: XXXVII).

If we leave out a few relative exceptions (Cordiè 1941; Petrocchi 1944; Chabod 1948; Morpurgo Tagliabue 1949), it is only between the end of the 1960s and the beginning of the 1970s that Ovidio Capitani, in his introductions to Huizinga's autobiographical and methodological writings on history (Capitani 1967, 1974), gave 'the best interpretation' of Huizinga's work (Manselli 1973), blaming the 'substantially concord choir of criticisms and perplexities, that was extraneous to the opposed signs of contrasting ideologies' in Italy, before, during and after the Second World War (Capitani 1974: IX). He could remember that even a distinguished scholar such as Corrado Vivanti, reviewing in 1967 the Italian translation of Huizinga's *My Way to History*, blamed its adhesion 'to extremely retrogressive cultural positions, even professed between 1934 and 1937' (Vivanti 1967: 284). It was a condemnation, as Capitani wrote, 'say in the manner … Croce and Antoni and their minor followers were firing, even in the Fifties, the dissenting views about "historicism" of Italian idealistic philosophy'.[19]

More recently, Daniela Coli has put in relation the idea of Croce, that 'culture is more than civilization', with Huizinga's on the *Fundamentals of Culture*, stressing that there was an ideal type of *Kultur* shared by many personalities like Mann, Croce, Weber, Löwith, Wittgenstein, Sorel, Aron and Huizinga (Coli 2002: 39; see Weintraub 1969). And talking about the common membership of Croce, Mann, Ortega y Gasset and Huizinga to a school of thought that the centre had the idea of freedom, Girolamo Cotroneo has underlined that in 1935 Huizinga wrote to denounce 'the danger of cultural irrationalism', and to affirm that 'it would not come as a surprise to anyone if tomorrow the madness gave way to a frenzy':[20]

> Intorno a questi autori, i quali, come Croce, denunziavano la 'rozzezza' e la 'stupidità' dei tempi (ma anche la loro ferocia: nel 1930 Croce parlava dell''odierno antistoricismo', impregnato di attivismo, 'tutto sfrenatezza di egoismo o durezza di comando', il quale 'par che celebri un'orgia o un culto satanico'); intorno a questi autori, dunque, ha finito con il crearsi – si pensi al giudizio che nel 1936 Delio Cantimori dava di Huizinga … – una triste leggenda: che alla resa dei conti, essi fossero – magari 'oggettivamente' – filofascisti; dimenticando o trascurando il fatto che la loro analisi, anche se coinvolgeva spesso, soprattutto in Huizinga (ma anche in Ortega e in Croce) il comunismo (sovietico), era soprattutto diretta contro l'incultura, la volgarità intellettuale di cui il fascismo – come l'uomo-massa di Ortega – menava vanto. Ben altri erano allora gli autori che alimentavano la cultura fascista o criptofascista: basta ricordare i nomi di Oswald Spengler, di Ernst Jünger, di Carl Schmitt…

Conclusion

Opposition to Carl Schmitt and to his *Der Begriff des Politischen* (1927) characterizes Huizinga's book.[21] We may look at the chapters entitled *Life and Battle* and *Regna Regnis Lupi?* which constitute a real essay on the crisis of politics and public law tradition in the West. Against Schmitt's polemological theory of law and politics, Huizinga recalls the 'extremely simple reasoning' by which the German theorist eliminates from interstate relationship 'any and all elements of human malice', by the vindication 'of the impeccability of political hostility in general or, in other words, of the good right of a state to wage war for its own interests' (Huizinga 1936a: 118–19). Schmitt's simplistic reasoning is therefore laid bare and deprived of a true conceptual significance in the close Huizinga's rebuttal (Huizinga 1936a: 119–22):

> To do this all that is necessary is to construct an *a priori* which places the State as an absolute independent object on a level of philosophical equivalence with the spiritual domain to which the concept of truth and justice belong. This is what Carl Schmitt, with great ingenuity, has set out to do in his treatise, *Der Begriff des*

> *Politischen*. The discussion opens with the following words: 'The essential political distinction is that between Friend and Foe. It gives human actions and motives their political meaning. All political actions and motives can, in ultimate instance, be traced to this distinction. In so far as the opposition is not to be derived from other characteristics, it corresponds as a political concept to the relatively independent characteristics of other contrasts: good and wicked in the ethical domain, beautiful and ugly in the æsthetic, useful and harmful in the economic; it is, at any rate, an absolute category. . .'. Now, it seems to me that in the construction of the political as an absolute category we have a case of an express and implicitly admitted *petitio principii* .... If it were admissible that in general the opposition friend-foe were of the same category as the others mentioned above, it would indeed follow that in the political field for which this opposition is held to be decisive, the friend-foe opposition would over-ride all other oppositions. ... Is not this over-rating the power of the logical argument as such, in a manner which is strongly reminiscent of the infancy of scholasticism? Is not the thinking of this shrewd jurist from the outset caught in the most vicious of vicious circles?

Caught in the most vicious of vicious circles, Schmitt – as a prophet of political totalitarianism standing by the advocates of war for war's sake – could not recognize 'that the theory of the absolute nature of the political, rooted in and governed by the friend-foe opposition', meant 'a defection from the spirit leading far beyond the sphere of a naïve animalism to a Satanism which sets up evil as a beacon and a guiding star for a misguided humanity' (Huizinga 1936a: 127). It was, if not 'the end of law', as in one of his vicious verbal jokes: the end of the Western legal tradition. That's why Huizinga also attacks directly the vulgar concept of the omnipotence of the State and of the so-called Reason of State, depriving once more of every significance Schmitt's key-formula 'friend-foe' (Huizinga 1936a: 143–4):

> 'The State can do no wrong'. So runs a political theory which at present enjoys a popularity extending far beyond the sphere of the Modern Despotism. The State, according to this view, cannot be considered bound by the moral standards of human society. All attempts to submit it to the verdict if ethical judgment must break down on the absolute independence of the political as such. The State stands outside all ethics. One might ask: above all ethics too? Perhaps the theorist of the amoral State will avoid affirming this. He will take recourse to the construction of the political as an absolute category solely governed by the friend-foe opposition, that is to say by an opposition which merely expresses danger and obstruction and the striving to eliminate them. For as we have pointed out before, 'friend' in this opposition means no more than potential foe. The State must be solely judged, therefore, by its achievement in the exercise of Might. Though the particular construction is novel, the theory of the amoral State itself is anything but new. With more or less justification it can be said to derive from thinkers like Machiavelli, Hobbes, Fichte and Hegel. In history itself the theory finds seemingly valuable support. For it is true that history shows little else than greed, lust for power, self-interest, and fear, as the motives governing the actions of States against

> and amongst each other. The age of systematized absolutism summed up such all motives under the term *raison d'état.*

Huizinga recalls that in former centuries the contrast between *ethos* and *kratos* (to phrase it in the same terms of Friedrich Meinecke's *Staatsräson*) (Meinecke 1924), or between Christian political theories and practice of power, was viewed as the perennial tragedy of violence and injustice 'of a State which failed to sanctify itself'; but the principle that States and governments owed the duty to live after the precepts of justice remained unimpaired: 'The State could not be permitted to dissociate itself from morals' (Huizinga 1936a: 145). That's why as a reaction against the early modern 'realistic' political theories, a new conception of international law and order grew up on the foundations of Christian ethics and juridical theory, regarding the nations 'as the members of a community in duty bound to observe the same mutual respect and rules of conduct as law demands from individual members of a community of human beings' (Huizinga 1936a: 145–6).

If Grotius's 'shining example' didn't prevent the theorists of political amorality to emphatically deny 'both the Christian and the juridical grounds for a moral law and a code of duty for the State' (Huizinga 1936a: 146), it allowed Huizinga, in a close dialogue with Gerhard Ritter, to discuss the 'moral autonomy' of the secular State, an expression that Ritter himself had employed in order to define the historical background of the Reformation in Germany. Huizinga was impressed in a very favourable way by Ritter's dictum, that the 'age-old tradition' had not yet completely disappeared from English politics while the great Continental nations generally admitted 'the purely biological … character of all striving for worldly power without any great qualms of conscience', were 'all essentially medieval-Christian thoughts' (Huizinga 1936a: 147). (In a letter Ritter made clear to Huizinga 'that the term "moral autonomy" should not be understood as implying an unqualified acceptance of the amoral State on his part', and furthermore, that he regarded 'the persistence of mediaeval conceptions of "eternal right" in English political thought rather as a superiority over Continental ideas than as a sign of backwardness'.)[22]

Huizinga's idea of the crisis of the Western legal tradition appears with a major evidence at this point, where he blames the ominous notes coming from the voice of practical politics of his time: 'On the occasion of the solemn installation of a new chair for German law', he recalls, 'the Reich Commissioner for Justice is reported by the Press to have stated "that it was not true that one could make politics by appealing to a certain idealistic justice. It was high time to have done with the ludicrous theory that anything less than the hard necessity of assuring the position of the State could determine what is and what is not justice. The earth belongs to the heroic, not to the decadent!"' (Huizinga 1936a: 149–50). 'The State, then, according to these views', Huizinga concludes, 'may do anything and everything. No falsehood, no deception, no breach of trust, no cruelty, whether against outsiders or nationals, can be held against it as wrong when it serves its own ends thereby. It may combat the enemy with any means useful to its purpose and go to any lengths, including such fiendish extremes as bacterial warfare' (Huizinga 1936a: 150). The final message of Huizinga's book, that one more time sounds like a prophecy, goes to the most dangerous of all tendencies in the crisis of the Western civilization, as 'the denial of every principle of truth, honour and justice as *universal* human principles' (Huizinga 1936a: 152–3).

Notes

1 See, for instance, what Huizinga says about the *Normandie*, the gigantic French ocean liner which entered into service on 29 May 1935 and held the Blue Riband for the fastest transatlantic crossing, taken by Huizinga as an example of puerilism (Huizinga 1936a: 171).

2 Richard 2012: 243. The final quotation into single quotation marks is from Paul Valéry's opening address (reprinted in Valéry 2010: 171).

3 Huizinga 1950: 261–2. ('The history I like, is not this parade of history that sounds the bugle and pretends to give lessons to mankind for the future. I like the past itself and, basically, I think the past thousand years ago is not much farther from us than the past today, in the time we walked into this room.') All translations mine.

4 Huizinga 1950: 266. ('Today's Europe is more exposed to a force that threats it of a return to barbarism .... Technical progress has allowed a speed and an organizational strength of the masses of which benefit the madness and crime as well or better than the wisdom and law .... A worrying weakening of ethical principles in the lives of nations as in that of individuals, has continued to emerge. When comparing the ideal professed by the nations of the present time to the conceptions that animated the great epochs of the past, the contrast is obvious. It is the economic well-being, the political power, the purity of race, who took the place of the generous aspirations of freedom or truth of the past. Realism, it will be said, instead of illusions and fictions. The fact remains that these old concepts had in general an obvious ethical value. It is the practice of morality, after all, by communities as by individuals, which alone can heal our poor world so rich and so infirm.')

5 On Lewis Mumford (1895–1990) and his optimistic idea of humanity as 'organic humanism', see Miller 1986; Miller 1989; Hughes and Hughes 1990; Halton 1995.

6 McCord Lowes 1933: 493. See Thomas 1973; Thompson 1993; Hodgson 2010; Rees 2016: 188: 'The publication of John Strachey's *The Menace of Fascism* was the signal for many echoing alarms and excursions on this theme.'

7 Marcel 1939–1946: 9–10. ('This time appears to younger generations, in a very large part of Europe, as a senile age, and I do not think there is much exaggeration in saying that they tend to subject the democratic and scientistic creed of the nineteenth century to the same verdict that Nazis give on the Weimar Republic.')

8 Marcel 1939–1946: 12–13. ('It is, nearly said Mr. Huizinga, only on the basis of a metaphysical conception of life that it will be possible to build a notion of truth from which to derive undisputed moral standards. We cannot say it better. But the word *metaphysical* has meaning only provided it aims to an intelligible challenge of life and to involve therefore the restoration of the ancient concept of salvation, a salvation that could not come from progress as conceived in the nineteenth century .... In other words, it is universalism that must be restored – not without having thought about the underlying reasons why the nineteenth century unwittingly betrayed it, why specifically rationalism conveyed by the French Revolution spawned the way to particularities that were erected in mystique and actually began serving the most destructive irrationality. My diagnosis of philosophy that after all

doesn't contradict in any way that of Mr. Huizinga would be to detect at the heart of the universal idea an ambiguity that can become fatal as long as thought has not exposed it. The triumph, momentary, we are sure of Hitler's enterprise, by remaking through lies and blood a Europe that democratic and Wilsonian ideology could only dissolve, appears to us as a caricatural anticipation, reversed and hideous, of an imperium which would establish itself not on abstractions where hypocrisy ferments, but on the fiery unity of faith. Europe is forever lost, and with it everything that can give life its meaning, its content, its fullness, if Christianity does not resurrect in still unthinkable forms – after what convulsions, what slaughter, what earthquakes?')

9 Marcel 1939–1946: 14. ('death toys which man still doesn't know how to use, except to spread the stupidity and perfecting the extermination techniques').

10 Huizinga 1937; a revised edition was made in 1938; the attribution of the Italian translation to Barbara Allason appeared only in Huizinga 1962.

11 Johan Huizinga to Luigi Einaudi, Leiden, 6 December 1937 (Document nr. 11, in Endrizzi 2006 and Carta 2006. (With some errors of the Editors, they believe, for instance, that a French translation never appeared): 'My dear Einaudi, You could not have offered me the Italian edition of my little book in a more delightful way .... So both my wife and I want to express our warmest thanks to you and to your son. It is only now I learn that you did the translation yourself. This is an honour quite weighing down the small boy I just shore of. The printing looks nice and I like the simple title page and cover. If you should see reviews of the book worth reading either for blame or praise, I should be grateful for being enabled to read them.')

12 Johan Huizinga to Luigi Einaudi, Leiden, 13–15 September 1937, with attached the English text of the Preface for the Italian edition (Documents nr. 8 *a–b* and nr. 9, in Endrizzi 2006 and Carta 2006): 'My dear Einaudi, It was a pleasant surprise to me to receive the press-proofs of the translation of my book. I had not yet expected them at all .... As far as I can make out at a rapid glance the translation has been admirably done. There is no French edition! At least I do not know anything of it. You may call the Italian edition something peculiar, because it is the only one made after the English text, which I consider as an improvement of the original. It was made by my son, in constant collaboration with me. Shall give you the new preface I wrote for the Czech and Norwegian edition under way of publication, and shall try to add a phrase for the Italian public. Your son may expect it in a few days, or rather I shall send it you to Dogliani'; 'I wrote the Preface yesterday and am including it. If it does not suit you, especially the phrase you wanted, please suggest alteration.'

13 Johan Huizinga to Luigi Einaudi, Leiden, 3 October 1937 (Document nr. 10, in Endrizzi 2006 and Carta 2006): 'My dear Einaudi, I fully approve the frontispiece you sent me. The original edition published October 1935 by H. D. Tjeenk Willink & Zoon, Haarlem beard the title: In de schaduwen van morgen, een diagnose van het geestelijk Lijden van onzen tijd. Suppose you got all right my approval of the proofs you sent me. Yours cordially, J. Huizinga.'

14 On Cantimori's controversial cultural parable see Berengo 1967; Miccoli 1970; and Sasso 2002: 178; more recently see D'Elia 2007; Simoncelli 2008; Di Rienzo and Perfetti 2009 and Chiantera Stutte 2011.

15 Cantimori 1936a: 383; Cantimori 1962: VIII (reprinted in Cantimori 1991: 315); see also Cantimori 1971: 343–64.

16 Cantimori 1962: XXIX–XXX and XXXI–XXXII. ('Huizinga's position is clear: his point of view is like that of someone who is in a high guard sentry box on three pil-

lars, composed of heterogeneous materials, but competing in giving stability to its base. Metaphors aside: 1) fundamental ethical values of Christianity, in a way very close to those of the famous *Perché non possiamo non dirci cristiani* of Croce; that to some Puritans Huizinga's conception may seem a little modern and pro-Catholic, and to some Roman Catholics in the traditional sense may seem a bit too Puritan, that's secondary. 2) Dutch civic patriotism made of taste for the language, the sentiment, the costumes and the sense of tradition; it is a "patriotism of the small state" which in essence is the same with that other "European patriotism", both reducible to a very solid relationship with the ideal cosmopolitan and liberal country, inhabited by the intellectual aristocracy in which and for which so often Huizinga worked and wrote. 3) Loyalty to the criteria and values of positive and rational philosophical and historiographical tradition, which did not exclude, though devoid of confessional claims, the sense of the religious and the transcendent; fidelity to the canons of careful and precise research and objectivity and impartiality, as well as the systematic and free examination of the material that one is studying, and the striking and evocative narration .... Of course, in Huizinga's book there are so many lines that appear prophetic. But the catharsis has not come as Huizinga expected: because there is no catharsis, the one and the same catharsis that many people, including Huizinga himself, think is obvious and accepted that there may be; and there is even a series of disasters and catharsis, as historians know. However, it's not without importance, we repeat, that he did feel how huge was the looming racist barbarity, foreseeing the horrors of what was coming, warning everybody the best that he could "shouting on rooftops"').

17 Capasso 1943, remembered by Garin 1953: XXVIII, only as 'a document of a mentality and of a custom'.

18 Morandi 1947: XX–XXI. For a similar criticism see Garin 1953: VII and XV, with judgements that oscillate between praise ('Huizinga ... was the most noble defender of freedom in dark times, from his chair, in his books, in his prisony') and blame, mostly underlining Huizinga's 'lack of logic strongness', 'fundamental theoretical weakness', and the 'great fragility' of works like *La crisi della civiltà* and *Homo ludens*.

19 Capitani 1974: IX. Similar views, although expressed less explicitly, in Eco 1973.

20 Cotroneo 2002: 29–30. ('Around these authors, who, like Croce, denounced the "brutality" and "stupidity" of the times (but also their ferocity: in 1930 Croce spoke of "today's anti-historicism", impregnated with activism, "all licentiousness of selfishness or command hardness", which "seems to celebrate an orgy or a satanic cult"); around these authors, therefore, a sad legend has ended up being created – think of the judgement given on Huizinga in 1936 by Delio Cantimori ... – that at the end of the day, these authors were – maybe "objectively" – pro-fascist; forgetting or ignoring the fact that their analysis, even if it often involved (Soviet) communism, especially in Huizinga (but also in Ortega and Croce), was primarily directed against the lack of culture, the intellectual vulgarity of which fascism – as Ortega's mass-man – was the leading boast. Others indeed were the authors who fed the fascist or crypto-fascist culture: just remember the names of Oswald Spengler, Ernst Jünger, Carl Schmitt.')

21 Huizinga read it in its third edition (Schmitt 1933), the year Schmitt joined the Nazi Party; see Schmitt 2007. On Schmitt's controversial life and works see Scheuerman 1999 and Müller 2003. See also Krumm 2011: 227.

22 Huizinga 1936a: note *. Huizinga refers to Ritter 1934.

References

Antoni, C. (1940), *Dallo storicismo alla sociologia*, Firenze: Sansoni.

Berengo, M. (1967), 'La ricerca storica di Delio Cantinori', *Rivista storica italiana*, 79: 902–43.

Berman, E. (1936), 'Review of H. F. Simon, *Revolution. Whither Bound?* (New York: Farrar & Rinehart, 1935)', *The Annals of the American Political Academy of Political and Social Science*, 187: 221–5.

Bianchi Bandinelli, R. (1976), *Dal diario di un borghese*, Roma: Editori Riuniti.

de Boer, W. (1993), 'Prefazione', in J. Huizinga (ed.), *Le immagini della storia. Scritti 1905–1941, a cura di W. de Boer*, XIII–XLI, Torino: Einaudi.

Boone, M. (2008), 'L'Automne du Moyen Âge: Johan Huizinga et Henri Pirenne', in P. Moreno and G. Palumbo (eds), *Autour du XVe siècle. Journées d'étude en l'honneur d'Alberto Varvaro*, 28–42, Genève: Droz.

Brucculeri, A. (1938), 'La crisi odierna', *La civiltà cattolica*, 89: 326–39.

Cantimori, D. (1936a), 'Review of J. Huizinga, *Im Schatten von Morgen. Eine Diagnose des kulturellen Leidens unserer Zeit*. Deutsch von W. Kaegi (Bern – Leipzig: Gotthelf Verlag)', *Leonardo*, 7: 383.

Cantimori, D. (1936b), 'Note sul Nazionalsocialismo', in C. Schmitt, *Principi politici del Nazionalsocialismo. Scritti scelti e tradotti da D. Cantimori*, 1–42, Firenze: Sansoni.

Cantimori, D. (1962), 'Nelle ombre del domani', in J. Huizinga (ed.), *La crisi della civiltà. Saggio introduttivo di D. Cantimori. Traduzione di B. Allason*, VII–XXXII, Torino: Einaudi.

Cantimori, D. (1971), *Storici e storia*, Torino: Einaudi.

Cantimori, D. (1991), *Politica e storia contemporanea, a cura di L. Mangoni*, Torino: Einaudi.

Capasso, A. (1943), 'Errori di Huizinga. Cattive e sintomatiche premesse di un pensatore del "vecchio mondo"', *Augustea. Rivista imperiale del nostro tempo*, 18: 50–2.

Capitani, O. (1967), 'Introduzione', in J. Huizinga (ed.), *La mia via alla storia. Traduzione di P. Bernardini Marzolla*, V–LI, Bari: Laterza. Reprinted in Capitani, O. (1979), *Medioevo passato prossimo. Appunti storiografici tra due guerre e molte crisi*, 9–53, Bologna: Il Mulino.

Capitani, O. (1974), 'Introduzione', in J. Huizinga (ed.), *La scienza storica. Traduzione di P. Bernardini Marzolla*, VII–XXX, Roma and Bari: Laterza. Reprinted in Capitani, O. (1979), *Medioevo passato prossimo. Appunti storiografici tra due guerre e molte crisi*, 55–73, Bologna: Il Mulino.

Capitani, O. (1979), *Medioevo passato prossimo. Appunti storiografici tra due guerre e molte crisi*, Bologna: Il Mulino.

Carta, P. (2006), 'Politica e morale ne *La crisi della civiltà* di Johan Huizinga', *L'épreuve de la nouveauté, Laboratoire italien*, 6: 213–36.

Chabod, F. (1948), 'Johan Huizinga', *Rivista storica italiana*, 2: 342–4.

Chiantera Stutte, P. (2011), *Delio Cantimori. Un intellettuale del Novecento*, Roma: Carocci.

Coli, D. (2002), *Il filosofo, i libri, gli editori: Croce, Laterza e la cultura europea*, Napoli: Editoriale Scientifica.

Colie, R. L. (1964), 'Johan Huizinga and the Task of Cultural History', *The American Historical Review*, 69: 607–30.

Copsey, N. (2011), 'Communists and the Inter-War Anti-Fascist Struggle in the United States and Britain', *Labour History Review*, 76: 184–206.

Cordiè, C. (1941), 'Immagini di Huizinga', *Letteratura*, 5 (20): 13–22.

Cotroneo, G. (2002), 'Introduzione. Una teoria filosofica della libertà', in B. Croce (ed.), *La religione della libertà. Antologia degli scritti politici, a cura di G. Cotroneo*, Soveria Mannelli: Rubbettino.

D'Elia, N. (2007), *Delio Cantimori e la cultura politica tedesca (1927–1940)*, Roma: Viella.

Diggins, J. P. (1972), *Mussolini and Fascism: The View from America*, Princeton: Princeton University Press.

Di Rienzo, E. and Perfetti, F., eds. (2009), *Delio Cantimori e la cultura politica del novecento*, Firenze: Le Lettere.

Eco, U. (1973), '"Homo ludens" oggi', in J. Huizinga (ed.), *Homo Ludens. Traduzione di C. van Schendel*, VII–XXVII, Torino: Einaudi.

Endrizzi, L. (2006), 'La crisi della civiltà in Italia: l'epistolario Einaudi-Huizinga', *L'épreuve de la nouveauté, Laboratoire italien*, 6: 201–11.

Foa, V. (1998), *Lettere della Giovinezza dal carcere 1935–1943, a cura di F. Montevecchi*, Torino: Einaudi.

Garin, E. (1953), 'Introduzione', in J. Huizinga (ed.), *L'autunno del Medioevo. Traduzione di B. Jasink*, 2nd edn, VII–XXXI, Firenze: Sansoni.

Halton, E. (1995), *Bereft of Reason*, Chicago: University of Chicago Press.

Hodgson, K. (2010), *Fighting Fascism: The British Left and the Rise of Fascism, 1919–1939*, Manchester: Manchester University Press.

Hughes, T. P. and Hughes, A. C., eds. (1990), *Lewis Mumford: Public Intellectual*, New York: Oxford University Press.

Huizinga, J. (1934), 'Discours sur l'avenir de l'esprit européen', in *L'avenir de l'esprit européen (Entretiens de Paris, 16–18 octobre 1933)*, 64–5, Paris: Institut International de Coopération Intellectuelle. Reprinted in Huizinga, J. (1950), *Verzamelde Werken, 7, Geschiedwetenschap. Hedendaagsche cultuur*, 261–8, Haarlem: Tjeenk Willink.

Huizinga, J. (1935a), *In de schaduwen van morgen. Een diagnose van het geestelijk lijden van onzen tijd*, Haarlem: H. D. Tjeenk Willink & Zoon. Reprinted in Huizinga, J. (1950), *Verzamelde Werken, 7, Geschiedwetenschap. Hedendaagsche cultuur*, 313–428, Haarlem: Tjeenk Willink.

Huizinga, J. (1935b), *Im Schatten von Morgen. Eine Diagnose des kulturellen Leidens unserer Zeit. Deutsch von W. Kaegi*, Bern and Leipzig: Gotthelf Verlag.

Huizinga, J. (1936a, repr. 1964), *In the Shadow of Tomorrow. Translated from the Dutch by J. H. Huizinga*, New York: W. W. Norton & Company.

Huizinga, J. (1936b), *Entre las sombras del mañana. Diagnóstico de la enfermedad cultural del nustro tiempo. Traducción del holandés por M. de Meyere*, Madrid: Revista de Occidente.

Huizinga, J. (1937), *La crisi della civiltà*, Torino: Einaudi.

Huizinga, J. (1938), *Der Mensch und die Kultur*, Stockholm: Bermann-Fischer Verlag.

Huizinga, J. (1939–1946), *Incertitudes. Essai de diagnostic du mal dont souffre notre temps. Préface de G. Marcel. Traduit du Néerlandais par J. Roebroek, S. J.*, Paris: Librairie de Médicis and Bruxelles: Presses de Belgique.

Huizinga, J. (1948), *Schriften zur Zeitkritik*, Zürich: Occident-Verlag and Brüssel: Pantheon.

Huizinga, J. (1950), *Verzamelde Werken, 7, Geschiedwetenschap. Hedendaagsche cultuur*, Haarlem: Tjeenk Willink.

Huizinga, J. (1962), *La crisi della civiltà. Saggio introduttivo di D. Cantimori. Traduzione di B. Allason*, Torino: Einaudi.

Kaegi, W. (1946), 'Das historische Werk Johan Huizingas', in *Historische Meditationen*, vol. II, 257–85, Zürich: Fretz & Wasmuth.

Kammen, M. (1987), *Selvages & Biases: The Fabric of History in American Culture*, Ithaca and London: Cornell University Press.

Krumm, C. (2011), *Johan Huizinga, Deutschland und die Deutschen. Begegnung und Auseinandersetzung mit dem Nachbarn*, Münster, New York, München, and Berlin: Waxmann.

Manselli, R. (1973), 'Huizinga, Johan', in *Enciclopedia dantesca*, 3, 301, Roma: Istituto della Enciclopedia Italiana.

Marcel, G. (1939–1946), 'Préface', in J. Huizinga (ed.), *Incertitudes. Essai de disgnostic du mal dont souffre notre temps. Traduit du Néerlandais par J. Roebroek, S. J.*, 7–14, Paris: Librairie de Médicis and Bruxelles: Presses de Belgique.

McCord Lowes, M. (1933), 'Mr. Strachey's "Fascism"', *The American Review*, 489–93.

McCord Lowes, M. (1934), 'The Blind Emperor, Napoleon III', *The American Review*, 620–4.

McCord Lowes, M. (1935), 'Pious Hopes and Drunken Assumptions', *The American Review*, 236–41.

McCord Lowes, M. (1936), 'The Modern Disease', *The American Review*, 251.

Meinecke, F. (1924), *Die Idee der Staatsräson in der neueren Geschichte*, München and Berlin: R. Oldenbourg.

Messner, A. C. (2015), 'Transforming Chinese Hearts, Minds, and Bodies in the Name of Progress, Civility, and Civilization', in M. Pernau et al. (ed.), *Civilizing Emotion. Concepts in Nineteenth-Century Asia* and *Europe*, 231–47, Oxford: Oxford University Press.

Miccoli, G. (1970), *Delio Cantimori*, Torino: Giulio Einaudi Editore.

Midglay, A. (2012), 'Cultural History and the World of Johan Huizinga', *Saber and Scroll*, 1: 109–22.

Miller, D. L., ed. (1986), *The Lewis Mumford Reader*, New York: Pantheon Books.

Miller, D. L. (1989), *Lewis Mumford. A Life*, New York: Weidenfeld & Nicolson.

Morandi, C. (1947), 'Prefazione', in J. Huizinga (ed.), *L'uomo e la cultura. Traduzione di U. Arlotta*, XI–XXII, Firenze: La Nuova Italia.

Morpurgo Tagliabue, G. (1949), 'Le opinioni sulla storia di J. Huizinga', *Rivista di storia della filosofia*, 4: 104–17.

Müller, J.-W. (2003), *A Dangerous Mind: Carl Schmitt in Post-War European Thought*, New Haven and London: Yale University Press.

Mumford, L. (1936), 'The Shadow of Yesterday', *The New Republic*, 30 September 1936: 230–1.

Petrocchi, M. (1944), 'Ricchezze di Johan Huizinga', in R. Chiacchella and G. F. Rossi (eds), *L'uomo e la storia. Studi in onore di M. Petrocchi*, 139–42, Bologna: Zanichelli.

Rees, P. (2016), 'Changing Interpretations of British Fascism: A Bibliographical Survey', in K. Lunn and R. C. Thurlow (eds), *British Fascism. Essays on the Radical Right in Inter-War Britain*, 187–204, London: Routledge.

Richard, A.-I. (2012), 'Intellectual Cooperation and the Spirit of Europe, 1933–1945', in M. Hewitson and M. D'Auria (eds), *Europe in Crisis: Intellectuals and the European Idea, 1917–1957*, 243–56, Oxford: Berghahn Books.

Ritter, G. (1934), 'Die Ausprägung deutscher und westeuropäischer Geistesart im konfessionellen Zeitalter', *Historische Zeitschrift*, 149: 240–52.

Rival, P. (1930), *The Madcap Queen: The Story of Marguerite of Navarre. Translated from the French by M. McCord Lowes*, New York and London: Putnam.

Rossi, M. M. (1939), 'Review of J. Huizinga. 1937. *La Crisi della Civiltà* (Torino: Einaudi)', *Nuova Rivista Storica*, 23: 144–6.

Sasso, G. (2002), *Il guardiano della storiografia. Profilo di Federico Chabod e altri saggi*, Bologna: Il Mulino.
Scheuerman, W. E. (1999), *Carl Schmitt: The End of Law*, Lanham, Boulder, New York, and Oxford: Rowman & Littlefield Publishers.
Schmitt, C. (1933), *Der Bregriff des Politischen*, Hamburg: Hanseatische Verlagsanstalt.
Schmitt, C. (2007), *The Concept of Politics. Translated and with an Introduction by G. Schwab. With a Foreword by T. B. Strong and Notes by L. Strauss*, Chicago: The University of Chicago Press.
Seideman, D. (1986), *The New Republic: A Voice of Modern Liberalism*, New York: Praeger.
Sheng-Cheng (1930), *A Son of China: Translated from the French by M. McCord Lowes. Preface by P. Valéry*, New York: W. W. Norton & Company.
Simoncelli, P. (2008), *Cantimori e il libro mai edito. Il movimento nazionalsocialista dal 1919 al 1933*, Firenze: Le Lettere.
Spofford Morgan, B. (1936), 'A Choice of Revolutions', *The Saturday Review*, 16: 23.
Stone, Jr., A. E. (1960), 'Seward Collins and the American Review: Experiment in Pro-Fascism, 1933–37', *American Quarterly*, 12: 3–19.
Strupp, C. (2000), *Johan Huizinga*, Göttingen: Vandenhoeck & Ruprecht.
Thomas, H. (1973), *John Strachey*, London: Eyre Methuen.
Thompson, N. (1993), *John Strachey: An Intellectual Biography*, London: Macmillan.
Tucker, M. J. (2006), *And Then They Loved Him: Seward Collins and the Chimera of an American Fascism*, New York: Peter Lang.
Valéry, P. (2010), 'L'Avenir de l'esprit européen', in P. Valéry (ed.), *Souvenirs et réflexions. Édition établie, présentée et annotée par M. Jarrety*, 171, Paris: Bartillat.
Vivanti, C. (1967), 'Review of J. Huizinga, *La mia via alla storia*. Traduzione di P. Bernardini Marzolla. Introduzione di O. Capitani (Bari: Laterza)', *Rivista storica italiana*, 79: 280–5.
Weintraub, K. J. (1969), *Visions of Culture: Voltaire, Guizot, Burckhardt, Lamprecht, Huizinga, Ortega y Gasset*, Chicago: The University of Chicago Press.
Wesseling, H. L. (2002), 'From Cultural Historian to Cultural Critic: Johan Huizinga and the Spirit of the 1930s', *European Review*, 10: 185–499.

11

Roman Law as Wisdom: Justice and Truth, Honour and Disappointment in Franz Wieacker's Ideas on Roman Law

Ville Erkkilä[1]

Introduction

Franz Wieacker's *Privatrechtsgeschichte der Neuzeit* (1952) is a seminal legal–historical work on twentieth-century Europe from one of the greatest Romanists of our time. In this book Wieacker, with incomparable sophistication, knitted together his works and learning from preceding decades in order to illustrate not only the legal history of modern Europe but also the influence of Roman law in the Continent's destiny. While preparing his magnum opus, Wieacker lived through the social and political upheaval of Germany: National Socialism, the Second World War and the 'Point Zero' of post-war German society. Thus, *Privatrechtsgeschichte* is the end result of a decades-long interaction between the scholar, the tradition of Roman law and the disarray of social structures.

Wieacker's tool for understanding and categorizing the social phenomena he personally experienced was always his ideas on Roman law. With the help of this idealized form of thinking he attempted to explain new ideological streams, the shifting relations between politics and justice, as well as concrete changes in his position as a lawyer, scholar and citizen. In this chapter, I will review Wieacker's works as a means of making sense of the turbulent social reality of a scholar, not merely the jurisprudential context but also the feeling of social prestige and disappointment. In practice, my hermeneutical task is conducted via scrutinizing Wieacker's relation to two other theorists of the twentieth century, namely Carl Schmitt and Hans-Georg Gadamer. This chapter scrutinizes the meanings – on the one hand shifting and on the other hand enduring – that Wieacker attached to Roman law in the light of the social and historical circumstances which he faced as a lawyer, scholar and German citizen. Wieacker's relation to the thoughts of Schmitt and Gadamer are examples of different usages of the idea of Roman law and of the connotations associated with it during the turbulent twentieth century.

Like most of the prominent twentieth-century scholars of Roman law, Wieacker witnessed at first hand the collapse of traditional German society. But unlike Fritz Pringsheim, David Daube and Fritz Schulz, he did not experience exile. On the contrary, he was able to stay in totalitarian Germany, publish works dealing with Roman law and concurrently even advance in his career. It is not accurate to categorize Wieacker as a supporter of National Socialism, but he had to, and he was willing to, reconcile with some of the ideological streams of the Third Reich. However, after the Second World War, it was Wieacker who became perhaps the most renowned proponent of the idea of a pure and shared European legal heritage founded on Roman law (Winkler 2014; Behrends 1995).

It is difficult to overstate the influence of Wieacker's contribution to the discipline. Moreover, his works continue to have an effect in the fields of Continental legal history and legal hermeneutics. The shift in Wieacker's intellectual context – from an acknowledged scientist in a fascist society to a leading voice in the post-war search for sustaining the premises of European justice – seems to necessitate a similar abrupt change in the perennial principles guiding the scholar's research stance. In Wieacker's case, however, no such transformation took place. From his 1937 inaugural lecture 'Vom Römischen Juristen' to the second edition of his magnum opus *Privatrechtsgeschichte der Neuzeit* in 1967, his personal view on the essence of the fundamental virtues of liberty, communality and social justice did not really alter. Moreover, he never ceased to emphasize that within the European legal tradition these virtues were a reflection of the historical paragon of 'true Roman jurisprudence'.[2]

To Wieacker, Roman law in its purest form was an embodiment and expression of a superior model of thinking which had surfaced in the later Roman Republic. He perceived the jurisprudence of the later Republic as a result of a historically exceptional interplay between socially originated virtues and legal craftsmanship which produced authoritative, just norms for society. The legal reasoning of Rome's 'great jurists' managed to combine the collective 'experience' of jurists to their 'social reality' in an incomparable way (Wieacker 1939). In his legal–historical works he then further applied this principle of an ideal mode of thinking to the changing circumstances within the European continent, often dealing with questions of truthful legal interpretation and social justice.

The intellectual core in Wieacker's scholarship – belief in the organic constitution of society and distinguished position of legal scholars within societies – was not only concise but also easy to combine with various theoretical openings in the field of legal science (Wolff 2007). Wieacker did adjust this belief in congruence with contemporary social change and theoretical streams in legal disciplines. Thus, even if the core remained unchangeable, the sentiments, meaning and contemporary relevance, which Wieacker attached to 'true Roman jurisprudence' in his works, varied over time. Depending on his intellectual context, the audience and the political atmosphere, Wieacker presented the wisdom of Roman law either as an ultimate communal form to reach a socially sustainable and legally binding decision, or as a paragon for a style of thinking in achieving truth, or as a mental asset which uplifted those who expressed it to social prominence, or as a virtuous orientation which modern legal science had failed to follow.

Thus, during the years from the 1930s to the late 1960s there was no paradigmatic rupture in Wieacker's idea of Roman law. While emphasizing different aspects from the 'true great jurisprudence' of the late Roman Republic he was always able to present Roman law as significant in relation to actual and contemporary political and juridical issues, notwithstanding that the political constitution of German society changed between absolute polarities. Nor was this approach opportunism; rather, Wieacker sincerely believed in the superior rationality of legal thinking cultivated by Roman law which, to him, never became outdated as an administrative tool in the modern search for social justice.

Interest on the themes of 'social justice' and 'objective truth' connected Wieacker's works to the theories of Schmitt and Gadamer. Wieacker reflected and sharpened his view on the European legal past in relation to their works and borrowed to some extent from both of them, thus constructing his 'way' on principles which are often connected to Gadamer and Schmitt. In Wieacker's personal history the attachment first to Schmitt's work and then later to Gadamer's manifests a shift in his intellectual context. Schmitt's anti-parliamentarism and Gadamer's dialogical hermeneutics presented two opposites in the politics of legal science. Schmitt contributed significantly to the ideological 'battle' of National Socialist *Gleichschaltung* and provided a 'bourgeois façade' for the fascists in their attempts to transform Germany into a totalitarian nation (Mehring 2014; Stolleis 2004). Although Schmitt was later turned down by the administrative and political elite of the NSDAP, he never abandoned his revolutionary conservatism or his offensive on democratic society. Gadamer, on the other hand, has been considered as a thoroughly apolitical figure, and was later even criticized for acquiescing in the consensus over social emancipation (Mendehlson 1979). While the collegiality between Wieacker and Schmitt was intense from the 1930s to 1945, Gadamer's influence on Wieacker's texts is most evident from the 1950s onwards.

Wieacker, Schmitt and Gadamer shared common social premises. As scholars in Weimar Germany, they perceived a fundamental change in social circumstances which obliged them to rethink the tradition of legal science. All of them were convinced of the incapability of contemporary or previously upheld models of argumentation to meet the needs of a rapidly changing community. Wieacker, Schmitt and Gadamer evaluated contemporary legal theories (and in particular positivistic theories) as incapable of depicting the essence of post-imperial society and in guiding jurisprudence in a 'healthy' direction. Along the lines of genuine historical change which they were experiencing as German scholars and citizens, they sought to re-evaluate the relationship between human sciences and social reality. They asserted that the extent to which European jurisprudence and politics was ready to accept and utilize the traditional, yet newly discovered, way of communal knowledge production would very much define the destiny and the moral essence of the Continent. So, neither the theoretical constructions of respected scholars nor Wieacker's attachment first to Schmitt's concepts and later to Gadamer's thinking should be taken as a rootless play of ideas. The academic works of Schmitt, Gadamer and, in particular, Wieacker should be interpreted in relation to their context – the social disarray of Weimar and the consequent different phases of the social history of Germany.

Carl Schmitt and Franz Wieacker: Honourable lawyers and justice as an institution

Wieacker's acquaintance with Schmitt started in the early 1930s and lasted for a decade.[3] Schmitt's writings and thoughts had a decisive effect on Wieacker's vision of historical meaning and the structuring of modern (German) society, which is most evident in Wieacker's earlier texts, and in a vaguer form even in his post-war works (Winkler 2014). Many of Wieacker's texts from the 1930s disclose a merger between 'fashionable' theoretical streams, contemporary jurisprudential and political need, on the one hand, and Wieacker's legal scientific scholarship, on the other. Although originally a Roman law scholar, in the years following the National Socialist *Machtergreifung* ('seizure of power'), Wieacker was commonly associated with the younger generation of legal scholars who, from a neo-Hegelian base, attempted to overcome the alleged – and factual – shortcomings of the then dominant positivist view of law (Meinel 2012).

In the early 1930s, Wieacker, like his peer group of young academics born in the first decade of the twentieth century, desperately pursued a permanent position as a professor, *Ordinariat*, in any decent German university with a law faculty. Wieacker and his generation comprehended the liberal Weimar social order as a perennial failure. Their scepticism was born in the collapse of the common German value system when the estates of Imperial Germany were replaced by inefficient Weimar parliamentarism, but was decisively strengthened through the social consequences of the 1923 hyperinflation and the looming threat of Bolshevik Revolution. In 1935, when Wieacker and Schmitt engaged for the first time in collegial correspondence, Wieacker was affiliated as a private docent with the University of Kiel and contributed to the teaching and writing of a loose group of young scholars known as the *Kieler Schule* (Winkler 2014). The *Kieler Schule* was not an insignificant institution in the legal scientific field, but occupied a distinguished place in the 'legal renewal' of the Third Reich. The *Schule* had been tasked by the new government with redefining legal education and the concepts of German legal science to meet the ideological standards of the fascist regime (Eckert 1992).

For this revolutionary conservative endeavour aligned with fascist interests, Schmitt was a convenient mentor. Thus, in their task the *Schule*, and Wieacker among others, leaned heavily on Schmitt's theory of the institutional nature of proper jurisprudence and law. Nevertheless, even Schmitt's contemporaries found it difficult to categorize his ideas. Depending on the interpreter, he appeared either as a consistent anti-positivist, revolutionary existentialist or as a political opportunist. In his 1930s works, Schmitt was concurrently socially conservative, intellectually provocative and explicitly racist. In 1935 Schmitt was at the height of his national career. He was widely cited, appreciated and referred to as *Staatsrat* or 'state-counsellor' (Mehring 2014). Although from his own perspective he was being ignored and sidelined in the bitter power struggles of German academia, to an outside observer he seemed to represent *the* epitome of a 'legal scientist of the Third Reich'.

In his works preceding the National Socialist *Machtergreifung*, Schmitt had attacked the hollowness of the positivist view on law and distinguished between the 'absolute', legitimate, constitution and written statutes. As a 'state-counsellor' of the

Third Reich he pushed his interpretation even further and turned the enlightened idea of democratic legislation upside down. To Schmitt, parliamentarism was a later aberration of the pure expression of the will of the people (Schmitt 1996 [1932]). In his search for proper premises for an authoritative, just decision, Schmitt returned to groups or units distinguished by their shared set of values. He maintained that these communities usually upheld a practice of pursuing social justice, which furthermore was impossible to evaluate by means of (positivistic) legal theory (Shapiro 2008: 19–36). Consequently, on the level of legal culture, the law-giver should take into account those interpretations of norms and social orders within the societies it sought to regulate (Schmitt 2004 [1934]: 20). In the social reality of a people, questions of scientific truth and legal justice were to be resolved by analysing the existence of these traditions.

This 'concrete-order thinking', so prominent in 1930s German jurisprudence, was perfected by Schmitt in his *Über die drei Arten des rechtswissenschaftlichen Denkens* (1934). Schmitt asserted that the jurisprudential 'concrete orders', juridical traditions, in the end safeguarded the justness of entire legal systems. Here, by jurisprudential tradition Schmitt actually meant the level of responsibility, dignity and influence which lawyers as a group possessed in a given society. The higher status and greater political power of the jurist class correlated with the 'justness' of the community. In comparing the legal cultures of France, Great Britain and Germany, Schmitt attempted to show that each distinct legal community had its own tradition, which remained superior to any attempt at imposing outside legal doctrines on its traditional practice. To Schmitt the British legal tradition was closest to a system which secured the achievement of social justice within the level of the nation. Schmitt took the view that, in Britain, lawyers were the actual law makers. They were in charge of implementing social justice, which they did according to the interpretation of the norms abiding within their order (Schmitt 2004 [1934]; Schmitt 1995 [1941]). British jurisprudence was guided by 'jurisdictional authority, hierarchy of offices, inner autonomy, internal counterbalance of opposing forces and tendencies, inner discipline, honour and official secrets'. Thus, it embodied a perfect 'example of concrete order thinking' (Schmitt 2004 [1934]: 88).

The tradition of jurisprudence in Britain was a 'concrete order', which was able to evade the factual state of conflict characteristic of modern communities (cf. Schmitt 1996 [1923]: 74–80). In the perspective of Schmitt's vast output, the idea of material 'concrete orders' was more or less a side effect. Indeed, he never used the concept again. It has also been noted that the concept in itself is more an example of outstanding rhetorical skill than a social-scientific breakthrough. Along with the rocketing status of Schmitt and enthusiastic deployment by his disciples, the concept quickly became a mere fashionable slogan, which was used to describe pretty much everything (Mehring 2014). Soon the actual explanatory value of the phrase was being exploited.

However, the 1934 book, and the concept within it, was crucial in that it shaped the presuppositions and ontological stances of a whole generation of young scholars, among them Wieacker, who – like so many legal scientists of his generation – was assured by Schmitt's revolutionary conservatism and fascinated by his aggressive yet sophisticated style of writing (Rüthers 2012: 99–101, 270–317; Müller 2003: 1–4; Meinel 2012: 36–47). Schmitt's untiring attack on the alleged incongruity between (positivist) legal science and social reality was, in its conservatism, an orientation which fitted very well with Wieacker's perspective of German society. As a textbook representative of the bourgeois values of German *Bildungsbürgertum*, Wieacker witnessed at first hand the inability of modern society to maintain circumstances which it promised in its democratic ethos and interpreted this as a failure in the value-base of the legal system. As a young scholar, Wieacker experienced personally the obvious incoherence between the social reality of Weimar and dogmatic legal science.[4]

The experience of the distance between national values and law was a feature which provided common ground for young, conservative legal scholars in their attempts to textually contribute to and influence the National Socialist 'revolution'.[5] It has to be acknowledged that during the *Gleichschaltung* of German society, the NSDAP assigned to these young scholars the task of translating legal language to coincide with National Socialist ideology, while the young scholars perceived themselves as the vanguard and elite of the 'new stance' in legal science. Nevertheless, their pursuit of resolving the incongruence between law and reality – providing legal bases for social justice – was sincere. From the basis of their Weimar experience, the members of the *Kieler Schule* were convinced of the necessity for their 'legal renewal'. So, like Ernst Rudolf Huber and Ernst Forsthoff, Wieacker – leaning heavily on Schmitt's theories – outlined 'new' jurisprudence which would meet the consciousness of the German people (See Forsthoff 1933; Wolf 1934; Huber 1935). What distinguished Wieacker's contributions from most contemporary texts is the absence of racist rhetoric and a persistent adherence to antique (Roman) examples in legal–historical comparison.

Judging by their correspondence, it is clear that Wieacker appreciated Schmitt and sought his favour. There were, however, significant disagreements between them, of which the perception of the meaning given to Roman law might have been the most crucial. Schmitt was a vehement opponent of Roman law.[6] He saw Roman law as an arbitrary theoretical construction, which during its reception in Europe disturbed and overruled the natural, sacred and organic legal systems or orders of the Germanic kingdoms. To Schmitt, applied Roman law became a symptom of the process of 'scientification', where the traditional relation between the people and power had been misplaced. Needless to say, this point by Schmitt was backed up by the Nazi party, who as early as their party programme of 1919 had expressed their revulsion towards 'foreign' Roman law.

Wieacker, however, as a Romanist first and foremost, sought to prove that Roman law was not a hostile intruder but a tradition which had been 'Germanized' over the centuries, and thus its study was to analyse the foundations of the national legal system (Wieacker 1967: 8–24). The biggest practical obstacle blocking an agreement between Wieacker and Schmitt was the 'reputation' of Roman law. The nineteenth-century Pandectists had emphasized the dogmatic and hierarchical aspect within Roman law, which became a synonym for a stiff understanding and idea of jurisprudence, compressing the law as a collection of norms, unable to adapt to changing social reality. This picture was the precise target of Schmitt's attack; he defended law's dignity, tradition and sacredness against 'over-theoretical' constructions (Ojakangas 2009: 34–54). Wieacker was well aware of all this; thus his aim was to prove that Roman law was not an unnatural construction but actually in itself a concrete order. In his letter to Schmitt in 1935 Wieacker argued[7] that the alleged influence of Greek theories (which was supposedly the reason for Roman law becoming distinct from social reality), far from being the defining *essence*, was an external, late and misleading trait in the entity of Roman law:

> [Greek systematization] produces a legal theory from a Greek model for the relationship of natural and civil law that is rather subordinate to classical Roman law. It leads on the other hand to a rationally and logically arranged survey of legal concepts that have been handed down, as they are self-evident to the Greek-educated Roman, and thereby make the somewhat archaic guild-like thinking style of the pre-classical lawyers (comparable to the English Inns of Court) much more interesting. In comparison, I think that the inner structure of the classic jurisprudence almost completely refused to give itself to these influences, and it maintained the ancient Roman style up to Julian's former revision of the Roman edicts.[8]

Wieacker described Roman law as being composed of living, organic edicts which resisted any attempts at theorization. On the contrary, as an entity it could be better described through its 'inner feeling'. Moreover, it was held together by the guild-like community of the late Republican lawyers, and their distinguished style of seeing the world. In his letter Wieacker drew a straight analogy between Roman lawyers as a class and the English Inns of Court. As presented above, to Schmitt these Inns of Court were the clearest example of a juridical concrete order. Wieacker likewise held that the relative social status which lawyers allegedly possessed in the Roman Republic, as an exclusive and coherent social unit, was both the result of and the key to their success in Roman culture. On the other hand, the evident failure of contemporary modern legal systems, in terms of their ability to connect the language of law to the 'life' of the people, was not a Roman trait. On the contrary, Roman law was an insurmountable example of the 'facts that have a real and independent existence in the legal world', and the Pandectists' failure was a result of later Greek corruption.[9]

In 1939 Wieacker elaborated this idea on the inner 'spirit' of the Roman lawyer class in his article 'Vom Römischen Juristen', where he described Roman culture as a seedbed for European legal ideas. It was lawyers who had cultivated the Roman mentality towards rational problem-solving and the idea of social justice, opposing and substituting the previous superstitious and violent worldview of pre-modern generations. The lawyers of the later Republic invented and practised the law as casuistic mind-setting, through which they were able to apply their internalized body of knowledge in different situations in order to reach a just result (Wieacker 1939: 440, 445, 448). Their achievement was not due to mere academic dogmatism. To Wieacker, Roman law was not based on a theoretical or conceptual construction but on a *phronesis*, a skill. This lawyering skill was a synthesis of lawyers' education and social status.[10] Even in ancient Rome, the intellectuals in general were usually capable of deciding and ruling according to their accumulated knowledge, a tradition which was a prerequisite provided by their Hellenistic education. But lawyers, in distinction from other educated, upper-class people, had the social, communal knowledge which enabled them to understand the meaning of justice in different circumstances. This knowledge, which Wieacker later labelled as *Lebenskunde* ('science of life'), was a compilation of virtues, acquired first hand from their noble way of life. They served, experienced, and lived the law.

> Through military service and political speeches he [the Roman lawyer] is of the highest virtue, a legitimated public agent.... [He conducts] free service for the community that is exercised through expert opinion and instruction and of which the strictest guarantee is the predominant lack of fees. Just this distinguishes the 'honos' from the highest professions, especially the literate ones, even legally trained court speakers, who he looks down on with the cold contempt of the real expert.[11]

Thus the European legal tradition, descending from Rome, was based on the experience of law and on law (Wieacker 1939: 455–7; Avenarius 2010). But more than a knowledge of statutes, examples or texts, this knowledge, this experience, was based on a sense of virtuous social being appearing within a class of people. A true European legal tradition embedded the *authority* of both the law and lawyers.

Why, then, was Wieacker ready to accept Schmitt's polemic, and aggressive, approach to jurisprudence and why did he employ Schmitt's conceptualizations in his texts? Wieacker's 1930s works loyally repeated the 'fighting stance' towards the liberal order, but no signs of racist infiltration are evident in his methodology, while the obligatory references to the Führer are few and notably perfunctory. Nevertheless, Wieacker did agree with Schmitt that something was not right in the contemporary legal system in Germany. Judges did not have the power or the ability to decide according to the meaning of the law. They were content or obliged merely to follow norms but not to develop or interpret the law in a given case. Contemporary German jurisprudence lacked an acknowledgement of the traditional mindset of a lawyer, which had originated from the experience of the law. There was no space for *phronesis* in the mentality which now prevailed in German academia. In his letter to Schmitt of 1942, Wieacker agreed with the former's thoughts on the complete inability of the German legal system to meet the needs of the new world and to teach lawyers capable of securing the moral core of society.

> However one wonders if, in each German systematic-philosophical structure, the pervasiveness of magistrates with the role, which the basic political order assigns to lawyers, has not failed until now, due in fact to each systematic teaching approach. It is conceded that the systematic-normative approach of life is, for better or worse, characteristic of the Germans in their lives and deeds, as well as for government policy.[12]

It is important to notice that neither Schmitt nor Wieacker meant National Socialism when they wrote about the crisis in the legal system. Both placed the starting point of the crisis to times well before the Nazis and complained about the ongoing crisis long after 1945 (Wieacker 1967: 482). To them, the German system produced lawyers unable to work as a political 'estate' because of the systemic-philosophical ideology which had nullified the space for individual interpretation and consideration. Wieacker and Schmitt agreed that educating young law students was the most important task in reviving German legal science and the status of lawyers along with it.[13] What the legal system needed was prestige, education and restoration of the priority of practical legal thinking.

Furthermore, in the 1940s Wieacker continued defining his idea of the spiritual heritage of Roman law in European legal history as appearing in the 'estates' of lawyers. In his article 'Das römische Recht und das deutsche Rechtsbewusstsein' (1944) Wieacker defended Roman law from the accusations of Germanistic legal scholars (not far from Schmitt) who blamed it as originally constituting the rift between the people's everyday reality and the legal system. Wieacker sought to prove that Roman law was not responsible for this twist of the modern world, but rather that, without Roman law and lawyers trained in Roman law, this distortion would have been far worse. He argued that the ethical sustainability of a particular judgement, happening in the reality framed by a collection of norms, depended on whether the given judge had applied *Rechtsgewissen* ('legal conscience') in weighing that particular case (Wieacker 1944: 42).[14] According to Wieacker, German lawyers were able to cultivate *Rechtsgewissen* ever since they obtained training in Roman law. This was a skill which enabled them to interpret existing norms and execute decisions, concurrently maintaining and cultivating righteousness in the reality of society. Again, *Rechtsgewissen* was not just about formal education. Wieacker asserts that whether an individual was further capable of using this mental tool depended on their personal moral stance and adjustment to the 'guild' of lawyers (Wieacker 1944: 24, 31–2, 41). A disinclination or inability to subordinate one's legal act to the virtues of the class resulted in bad decisions, injustice and oppressive laws. On the other hand, following, learning and contributing to the tradition stemming from Roman law not only provided ethically sustainable judgements but also cultivated the European legal heritage (Wieacker 1944: 28, 41).

Hans-Georg Gadamer and Franz Wieacker: The hermeneutics of truth

From our perspective it is easy to argue that the assumption of power by the NSDAP and the resulting construction of a totalitarian nation after 1933 was in principle misunderstood by many legal scholars. Undoubtedly, the vast majority of academics concentrated on the abolition of the loathed Weimar Republic, welcomed social conservatism – which the new order appeared to bring about – and were delighted by the career possibilities which the expulsion of Jewish university staff offered for young scholars. Like Wieacker, many of the 'Aryan' scholars could not predict or accept the totalitarian reality into which the NSDAP turned German society. Their miscalculation is in one sense understandable, since not even legal scientists can foresee the future. At the same time, the general incapability to read and later to cope with the 'aberration of social justice' does tell us something about the then prevailing scholarly culture of legal science.

If one leaves aside anti-Semitism and appreciation of militant fascism – which were true and widespread motivators for some legal scientists – many, like Wieacker, sincerely believed that the new order would accept the lawyer-estate as its administrative trustee, and the 'guild' of legal scholars would in practice steer the moral consciousness of the nation. When the true nature of the fascist regime reached legal academia, many resorted to a form of apologetic existentialism.

Disappointed by National Socialism, scholars like Ernst Forsthoff and Schmitt in their writings of the early 1940s concentrated on the 'pure core' of legal science – unchanged premises, which would enable scholars to interpret and develop law according to tradition, national culture and ideals of social justice (Meinel 2012). These scholars tried deliberately to put aside their previous alliance with fascism – which at a rhetorical level had been presented as an attempt to revive an age-old idea of national 'social justice' – and instead turned their attention to the dilemma of 'objective truth'. Many legal scientists, Wieacker among them, focused on 'conscience' (see, for example, Welzel 1947).[15] This was a concept which, when employed in legal–historical and criminal law study, enabled a metaphysical and existentialist approach to jurisprudential questions.

In all of these approaches scholars reluctantly and indirectly concurred that the 'legal awareness of the people', on which scholars had built their 1930s explorations, was apparently indiscernible and an insufficient starting point for legal scientific research. Instead, academics started to distinguish their pure, 'conscientious' scholarship from the irrational political sphere and the oblivious will of the people. The 'people' was no more a source of inspiration and appeared as the opposite to scholarly views and thinking. Proper, scholarly wisdom was able to read the signs and circumstances of its time and analyse contemporary reality. 'Truth' was not with the people, but it could be extracted from the people by means of learned legal skill. Wieacker wrote to Gadamer in early 1945 in describing the people of Germany and Italy:

> The condition of the public of this country is so abominable. These people, without soul, without conscience and destiny in the good and the bad, without humour in the proper meaning of the word, without sentimentality, and without the need to see a new reality that is only visibly transcendent of their own souls behind their own reality – these people are peculiarly a comforting and exhilarating form, and also likeable in the everyday world. To understand the judgement 'here without conscience', I must use these words: instead of the soul, a bright cheerfulness, instead of responsibility, absolution, instead of the conscience, the law, instead of destiny, grace.[16]

The fact that Wieacker sent to Gadamer this letter – written in the front line in northern Italy – in which he expressed his disappointment with the idealized 'people', is in many ways revealing. During the last year of the Second World War, Wieacker was deeply tired of and cynical towards any nationalistic rhetoric. To Gadamer, such language had always appeared hollow, and in his philosophy he searched for historical meaning outside political history, national communities and ethnic distinctions. Not even Gadamer was uninfluenced by public opinion and the social reality of totalitarian

Germany, but he seemed to remain uninterested in the politics of human sciences. Indeed, the influence of National Socialism in his works is either non-existent or very well camouflaged (Hausmann 2008; Grondin 2003). As a student of Martin Heidegger, Gadamer's thoughts on history, philosophy, philology and law reflected the ideas of his teacher. Additionally, he further developed and fine-tuned Heidegger's theses on metaphysics to a universal science of interpretation and hermeneutics. During the Second World War Gadamer worked at the University of Leipzig, where Wieacker held the professorship in Roman law (Grondin 2003). This era marked the beginning of their friendship and connection which continued throughout the century. In Gadamer's massive output, the questions of legal application and historical interpretation link him to the theme of this compilation, which he frequently discussed with Wieacker in their correspondence (Avenarius 2013).

The 'Point Zero' of 1945 shook the foundations of German legal science. Due to the enormous influence of Martin Heidegger, the existentialist orientation in German legal science was already a significant stream in the 1930s, but war and disappointment had drawn increasing attention towards the ontological sides of law. So Gadamer's theory of truthful interpretation was a current reality for many legal scientists during the later war years. Nevertheless, the end of the Second World War meant that legal scientists had to redefine the 'existence' of, and provide justification for, their *own* scholarship and discipline. The de-Nazification of German universities put legal scholars into an unprecedented situation. Suddenly, they were accused of enabling the crimes of the Nazis. The academics reacted with denial and felt offended. Surely their project had nothing to do with politics. With growing determination, they struggled to prove that the legal havoc of the 1930s was a result of theoretical dogmatism, not academic opportunism. Legal positivism was to be blamed for the misreading and mal-development of law. With its 'cold' and 'heartless' approach, it had perverted the meaning of law (Foljanty 2013). The search for that 'meaning', of sustaining premises for just legal interpretation, became the purpose of legal science in the decades following the 'Point Zero' of 1945. However, this task had actually already started earlier, during the later years of the Second World War.

Similarly to Wieacker's work, there is no war-related, clear rupture in Gadamer's methodological approach before and after the Second World War. In Gadamer's understanding, a similar understanding of a particular source or historical phenomenon was always historically situated and affected by the prejudices of each interpreter. Gadamer based his theory of understanding on the preceding tradition of hermeneutics and historians. This meant that he also saw the interpretative work of a scholar taking shape in a hermeneutical circle where a particular event has to be understood as a part of, and deriving from, a larger entity. But unlike Schleiermacher or Willem Droysen, he emphasized the role of the interpreter's culture (Gadamer 2000; Froeyman 2014). A scholar always approaches a research question from a distinct worldview or perspective. Thus their understanding of a phenomenon in a past culture or alien language is determined by certain prejudices, which Gadamer named 'preconception' (*Vorurteil*). The prejudices of a given scholar are consequently shaped by the historical situation of its culture (Gadamer 2000: 277–84). Our understanding of the world, history and human activity is irreversibly bound to the history of long-term effects, *Wirkungsgeschichte*, of their surroundings and culture. By this Gadamer did not solely mean specific social or political changes in the past of a particular community, but meaningful effects extending to the realms of understanding and interpretation (Gadamer 1986a: 115–17; Gadamer 2000: 297).

To Gadamer, humanist research was a dialogical task. He asserted that although scholars were always bound to their historical situation, their horizon was not fixed. This horizon could and should evolve and change along with the research process. Questions one poses as to the subject matter produce answers that speak of or appeal to the scholar. In turn, this produces more questions as to the phenomena or text under scrutiny (Gadamer 1986b: 57–65). For example, the research process in studying Roman law should take a form of a dialogue. This dialogue would incorporate the tradition – thus Roman law as events and interpretation – and the historical situation of the scholar. What clearly distinguished Gadamer from scholars like Emilio Betti and Wieacker, however, was his rejection of a complete and correct understanding (Betti 1962). An interpretative act could never reach the final meaning of a particular event or text. To him, the search for 'objective truth' was futile. A historical distance from the phenomenon one was analysing was in practice helpful, since time has a tendency to fade certain irrelevant opinions about a historical event. Nevertheless, the process of interpreting and reinterpreting history was a never-ending business. An objective truth about a distinct meaning or event was a 'phantom' that scholars kept on chasing (Gadamer 1986b: 65; Veith 2015: 119–22). Consequently there was no method that could lead a scholar to an 'absolutely correct' interpretation of history, or indeed law either (Gadamer 1986a: 107–10).[17] A lawyer or historian might reach an agreement between their heritage and a tradition whose understanding they pursued, but nonetheless all attempts at understanding were bound to the dialogical and incomplete process of truth-seeking.

After the war, Wieacker continued his involvement in the theme of the rightful application of law and frequently discussed Gadamer's ideas in his academic texts.[18] The correspondence between the two stayed irregular but continued. In a scholarly sense, Gadamer's phenomenal contribution to the post-war discussion on legal hermeneutics was naturally a reason in itself for Wieacker to take an interest in the former's ideas, but at the same time Gadamer's writings converged in an important way with some of Wieacker's arguments. Wieacker stuck to his 'existential' – originally 'Schmittian' – approach to law. In the end, and for Wieacker, law was the embodiment of the questions people presented to their *being*. In law, the achievements, as well as the limits of human understanding, became visible. Legal history was a tool to compare and understand different views and ways of thinking, not only in the legal sphere but also within the wider spectrum of different cultures.

In the first edition of *Privatrechtsgeschichte der Neuzeit* in 1952, Wieacker proposed that the task of the legal historian should be to track 'time-transcending legal ideas' (*überzeitliche Rechtsidee*), from the European past (Wieacker 1952: 8). Although he removed that conceptualization from the second, 1967 edition of *Privatrechtsgeschichte*, the tone even in the second edition of the classic book remained the same; every historical situation was unique and could not be reproduced in our present, but there resided a historical paragon of legal thinking that could serve as a model for modern legal science. That 'time-transcending model' was naturally the 'great jurisprudence' of late Republican Rome. To Wieacker, the true brilliance of classical Roman lawyers was in the way they adjusted their knowledge to changing circumstances through method. In the end it was about interpreting the tradition in a new situation. It enabled Roman lawyers be in touch with reality, while concurrently conducting a just and correct interpretation (Wieacker 1939; Wieacker 1956). This congruence between thinking and reality was desirable, not sophistication in legal expression or universality of legal definition, as some Roman law scholars explained the continuing importance of Roman jurisprudence to modern legal science. Thus, to Wieacker, Roman legal sources presented a paragon for European legal cultures in the sense that they were a (pale) reflection of the superior legal skill and wisdom of Roman law.[19]

Gadamer's idea of a universally incomplete understanding not only diminished the value of classical Roman lawyers but also cast a shadow over Wieacker's whole reconstruction of European legal history. The problem concerned in particular Gadamer's idea of 'preconception' (Avenarius 2010). To Wieacker, the problem of interpretation in a particular legal case concerned the appropriateness or solidity of the methods deployed; a truthful judgement could be achieved only through certain, correct methods. The question of methodology also extended beyond jurisdiction and to the morality of legal science (Wieacker 1967). According to Wieacker, the post-war 'crisis of justice' was partly due to an incorrect interpretation of the law, that is, legal science (more precisely, legal positivism) had become disoriented in its methods. He wrote to Gadamer in 1965:

> This [crisis] could be related to the generally accepted discrediting and "unmasking" conducted by legal positivism. These things [methodology] are now in such disarray that the old fundamental relations between law and dogma are at the moment nothing but blurred.[20]

In *Privatrechtsgeschichte* Wieacker continued to study the form of legal wisdom which would enable just decisions despite historical and social confusion. With unprecedented explicitness he called this skill *Rechtsgewissen*. In comparison to his wartime writings, Wieacker linked *Rechtsgewissen* more closely to the long line of *European* legal tradition and to correct jurisprudential methods, but nevertheless it was the inner instinct of the judge that enabled him to accomplish a sound interpretation of the law and let justice happen. So in Wieacker's theory there was a connection between feeling and interpretation, and to be more precise, a just understanding could not be achieved by means of pure reason (Wieacker 1967: 619). Justice involved such sentiments as respect, modesty and dignity. Again, Wieacker wrote about the post-war 'crisis of justice' to Gadamer:

> Modern law does not seem to give such an experience [of prestigious relation to tradition] for today's lawyers. I cannot think of any other reason for this very peculiar phenomenon than particular disrespect on behalf of contemporary theories of interpretation against the authority of the word of law.[21]

Partly this idea of just, truthful interpretation was difficult to translate to Gadamer's hermeneutical model. To Gadamer, true interpretation existed in dialogue. When scholars engaged in discussion or reading, the quest for understanding was a dialectic one. A change occurred, in terms of both the understanding of the phenomenon involved *and* the scholar's own prejudices. The whole core of Wieacker's historical view was that a model of just interpretation had existed in the history of Europe and should also be used as such in contemporary society in order to correct 'the crisis of justice' (Wieacker 1967).

In the end the disagreement between Wieacker and Gadamer was about the nature of historical time. Gadamer was ready to abandon historical knowledge as 'beyond-temporal'; it had no pre-given direction. Written history was a series of acts of interpretation where people tried to understand their past and present. For sure there were some consistent elements in human beings that had remained unchanged through time, but in his view historical narrative was more about the present than the past. Wieacker's idea about history was, as Reinhard Zimmermann rightly asserts, distinctively constructive in its nature (Zimmermann 1995). Rather than identifying the possible divergent lines of development in European legal history, Wieacker emphasized the unity and similar features of different legal cultures distinguished by time and place.

In all his post-war works, Wieacker tried to re-establish something that the modernization process had broken or questioned. The majority of Wieacker's 1950s and 1960s works dealt with the rational mind of Europe and Europeans. History was an 'onward march' of rationality, and legal history worked as an 'iron ratio' which conserved the wisdom of past generations (Wieacker 1967: 619–25). The task for the modern legal historian was to find the appropriate sources, understand them correctly and then apply this wisdom to their present society. To Wieacker, this triumph of the will and reason was a fact in European history, which renewed itself in countless conditions and environments through history. The methodological superiority of the Roman lawyers over a superstitious and magical worldview was the first and most evident example of this historical direction.[22]

Why, then, did Wieacker pay such strong attention to Gadamer's thoughts, which rejected the existence of any particular 'correct' methodology in distinguishing a 'proper understanding' of legal history? To Wieacker, who consistently opposed any Gadamerian hesitation as to the possibilities of legal science to reach the ultimate truth about history and society, Gadamer's theory nevertheless offered support in his attack on the genuine nemesis: legal positivism (Betti 1962: 52). Gadamer emphasized the practical wisdom of adjusting and interpreting the law in differing historical situations as a means of achieving a solid interpretation. This wisdom was embedded in the idea of 'sensus communis'. This meant that a group of properly informed, learned people could reach a consensus, which could serve as a truthful and just decision in a particular situation. If the community of scholars was able to apply their common 'tact' and knowledge in a dialogical enquiry, their jurisprudence was in congruence with reality and truth. To Gadamer, the dialogical research process and decision-making should be directed by virtues, which were neither impulses nor calculations. 'Sensus communis' was close to conscience or ethos. Furthermore, in elaborating this 'sensus communis',

Gadamer used examples from the Stoic philosophers and Wieacker's presentation of the Roman world and 'conscience' of the guild of lawyers. Wieacker's *Rechtsgewissen*, practical legal wisdom and Gadamer's 'common sense' were different elaborations of the same phenomenon – legal wisdom – but to Wieacker, it was always associated with Roman law, and more precisely with the common knowledge and mentality of the guild of Roman lawyers.

The multifaceted idea of Roman law in Franz Wieacker's academic texts

Different phases, multiple interpretations and a continuous attempt to bridge the domains of social reality and jurisprudence all appear in Wieacker's idea of Roman law. His view on late Republican jurisprudence was never complete, and he did not cease to compare and connect that idea to contemporary social events and new theoretical openings in legal science. The idea of Roman law offered a 'fixed position' from where he could observe and comment on historical change and legal scientific discourse. Likewise his engagement with the thoughts of Schmitt and Gadamer can be seen as different phases in his scholarly career. However, they are not hierarchical stages in a linear development of scholarly identity. Wieacker interpreted and re-interpreted Schmitt's and Gadamer's ideas, abandoned them and returned to them, whenever a changed social situation or paradigmatic change in legal science necessitated rethinking the core values of his scholarly principles. There was, however, such a core, which was both irreplaceable and irremovable. To Wieacker, the correct kind of jurisprudence was not only learned but also, and always, virtuous. What distinguished Roman law among other legal cultures and elevated it to wisdom was its strong relation and interdependence with the noble values of Roman society. Law should have been shaped by the feelings and qualities of dignity, piety, maturity and humility. Moreover, law should have been guarded and developed by a group of people who embodied those virtues. In Wieacker's historical view, Roman law was nothing less than that, whereas modern law was barely related at all.

Although the theories of Wieacker, Schmitt and Gadamer diverged in many places, they converge in their aim to fight against the positivistic ideas of law and society. Schmitt, Wieacker and Gadamer attempted to defend the humanist tradition against Cartesian and inductionist theories in jurisprudence, social sciences and philosophy. They saw this humanist tradition in very different ways but found their adversaries in academics and streams of thought (imaginary or real) from the field of positivistic induction and pure reason. Likewise, according to these scholars, those guilty of inconsistency between reality and science included scholars who disembodied scientific reasoning from traditional values and virtues.

Accordingly, Wieacker saw the legal and social turmoil of the twentieth century deriving from an ontological incoherence in society, an incoherence which was also the constitutive factor behind the tragic political events of the modern era. Political and legal tragedies were a symptom of a deeper imbalance in social relations and awareness. Thus his ideas on legal science and justice were 'resurrective' in the sense that he believed that a simple misinterpretation of tradition had caused injustice in society. European legal tradition simply needed to be reminded again of its founding virtues in order to achieve social justice.

This construction of European legal history and legal–historical knowledge emphasized the meaning of law, further interpreted by legal scholars. Alongside this view, and contrary to the legal positivists, Wieacker maintained that, while interpreting the law, lawyers simultaneously created it and that their process of creation should be conducted unattached (and superior) to the political sphere. This view of European legal tradition put lawyers and legal scientists as the subjects, the makers, of not only law but history as well. At the same time, it emphasized the role of legal historians. Since European legal history was based and built on the experience, knowledge and interpretative acts of lawyers, reliable information about one's own legal reality could be obtained by comparing the legal experience of the present to that in the past.

Notes

1 This research has made been possible by the European Research Council under the European Union's Seventh Framework Programme (FP7/2007-2013)/ERC grant agreement n°313100 (Reinventing the Foundations of European Legal Culture 1934–64).

2 Cf. Chapter 4 in this book.

3 Their relationship as colleagues may have started as early as 1933, but the first letter from Wieacker to Schmitt is from August 1935. See Franz Wieacker to Carl Schmitt on 13 July 1935, Nachlass Carl Schmitt, RW 265–17971/2, Landesarchiv Nordrhein-Westfalen, Duisburg.

4 See Franz Wieacker's letter to Erik Wolf on 18 April 1934, NL Erik Wolf 66/3044, Freiburg-Albert-Ludwig-Universitätsarchiv, Freiburg im Breisgau; also Wieacker 1936: 74–80.

5 Here by the 'network of young scholars', including Franz Wieacker, I mean the members of *Kieler Schule* – and especially Ernst Rudolf Huber – Erik Wolf and Ernst Forsthoff. These scholars not only were close professionally but also remained friends way up to the late decades of the twentieth century (Winkler 2014; Meinel 2012). Their 'orientation' was firmly fascist but less party oriented (Ralf Walkenhaus 1997).

6 See Fritz Pringsheim's open letter to Carl Schmitt (Pringsheim 1960: 532–8).

7 Wieacker to Carl Schmitt, 13 July 1935, Nachlass Carl Schmitt, RW 265–17971/2, Landesarchiv Nordrhein-Westfalen, Duisburg. The letter is more a review of Johannes Stroux's article 'Griechische Einflüsse auf die Entwicklung der römischen Rechtswissenschaft gegen Ende der republikanischen Zeit' (1934) that Schmitt had sent to Wieacker. In the text, Stroux asserts that Greek philosophy, and in particular the Stoic parts of it, had a decisive influence on Roman legal thinking even during the time of the late Republic. Wieacker rejected this claim as fundamentally inaccurate.

8 Wieacker to Carl Schmitt, 13 July 1935, Nachlass Carl Schmitt, RW 265–17971/2, Landesarchiv Nordrhein-Westfalen, Duisburg: 'dies System bringt einmal eine für das klassische römische Recht ziemlich untergebliche Rechtstheorie griechschen Musters über das Verhältnis von natürlichem und bürgereigenem Recht hervor. Sie führt auf der anderen Seite zu einer rationaleren und logisch durchgegliederten Erfassung

überlieferter Rechtsvorstellungen, wie sie dem hellenistisch gebildeten Römer selbstverständlich ist, und lokert dadurch den etwas zopfigen zünftlerischen Denkstil der vorklassischen Juristen (vergleichbar etwa dem englischen Inns) stark auf. Dagegen glaube ich, dass das innere Gefüge der klassischen Jurisprudenz sich diesen Einwirkungen fast gänzlich versagte und den altrömischen Stil bis zu Julians Ediktredaktionen wahrte.'

9 Wieacker to Carl Schmitt, 13 July 1935, Nachlass Carl Schmitt, RW 265–17971/2, Landesarchiv Nordrhein-Westfalen, Duisburg: 'Sachverhalts, die in der Rechtswelt eine reale eigenständige Existenz haben.'

10 Wieacker 1939: 449. 'Denn ein Präjudiz kann nur angewendet werden, wenn man den gemeinsamen Grundgedanken, das *tertium comparationis* erkennt. Dieser Grundgedanke kann mit unbewusster Anschauung angewendet, aber auch ausdrücklich als Regel formuliert und überliefert werden. Solche Regeln sind noch keine abstrakten Obersätze, sondern durch Anschauung und Erfahrung gewonnene Richtschnuren künftiger Praxis: wie Sprichwort, Wetterregel oder Rezept, zusammengedrängte Weisheit von Generation. Mit dem Auftreten dieser Regularjurisprudenz im 2.Jahrhundert beginnt das *Rechtswissen* um seiner selbst willen [.]'

11 Wieacker 1939: 447. 'Dem freien Dienst am Gemeinwesen, der durch Gutachtung und Unterweisung geübt wird, und dessen strengste Gewähr die überwiegende Unentgeltlichkeit ist. Eben dies dies unterscheidet den honos vom Erwerb auch höherer Art, besonders auch vom gebildeten, aber rechtskundigen Prozessredner, auf den er mit der stillen Geringschätzung des wirklich Sachkundigen herabblickt.'

12 Wieacker's letter to Schmitt, 25 August 1942, Nachlass Carl Schmitt RW 265–17971/5, Landesarchiv Nordrhein-Westfalen, Duisburg: 'Freilich fragt man sich, ob in jenem deutschen systematisch-philosophischen Typ die Durchdringung des Richteramts mit der Funktion, welche die politische Grundordnung dem Juristen zuweist, nicht bisher misslungen ist, und zwar eben wegen jener Gelehrt-systemalischen Betrachtung. Zuzugeben ist, dass die systematisch-normative Betrachtung des Lebens im Guten wie im Bösen auch für das Leben und Handeln, auch das politische Handeln der Deutschen bezeichnend ist.'

13 Wieacker to Schmitt, 25 August 1942, Nachlass Carl Schmitt RW 265–17971/5, Landesarchiv Nordrhein-Westfalen, Duisburg.

14 In 'Das römische Recht und das deutsche Rechtsbewusstsein' Wieacker describes *Rechtsgewissen* also as 'geistige technik' and 'Geistige Macht der Wissenschaft'.

15 Like Wieacker's, Hans Welzel's post-war works were grounded on the earlier texts and philosophical openings. See Loos 2004: 1118.

16 Wieacker to Hans-Georg Gadamer, 14 March 1945. Nachlass Hans-Georg Gadamer, Deutsches Literatur Archiv, Marbach am Neckar: 'So abscheulich der öffentliche Zustand des Landes ist, dieser Mensch, ohne Gemüt, ohne Gewissen und Schicksal im Guten und im Bösen, ohne Humor im eigentlichen Sinne und ohne Sentimentalität, ohne das Bedürfnis, hinter seiner Wirklichkeit eine neue, nur der Einzelseele sichtbare transzendierende Wirklichkeit zu sehen, – dieser Mensch ist sonderbarerweise ein tröstliches und erheiterndes Bild, und und auch im Täglichen sympathisch. Wie das Urteil "ohne Gewissen hier" zu verstehen ist, muss ich doch wohl ausdrücken: statt des Gemüts die helle Heiterkeit, statt der Verantwortung die Absolution, statt des Gewissens das Gesetz, statt des Schicksals die Gnade.'

17 Gadamer 1986a: 107–10.

18 In this dilemma he was not alone. The coup of National Socialism and their distorted fashion of interpreting and adjusting the legal system was a memory and a fact that

led legal historians such as Helmut Coing or Gustav Radbuch to rethink and re-evaluate the basis of the German legal system. See Coing 1950; Radbruch 1946.

19 Wieacker to Hans-Georg Gadamer, 14 July 1965. Nachlass Hans-Georg Gadamer, Deutsches Literatur Archiv: 'Den alten römischen Texten (für die dogmatische Auslegung) mit zunehmenden Zeitenabstand wirklich ein neurer, gerechterer Sinn sich entfalten kann; (wie im Abstand Hochgipfel hinter den vorgrelagerten Hügelketten aufsteigen).'

20 Wieacker to Gadamer, 14 July 1965. Nachlass Hans-Georg Gadamer, Deutsches Literatur Archiv, Marbach am Neckar: 'diese könnte zusammenhängen mit der allgemein akzeptierten Diskreditierung und "Entlarvung" des Gesetzespositivismus. Diese Dinge sind heute so in Unordnung, dass die alten Grundverhältnisse von Gesetz und Dogmatik heute nur in Trübung erscheinen.'

21 Wieacker to Gadamer, 14 July 1965. Nachlass Hans-Georg Gadamer, Deutsches Literatur Archiv, Marbach am Neckar: '... für die modernen Gesetze scheint der heutige Jurist eine solche Erfahrung nicht zu machen. Ich wüsste für diese sehr eigentümliche Erscheinung im Augenblick keinen anderen Grund anzugeben als die besondere Respektlosigkeit der heute herrschenden Auslegungslehren (Interessen – oder Wertungsjurisprudenz; teleologische, selbst "verfassungskonforme" Auslegung) gegen die im Gesetzeswort erscheinende Autorität.'

22 Franz Wieacker to Carl Schmitt, 16 May 1943, Nachlass Carl Schmitt RW 265–17971/6, Landesarchiv Nordrhein-Westfalen, Duisburg: 'Was ich im "Römischen Juristen" über die eigentümliche Rechtsontologie der Römer sage, nicht hinaus gehen, also keineswegs zugeben, dass die autonome, lebensheilige Geltung der überlieferterten und fachlich fortgebildeten Rechtsform in Altrom in die Bewusstseins-Kategorien des Magischen, Numinösen, des Tabu, Orenda und ähnlicher ethnologischer Hilfsvorstellungen fällt.'

References

Avenarius, M. (2010), 'Verwissenschaftlichung als "sinnhafter" Kern der Rezeption: eine Konsequenz aus Wieackers rechtshistorischer Hermeneutik', in O. Behrends and E. Schumann (eds), *Franz Wieacker. Historiker des modernen Privatrechts*, 119–80, Göttingen: Wallstein.

Avenarius, M. (2013), 'Universelle Hermeneutik und Praxis des Rechtshistorikers und Juristen. Die Entwicklung ihres Verhältnisses im Lichte der Diskussion zwischen Gadamer und Wieacker', in S. Meder, G. Carlizzi, C.-E. Mecke and C. Sorge (eds), *Juristische Hermeneutik zwischen Vergangenheit und Zukunft*, 59–104, Baden-Baden: Nomos Verlagsgesellschaft.

Behrends, O. (1995), 'Franz Wieacker 5.8.1908 – 17.2.1994', *Zeitschrift der Savigny-Stiftung für Rechtsgeschichte. Romanistische Abteilung*, 112: XIII–LXII.

Betti, E. (1962), *Die Hermeneutik als allgemeine Methodik der Geisteswissenschaften*, Tübingen: J. C. B. Mohr.

Coing, H. (1950), *Grundzüge Der Rechtsphilosophie*, Berlin: Walter de Gruyter.

Eckert, J. (1992), 'Was war die Kieler Schule?' in F. J. Säcker (ed.), *Recht und Rechtslehre im Nationalsozialismus*, 37–70, Baden-Baden: Nomos.

Foljanty, L. (2013), *Recht oder Gesetz. Juristische Identität und Autorität in den Naturrechtsdebatten der Nachkriegszeit*, Tübingen: Mohr Siebeck.

Forsthoff, E. (1933), *Der totale Staat*, Berlin: Schlieffen-Verlag.

Froeyman, A. (2014), 'Hermeneutics, Life and Dialogue: A Sketch of a Buberian Dialogue with the Past', *Journal of the Philosophy of History*, 8: 407–25.

Gadamer, H.-G. (1986a), 'Klassische und philosophische Hermeneutik', in H.-G. Gadamer (ed.), *Gesammelte Werke, Bd. 2*, 92–117, Tübingen: J. C. B. Mohr.

Gadamer, H.-G. (1986b), 'Vom Zirkel des Verstehens', in H.-G. Gadamer (ed.), *Gesammelte Werke, Bd. 2*, 57–66, Tübingen: J. C. B. Mohr.

Gadamer, H.-G. (2000), *Truth and Method*, trans. J. Weisheimer and D. G. Marshall, 2nd rev edn, New York: Continuum.

Grondin, J. (2003), *Hans-Georg Gadamer: A Biography*, New Haven: Yale University Press.

Hausmann, F.-R. (2008), *Deutsche Geisteswissenschaft im Zweiten Weltkrieg. Die 'Aktion Ritterbusch' (1940–1945)*, Heidelberg: Synchron.

Huber, E. R. (1935), *Wesen und Inhalt der politischen Verfassung*, Hamburg, Hanseatische Verlagsanstalt.

Loos, F. (2004), 'Hans Welzel (1904–1977)', *Juristenzeitung*, 22: 1115–19.

Mehring, R. (2014), *Carl Schmitt: A Biography*, trans. D. Steuer, Cambridge: Polity Press.

Meinel, F. (2012), *Der Jurist in der industriellen Gesellschaft. Ernst Forsthoff und seine Zeit*, Berlin: Akademie Verlag.

Mendelson, J. (1979), 'The Habermas – Gadamer Debate', *New German Critique*, 18: 44–73.

Müller, J.-W. (2003), *A Dangerous Mind: Carl Schmitt in Post-War European Thought*, New Haven: Yale University Press.

Ojakangas, M. (2009), 'Carl Schmitt and the Sacred Origins of Law', *Telos*, 147: 34–54.

Pringsheim, F. (1960), 'Die Haltung der Freiburger Studenten in den Jahren 1933–1935', *Die Sammlung. Zeitschrift für Kultur und Erziehung*, 15: 532–8.

Radbruch, G. (1946), 'Gesetzliches Unrecht und übergesetzliches Recht', *Süddeutsche Juristen-Zeitung*, 1: 105–7.

Rüthers, B. (2012), *Die Unbegrenze Auslegung. Zum Wandel der Privatrechtsordnung im Nationalsozialismus, 7. Auflage*, Tübingen: Mohr Siebeck.

Schmitt, C. (1923, repr. 1996), *Roman Catholicism and Political Form*, Westport: Greenwood Publishing Group.

Schmitt, C. (1932, repr. 1996), *The Concept of the Political*, trans. Georg Schwab, Chicago: The University of Chicago Press.

Schmitt, C. (1934, repr. 2004), *On Three Types of Juristic Thought*, trans. Joseph W. Bendersky, Westport: Praeger.

Schmitt, C. (1941, repr. 1995), 'Das Meer gegen das Land', in C. Schmitt (ed.), *Staat, Grossraum, Nomos. Arbeiten aus den Jahren 1916–1969*, Berlin: Duncker & Humboldt.

Shapiro, K. (2008), *Carl Schmitt and the Intensification of Politics*, Lanham, MD: Rowman & Littlefield Publishers.

Stolleis, M. (2004), *A History of Public Law in Germany, 1914–45*, Oxford: Oxford University Press.

Stroux, J. (1934), 'Griechische Einflüsse auf die Entwicklung der römischen Rechtswissenschaft gegen Ende der republikanischen Zeit', *Atti del Congresso internazionale di diritto romano*, 1934: 114–32.

Veith, J. (2015), *Gadamer and the Transmission of History*, Bloomington: Indiana University Press.

Walkenhaus, R. (1997), 'Totalität als Anpassungskategorie. Eine Momentaufnahme der Denkentwicklung von Carl Schmitt und Ernst Rudolf Huber', in R. Walkenhaus, A. Söllner and K. Wieland (eds), *Totalitarismus, Eine Ideengeschichte des 20. Jahrhunderts*, 77–104, Berlin: Akademia Verlag.

Welzel, H. (1947), 'Über die ethischen Grundlagen der sozialen Ordnung', *Süddeutsche Juristen-Zeitung*, 2: 409–16.

Wieacker, F. (1936), 'Kitzeberger Lager junger Rechtslehrer', *Deutsche Rechtswissenschaft*, 1: 74–80.

Wieacker, F. (1939), 'Vom Römischen Juristen', *Zeitschrift für die gesamte Staatswissenschaft*, 99: 440–63.

Wieacker, F. (1944), *Das römische Recht und das deutsche Rechtsbewusstsein*, Leipzig: Johann Ambrosius Barth Verlag.

Wieacker, F. (1952), *Privatrechtsgeschichte der Neuzeit unter besonderer Berücksichtigung der deutschen Entwicklung*, Göttingen: Vandenhoeck & Ruprech.

Wieacker, F. (1956), 'Ursprünge und Elemente des europäischen Rechtbewusstseins', in M. Göhring (ed.), *Europa, Erbe und Aufgabe. Internationaler Gelehrtenkongress Mainz 1955*, Wiesbaden: Franz Steiner.

Wieacker, F. (1967), *Privatrechtsgeschichte der Neuzeit. 2. Auflage*, Göttingen: Vandenhoeck & Ruprecht.

Winkler, V. (2014), *Der Kampf gegen die Rechtswissenschaft. Franz Wieackers "Privatrechtsgeschichte der Neuzeit" und die deutsche Rechtswissenschaft des 20. Jahrhunderts*, Hamburg: Verlag Dr. Kovac.

Wolf, E. (1934), *Richtiges Recht im nationalsozialistischen Staat*, Freiburg: Wagner.

Wolff, J. G. (2007), 'Franz Wieacker (5. August 1908–17. Februar 1994)', in S. Grundmann (ed.), *Deutschsprachige Zivilrechtslehrer des 20. Jahrhunderts in Berichten ihrer Schüler. Eine Ideengeschichte in Einzeldarstellungen. Bd. 1*, 73–86, Berlin: De Gruyter.

Zimmermann, R. (1995), 'Foreword', in F. Wieacker (ed.), *A History of Private Law in Europe: With Particular Reference to Germany*, trans. T. Weir, Oxford: Oxford University Press.

12

Conceptions of Roman Law in Scots Law: 1900–60

Paul J. du Plessis

Introduction

Although Scotland is geographically situated on the edges of Europe, it has nonetheless come to play an important role in the narrative of a new European *ius commune* during the course of the twentieth century. Perhaps a view from the edge provides greater clarity than being *in medias res*. Few scholars working on the civilian tradition or comparative law more generally in 2018 will be unaware of the peculiar nature of the Scottish legal tradition.[1] As a non-codified 'mixed jurisdiction' in which legal principles have been drawn from both the civilian (i.e. Roman law) and common law traditions, Scots law has become a veritable cornerstone in contemporary debates about harmonization of different legal traditions and the utility of 'mixtures'. Within this debate, the scholarship of Reinhard Zimmermann has played a central role, primarily owing to his support for the idea of a living, non-codified civilian tradition based on the principles derived from Roman law. Zimmermann's involvement with the Scottish project can be traced back to at least the 1990s and, while it has done much to support the cause of the civilian tradition in Scotland (and is therefore deserving of great praise and admiration), it is by no means the entire story of Roman law in Scotland during the twentieth century. Since the focus of this collection is the first part of the twentieth century, this chapter will attempt to show how earlier scholarship during this period laid the groundwork for the notion of the 'mixed jurisdiction'. In doing so, I will engage with some of the broader themes raised elsewhere in this volume.

The other main reason for the inclusion of Scotland in a collection of this kind relates to the legal history of Scotland. Although the focus of this volume is the first half of the twentieth century, the nature of contemporary Scots law cannot be understood without some remarks about its legal history. As a separate country from England before the union of crowns in 1603 and the union of parliaments in 1707 by which the United Kingdom was created, Scotland had experienced a reception of Roman law from the late medieval period onwards.[2] Initially in its *ius commune* form, but later also in its humanist form,[3] Roman law had a profound impact on the formation of the municipal law of Scotland during the early modern period, to the extent that the drafters of the Treaty of Union of 1707 specifically provided legal measures to ensure the recognition and continuation of the civilian tradition post 1707.[4] While it cannot be denied that the post-1707 settlement led to a substantial influence of English law in some fields (especially commercial law), the civilian tradition in Scots law has survived and continues to be at the very core of the national legal identity that separates Scots law from English law.

Despite these shared origins in Roman law, however, Scots law took a different developmental route from its Continental sister jurisdictions. What separates Scots law from most of these jurisdictions (and indeed also from English law, but for different reasons) is the manner in which Scots law has come to and continues to use Roman law. For, unlike most Continental jurisdictions, Scotland (and indeed the United Kingdom as a whole) did not codify branches of its law during the course of the nineteenth century. Thus, unlike most of these jurisdictions, where the 'practical' use of Roman law as a source of law ceased upon codification, to be replaced by a civil code of some description consisting of general rules of law (often very heavily based on nineteenth-century Pandectist conceptions of Roman law), Roman law continues to have 'practical' utility in Scottish courts. It cannot be denied, of course, that Roman law as the object of academic study and the 'practical' uses of it by advocates in Scottish courts are two separate (if not unrelated) things, and yet the application of Roman law as a source of modern law is unique in Europe and is deserving of study. It also bears repeating that precisely because Roman law continues to have a 'practical' application in Scots law, it has not been immune to shifts in legal theory during the course of the twentieth century concerning the nature of law and the nature of sources of law.[5]

This chapter will focus on statements made in a variety of contexts (textbooks, case law etc.) about the place of Roman law in Scots law during the first part of the twentieth century. The aim of such a text-based investigation is to demonstrate perceptions about the place of Roman law in Scots law to assess whether any changes are visible in the period under discussion. While it would of course be possible to write a history of the place of Roman law in Scots law against the backdrop of larger historical events of this period, such as the Industrial Revolution in Britain in the nineteenth century (and its lingering effect also in the first part of the twentieth) as well as the social and economic upheavals brought about by two world wars and the loss of an empire, such an investigation would require different types of evidence. Since law is, however, to some extent a reflection of society, even if not a perfect and clear reflection, these larger historical events will be mentioned in passing and where they have had a demonstrable impact on the main narrative of this chapter.[6]

A tale of reception

The formative period

The extent to which Roman law contributed to the creation of a municipal law of Scotland is a long and complex tale, the start of which can be traced to (at least) the fourteenth century. It is not my intention to provide a comprehensive overview of this process, since the matter is well documented in a number of recent works, but it bears repeating that there is strong and incontrovertible evidence that Scottish legal culture is historically based on Roman law. In providing a brief overview, I wish to highlight three broad themes.

First, the reception of Roman law in Scotland covers the early modern period and the concomitant rise of the nation state (Birks, Evans-Jones and Stair Society 1995: 185–200). In second place, the reception of Roman law in Scotland occurred against the backdrop of the rise of the European *ius commune* in the later medieval period and continued through the humanist and *Usus Modernus* movements of the early modern period into the natural law movement of the mid-eighteenth and beyond (Robinson, Fergus and Gordon 1994: 230). Thus, in the teaching manuals used in Scotland and abroad as well as in the lecture notes, the main tenets of these movements (and especially the jurists who are representative of these) can be found across different periods. These also influenced the way in which Scottish jurists wrote about Roman law, especially in the so-called institutional writers, a group of prominent jurists covering the seventeenth to the nineteenth centuries whose works have, since the nineteenth century, been used by Scottish courts to discover basic principles of Scots law (Robinson, Fergus and Gordon 1994: 234). Finally, it should be remembered that the reception of Roman law in Scots law was not wholly a juristic reception. In fact, there is good evidence to suggest that the main vehicle of reception, at least in the late medieval and beginning of the early modern period, was through legal practice (Cairns 2000: 86–7).

For the purposes of this chapter, the first phase of reception (i.e. the fourteenth to the nineteenth centuries) will only be dealt with in outline. The initial reception of Roman law occurred via canon law (Robinson, Fergus and Gordon 1994: 229; Cairns 2000: 29–33). During the first part of the period there was no conception of Scots law as a coherent body of municipal law founded on its own principles. Rather, a pan-European *ius commune* also applied to Scotland subject to certain 'national' deviations, the *ius proprium*.[7] This notion of a 'European common law' was rooted in and reinforced by the practice of studying law on the Continent. Already by 1496, a statute had dictated that 'barons and free-holders of substance' had to provide their sons with at least three years of university training in arts and law.[8] This generally entailed a period of study abroad, an expensive undertaking. Canon law and church courts continued to have a substantial impact on the reception of Roman law during this period until the Reformation occurred by act of parliament in 1560, after which the study of canon law declined and the jurisdiction of church courts were gradually folded into that of secular courts (Cairns 2000: 76).

The second half of this period of reception, from the beginning of the eighteenth to the end of the nineteenth centuries, opens with the Treaty of Union in 1707 that created the United Kingdom. Two articles of this treaty require specific mention in the context of the development of Scots law and the place of Roman law. The first, Article 18, ensured that, with the exception of revenue and trade law (commercial law), the two systems of private law would continue to exist separately, but subject to the laws promulgated thereafter by the Westminster parliament.[9] This latter point is especially significant as this period saw the rise of legislation as the prime source of law in the

United Kingdom. The other, Article 19, provided that the Westminster parliament, in its configuration as the House of Lords, would not have jurisdiction to hear cases on appeal from the Court of Session, the highest court in civil matters in Scotland, although this became the norm in the years thereafter (Robinson, Fergus and Gordon 1994: 241).

The reception of Roman law in Scotland in this period was affected by three factors. The first of these was changes to the legal profession manifested in the growing influence of the Faculty of Advocates.[10] The second factor was changes to the court system introduced towards the end of the seventeenth century by act of parliament. The Court of Session was divided into an Outer House and Inner House and changes were made to the procedure used in the court (Robinson, Fergus and Gordon 1994: 238). It was also during this period that the first attempts at reporting and publishing of court decisions were made. It would continue in this form until the first part of the nineteenth century when further changes were introduced, mainly of a jurisdictional nature, to settle the structure of the different levels of court in Scotland (Cairns 2000: 153–5). It is also worth noting that by the first part of the nineteenth century, it had become a legal requirement for students to obtain a degree in law from a Scottish university in order to practice in Scottish courts.

The final factor that may be said to have affected the reception of Roman law during this period is the rise of national legal systems. The Scottish situation here is quite complex, given that Scotland formed part of the United Kingdom, but as already mentioned above, the autonomy of Scots private law as set out in the Treaty of Union allowed for the formation of Scots private law along the lines of a national legal order. It is difficult to map out the complete route whereby Scots law became a national legal order. As an end point, one might cite the year 1750 when the Faculty of Advocates introduced a compulsory examination in Scots law as an entry requirement to the bar (Robinson, Fergus and Gordon 1994: 245). The introduction of this requirement (in addition to the requirement of a pass in Roman law, which had been introduced in the seventeenth century) indicates that the process whereby the national law of Scotland had been created was now complete.

Intellectual movements in legal theory played an important role in the formation of Scots law. The initial interest in legal humanism and the *Usus Modernus* following the restoration of the monarchy eventually commutated into the natural law movement during the course of the eighteenth century (Robinson, Fergus and Gordon 1994: 253–4). Given the importance of natural law for the Enlightenment, a philosophical movement, which dominated Scotland and the world for much of this century, it stands to reason that it had a profound impact on the latter history of Roman law in Scotland.[11] It would be foolish to attempt a definition of 'natural law' in this context.[12] Suffice it to say that the supporters of this movement placed an emphasis on reason as the basis for all rules of law and that the natural law movement was generally in favour of clear, uncomplicated rules of law that could be collected into a gapless body, hence their impact also on the codification movement in Europe during the course of the nineteenth century. The opponents of this movement, the historical school spearheaded by Savigny, argued against codification and in favour of an organic development of private law rooted in the 'Geist' of the people.[13] Two trends are visible in the development of Scots law during this period. The first is a decline in the citation of Roman law sources by the Scottish jurists. This is in line with the notion of natural law and the rise of Scots law as a national legal system. In second place, during the course of the nineteenth century, when the notion that law should be an instrument of change in society begins to take hold, Scottish jurists increasingly focus on English law as a source for such ideas. At the same time, and given the importance of precedent in English court decisions, the 'institutional writers' become an important vehicle in Scottish court decisions through which certain basic civilian underpinnings of Scots private law could be conveyed.[14]

From the Edwardian period to the 1960s

The period 1890–1914 straddles the end of the Victorian and the entire Edwardian period. Although the Industrial Revolution had made Great Britain wealthy, her economic supremacy had begun to wane (Gilbert and Large 1991: 3–24). Domestically, while relatively peaceful, social change was afoot. The great wealth produced by the Industrial Revolution had not resulted in the improvement of the lives of ordinary workers. Thus, the early part of the twentieth century in Great Britain is marked by the rise of the social function of law. Unions are formed to alleviate the plight of ordinary workers and the progressive extensions of voting rights from the (male) aristocracy to the (male) middle classes and then also to women became a leitmotiv of domestic British politics. Politically, the prevailing policy in Great Britain is one of imperialism.

The First World War had profound socio-economic consequences on Britain and her Empire. Domestically, the First World War led to the demise of the liberals in Great Britain and to the rise of the labour party, briefly in the early 1920s and then for longer periods. Internationally, the First World War has caused rifts between Great Britain and her European neighbours. This, combined with the terms of the Treaty of Versailles, especially in relation to war reparations imposed upon Germany, meant that matters of diplomacy and indeed contact between Great Britain and Germany remained rather strained. This matter remains to be studied more thoroughly in the context of Roman law scholarship, especially since many of the late Victorian professors of Roman law such as James Muirhead and his successor Henry Goudy had studied in Germany. This would no doubt have had an impact on their academic contacts with scholars there.[15]

Arguably the biggest consequence of the First World War, however, was economic (Gilbert and Large 1991: 152–3, 157, 174). Without going into specific details, speculation on the American stock exchange led to the economic crash of the 1930s and the subsequent depression. This economic malaise eventually also had an impact on Europe (Gilbert and Large 1991: 202–3). Many banks in Europe and in Great Britain were left exposed leading to a global financial disaster. Much has been written about the extent to which the financial penalties of the Treaty of Versailles, combined with the effects of the economic problems of the 1930s, gave rise to the rise of Nazism in Germany.

The reasons for and the effects of the Second World War are well documented and will not be elaborated upon here. Suffice it is to say that the economic consequences of this conflict were as dire as those of the First World War and it took the second half of the 1940s and the start of the 1950s to overcome the immediate effects. The 1950s in Great Britain saw the creation of the welfare state in its modern form as well as an attempt, through labour governments, to improve the lives of the average citizen through better housing and employment opportunities. The 1950s also played host to a number of technological advances (e.g. the jet engine), thereby laying the foundations for a move away from traditional industries such as shipbuilding and the like towards innovations in technology. In many ways, Great Britain emerged as a leader in many technologies and this would continue into the early 1960s, culminating in Harold Wilson's famous 'white heat of technological innovation' speech to the labour party conference in 1963. The second factor that had an impact on domestic politics in Great Britain was the slow demise of the British Empire. While Britain's colonies had played a vital role during the Second World War, the end of the conflict and the redrawing of the world map had made it clear that colonialism was a spent force. To that end, for much of the late 1940s and the bulk of the 1950s, ways were explored (not always peacefully) whereby the former colonies could be given self-determination. Although many of these colonies did not achieve independence until the 1960s, following the iconic 'winds of change' speech delivered by Harold MacMillan, the groundwork had already been laid in the 1950s through notion of a British commonwealth (rather than Empire).

The 'idea' of Roman law

Before progressing to specifics, a few observations about conceptions of 'law' in Great Britain during the first part of the twentieth century are required. It is of course incorrect to speak of 'a law of Great Britain' as in reality there has never been a unified law of this kind. Nevertheless, despite the separation between the two bodies of private law (England and Scotland), neither remained unaffected by the prevailing conceptions of law espoused by prominent legal theorists. In terms of legal theory, this period (i.e. 1900–60) is the apex of legal positivism in the United Kingdom,[16] originating in the work of Jeremy Bentham (1728–1832)[17] and developing through a succession of scholars such as John Austin (1790–1859), Hans Kelsen (1881–1973) and, ultimately, H. L. A. Hart (1907–92). It is not my intention to attempt an overview of the complexities of the subtle differences in theory proposed by these scholars. Rather, my argument is merely that these legal philosophers, because of their significant influence on how law should be understood (and indeed the distinction between 'law' and 'other') during the first part of the twentieth century, provide the milieu within which the developments in Scotland should be understood. Whereas the English common law had traditionally been understood in terms closer to that advocated by Savigny and the German historical school,[18] namely as an organic (often unclear) primordial soup from which rulings (never principles) could be drawn through judicial decision, the legal positivists advocated a different approach to law, namely one of simplification and systematization based on the identification of clear rules of law. These rules draw their power from some higher authority (usually the state) and fit together as a harmonious whole in a 'system' (in the scientific sense). In identifying and discussing these rules of law, these legal theorists maintained, legal scholars should draw a clear distinction between a rule of law and other non-legal considerations such as ethics and morality. The latter, as a rule, have no place in discussions of law.

It is not difficult to fathom why this school of legal philosophy had such a profound effect on legal scholarship in Great Britain during the first half of the twentieth century. Two world wars and the socio-economic problems brought about by these conflicts had swept away the last vestiges of natural law thought. If law were to function as a tool to improve society, it had to be clear and unambiguous, the more scientific the better. Recent research has again reinforced the relationship between post–Second World War labourism and Hart's notions of legal positivism.[19]

It is against this backdrop that some remarks about the teaching of law more generally in Edinburgh and of Roman law more specifically are required. My focus on Edinburgh is because of its importance for Scottish law teaching (both historic and contemporary) and also because so much work has been done by Cairns on the teaching of Roman law at this university across centuries.

The nineteenth century is an interesting period in this history of law teaching at Edinburgh. During the first part of this century, the quality of teaching at Scottish law faculties had been called in to question and, since many Scots still studied abroad (especially in Germany during the nineteenth century), it had been suggested that Scottish law teaching should be reformed along German lines to make it more scientific. As Cairns and MacQueen write,

> The Scottish universities had been the subject of increasing dissatisfaction from 1820 or so onwards. Within the British context, they were compared unfavourably with Oxford and Cambridge (themselves not immune for criticism at this period), while the tremendous development of the universities of Germany provided a model for the rest of Europe to admire and attempt to emulate. (Cairns and MacQueen 2000: section III.)

This sense of dissatisfaction eventually led to the promulgation of the Universities (Scotland) Act of 1858 which was drafted to reform Scottish universities (Cairns and MacQueen 2000: sections III and IV). Not long thereafter, a new standardized LLB degree was introduced. It was a part-time graduate degree (meaning that students could only be admitted once they had obtained an MA beforehand) and the focus of teaching was on academic subjects (part of the drive towards greater scientification). It is worth pointing out that the foremost scholars of Roman law at the University of Edinburgh during this period were James Muirhead (appointed to the chair of civil law in 1862 and who held it until his death in 1889), succeeded by Henry Goudy (who held the chair from 1889 until he resigned to take up the position of Regius chair of civil law at Oxford in 1894). The first two had studied Roman law in Germany. As Cairns and MacQueen write of James Muirhead,

> Muirhead established modern Roman law teaching in Edinburgh, drawing on the best contemporary, essentially German, scholarship, with which he kept up-to-date all his life, and on which he himself wrote … (Cairns and MacQueen 2000: section IV.)

When Goudy left for Oxford in 1894, James MacKintosh was appointed to the chair. MacKintosh, a practicing advocate who had not studied abroad, occupied the chair for a considerable period of time and resigned the chair only in 1938, shortly before his death. But whereas Muirhead and Goudy had looked towards Germany for their scholarly inspiration, MacKintosh looked locally. No doubt one of the main consequences of the First World War had been to reduce academic ties with Germany.[20] MacKintosh is primarily known for the publication of *Roman Law in Modern Practice* (Edinburgh, Green and Son 1934), an archetypal positivist work, which is telling of the intellectual trends in law teaching during this period. This book contains the transcriptions of a series of lectures he delivered in Calcutta as a visiting professor. In the Preface, MacKintosh stated,

> I am going to present to you some aspects of Roman Law as applied in the law of Great Britain and adopted to a considerable extent in your Courts, where I am informed the voice of the Digest, or its echoes in the Law Reports, may still at times be heard. … I note among the legal luminaries on the Bench some divergence of opinion, or at any rate some difference of emphasis, with regard to the value and authority of the Roman Law for present-day purposes. … The real question is what weight do the Civil Law and its commentators carry in the actual adjudication of disputed issues? … The main purpose of these Lectures is to supply some materials for an answer to this question … (MacKintosh 1934: 1–2.)

Following this rousing introduction, MacKintosh proceeded to deal with matters such as the importance of legal history, the relationship between Roman and English equity and the transmission of Justinian's project in the medieval period. These were followed by a comprehensive account of various aspects of Roman private law with reference to English and Scottish case law of the period.[21] Thus, to MacKintosh, Roman law served a thoroughly practical purpose in the context of legal practice in Great Britain.

This model of law teaching continued throughout the first part of the twentieth century. The LLB remained a graduate degree that was in practice only offered on a part-time basis. Most professors at the faculty were also practicing advocates or solicitors and most students were engaged in legal practice as trainees. This practice prevailed until after the Second World War when reform of the LLB was once again on the cards. Although the reform did not become final until 1960, it was widely discussed in academic circles in the post-war years and the end result was a full-time undergraduate degree (i.e. dispensing with the requirement of having an MA before enrolling into the LLB) in which law was taught, according to the prevailing legal positivist fashion, predominantly in terms of rules of law and their system. As Cairns and MacQueen write,

> A desire developed for a more academic and sophisticated law degree, with a higher level of teaching than had sometimes prevailed, and a curriculum that gave a more balanced legal education, with greater scope for more advanced, specialised teaching. (Cairns and MacQueen 2000: section V.)

Two figures involved in the teaching of Roman law at Edinburgh are deserving of specific mention (Cairns and MacQueen 2000: section V). The first, Matthew Fisher, the successor to MacKintosh, held the chair from 1938 to 1958 when T. B. Smith was appointed to it. As for scholarly output, it appears to have been negligible, although as a part-time academic and with the disruption of war, this is perhaps understandable. The other, an energetic man whose legacy has divided academic opinion sharply, is T. B. Smith, who became professor of civil law at the University of Edinburgh in 1958. It must not be forgotten that in the interwar period, from roughly the mid-thirties onwards, Roman law as an academic discipline in Great Britain had benefitted from the arrival of Jewish-German émigrés at Oxford and Cambridge such as Fritz Schulz and David Daube who were to have a profound impact on the landscape of Roman law in Britain.[22] Not only did their work influence the scholarly landscape of Roman law but in very real terms the pupils of Daube (e.g. Alan Watson) had a profound effect upon Roman law in Britain post 1960. Although in Scotland the impact of Schulz was indirect only via his textbooks (since the chair in Edinburgh was filled throughout the interwar period by MacKintosh and then Fisher), Daube, through his association with the University of Aberdeen, where he was first appointed to the newly created chair of jurisprudence through the intervention of the then dean of the law faculty, T. B. Smith, also had an impact on Scotland.

At this point, a few comments about perceptions of Roman law in Scots law during the first part of the twentieth century are required. As mentioned before, Cairns has shown that there had been a general downplaying of Roman law in the works of the scholars of natural law towards the end of the eighteenth and into the nineteenth centuries. Given the decline of natural law and its commutation into legal positivism through the works of Bentham and his followers, it stands to reason that a new role had to be found for Roman law in Scots law. Four pieces of evidence will be presented in this regard. The first is a statement in the 1927 edition of the standard Scots law textbook, *Gloag and Henderson* (Gloag and Henderson 1927: paragraph 17). Here we are told that Scots law consists of enacted (= statute) law and non-enacted (= common) law. Given the historical development of Scots law as a national legal system, the authors observe that it can be difficult to work out in any given case what the 'common law' of Scotland is. Despite the dominance of English law, however, the authors maintain that the 'common law' of Scotland is 'in large measure derived from the civil law' (Gloag and Henderson 1927: paragraph 17). Shortly thereafter in 1932, an entry in the *Encyclopaedia of the Laws of Scotland*, in a comprehensive and nuanced discussion of Roman law as a source in Scots law, explained that Roman law acted as a buffer to the development of the English common law during the formative period of Scots law, thereby restricting the extent of its influence upon Scots law (Murray 1932: 74). After setting out in detail the historical process whereby Scots law came to be influenced through canon law and latterly the institutional writers, the reader is reminded, using a dictum from Lord Dunedin in the case of *Sinclair v Brougham* [1914] AC 398, that Roman law was not authoritative, but merely instructive (Murray 1932: 74). The third piece of evidence comes from 1936 in which Lord MacMillan, in the first publication of the Stair Society, set out the sources of Scots law.[23] This account of the sources of Scots law clearly shows that Lord MacMillan was a legal positivist as well as a legal nationalist. Evidence of this can be seen, for example, in his distinction drawn from 'native' and 'non-native' sources. Statute law, precedent and institutional writers are listed in this category, while 'non-native' sources include Roman law. Furthermore, in his discussion of the place of Roman law, he is at pains to stress, following the dictum of Lord President Dundas in the *Cantiere San Rocco case*, that Roman law is only useful inasmuch as it sheds light on the development of Scots law and that it should not be used as a cover under which to over-Romanise Scots law (McKechnie, Brown and Stair Society 1936: 175). The final piece of evidence comes from a booklet by Lord Cooper of Culross, *The Scottish Legal Tradition*, first published in 1949. When read in the context of the aftermath of the Second World War and of strength of the legal positivist tradition through the work of Hans Kelsen during this period, this book takes on a new significance.[24]

After extolling the virtues of Scots law as a system to be studied by others, Lord Cooper went on to say, 'the difficulty is that times are hard and Scotland is small, and this is not the day for small things. … The fertilising foreign contacts upon which Scots law has thrived for ages can only with difficulty be maintained, and there is a visible risk that the old breadth of vision may be succeeded by insular parochialism and a disposition to rest content without inherited capital of ideas' (Meston, et al. 1991: 87–8). The message is clear. To Cooper, the continued civilian nature of Scots law was in danger. The influence from English law had become overwhelming and something needed to be done in order to prevent the onset of 'parochialism'. It is difficult to identify the reasons behind Cooper's statement in this regard (MacQueen 2005b: 53). No doubt the experience of the Second World War combined with the increasing hegemony of English law over areas of Scots law contributed to this views.[25] It would be through Cooper's pupil, T. B. Smith, appointed to the chair of civil law at the University of Edinburgh in 1958, that a vision as to how to save Scots law would be crystallized.[26]

Smith had a profound impact on the development of Scots law during the course of the 1950s and 1960s (Reid 2005: 4). As mentioned above, it was during this period that the part-time, graduate LLB was increasingly under pressure and would eventually be replaced by the full-time, undergraduate degree. Smith should be seen in the context of the rise of the professional legal academic. After a brief career at the Scottish bar immediately following the Second World War, he was appointed to the first full-time chair of law at Aberdeen in 1949, where he would remain for a number of years and ultimately, in his capacity as dean of the faculty of law, would be instrumental in the appointments of David Daube and his pupil, Peter Stein, there.[27]

In terms of Smith's views on the civilian tradition in Scots law, these appear to have been influenced by the views of his teacher, Lord Cooper, as well as by Smith's own experiences in the period immediately post–Second World War. He had spent time both in Louisiana and in South Africa during the late 1950s and had come to the conclusion that English common law presented a threat to the continued civilian character of Scots law (Reid 2005: 10). He therefore advocated that the civilian principles should be infused into Scots law once more using not only Roman but also Roman–Dutch law as visible in South Africa.[28] The analogy with South Africa, though useful at the time, would in retrospect become difficult to sustain. As Chanock observed about the creation of South African legal culture in the first part of the twentieth century,

> There are two important things about this pedigree [i.e. tracing the history of South African law back through the Dutch Republic to Justinian]. First, and this it has in common with the pedigree of English common law, it is long and *old*. Secondly, it is presented as having its essential roots in Europe, and in two basic European traditions, Roman and German. In this conception the law was both established as a sort of organic heart in the body of the state, and also situated in an external, non-African, European heritage. ... This way of presenting the history of the law had two effects. One was instrumental, in that it was resurrected and developed to combat another narrative and pedigree, that of the English common law. A second was that it drew attention away from the local situations in which the law was developed in response to contemporary needs and conflicts. (Chanock 2008: 155.)

The benefit of hindsight is that it sharpens the focus, but at the time Smith saw much in South African legal culture to admire. What Scotland lacked in legal literature, he maintained, could be obtained via the extensive bodies of legal literature in South Africa and to some extent also in Louisiana. Many of his explicitly legal-nationalist views can be seen in his inaugural address in 1958 when he was appointed to the chair of civil law at Edinburgh. This address, the title of which is 'Strange gods', he referred to the creeping influence of English law and how this had negatively impacted upon the civilian doctrinal heritage of Scots law.[29] Smith's plan for the future of Scots law did not bear fruit in the short term. He could of course not have known that a merely couple of years later, in 1961, South Africa would withdraw from the British commonwealth and, following the growing body of Apartheid legislation enacted during the 1960s, combined with the international condemnation following the Sharpeville massacre in 1960, would become an international pariah until democracy was restored in 1994. Furthermore, as argued by Reid in his assessment of the legacy of Smith, his nationalist views were not shared by his colleagues and many did not agree with his assessment as to the state of Scots law and the decline of its civilian heritage (Reid 2005: 13–14, 20).

Given the subsequent history of Scots law and the politics of Scottish devolution, it seems somewhat ironic to end this chapter at the advent of 1960. With that said, 1960 is perhaps a good place for a caesura, precisely because of the rather complex events thereafter.[30] One thing is clear, though. Even if Smith's flavour of legal nationalism was not popular with many of his contemporaries in the legal teaching profession at the time, it cannot be denied that 1950s Scotland was beginning to experience the first flushes of political nationalism.[31] Thus, for example, although the Scottish National Party, created in the mid-1930s, initially did not pursue an independent Scotland, by the mid-1950s, the mood music had changed. The reasons for this new impetus are difficult to pin down, but seems likely to have been connected to a general decline of large industry in Scotland during the 1950s and into the 1960s, creating economic challenges (Devine 1999: 568–9), and, to some extent also the decline of the notion of a British Empire and a sense of global purpose in for Great Britain in the world (Devine 1999: 618–19). Of course the relationship between legal nationalism and political nationalism is by no means straightforward and continues to be a point of contention even in the present. Nonetheless, there are certain indications of a growing sense of national identity connected to the separate nature of Scots law. This can be seen, for example, in the 1953 case *MacCormick v. Lord Advocate* 1953 SC 396 concerning the Royal Prerogatives, which centred on a claim that the newly crowned Queen Elizabeth II had no right to style herself as Elizabeth II in Scotland, since there had never been an Scottish queen by the name of Elizabeth, or, for example, in the circumstances surrounding the theft of the stone of destiny from Westminster Cathedral by a group of Glaswegian Scots in 1950.

Conclusion

The place of Roman law in Scots law during the first half of the twentieth century is a fascinating subject that can only be understood within the context of larger debates about the nature of law and the place of Scotland within the union of Great Britain.[32] As this account clearly shows, while the history of Roman law as a practical component of the Scottish legal culture is a long and hallowed one, it is not without controversy. This is most clearly evident in discussions concerning the role of Roman law in the post-natural law period of Scots law covering the first half of the twentieth century. In legally positivist environments, Roman law was relegated to the DNA of Scots law to be viewed through the lens of the institutional writers, not as authoritative in its own right but merely as an addition. Of course, since the end of the 1950s, much has changed in Scotland and with Scots law and the recent attempt by the supporters of Reinhard Zimmermann to 'revive' the civilian tradition in Scotland cannot be ignored. The fundamental tenets of this attempt are that Scotland is the model as it contains a unique blend of civilian and English common law principles. In a post-national state environment such as the European Union, the 'mixture' could be used as a template for modern Continental civilian systems. This vision of the future of Scots law has not found favour universally in academic circles in Scotland.[33] One thing is clear, however. Not only has it left many unconvinced in practical terms, but the nationalist underpinnings of the idea that the civilian tradition should be used as a bulwark against Anglicization is difficult to sustain in 2018. Furthermore, the association between legal nationalism and the narrative of the South African legal culture make for uncomfortable reading. With that said, it is an indisputable historical fact that Roman law has played (and continues to play) a significant role in Scottish legal culture. Perhaps the time has come to celebrate it for what it is and to reflect on its place in the history of the formation of Scots law on its own terms, rather than try to use it for teleological or ideological purposes.

Notes

1 See now the excellent survey of Simpson 2017. Although precedent plays an important part in the creation of legal norms in Scotland, it has not always been seen as a welcome source of law; see Whitty 2003. For a discussion of 'legal culture' in relation to the Scottish academic T. B. Smith, discussed below, see Blackie 2005: 86.

2 Robinson, Fergus and Gordon 1994: 229. The dating for the first signs of a reception is variously given either as the fourteenth or the fifteenth century; see Cairns 2000: 28. As to whether the Scottish reception was continuous or fitful, see Cairns 2000: 15. Two opposing views, one by Cooper (fitful) the other by Sellar (continuous), may be identified in this debate. For an overview of the Sellar position, see Sellar 2000.

3 Cairns 2000: 126. For a recent assessment of this entire movement, see Du Plessis and Cairns 2016.

4 Robinson, Fergus and Gordon 1994: 231 for an account of the various 'schools' of Roman law during the early modern period. Stein 1988: 269–353. Also see now Simpson and Wilson 2017: chapters 9, 15, 16.

5 Birks 1997. See also Birks, Evans-Jones and Stair Society 1995.

6 This view about the relationship between law and society is a paraphrase of the celebrated statement by Crook 1967: 7.

7 Cairns 2000: 47. The attraction of Roman law in its *ius commune* form as a source of law was connected to its written nature; see Cairns 2000: 100–1.

8 Cited in Robinson, Fergus and Gordon 1994: 230.

9 Robinson, Fergus and Gordon 1994: 239. Interestingly, Cairns 2000: 78 mentions that discussions did take place post 1603 about the harmonization of the laws of the two kingdoms, but the project was unpopular and never came to fruition.

10 Cairns 2000: 128. See now Cairns and Baston 2015. See also now the collection in Cairns 2014b.

11 Cairns 2000: 125. See also now the essays collected in Cairns 2014a.

12 See now Finnis 2016.

13 Robinson, Fergus and Gordon 1994: 271 for a summary of Savigny's opposition to codification. See now Beiser 2015: especially chapter 5.

14 See the Introduction to Reid and Zimmermann 2000 for an account of how legal doctrine develops in a mixed legal system. See also Cairns 2000: 161–77 for an account of the influence of English law in the nineteenth century.

15 In the first edition of James Muirhead's *Historical Introduction to the Private Law of Rome* (1886), the author cites many German works, as can be seen from the list of abbreviations in the front of the work. Muirhead had scholarly links to Germany, having studied there. On Muirhead and this point more generally, see Cairns 2013.

16 Robinson, Fergus and Gordon 1994: 253–4. For a good survey of the main features of legal positivism, see now Green 2009. See now also Schauer 2011.

17 Robinson, Fergus and Gordon 1994: 254. For a good overview of Bentham's philosophy and its impact, see now Crimmins 2017.

18 Crimmins 2017: 271. See also van Caenegem 1991: 165–83. See also Kantorowicz 1937. I wish to draw the attention of the reader here specifically to the rather wonderful introduction in Buckland 1925: ix–xxvii, which contains a veritable tour of positivist theories of law prevalent during the time and an assessment as to whether the force of rules of law the Roman context can be explained using these theories.

19 Edgeworth 1989. See also now Roberts 2005.

20 That German scholars were aware of this can be seen, for example, in the Introduction to Schulz 1936, where the author notes that in translating this book into English, certain issues that would not be of interest to British or American scholars have been removed. A comparison between the German and the English versions of this text should be undertaken to examine the extent of these changes.

21 It is worth pointing out that this work by MacKintosh was not dissimilar to that produced by Sherman 1937, after the First World War and which by this time had seen two editions (soon to have a third edition in 1937).

22 See Birks 2004 for an assessment of all this.
23 See the Introduction to McKechnie, Brown and Stair Society 1936.
24 MacQueen 2005a: 396–402 argues that Cooper's views may be traced back to before the Second World War and should be viewed in the context of the rise of comparative law in Britain. On this latter point, see now comprehensively Cairns 2006, especially on the relationship between the rise of comparative law and legal positivism as well as the relationship between comparative law as a scientific discipline and the legal demands of the British Empire. See also Zweigert and Siehr 1971.
25 Reid 2005: 9 shows that it was Lord Cooper, the teacher of T. B. Smith that first raised the idea of Scotland as a 'mixed legal system' in an article published in the 1950 *Harvard Law Review*.
26 See the chapter by Willock 1976.
27 Reid 2005: 7–8; MacQueen 2005b: 55–6 shows that T. B. Smith had never studied Scots law. He had been educated at Oxford where he had been influenced by prominent Roman law, Roman–Dutch law and comparative law scholars such as Francis de Zulueta, Robert Warden Lee and Frederick Henry Lawson.
28 Fagan 1996; Van der Merwe 2012. For a defence of the continued relevance of Roman–Dutch law in South Africa, see now Scott 2016.
29 Reid 2005: 11–12. A subsequent appraisal of his legacy by Gretton has pointed out that the phrase 'nationalism' is almost always used in a pejorative sense, see Gretton 2005: 32–3. Similarly Visser 2005: 271 do not see him as legal nationalist in the sense.
30 For an assessment of the continuing relevance of the civilian tradition in modern Scots law, see the chapters collected in Evans-Jones and Stair Society 1995. See also the collected works of William (Bill) Gordon: Gordon 2013.
31 See now the interesting chapter by Kidd and Petrie 2016.
32 There are also clear links with the rise of comparative law as an academic discipline in Great Britain during this period. On all this, see Cairns 2006.
33 Evans-Jones 1998. See also Du Plessis 2010.

References

Beiser, F. C. (2015), *The German Historicist Tradition*, Oxford: Oxford University Press.

Birks, P. (1997), 'More Logic and Less Experience: The Difference between Scots Law and English Law', in D. L. Carey Miller and R. Zimmermann (eds), *The Civilian Tradition and Scots Law: Aberdeen Quincentenary Essays*, 167–90, Berlin: Duncker and Humblot.

Birks, P. (2004), 'Roman Law in Twentieth-Century Britain', in J. Beatson and R. Zimmermann (eds), *Jurists Uprooted: German-Speaking Émigré Lawyers in Twentieth-Century Britain*, 249–68, Oxford: Oxford University Press.

Birks, P., Evans-Jones, R. and Stair Society (1995), *The Foundation of Legal Rationality in Scotland*, Edinburgh: Stair Society.

Blackie, J. W. G. (2005), 'T. B. Smith as a Legal Historian', in E. Reid and D. L. Carey Miller (eds), *A Mixed Legal System in Transition: T. B. Smith and the Progress of Scots Law*, 73–99, Edinburgh: Edinburgh University Press.

Buckland, W. (1925), *A Manual of Roman Private Law*, Cambridge: Cambridge University Press.

van Caenegem, R. C. (1991), *Legal History a European Perspective*, London: Hambledon Press.

Cairns, J. W. (2000), 'Historical Introduction', in K. Reid and R. Zimmermann (eds), *A History of Private Law in Scotland*, vol. 1, 14–184, Oxford: Oxford University Press.

Cairns, J. W. (2006), 'Development of Comparative Law in Great Britain', in M. Reimann and R. Zimmermann (eds), *Oxford Handbook of Comparative Law*, 131–73, Oxford: Oxford University Press.

Cairns, J. W. (2013), 'English Torts and Roman Delicts: The Correspondence of James Muirhead and Frederick Pollock', *Tulane Law Review*, 87: 867–86.

Cairns J. W. and Baston, K. G. (2015), 'An Elegant Legal Education: The Studies of Charles Binning, a Scottish Pupil of Cornelis van Eck', *Tijdschrift Voor Rechtsgeschiedenis*, 83 (1–2): 179–201.

Cairns, J. W. and MacQueen, H. L. (2000), *Learning and the Law: A Short History of Edinburgh Law School*, privately published by the Faculty of Law. http://www.research.ed.ac.uk/portal/en/publications/learning-and-the-law(7617657e-1d1e-4961-aa53-bceea1404dab).html.

Cairns, J. W. (2014a), *Enlightenment, Legal Education, and Critique: Selected Essays on the History of Scots Law*, Edinburgh: Edinburgh University Press.

Cairns, J. W. (2014b), *Law, Lawyers and Humanism: Selected Essays on the History of Scots Law*, Edinburgh: Edinburgh University Press.

Chanock, M. (2008), *The Making of South African Legal Culture 1902–1936: Fear, Favour and Prejudice*, Cambridge: Cambridge University Press.

Crimmins, J. E. (2017), 'Jeremy Bentham', in E. N. Zalta (ed.), *The Stanford Encyclopedia of Philosophy* (Spring 2017 Edition). https://plato.stanford.edu/archives/spr2017/entries/bentham/ (accessed 23 April 2017).

Crook, J. A. (1967), *Law and Life of Rome*, Ithaca, NY: Cornell University Press.

Devine, T. M. (1999), *The Scottish Nation 1700–2000*, London: Penguin Books.

Du Plessis, P. J. (2010), 'Legal History and Methods', in P. J. Thomas, R. Van den Bergh, G. J. Van Niekerk and L. Wildenboer (eds), *Libellus ad Thomasium: Essays in Roman Law, Roman-Dutch Law and Legal History in Honour of Philip J. Thomas*, 47–55, Pretoria: UNISA Press.

Du Plessis, P. J. and Cairns, J. W. (2016), *Reassessing Legal Humanism and Its Claims: Petere Fontes?*, Edinburgh: Edinburgh University Press.

Edgeworth, B. (1989), 'H. L. A. Hart, Legal Positivism and Post-War British Labourism', *University of Western Australia Law Review*, 19: 275–300.

Evans-Jones, R. (1998), 'Receptions of Law, Mixed Legal Systems and the Myth of the Genius of Scots Private law', *Law Quarterly Review*, 114: 228–49.

Evans-Jones, R. and Stair Society (1995), *The Civil Law Tradition in Scotland*, Edinburgh: Stair Society.

Fagan, E. (1996), 'Roman-Dutch Law in Its South African Historical Context', in R. Zimmermann and D. Visser (eds), *Southern Cross: Civil Law and Common Law in South Africa*, 33–64, Oxford: Oxford University Press.

Finnis, J. (2016), 'Natural Law Theories', in E. N. Zalta (ed.), *The Stanford Encyclopedia of Philosophy* (Winter 2016 Edition). https://plato.stanford.edu/archives/win2016/entries/natural-law-theories/ (accessed 23 April 2017).

Gilbert, F. and Large, D. C. (1991), *The End of the European Era: 1890 to the Present*, New York: W. W. Norton and Co.

Gloag, W. M. and Henderson, R. C. (1927), *Introduction to the Law of Scotland*, Edinburgh: W. Green & Son.

Gordon, W. (2013), *Roman Law, Scots Law and Legal History: Selected Essays*, Cambridge: Cambridge University Press.

Green, L. (2009), 'Legal Positivism', in E. N. Zalta (ed.), *The Stanford Encyclopedia of Philosophy* (Fall 2009 Edition). https://plato.stanford.edu/archives/fall2009/entries/legal-positivism/ (accessed 23 April 2017).

Gretton, G. (2005), 'The Rational and the National: Thomas Broun Smith', in E. Reid and D. L. Carey Miller (eds), *A Mixed Legal System in Transition: T. B. Smith and the Progress of Scots Law*, 30–43, Edinburgh: Edinburgh University Press.

Kantorowicz, H. (1937), *Savigny and the Historical School of Law*, London: Stevens.

Kidd, C. and Petrie, M. (2016), 'The Independence Referendum in Historical and Political Context', in A. McHarg, T. J. Mullen, A. C. Page and N. Walker (eds), *The Scottish Independence Referendum: Constitutional and Political Implications*, 29–49, Oxford: Oxford University Press.

MacKintosh, J. (1934), *Roman Law in Modern Practice*, Edinburgh: W. Green & Son.

MacQueen, H. L. (2005a), 'Legal Nationalism: Lord Cooper, Legal History and Comparative Law', *Edinburgh Law Review*, 9 (3): 395–406.

MacQueen, H. L. (2005b), 'Two Toms and an Ideology for Scots Law: T. B. Smith and Lord Cooper of Culross', in E. Reid and D. L. Carey Miller (eds), *A Mixed Legal System in Transition: T. B. Smith and the Progress of Scots Law*, 44–72, Edinburgh: Edinburgh University Press.

McKechnie, H., Brown, J. C. and Stair Society (1936), *An Introductory Survey of the Sources and Literature of Scots Law*, Edinburgh: The Stair Society.

Meston, M. C., David, W., Sellar, H., Cooper, T. M. and Styles, S. C. (1991), *The Scottish Legal Tradition*, Edinburgh: The Saltire Society.

Muirhead, J. (1886), *Historical Introduction to the Private Law of Rome*, Edinburgh: Ballantyne, Hanson and Co.

Murray, A. (1st Viscount Dunedin), ed. (1932), *Encyclopaedia of the Laws of Scotland*, Edinburgh: W. Green & Son.

Reid, K. (2005), 'While One Hundred Remain: T. B. Smith and the Progress of Scots Law', in E. Reid and D. L Carey Miller (eds), *A Mixed Legal System in Transition: T. B. Smith and the Progress of Scots Law*, 1–29, Edinburgh: Edinburgh University Press.

Reid, K. and Zimmermann, R. (2000), *A History of Private Law in Scotland*, vol. 1, Oxford: Oxford University Press.

Roberts, T. (2005), 'Legal Positivism and Scottish Common Sense Philosophy', *The Canadian Journal of Law and Jurisprudence*, 18 (2): 277–306.

Robinson, O. F., Fergus, T. D. and Gordon, W. M. (1994), *European Legal History: Sources and Institutions*, London: Butterworths.

Schauer, F. (2011), 'Positivism before Hart', *The Canadian Journal of Law and Jurisprudence*, 24 (2): 455–72.

Schulz, F. (1936), *Principles of Roman Law*, Oxford: Clarendon Press.

Scott, H. (2016), 'The Death of Doctrine?', in J. Basedow, H. Fleischer and R. Zimmermann (eds), *Legislators, Judges, and Professors*, 223–48, Tübingen: Mohr Siebeck.

Sellar, W. D. H. (2000), 'Scots Law Mixed from the Very Beginning: A Tale of Two Receptions', *The Edinburgh Law Review*, 4: 3–18.

Sherman, C. P. (1937), *Roman Law in the Modern World*, New York: Baker, Voorhis & Co.

Simpson, A. R. C. (2017), 'An Introduction to Scottish Legal Culture', in S. Koch, K. E. Skodvin and J. Øyrehagen Sunde (eds), *Comparing Legal Cultures*, 87–130, Bergen: Fagbokforlaget.

Simpson, A. R. C. and Wilson, A. L. M. (2017), *Scottish Legal History: Volume 1: 1000–1707*, Edinburgh: Edinburgh University Press.

Stein, P. (1988), *The Character and Influence of the Roman Civil Law: Historical Essays*, London: Hambledon Press.

Van der Merwe, V. (2012), 'The Origin and Characteristics of the Mixed Legal Systems of South Africa and Scotland and Their Importance in Globalisation', *Fundamina: A Journal of Legal History*, 18 (1): 91–114.

Visser, D. 'The Ties That Bind: T.B. Smith as a Comparative Lawyer', in E. Reid and D. L. Carey Miller (eds), *A Mixed Legal System in Transition: T. B. Smith and the Progress of Scots Law*, 272–92, Edinburgh: Edinburgh University Press.

Whitty, N. R. (2003), 'From Rules to Discretion: Changes in the Fabric of Scots Private Law', *Edinburgh Law Review*, 7 (3): 281–339.

Willock, I. D. (1976), 'The Scottish Legal Heritage Revisited', in J. P. Grant (ed.), *Independence and Devolution: The Legal Implications for Scotland*, 1–14, Edinburgh: W. Green & Son.

Zweigert, K. and Siehr, K. (1971), 'Jhering's Influence of the Development of Comparative Legal Method', *The American Journal of Comparative Law*, 19: 215–31.

13

The Search for Authenticity and Singularity in European National History Writing: 1800 to the Present

Stefan Berger

Introduction: Why everyone wants to be special

In the debates surrounding the referendum on the British exit from the European Union (EU), the Brexiteers routinely referred to history. A sense of British history as being different and far removed from Continental European history was an important sub-theme of the debate. In particular, nostalgia for Empire and a vague longing for the imagined community of the Second World War played a key role.[1] Britain's long-term internationalist free-trade orientation was also a bulwark against those Remain campaigners who were warning of the dangers of Britain leaving the European free-trade zone. Furthermore, the British self-image as the motherland of liberal democracy and parliamentary government was also frequently underlined by Brexiteers. These historical undertones reflect a long-standing concern in right-of-centre historical accounts that have pondered the role of (largely) English (as opposed to British) history in a wider European narrative. David Starkey, one of the most powerful television historians in the UK, in his Medlicott Lecture given to the Historical Association in 2001, wrote, 'Maybe we have a future as a series of disparate regions of the European Union, perhaps as a greater city state, in other words, a greater London. But where a history – where an English history, fits in … a sense of England as a place that once existed, that once mattered, that was once glorious – I'm really not sure' (Starkey 2001).

This sense of tension between commitment to a particular national historical master narrative and challenges by supranational institutions and their historical narratives can also be found elsewhere in Europe. This very tension reflects a deep-rooted concern in European national histories that sought to legitimate nation states vis-à-vis a unique or special national path of development, a path that provided authenticity to national narratives and shaped alleged national characters. Supranational institutions, such as the EU, can easily be perceived as a threat to these cherished national narratives, as indeed we can observe in many European states today. This chapter will trace the development of these particularisms from the late eighteenth century to the present day. In doing so, it highlights the idiosyncrasies between the appeal to the particular and the narrative structuring of those particularist histories according to oft-repeated patterns across diverse European national histories. Arguably, the power of those histories over national imaginations today has waned. Nevertheless, it remains a powerful threat to the EU and begs the question how historians today should deal with national historical master narratives.

Romantic national history writing and authenticity

The Romantic tradition of writing history starts in the late eighteenth century with Johann Gottfried Herder's reaction against the Enlightenment. Himself very much a child of the Enlightenment and unthinkable without it, he had grown suspicious of certain elements within it, including its penchant for universalisms and for a belief in progress. In historical writing this had led representatives of the Enlightenment to trace the progress of mankind throughout the ages, leading to forms of universal history writing in which the authors attempted to follow the most advanced civilizations of their time, whom, they believed, were the carriers of progress. This made for histories that ranged widely, in terms of space and thematically; it also made for histories that privileged the successful and the powerful over the marginal and the powerless. Herder's cosmopolitanism was one that took offence at this idea and instead sought to put all civilizations on an equal par. He did this by arguing that people were naturally organized into nations and that these nations possessed distinct characteristics from other nations that endowed them with their own worth and value. As Herder abandoned the idea of universal values, one was not necessarily better or worse than the other. In typically Herderian organicist language, world civilization was presented as a tree from which various branches grew that were quite different in shape, strength and outlook; yet each branch claimed its own value and worth in itself and helped to make up the entirety of the tree.[2]

Unsurprisingly, this revolutionary idea was picked up with a vengeance, especially by those peoples who had been marginal and weak in the universal histories of the Enlightenment. Throughout nineteenth-century Europe we find a proliferation of Herders in many places whose writings all aimed at establishing what characterized their own nations. Therefore national history not only became the centre of attention; it also was, indeed above all, concerned with authenticity and uniqueness. Whereas Enlightenment historians could and did write national history as well, their concern was with tracing how the nation advanced the whole of mankind, how it was marching at the helm of progress. Now, in Romantic historical writing, this was turned on its head. The success of this exercise was not merely rooted in intellectual fashions, but happened against the concrete backdrop of the experience of the French Revolution and the Napoleonic attempt to conquer Europe. Apologists for both the French Revolution and Napoleon argued within a strongly universalist framework. National history was an important means of rejecting these universalisms along with French armies and for preparing an intellectual defence against occupation.[3]

Thus, for example, Fichte specifically called for a national history of the Germans as the best defence against French universalism: 'Amongst the means of strengthening the German spirit, a powerful one would be an enthusiastic history of the Germans, which would be a national as well as a people's book, just like the Bible or the Song Book' (Fichte 2008 [1808]: 106). Fichte's idea of history as a bulwark against the French Revolution found its parallels elsewhere, for example, in the thought of Joseph de Maistre in France and of Edmund Burke in Britain. For all of them, the study of national history allowed access to a vision of a nation fundamentally at odds with that created in the French Revolution. With their emphasis on the continuity of national historical evolution, Friedrich Schlegel's 1811 Vienna lectures on modern history summarized some of the key characteristics of Romantic historiography. Invariably, each state and nation had its own individuality and each *Volk* its own unique authenticity. The totality of Christian Europe was made up of such national individualities. Overall, authenticity, longevity, unity and homogeneity became the hallmarks of Romantic national history-writing. 'Growth' and 'evolution' were its key metaphors, stressing the durability of national characteristics and the permanence of the *Volk*. Tradition, as represented by history, was juxtaposed with sovereignty as formulated by the French revolutionaries.

Ironically, the search for national features produced, in European national historiography, a patterning applicable to many national histories. While the narratives that were produced aimed for distinctiveness, they in fact resulted in narrative tropes and structures that can often be traced back to pre-modern forms of national history writing. These same narratives established an enduring legacy for national historiographical traditions well into the second half of the twentieth century and beyond. Thus, to give a few examples, many Romantic national histories became obsessed with defining the territory of the nation. The German cultural historian Wilhelm Heinrich Riehl argued that the national characters of all peoples were rooted in the soil and landscape they inhabited. He juxtaposed the wild, warlike and freedom-loving peoples of the forest with the tame, civilized and peaceful peoples of the field (Riehl 1897; also Riehl 1990). In the larger nations of Europe, territorial definitions of the nation incorporated the idea of the nation being made up of diverse regions. Michelet was all too aware of the wealth of regional and local historical studies and the diverse possibilities of conceptualizing national history, when he started the second volume of his *History of France*, published in 1833, with a 'tableau de la France', in which he surveyed the different regions of his country, describing their diversity but ultimately reassuring his readers that the regional differences came together in a homogeneous whole called 'France' (Thiesse 1999; Brakensiek and Flügel 2000).

Apart from an obsession with defining national territory, many national histories were either strongly oriented towards the state, mainly if they could look back on a long history of independent statehood, or referred back to the people as the backbone of the nation, mainly in areas where statehood had not existed at all or had been interrupted for a long time. Overall, state and people became the central axis around which national histories were organized. Furthermore, in their search for authenticity, virtually all national histories traced their histories as far back as possible until their stories were lost in the mists of time. The Middle Ages was a period when, with the exception of Italy and Greece, which harked back to ancient times, national history fully came into its own. The periodization of national histories often followed rise-and-fall narratives that ended either on the actual or on the predicted rise of the nation, whether in the present or the future. Canons of national heroes and enemies were constructed. Many national histories followed similar ideas. One popular notion, for example, was nationhood as the continuous extension of the idea of liberty. Invariably, across Europe, the idea of the nation had to position itself vis-à-vis a range of other, potentially rival master narratives, including those of class, ethnicity/race and religion. Indeed, a remarkable feature of Romantic national history writing across Europe consists of the extent to which the Romantic historians managed to incorporate those potential rivals into their national storylines, so that ethnic, religious and class characteristics became alleged hallmarks of national attributes.[4]

Legal historians, influenced by Romanticism, could play a crucial role in establishing national characteristics through distinct legal traditions. Carl Friedrich von Savigny, for example, was extremely important in arguing against rationalistic French jurisprudence. He was convinced that law developed historically according to national cultural logics which differed in disparate parts of Europe. Savigny's ideas paralleled those of Ranke, who also believed in diverse national trajectories rooted in historically specific primordial national types, for example, Celts, Germans and Latin and Slavic peoples.

The age of Romantic historiography also saw a range of historians forging legal documents in an attempt to invent legal traditions that were to prove specific national characteristics. Vaclav Hanka, for example, forged Czech legal documents in 1818 to prove the independent development (from the German one) of an ancient Czech legal tradition (Otáhal 1986). In early nineteenth-century Catholic Irish historiography, legal history was instrumental in preparing the road for the Catholic Emancipation Act of 1829 by arguing consistently against the body of Protestant Irish historiography that the 1691 Treaty of Limerick provided a contract guaranteeing legal rights (McCartney 1957).

Scientificity, nationalism and the need for 'being special'

Across Europe, the Romantic historiographical tradition was heavily criticized by subsequent generations of more professionalized historians. During the second half of the nineteenth century, the institutionalization of historical writing at universities and academies gathered pace, as states and governments came to perceive the usefulness of history for purposes of state integration and stabilization, especially in an age of mass politics. If we take the example of Romania, after the foundation of the Romanian state in 1862, the state administration quickly united the archives in Wallachia (founded in 1831) and Moldavia (founded in 1832) and vigorously promoted research into national history. The state expanded the University of Iaşi (1860) and founded the University of Bucureşti (1864), the *Muzeul Naţional de Antichităţi* (National Museum of Antiquities, 1864) and the Societatea Academică Română (Romanian Academy, 1867) and gave national history a prominent place everywhere. The Academy was to play a hugely influential role in publishing key sources of Romanian national history through the

Hurmuzaki collection, published in forty-five volumes between 1876 and 1942. It also organized yearly prizes for the best publications in national history and through its own yearbook participated actively in constructing a specific national master narrative that was to differentiate it clearly from its neighbours. The Comisia Istoricăa României (Historical Commission of Romania) was founded in 1910 by the Ministry of Education with the specific task of publishing more historical sources, especially critical editions of medieval manuscripts (Murgescu 2010: 100).

The training of historians became more formalized and the disciplinary methodological and theoretical arsenal of the historian became more refined. As a result, professionalized historians could claim that they were the only ones, *qua* trained specialists, who could speak authoritatively about the past and that therefore they were privileged in comparison to other disciplines and genres also dealing with the past. In an age of historicism, during the second half of the nineteenth century, they were remarkably successful in pushing through this idea. Yet their exclusive claims to scientificity did not see a significant break with historiographical nationalism across Europe. Quite the contrary, historians continued the Romantic tradition of acting as prophets and seers of the nation, devising strategies of ever greater authenticity and narrow specificity, only now with renewed scientific claims and enhanced authority (Feldner 2010).

Their strong orientation towards the nation and increasingly the nation state meant that historiographical nationalism even increased in the second half of the nineteenth century and up until the outbreak of the First World War. In Scotland, the development of a more self-consciously 'scientific' historical science went hand in hand with patriotic and civic education emphasizing the distinguishing features of Scotland (Anderson 2010). In Finland, the University of Helsinki, founded in 1825, became a hotbed of Fennoman nationalist history writing from the middle of the nineteenth century onwards, with two historians in particular, Georg Zacharias Forsman and Zacharias Topelius, constructing the canon of Finnish national history that was also characterized by its specific features (Haapala and Kaarninen 2010: 75).

Empires and multinational states alike often reacted to the challenges of national movements at their peripheries by promoting historical national master narratives foregrounding a central national storyline into which peripheral nations could be incorporated. Historians have for too long seen empires and multinational states only as 'victims' or 'oppressors' of national movements, ignoring the fact that these polities developed nationalizing strategies with the intention of keeping the empire together by establishing a unique and highly focused narrative about its national core and its peripheries (Berger and Miller 2015).

Professional historians, whether writing on empires or nations, stuck to the Romantics' obsession with specific national features. Yet at the same time national histories across Europe also continued their pattern of mutual resemblance. In other words, national history aimed at being unique but often produced more of the same. So, for example, the specifics of Polish, Romanian, Russian, Swedish, British, Spanish and other national histories in Europe resulted from an allegedly close and even unique affinity with religion, whether Catholicism, Orthodoxy or Protestantism. Yet the alleged special affinity of one nation with one religion was consistently reproduced elsewhere in Europe (Hermann and Metzger 2015). The same could be said for the racialization of national historical consciousness from the last third of the nineteenth century onwards. Many national historians sought to prove scientifically, by reference to history, the superiority of the specific racial characteristics of their own nation over others. The arguments were framed with a view to specificity and exclusiveness but they again followed a common patterning. To illustrate – if we take Hungarian national narratives – the Hungarian national master narrative was also bound up with notions of Hungarians as descending from 'tribes from the East'. If Hungarian historians of the early nineteenth century routinely depicted Hungary as a multi-ethnic nation state, the search for the 'Asian roots' of the Magyar nation was a direct attempt to homogenize the ethnic origins of the Hungarian nation and, at the same time, assimilate non-Magyar 'tribes' along often racialized and social-Darwinist lines (Zsolt 2010. See also von Klimó 2003: chapter 4).

The uniqueness of national paths could also be borrowed. If we take the example of German national history, German historians working on ancient Greek history did not tire of emphasizing how intimately related the German national character was to that of the ancient Greeks. Wilhelm von Humboldt, who formulated this idea at the beginning of the nineteenth century, could already draw on arguments put forward in the mid-eighteenth century by Johann Joachim Winckelmann and in the late eighteenth and early nineteenth centuries by Johann Wolfgang von Goethe, both of whom stressed the spiritual, cultural and educational proximities between ancient Greeks and contemporary Germans. Humboldt, following Goethe, still perceived the plurality of the German nation state as a direct parallel to the plurality of the ancient Greek city states. Ancient Rome had built an empire and might therefore be best compared with contemporary imperial nations such as Britain or France, but ancient Greece was characterized not by nation or empire building but by attempts to perfect human education: what the Germans came to refer to as *Bildung*. Nevertheless, ancient Greece also became a political model for contemporary Germany – a federal system united by culture. Analogies with the contemporary German *Kulturnation* were all too obvious. Moreover, later on, Droysen's writings on Alexander the Great were not shy in pointing out the parallels between Macedonia and Prussia. If it had been Macedonia's telos to unite all the Greek city states into one powerful nation state, so it was Prussia's telos to unite all the German tribes into one powerful German nation state which could defeat its enemies and secure Germany's 'rightful place' among the great nations of Europe (Funke 1998).

National uniqueness was rarely uncontested. Looking at Russia, in Russian national history, for example, we encounter one of the biggest and longest-running historical debates focused on this very question of Russia's peculiar position vis-à-vis Europe and the West. Historians such as Samarin argued that Westernizing influences in Russia's history had weakened the nation by subverting the spiritual and political foundations of the country, that is, Orthodoxy, the village community and Tsarism. His writings were full of vigorous attacks on what he perceived as lifeless cosmopolitanism. By contrast, his colleagues Solov'ëv and Boris Nikolaevič Čičerin emphasized that it would be impossible to maintain Russian traditions if the aim was to modernize the nation. Only the Western path promised a modernity that would, at long last, free Russia from its inferior and backward position vis-à-vis Europe. Not all Russian historians fit neatly into these two camps. A variety of intermediate positions could also be found. So, for example, Michail Petrovič Pogodin divided European history into a Western and an Eastern European path. They corresponded to a distinction between Rome and Constantinople. Russia, Pogodin argued, was the heir of the Eastern tradition. Hence Pogodin positioned his country to some extent in opposition to the West, but at the same time he was also full of praise for Peter the Great, who had allegedly brought Russia into the mainstream of European civilization. The uniqueness of Russia, according to Pogodin, lay precisely in its ability to reconcile Western and Eastern traditions.[5]

The prominence of legal history in the framing of national uniqueness continued with the growing professionalization of the historical sciences. Thus, for example, constitutional history in Britain was hugely important in framing the national master narrative. Stubbs's *Constitutional History of England*, published between 1874 and 1878 in three volumes, famously described thirteenth-century England as a location where the English people had united around the constitution and had formed a consensus unperturbed by divisions of class, race or language. Ever since, according to Stubbs, English history has amounted to one long struggle to maintain, defend and develop those constitutional rights (Mitchell 2000). Yet the importance of constitutional rights and legal traditions was also highlighted in many other national histories across Europe. In the nineteenth century, where national historical narratives were underpinned by massive source collections, many of those collections explicitly assembled legal documents related to the formation and development of the nation state. In England, the Whig story of ancient English liberties and constitutional progress simply had to be extended to incorporate the Scots and the Welsh and potentially, as in Seeley's national history, all white-settler communities in the Empire – a Greater Britain indeed. A narrative of a unique civilization and its civilizing mission underlay this revamped national history, which was to safeguard the multinational state against threats from nascent national movements and their historical master narratives in Ireland, Scotland and Wales (Mycock and Loskoutova 2015).

The high point of historiographical nationalism between the wars

Historiographical nationalism, based on assumptions of unique authenticity, reached a high point at the time of the First World War. Stories of national features and characteristics in aggressive juxtaposition to those of the enemy were vital for a wide variety of intellectual justifications of diverse war efforts. In 1915 Friedrich Meinecke (1862–1954) published a collection of his speeches and articles that justified the German war effort by reference to German history, which he interpreted as a long search for national independence against foreign enemies. The wars of liberation against Napoleon in 1812–13, the revolution of 1848 and the wars against Denmark (1864), Austria (1866) and France (1870–1) were all stepping stones to realizing the sovereign German nation state representing a unique spiritual heritage that was superior to all other national essences. Meinecke saw the specific German national character rooted in a combination of inner freedom (*Innerlichkeit*) and the ability to sacrifice selfish desires for the good of the community. In contrast to the historically developed higher German form of humanity stood the humanity of the 'West' which Meinecke identified with uniformity, egotism and degeneracy (Meinecke 1915. See also Stibbe 2003). Historians from the Allied nations replied in kind, constructing various historical missions delineated from their own specific national pasts (Wallace 1988; Krumeich 1996).

In the major struggles of the interwar period between democracy and the totalitarianisms of the twentieth century, a range of discursive constructions of national particularities were prominently present. In the struggle of the Italian anti-fascists, the idea took root that fascism emerged as a direct consequence of an allegedly unique national trajectory. The brothers Rosselli, for example, argued that the Risorgimento had been unfinished, and claims by the fascist regime to be its heir had to be contested historically. An alternative, republican and socialist Risorgimento had to be upheld against the rival claims of the fascist state. The Rossellis were influential in defining the anti-fascist struggle as a 'second Risorgimento', a trope that became popular in Resistance circles during the Second World War. It sought to expound the unity of the Italian nation on the basis of social justice and emancipation (Morgan 1999).

In Spain, the re-Catholicization of Spanish national historical consciousness under Franco saw new attempts to write national history in a uniquely Catholic key. This in turn found expression in the idealization of medieval Christendom, stress on the moral purity of Spanish Catholic nationality and the strong role of Opus Dei in history departments and historical education more generally. The nation became synonymous with the church and the monarchy (Boyd 1997: chapter 6). In Germany, the historian of the Catholic Centre Party, Carl Bachem (1858–1945) also described political Catholicism as an expression of the German national character, thereby confirming once again that similar patterns were the norm rather than the exception in framing national peculiarities in national historical master narratives in Europe (Kiefer 1989: 197ff).

In Britain, one of the bulwarks of interwar liberal democracy, liberal historians such as George Macaulay Trevelyan used their positions of public influence to stress the organic link between a special historical past and a contemporary political mission. In a speech written for George V and delivered on the occasion of the opening of Parliament in 1935, Trevelyan wrote,

> It is to me a source of pride and thankfulness that the perfect harmony of our parliamentary system with our constitutional monarchy has survived the shocks that have in recent years destroyed other empires and other liberties .... The complex forms and balanced spirit of our Constitution were not the discovery of a single era, still less of a single party or of a single person. They are the slow accretion of centuries, the outcome of patience, tradition and experience constantly finding outlets ... for the impulse toward liberty, justice and social improvement inherent in our people down the ages. (Cited in Hernon 1976: 86)

These sentences were a patriotic assertion of the Whig view of historiography that had associated constitutional liberties and democratic traditions with Englishness throughout the nineteenth century. This decidedly Whiggish view of British national history remained strong in popular historical writing in interwar Britain, not just among liberals.

Newly founded states in the interwar period were particularly prone to harnessing the power of uniqueness to justify their new-found statehood. Thus, historians close to the Kemalist revolution at the heart of modern Turkey stressed that Turkish was the original language of mankind and glorified Turkishness as the cradle of humanity. This view declared Turks to be Aryans and identified contemporary Turks with the ancient Hittites, thereby moving the foundation story of Turkey back by several centuries (Kieser 2005).

In Latvia, historians established an official national master narrative, in particular refuting the claims of Baltic German historiography over their territory. Focusing on agrarian history, their work sought to demonstrate that the claims of Baltic Germans to the land were spurious and that redistribution of land to Latvian smallholders was historically justified. The special status of a nation of small-holding peasants oppressed by a foreign occupier was, of course, an oft-repeated story in Europe, not just in the Baltic States. According to the argument of nationalist Latvian historians of the interwar period, the distinctive features of prehistoric pagan society of the Ur-Latvians, who were allegedly committed to social egalitarianism under wise leadership until the Crusaders put an end to it and established colonial rule over Latvia in the thirteenth century, could only be rediscovered after seven centuries of darkness with the formation of an independent Latvia at the end of the First World War (Šnē 2010: 82).

Notions of uniqueness could go hand in hand with justifying an internationalist and cosmopolitan mission. In interwar Switzerland, nationalist appropriation of the medieval past of the Old Confederacy reached its high point in and around the Second World War, when homeland defence against Nazi Germany became a key issue. This appropriation was depicted in terms of defence of ancient Swiss neutrality and freedoms. But by the 1920s many Swiss histories combined notions of the Alps as protector of the sources of major European rivers with ideas of Switzerland as the home of the new League of Nations. The specific feature of neutrality and ancient freedoms mixed with geographical location was used to lay claim to be a champion of internationalism (Marchal 2006).

To take another example, Belgium, as a crossroads of cultures, so Henri Pirenne argued after the First World War, was specially predestined to lead the way in an international examination of the methodological ground rules of historical writing (Harvey 2003: chapter 6). However, at the same time as Pirenne was promoting his native country as a unique cosmopolitan microcosm, he was faced with the rise of an ethnically rooted Flemish nationalism. Flemish historians regarded Belgian history à la Pirenne as an invention of early nineteenth century French diplomats and provided their own Flemish master narrative. The specific features of the region-cum-nation challenged the universalism derived from a specific construction of a Belgian national master narrative (Beyen 2007: 44f).

In the young Soviet Union, notions of Soviet distinctiveness vis-à-vis the West figured prominently in debates surrounding the revolutionary strategy to be pursued by the first Communist state. Those who followed a well-established trope in socialist historical discourse about the backwardness of Russia due to its specific historical trajectory argued that communism would not be able to survive in Russia unless the Russian Revolution was followed by revolutions in the more developed West. As this became increasingly illusory in the course of the 1920s, Stalin's idea of 'socialism in one country' was equally based on notions of the uniqueness of Russian history that predestined it to build communism unsupported by successful revolutions in the West. Russian Marxist historiography was best represented by Georgij Plechanov, whose *Istorija russkoj obščestvennoj mysli* (*History of Russian Social Thought*), published in 1909, paid much attention to Russian national history, which he described as deviating in major ways from the history of West European nation states. Russian national history was closer to certain oriental and Asiatic societies than West European ones, which explained much of Russia's backwardness. According to Plechanov, despotism and immobility became the hallmarks of Russian national development. Whereas in the West the Marxist idea of different stages of economic production succeeding each other until capitalism was reached was valid, in Russia primitive communism was followed directly by oriental despotism. In other words, Russia was not yet a developed capitalist country, which also made it the most unlikely location for a successful working-class revolution (Baron 1963). Michail Pokrovskij, who became the undisputed leader of Soviet Marxist historiography in the 1920s, nicknamed 'Supreme Commander of the Army of Red Historians', begged to differ. His *Russkaja Istorija v samom sžatom očerke* (*Brief History of Russia*) was approved by no less a figure than Lenin and served as a bible for the first generation of Marxist–Leninist historians in the Soviet Union. As a national history it indeed sought to establish a new national master narrative portraying the history of Tsarist Russia as a 'dark other', where not only the working classes but also the non-Russian nationalities were repressed. He contrasted the Russian past sharply with the bright Communist future of the Soviet Union under Bolshevism. In line with Marxist thinking, he depicted the history of Russia as a history of class struggle. However, contrary to Plechanov and Trotsky, Pokrovskij described Russian historical development as essentially following the same trajectory as that of Western Europe. By assimilating Russian history into the West European model, Pokrovskij gave historical explanation, justification and, not least, hope to the Russian Revolution of 1917 (Enteen 1978).

In the interwar period, legal history continued to play an important role in underpinning notions of uniqueness and specificity. In Hungary, for example, historians justified their country's post-war territorial ambitions via the 'Idea of the Holy Crown of St Stephen', a nineteenth century legal concept about the integrity of the lands of the Hungarian crown within the Habsburg monarchy. The Horthy regime generously supported the annual Saint Stephen's procession after 1920. The admiral himself marched ahead of the procession (despite being a Calvinist) every 20 August, and the military participated prominently in the festivities leading to militarization of the religious cult in the interwar period. On the occasion of the 900th anniversary of the death of Saint Stephen in 1938, the Catholic Eucharist Congress was held in Budapest and around 800,000 people participated in the procession. The mayor of Budapest, Ferenc Ripka, even commissioned a historical study in 1927 which was to prove once and for all that the annual Saint Stephen's procession was not an invented tradition as was claimed by Protestants and socialists (von Klimó 1999a; von Klimó 1999b).

Appeals to law, in this case international law, were also important in the context of justifying British involvement in the First World War. The University of Oxford's Faculty of Modern History published a pamphlet immediately after the outbreak of hostilities in which they argued that Britain was upholding the international rule of law against the authoritarian and militarist *étatisme* of Germany (*Why We Are at War: Great Britain's Case* (1914)).

The restitution of traditional national historical narratives after the Second World War

In the immediate aftermath of the Second World War, national histories found themselves deeply destabilized through the histories of fascism, war, occupation and collaboration in most parts of Europe. It is striking to what extent references to uniqueness and specificity were used to stabilize traditional national narratives in the post-war period. Sometimes these were new constructions. In the case of Austria, for example, the theory of Austria having been the 'first victim' of Hitler's aggression served the purpose of avoiding questions of perpetratorship and historical guilt. The National Socialist period of Austrian history could be externalized and made into something foreign. Austrian historians played a major part in shaping an independent and separate Austrian national consciousness that had been so manifestly absent in the interwar period. A 'coalition historiography' of Catholic and socialist historians stressed the common anti-fascism of the Austrian people and ignored the many incidents of voluntary collaboration with Germany (Utgaard 2003). The idea of a separate Austria, built on notions of 'special development' within the Babenbergian–Habsburg countries during the Middle Ages, highlighted the baroque period and enlightened Josephinism as 'formative phases' of Austrian national history. The Habsburg monarchy was now interpreted as a positive antidote to the aggressive nationalism of the German Empire and as a model for the bridging function that the independent and neutral Austria allegedly fulfilled in the Cold War – mediating between East and West (Marjanović 1998).

In a similar way, German post-war historical narratives externalized the question of guilt and responsibility by arguing that National Socialism was not rooted in positive and unique German national traditions, but in modern mass society, associated with the French Revolution and its aftermath, and in Italian fascism. For historians, such as Gerhard Ritter, Hans Rothfels and Herman Aubin, the good national tradition was represented by the national conservative opposition to Hitler, that is, those who had plotted to assassinate Hitler on 20 July 1944 (Cornelißen and Ritter 2001; Eckel 2005; Mühle 2005). Furthermore, memories of wartime bombing, of the suffering of ordinary soldiers and of ethnic cleansing were cultivated in order to allow a positive national historical consciousness to re-emerge after 1945 (Berger 2006).

In Italy we can observe a similar attempt to decouple a favourable national trajectory from the history of Italian fascism. The former was represented by the nineteenth-century Risorgimento (Levy 1999). Historians from the centre-left, such as Gaetano Salvemini, who had been exiled during the fascist years, and centre-right historians, such as Federico Chabod, united forces to preserve a good deal of the traditional national master narrative. As in Germany, the Resistance was key in allowing historians to locate favourable national traditions outside of fascism. The Resistance was routinely portrayed as a second Risorgimento. By concentrating on the period of German occupation after 1943, Italian historians could furthermore present a picture of a genuinely popular anti-fascism struggling against foreign occupiers and a small clique of Italian collaborators.[6]

In Communist Eastern Europe after 1945 most national histories, resting on understandings of uniqueness and specificity, were simply painted red. In other words, a Marxist–Leninist class interpretation of history was placed over the well-established national narrative, retaining most elements of the latter. In the GDR, for example, national histories still routinely referred to the wars of 1813–14 as national 'wars of liberation', the national movement of the first half of the nineteenth century was viewed as uniformly progressive, the war against France in 1870–1 was frequently portrayed as a defensive war, and the Bismarckian solution to the German question was presented as having lacked alternatives. All of these interpretations were harking back to traditional forms of Prussianism in national historical writing (despite the formal dissolution of Prussia in 1947), and were relatively unaffected by Communist reinterpretations (Iggers 1989: 69). An exception is the Romanian historical master narrative that emerged in the post-Second World War years. A marked negativity towards Romanian national history coincided with an emphasis on building Romanian communism entirely on the glorious Soviet example. The most important representative of this negative inversion of national history was Mihail Roller (Murgescu 2010: 100). This phase of national self-deprecation, however, lasted only until 1958 and was followed by a period of hypernationalism. Increasingly, historians merged the dictates of Marxism–Leninism with traditional nationalist narratives (Durandin 2002; Kellogg 1990).

In Britain, the traditionally forceful Whig narrative of British national history as an expansion of liberty and freedom survived in British historical thinking throughout much of the twentieth century (Bentley 2005), and now began to incorporate the national story of the emancipation of the working classes – nowhere more emphatically than in the work of the Communist Party Historians' Group, among which could be found some of the most influential Western Marxist historians, such as Eric Hobsbawm and Edward Palmer Thompson (Kaye 1984; Schwartz 1982; Elliott 2010).

Several of the countries that remained neutral in the conflict of the Second World War also appealed to the specific features and characteristics of their respective national histories. In Switzerland, for example, a strong self-image was the idea of a charitable Switzerland, home of the Red Cross, which had granted asylum to the 'victims' of National Socialist Germany. Switzerland as a nation had a long tradition of neutrality and its national narrative of the Second World War therefore fitted neatly with its construction of national tradition and identity (Zala 2003). Sweden's historians similarly emphasized the country's position as a peaceful oasis on the margins of Europe, conveniently forgetting Sweden's past as an early modern great power. Rather than participating in the horrors of the Second World War, Sweden, they argued, did the right thing in concentrating on the country's build-up of its model welfare state. The home front was lovingly depicted as strengthening solidarity under the ideal of the 'people's home'. The only aspect of war that was depicted positively was the willingness of Swedish volunteers to fight alongside the Finns in the Winter War – against Sweden's old enemy, the Russians (Liljefors and Zander 2004).

Challenging uniqueness amidst a crisis of national historiography

A significant break with particularist narratives underpinning positive constructions of national master narratives was only attempted in the course of the 1960s – in the context of profound institutional and political change. In Eastern Europe the diverse reform communisms of the 1950s and 1960s sought to challenge not only the Stalinist legacy of communism but also the red nationalism underpinning many national histories in East Central and Eastern Europe. In Western Europe, the political challenges loosely associated with 1968 combined with a massive expansion of the system of higher education to provide the conditions for a successful challenge to established historical master narratives based on notions of specificity and uniqueness.

In the Federal Republic of Germany, the Fischer controversy, a debate surrounding Fritz Fischer's claims about the Imperial German elite's responsibility for the start of the First World War, started a process in which a younger generation of social historians inverted the old *Sonderweg* theory and began to examine the long-term, nineteenth-century roots of the success of National Socialism (Moses 1975; Petzold 2011). One set of particularist assumptions was replaced with another, highlighting the continued appeal of exceptionalist arguments in national historical master narratives. In Italy, too, historians began to see continuities between nineteenth-century Risorgimento nationalism and the rise of fascism after the First World War. In both countries, the reception of Anglo-American historical works, which had been far more critical of the German and Italian national traditions, were important in furthering those critical historical writings inside the FRG and Italy. In West Germany, exiled historians, such as Hans Rosenberg, served as transmitters of the more critical Anglo-Saxon interpretations of the German past (Winkler 1989). And in Italy, it was an archetypal Oxbridge don, Dennis Mack Smith, whose history of Italy linked the Risorgimento directly to the rise of fascism, thereby drawing attention to the continuities in Italian national history. It was received well by Italian social historians who had already embarked on the road to more self-critical perspectives on Italian national history.[7]

Yet, this break with particularisms, often only resulting in the formulation of new particularisms, was again contested in the 1980s when a return to more traditional national historical master narratives could be observed in many parts of Europe. Thus, in France, for example, occurred an outpouring of national histories, of which arguably the most prominent was Fernand Braudel's 'L'identité de la France'. Here the undisputed leader of the post-war Annales school, who had strategically abandoned national history with his path-breaking book on the Mediterranean, returned to national history and ultra-traditional national history at that. Naturalizing the borders of France established in the twelfth and thirteenth centuries, alluding time and again to the ethnic origins of the nation, revelling in the regional diversities making up the allegedly unique French whole, Braudel argued in favour of the assimilation of immigrants and confirmed the Gaullist myth of the 'true France' in exile and opposition to Pétain's France under occupation (Braudel 1986).

In Italy, as more and more historians came to doubt the simplistic story of heroic Resistance between 1943 and 1945, the archive-based studies of Renzo de Felice (1929–96) put forward a revisionist interpretation of Italian fascism, which distanced it from German National Socialism and emphasized its genuinely revolutionary characteristics and popular appeal. It had been, in other words, a highly specific Italian affair and could not be subsumed under a generic understanding of European fascism.

In the FRG, the *Historikerstreit* ('Historians' Controversy') erupted in 1985, focused on the singularity of the Holocaust and the need to renationalize German identity. Conservative-liberal historians, such as Michael Stürmer, who acted as a political advisor to Chancellor Helmut Kohl during the 1980s, accentuated the more positive elements of German national history and argued that it was impossible to appreciate the characteristics of German national histories in all their manifold contradictions. According to him, an almost exclusive attention focused on the twelve years of National Socialism in German history had streamlined German history too much in the direction of a negative German special path. By contrast, critical left-liberal historians, led by the philosopher Jürgen Habermas (*1929), argued against any renationalization of German national identity and against the apologetic use of history. Instead they championed ideas of constitutional patriotism and post-nationalism – in themselves concepts that, by and large, set Germany apart from other European nation states in which these concepts were often seen as specific German features.[8] An important deviation from the discourse of particularity came about in a reunified Germany, when a broad alliance of right-of-centre and left-of-centre historians began to 'search for normality'. The best known expression of this was Heinrich August Winkler's two-volume *The Long Way West*, which argued that Germans had travelled a tortuous path to bring German national identity into line with 'normal' Western national identity. While both the history of Germany before 1945 and the histories of the divided Germany before 1990 represent deviations from Western 'normality', reunification in 1990 presented the Germans with a unique opportunity to develop a 'normal' national identity built on Western understandings of the nation state.[9]

Britain did not escape the trend towards renationalization in the 1980s. Right-wing historians in Britain had for some time established a conservative interpretation of Britain's past, which had been remarkably successful in permeating British national consciousness (Soffer 2009). Margaret Thatcher, who had no great interest in history per se, encouraged the heritage mania of the 1980s, making frequent positive references to Victorian values and Empire. The epic national historian Arthur Bryant (1899–1985) was a staunch supporter of Thatcher. He reached mass audiences with his pleas to save the unique national character from the allegedly all-devouring, all-flattening EU. He depicted the EU as a Brussels monster that was about to extinguish the British national identity. The latter, he argued, had grown organically over the centuries (Stapleton 2006). In line with the political mood of the times, Geoffrey Elton (1921–94), Regius professor of history at Cambridge University, denounced unpatriotic historians and called for a renewed commitment to teaching the glories of English political history.[10]

Yet, the return to national history was by no means an uncontested development. Everywhere it has been and continues to this day to be vociferously contested by those historians critical of apologetic historical writing that seeks to provide positive forms of national identity. While national history writing is blossoming in many parts of Europe today, we see at the same time a massive growth of global and transnational history. While the criticisms of national apologetic forms of criticism in the 1960s and 1970s often themselves harked back to explanations that fell back on national particularity, the more recent transnational and global approaches have successfully avoided the discourse of particularity, replacing it with a discourse of connectedness that seems precisely to question the validity of talking in terms of peculiarly national characteristics, revealing these to be constructions in the service of nation formation and development.

Conclusion: What place for national history in contemporary Europe?

The above analysis has demonstrated to what extent the development of national historical master narratives has depended on constructions of particularisms and special historical trajectories, despite the fact that any closer look at these quickly reveals patterns of national historical narratives that look remarkably similar across a range of different national histories in Europe. This highlights the ways in which such particularisms have been and continue to be used to contribute to nation formation and development. From a critical perspective towards such functional uses of national history, what role is national history to play in the future?

For a start, more recent national histories have started from a critical re-evaluation of national historical master narratives, often telling counter-stories to the traditional ones. Jakob Tanner's recent history of Switzerland is a good example of such a critical self-reflective national history that very effectively breaks open the national container and contextualizes notions of national uniqueness in a wider transnational framework (Tanner 2015). Several national histories have also been deliberately playful about identity as well as less homogenizing. The critical impetus continues in many places. Irish national history, for example, has witnessed vigorous debates since the 1970s – with Irish historians questioning the extent of Irish suffering, the levels of British oppression and the effectiveness of Irish resistance to the British, all topics of totemic significance for Irish nationalist narratives (Foster 2002).

Other examples of these self-critical and self-reflective forms of national historiography include the French desire to come to terms with the war in Algeria (Stora 1999), the tentative beginnings of problematizing the Francoist past in Spain (Sartorius and Alfaya 1999), the New Historians' attempts to undermine entrenched Zionist positions in Israeli historiography (Shapira and Penslar 2003) and Swedish research into violations of neutrality during the Second World War (Zetterberg 1992). Even in Eastern Europe, many of the renationalizing historiographies found it difficult to produce homogenous national master narratives. Instead, plurality has emerged out of very different attempts to narrate national history under post-Communist conditions. Amidst all the nationalist history writing of post-Communist Romania,

Lucian Boia's work has attempted to blur the line between fact and fiction in Romanian national history, thereby calling into doubt the very scientificity of national history writing on which its authority and political influence was based. His study on the relationship between myth and Romanian national history shows that the debunking of national myths remains controversial depending on place and context (Boia 2001).

Overall, therefore, there is ground for optimism. The debate between those wanting to use particularisms and special paths in order to legitimate proud constructions of national difference and instil in their readers feelings of national pride and those wanting to point to the constructed nature of national history and national identity reflecting particular political purposes is likely go on, but this is a healthy state of affairs in democratic nation states. Debates on who we are, who we have been and who we want to be in future can only be conducted in relation to a variety of 'others' and as long as we can openly debate the content and relationship of that 'us' and 'them' in a non-violent way, we have a lively polity.

Notes

1 http://www.historyworkshop.org.uk/the-brexit-syllabus-british-history-for-brexiteers/ (accessed 25 January 2017).
2 On Herder, see Nisbet 1999; Adler and Menze 1997. See also Berlin 2000; Adler and Köpke 2008. On Enlightenment historical writing compare Reill 1975; Bödeker, Iggers, Knudsen and Reill 1986; Abbatista 2012.
3 On Romantic nationalism, see the excellent overview of 'On the Development of National Thought in Europe' by Leerssen 2006, especially the pages on Romantic nationalism, and also his *Encyclopaedia of Romantic Nationalism* project: http://romanticnationalism.net/viewer.p/21 (accessed 25 January 2017).
4 For a more extensive discussion of this patterning of national history writing in the Romantic period, see Berger 2015b, chapter 3.
5 Thaden 1999: 90ff. On the different positionings of Russian historiography towards 'the West', see also Nolte 1999.
6 For a good introduction to Italian post-war historiography generally, see Pertici 2000.
7 Smith 1959. One of the best examples of a social history critical of the national tradition is Romano and Vivanti 1972–1978.
8 The literature on the Historians' Controversy is legion. Some of the most important documents of the debate can be found in English translation in *Forever in the Shadow of Hitler? Original Documents of the Historikerstreit, the Controversy Concerning the Singularity of the Holocaust* (1993); for two thoughtful book-length reflections on the debate in English compare also Evans 1989 and Maier 1989.
9 Winkler 2000. The English translation is *The Long Road West, 1789–1990* (2007); the French translation *Histoire de l'Allemagne, XIXe-XXe siècle: le long chemin vers l'Occident*, 2 vols (2005). See also Berger 2015a, for a detailed analysis and contextualization of Winkler's volumes. For the renationalization of historical consciousness in Germany generally, see Berger 2003.
10 Elton 1977 and Elton 1984. Elton, who was an immigrant with a Czech-Jewish background, just like Namier, with a Polish-Jewish background, always felt very warmly towards the British nation – they both contrasted it positively with their East Central European homelands.

References

Abbatista, G. (2012), 'The Historical Thought of the French *Philosophes*', in J. Rabasa, M. Sato, E. Tortarolo and D. Woolf (eds), *Oxford History of Historical Writing*, vol. 3, 406–27, Oxford: Oxford University Press.

Adler, H. and Köpke, W., eds. (2008), *A Companion to the Works of Johann Gottfried Herder*, Rochester, NY: Camden House.

Adler, H. and Menze, E. A. (1997), 'On the Way to World History: Johann Gottfried Herder', in H. Adler and E. A. Menze (eds), *Johann Gottfried Herder on World History: an Anthology*, 3–21, New York: M. E. Sharpe.

Anderson, R. (2010), 'University History Teaching and the Humboldtian Model in Scotland, 1858–1914', *History of Universities*, 25 (1): 138–84.

Baron, S. H. (1963), *Plekhanov: The Father of Russian Marxism*, Stanford, CA: Stanford University Press.

Bentley, M. (2005), *Modernizing England's Past: English Historiography in the Age of Modernism, 1870–1970*, Cambridge: Cambridge University Press.

Berger, S. (2003), *The Search for Normality. National Identity and Historical Consciousness in Germany since 1800*, 2nd edn, Oxford: Berghahn Books.

Berger, S. (2006), 'On Taboos, Traumas and Other Myths: Why the Debate about German Victims of the Second World War is not a Historians' Controversy', in B. Niven (ed.), *Germans as Victims: Remembering the Past in Contemporary Germany*, 210–24, Basingstoke: Palgrave Macmillan.

Berger, S. (2015a), 'Rising Like a Phoenix: the Renaissance of National History Writing in Britain and Germany since the 1980s', in S. Berger and C. Lorenz (eds), *Nationalizing the Past*, 426–51, New York: Palgrave Macmillan.

Berger, S. (2015b), *The Past as History: National Identity and Historical Consciousness in Modern Europe*, Basingstoke: Palgrave Macmillan.

Berger, S. and Miller, A., eds. (2015), *Nationalizing Empires*, Budapest: Central European University Press.

Berlin, I. (2000), *Three Critics of the Enlightenment: Vico, Hamann, Herder*, London: Pimlico.

Beyen, M. (2007), 'Natural-Born Nations: National Historiography in Belgium and the Netherlands between a Tribal and a Social-Cultural Paradigm, 1900–1950', *Storia della Storiografia*, 52: 17–25.

Boia, L. (2001), *History and Myth in Romanian Consciousness*, Budapest: Central European University Press.

Boyd, C. P. (1997), *Historia Patria: Politics, History, and National Identity in Spain, 1875–1975*, Princeton, NJ: Princeton University Press.

Bödeker, H. E., Iggers, G. G., Knudsen, J. B. and Reill P. H., eds. (1986), *Aufklärung und Geschichte*, Göttingen: Vandenhoeck & Ruprecht.

Brakensiek, S. and Flügel, A., eds. (2000), *Regionalgeschichte in Europa*, Paderborn: Schöningh.

Braudel, F. (1986), *L'Identité de la France*, 2 vols, Paris: Flammarion.

Cornelißen, C. and Ritter, G. (2001), *Geschichtswissenschaft und Politik im 20. Jahrhundert*, Düsseldorf: Droste.

Durandin, C. (2002), 'La function de l'histoire et le statut de l'historien à l'époque du national-communisme en Roumanie', in M.-É. Ducreux and A. Marès (eds), *Enjeux de l'histoire en Europe Centrale*, 103–12, Paris: L'Harmattan.

Eckel, J. (2005), *Hans Rothfels: eine intellektuelle Biographie im 20. Jahrhundert*, Göttingen: Vandenhoeck & Ruprecht.

Elliott, G. (2010), *Hobsbawm: History and Politics*, London: Pluto.

Elton, G. R. (1977), 'The Historian's Social Function', *Transactions of the Royal Historical Society*, 27 (5th series): 197–211.

Elton, G. R. (1984), *The Future of the Past*, Cambridge: Cambridge University Press.

Enteen, G. M. (1978), *The Soviet Scholar-Bureaucrat: M. N. Pokrovskii and the Society of Marxist Historians*, Pennsylvania: Penn State University Press.

Evans, R. J. (1989), *In Hitler's Shadow: West German Historians and the Attempt to Escape from the Nazi Past*, London: Routledge.

Feldner, H. (2010), 'The New Scientificity in Historical Writing around 1800', in S. Berger, H. Feldner and K. Passmore (eds), *Writing History: Theory and Practice*, 2nd edn, 3–21, London: Bloomsbury.

Fichte, J. G. (2008 [1808]), *Reden an die deutsche Nation*, Hamburg: Rowohlt.

Forever in the Shadow of Hitler? Original Documents of the Historikerstreit, the Controversy Concerning the Singularity of the Holocaust (1993), trans. K. James and C. Truett, Atlantic Highlands, NJ: Humanities Press.

Foster, R. (2002), *The Irish Story: Telling Tales and Making It Up in Ireland*, Oxford: Oxford University Press.

Funke, P. (1998), 'Das antike Griechenland: eine gescheiterte Nation? Zur Rezeption und Deutung der antiken griechischen Geschichte in der deutschen Historiographie des 19. Jahrhunderts', *Storia della Storiografia*, 33: 17–32.

Haapala, P. and Kaarninen, M. (2010), 'Finland', in I. Porciani and L. Raphael (eds), *Atlas of European Historiography: The Making of a Profession, 1800–2005*, 75, Basingstoke: Palgrave Macmillan.

Harvey, J. L. (2003), 'The Common Adventure of Mankind: Academic Internationalism and Western Historical Practice from Versailles to Potsdam', Ph.D. diss., Pennsylvania State University, University Park, PA.

Hermann, I. and Metzger, F. (2015), 'A Truculent Revenge: The Clergy and the Writing of National History', in I. Porciani and J. Tollebeek (eds), *Setting the Standards. Institutions, Networks and Communities of National Historiography*, 313–29, London: Palgrave Macmillan.

Hernon Jr, J. M. (1976), 'The Last Whig Historian and Consensus History', *American Historical Review*, 81 (1): 66–97.

Iggers, G. G. (1989), 'New Directions in Historical Studies in the German Democratic Republic', *History and Theory*, 28: 59–77.

Kaye, H. J. (1984), *British Marxist Historians: an Introductory Analysis*, Cambridge: Cambridge University Press.

Kellogg, F. (1990), *A History of Romanian Historical Writing*, Bakersfield, CA: Schlacks.

Kiefer, R. (1989), *Karl Bachem 1858–1945. Politiker und Historiker des Zentrums*, Mainz: Koehler & Amelang.

Kieser, H.-L. (2005), 'Die Herausbildung des nationalistischen Geschichtsdiskurses in der Türkei (spätes 19.–Mitte 20. Jahrhundert)', in M. Kroska and H.-C. Maner (eds), *Beruf und Berufung. Geschichtswissenschaft und Nationsbildung in Ostmittel- und Südosteuropa im 19. und 20. Jahrhundert*, 59–98, Münster: Aschendorff.

von Klimó, Á. (1999a), 'Die gespaltene Vergangenheit: die grossen christlichen Kirchen im Kampf um die Nationalgeschichte Ungarns, 1920–1948', *Zeitschrift für Geschichtswissenschaft*, 47: 871–94.

von Klimó, Á. (1999b), 'St. Stephen's Day: Politics and Religion in Twentieth-Century Hungary', *East Central Europe*, 26: 15–29.

von Klimó, Á. (2003), *Nation, Konfession, Geschichte. Zur nationalen Geschichtskultur Ungarns im europäischen Kontext (1860–1948)*, Oldenburg: De Gryuter.

Krumeich, G. (1996), 'Ernest Lavisse und die Kritik an der deutschen "Kultur", 1914–1918', in W. J. Mommsen and E. Müller-Luckner (eds), *Kultur und Krieg: die Rolle der Intellektuellen, Künstler und Schriftsteller im Ersten Weltkrieg*, 143–54, Munich: Oldenbourg.

Leerssen, J. (2006), *National Thought in Europe: A Cultural History*, Amsterdam: Amsterdam University Press.

Levy, C. (1999), 'Historians and the "First Republic"', in S. Berger, M. Donovan and K. Passmore (eds), *Writing National Histories: Western Europe since 1800*, 265–78, London: Routledge.

Liljefors, M. and Zander, U. (2004), 'Der zweite Weltkrieg und die schwedische Utopie', in M. Flacke (ed.), *Mythen der Nationen – 1945: Arena der Erinnerungen*, vol. 2, 569–92, Mainz: Koehler & Amelang.

Maier, C. (1989), *The Unmasterable Past: History, Holocaust and German National Identity*, Cambridge, MA: Harvard University Press.

Marchal, G. P. (2006), *Schweizer Gebrauchsgeschichte. Geschichtsbilder, Mythenbildung und nationale Identität*, Basel: Schwabe.

Marjanović, V. (1998), *Die Mitteleuropa-Idee und die Mitteleuropa-Politik Österreichs 1945–1995*, Frankfurt/Main: Suhrkamp.

McCartney, D. (1957), 'The Writing of History in Ireland, 1800–1830', *Irish Historical Studies*, 10: 347–62.

Meinecke, F. (1915), *Die deutsche Erhebung von 1914. Vorträge und Aufsätze*, Stuttgart: Meinders & Elstermann.

Mitchell, R. (2000), *Picturing the Past: English History in Text and Image, 1830–1870*, Oxford: Oxford University Press.

Morgan, P. (1999), 'Reclaiming Italy? Antifascist Historians and History in "Justice and Liberty"', in S. Berger, M. Donovan and K. Passmore (eds), *Writing National Histories. Western Europe since 1800*, 150–60, London: Routledge.

Moses, J. A. (1975), *The Politics of Illusion: The Fischer Controversy in German Historiography*, London: Prior.

Mühle, E. (2005), *Für Volk und deutschen Osten. Der Historiker Hermann Aubin und die deutsche Ostforschung*, Düsseldorf: Droste.

Murgescu, B. (2010), 'Romania', in I. Porciani and L. Raphael (eds), *Atlas of European Historiography: The Making of a Profession, 1800–2005*, 100, Basingstoke: Palgrave Macmillan.

Mycock, A. and Loskoutova, M. (2015), 'Nation, State and Empire: The Historiography of "High Imperialism" in the British and Russian Empires', in S. Berger and C. Lorenz (eds), *Nationalizing the Past*, 233–58, New York: Palgrave Macmillan.

Nisbet, H. B. (1999), 'Herder: the Nation in History', in M. Branch (ed.), *National History and Identity: Approaches to the Writing of National History in the North-East Baltic Region: Nineteenth and Twentieth Centuries*, 78–96, Tampere: Finnish Literature Society.

Nolte, H.-H. (1999), 'Russia in Russian Writing of World History', *Storia della Storiografia*, 35: 63–74.

Otáhal, M. (1986), 'The Manuscript Controversy in the Czech National Revival', *Cross-Currents*, 5: 247–77.

Pertici, R. (2000), *Storici Italiani del Novecento*, Pisa: Istituto editoriali e poligrafice internazionali.

Petzold, S. (2011), 'Fritz Fischer and the Rise of Critical Historiography in West Germany, 1945–1965', Ph.D. diss., University of Aberystwyth, Aberystwyth, Wales.

Reill, P. H. (1975), *The German Enlightenment and the Rise of Historicism*, New Haven: University of Berkeley Press.

Riehl, W. H. (1897), *Land und Leute*, 9th edn, Stuttgart: Cotta'scher Verlag.

Riehl, W. H. (1990), *The Natural History of the German People*, Lewiston: Edwin Mellen Press (first published in German in four volumes, 1862–1869).

Romano, R. and Vivanti, C., eds. (1972–1978), *Storia d'Italia*, 6 vols, Turin: Einaudi.

Sartorius, N. and Alfaya, J. (1999), *La Memoria Insumisa*, Madrid: Espasa.

Schwartz, B. (1982), '"The People" in History: The Communist Party Historians' Group, 1945–1956', in R. Johnson, G. McLennan, B. Schwartz and D. Sutton (eds), *Making Histories: Studies in History-Writing and Politics*, 44–95, London: Hutchinson.

Shapira, A. and Penslar, D. J., eds. (2003), *Israeli Historical Revisionism: From left to right*, London: Routledge.

Smith, D. M. (1959), *Italy: a Modern History*, Ann Arbor, MI: University of Michigan Press.

Šnē, A. (2010), 'Latvia', in I. Porciani and L. Raphael (eds), *Atlas of European Historiography: The Making of a Profession, 1800–2005*, 82, Basingstoke: Palgrave Macmillan.

Soffer, R. (2009), *History, Historians, and Conservatism in Britain and America: from the Great War to Thatcher and Reagan*, Oxford: Oxford University Press.

Stapleton, J. (2006), *Sir Arthur Bryant and National History in Twentieth-Century Britain*, Lanham, MD: Lexington Books.

Starkey, D. (2001), 'The English Historians' Role and the Place of History in English National Life', *The Historian*, 71: 6–15.

Stibbe, M. (2003), 'German Historians' Views of England During the First World War', in S. Berger, P. Lambert and P. Schumann (eds), *Historikerdialoge. Geschichte, Mythos und Gedächtnis im deutsch-britischen kulturellen Austausch, 1750–2000*, 235–54, Göttingen: Vandenhoeck & Ruprecht.

Stora, B. (1999), *Le transfert d'une mémoire. De l'Algérie française' au racisme anti-arabe*, Paris: La Découverte.

Tanner, J. (2015), *Geschichte der Schweiz im 20. Jahrhundert*, Munich: C. H. Beck.

Thaden, E. C. (1999), *Rise of Historicism in Russia*, New York: Peter Lang.

Thiesse, A.-M. (1999), *La Création des Identités Nationales. Europe XVIII–XIX Siècle*, Paris: Seuil.

Utgaard, P. (2003), *Remembering and Forgetting Nazism. Education, National Identity and the Victim Myth in Postwar Austria*, Oxford: Berghahn Books.

Wallace, S. (1988), *War and the Image of Germany: British Academics, 1914–1918*, Edinburgh: John Donald Publishers Ltd.

Why We Are at War: Great Britain's Case, by Members of the Oxford Faculty of Modern History; with an Appendix of Original Documents Including the Authorized English Translation of the White Book Issued by the German Government (1914), Oxford: Clarendon Press.

Winkler, H. A. (1989), 'Ein Erneuerer der Geschichtswissenschaft: Hans Rosenberg 1904–1988', *Historische Zeitschrift*, 248: 529–55.

Winkler, H. A. (2000), *Der lange Weg nach Westen*, 2 vols, Munich: C. H. Beck.

Winkler, H. A. (2005), *Histoire de l'Allemagne, XIXe-XXe siècle: le long chemin vers l'Occident*, 2 vols, Paris: Fayard.

Winkler, H. A. (2007), *The Long Road West, 1789–1990*, 2 vols, Oxford: Oxford University Press.

Zala, S. (2003), 'Geltung und Grenzen schweizerischen Geschichtsmanagements', in M. Sabrow, R. Jessen and K. G. Kracht (eds), *Zeitgeschichte als Streitgeschichte. Grosse Kontroversen seit 1945*, 306–25, Munich: C. H. Beck.

Zetterberg, K. (1992), 'Neutralitet till varje pris? Till frågan om den svenska säkerhetspolitiken 1940–42 och eftergifterna till Tyksland', in B. Hugemark (ed.), *I Orkanens Őga: 1941 - osäker neutralitet*, 11–36, Stockholm: Probus.

Zsolt, B. (2010), 'The Small Mirror of Hungarian Literature', in A. Ersoy, M. Górny and V. Kechriotis (eds), *Modernism: Representations of National Culture, vol. III/2 of Discourses of Collective Identity in Central and Southeastern Europe (1770–1945): Texts and Commentaries*, 26–32, Budapest: Central European University Press.

14

A Genealogy of Crisis: Europe's Legal Legacy and Ordoliberalism

Bo Stråth

Law as legacy and Europe's genealogy of crisis

This book is about the role of the legacy of Roman law in the transformation from fascism to the European integration project after 1945. The aim of this chapter is to extend the focus on Roman law to another connected legal foundation: ordoliberalism. The chapter will also extend the inquiry in time covering the crises in the 1970s and since 2008.

Ordoliberalism was an alternative point of reference to that of Roman law in order to mark the shift from fascism to European integration. Ordoliberalism provided a legal framework for a peaceful Europe with the aim of merging capitalism and democracy. Wilhelm Röpke, a protagonist in the elaboration of ordoliberalism, commented on the connection between Roman law and ordoliberalism, as we shall see. The key focus of this chapter is the ordoliberal and Roman legacy during the two crises of the 1970s and since 2008.

The point of departure of this book is that, during the war, exiled German scholars in Britain discovered Roman law as a European historical heritage on which one could build a new and peaceful post-war Europe. Simultaneously, Mussolini exploited the same Roman heritage in order to legitimize his fascist regime. *Romanitas*, the key concept of his outline of the Roman legacy, dealt with law, justice and order.

Hitler and the Nazis rejected the legacy of Roman law, instead hailing the myth of old Germanic law and proto-Germanic societies of free equals under a chieftain – supported by race biology, the geopolitical *Großraum* theory, and the search for the original Aryan home in a mythical North through philology, archaeology and anthropology.

This fascist-Nazi difference increases the complexity of ideological debates and the search for origin and roots, stability and continuity in a chaotic time. A general search was under way for historical points of reference and authority as an instrument to master the future. However, the decisive point was not whether the normative roots were Roman or Germanic, because both filled similar functions, but the fact that the search led to the derivation of very different origins among those who were looking for, for example, the Roman legacy.

Few outlined the Roman law basis of dreams of a future peaceful Europe in reaction to the horrors of the Second World War more emphatically than Paul Koschaker. In 1947, he published his most famous work, *Europa und das römische Recht*, and, before his death in 1951, he experienced the beginning of the debate on the connection between Roman law and a peaceful post-war Europe. After 1945, both Roman law and Europe were in a state of deep crisis and Koschaker's project dealt with the restoration of both in the construction of a common European legal culture. In his search for solutions to the crisis of both Roman law and Europe, Koschaker went backwards and ended in Savigny's historical school. He depicted European history and European legal culture as a teleological continuity from the Roman Empire via the Holy Roman Empire to the twentieth century. He thereby conflated pre-Christian Rome and Catholic Rome (Koschaker 1938; Koschaker 1947). His approach fitted well with the fact that the founding fathers of the European post-war integration project were Christian Democrats and Catholics. The doctrine of the Catholic Church acknowledged Roman law in its connection to natural law theory, which linked up with ideas of universalism and divinity as a legal origin as opposed to man-made positive law. The contours of a foundation myth emerged.

A problem exists with imageries of legal heritages and legacies. The search for the roots of the legal system is in vain. Centuries and millenia of political–legal entanglements constitute a powerful genealogy and a filter that sieves the search for the original, for the authentic roots of the present. In the past, not one original and undisputed original point of departure is available for our observations in the present. Many controversial layers of interpretations and reinterpretations of origin have constantly changed views on it and our attempt is only another contribution in that long chain. This fulfils the purpose of providing a better understanding of our own chaotic present. The search for legacies and roots is more about the present than the past.

In his article 'Foundations of European Legal Culture' (1990), Franz Wieacker shows the complexity of the millenary genealogy of Roman law, beginning with the replacement in the empire of the former individual freedom of the urban resident (*civis Romanus*) with diverse corporate freedoms. He shows how, after the fall of the Roman Empire, the heirs of Rome as well as the Romanized Iberians, Celts, Illyrians and the Germans, who had entered the empire, abandoned the high classical culture of Roman law. He shows how the transformation continued in the Middle Ages under the influence of the Catholic Church and by the creation of an autonomous legal science at the universities. In the early modern period up to the French Revolution, the conceptualization and systematization of law was built upon these foundations by means of the methodological tools of a new age, dedicated to mathematics and the natural sciences. The fragmentation of Christianity and the emergence of centralized states reflected the legal transformation in other ways. The modern age after the French Revolution, in the framework of the Industrial Revolution, where time seemed to accelerate, brought the definite collapse of Western legal metaphysics and the emergence of the *Rechtsstaat* for the protection of private property and the *Sozialstaat* for public welfare (Wieacker 1990). It is no easy task to discern what is Roman and original in this genealogy and to retrieve this argued legacy in today's European legal cultures marked by diversity.

Roman law was, as Wieacker has demonstrated, not a stable reference for all times. The crises in the 1970s and since 2008 have brought an intensification of the search for new legal points of reference in times when the Roman (and ordoliberal) legal foundations of integration had lost the capacity to convince. The search still continues.

The derivation of a Roman origin is not a matter of definition because there is no definition, as Nietzsche noted with his statement that what can be defined has no history.[1] The task is rather to retrieve the contentious meanings of Roman law in various historical situations. The term is full of contested meanings, which have emerged in political struggles for discursive power (Brunner, Conze and Koselleck 1979–1997). The discursive struggle about the meaning of key concepts is particularly intense in times of crisis, when old vocabularies break down and lose the capacity to convince, and the search for new legitimizing conceptualizations speeds up (Koselleck 1959).

Therefore, the European genealogy of crisis is important. The (West) European unification project after 1945 was built on the experiences of the crisis in the 1930s (and, of course, of the two world wars). An argument in the post-war work on unification was that integration in legal terms was based on Roman law. The aim was evidently to derive a different Roman past for Europe's future than Mussolini's. But what, more precisely, was this Roman heritage? How stable was it as legitimizing cement? How did later crises and challenges influence the connection to Roman law?

The value crisis of the 1930s

The implication of the value crisis of the 1930s was a loss of orientation at a time when various versions of democracy, authoritarianism and totalitarianism were competing intensely over providing a key to the future. The subsequent world war re-established values in terms of good and evil in Western and Eastern European versions. However, the question remained of how evil could acquire the power of persuasion that it actually did obtain. That question permeated the post-war search for meaning and for the final repression of evil.

In the conventional teleological understanding of Europe, democracy broke through slowly but inexorably during the nineteenth century, from the stabilizing restoration in Vienna after revolutionary and Napoleonic chaos, via the binding of monarchical power through constitutions.

A more realistic view on the nineteenth century discerns general constitutionalization after Vienna as a successful instrument of restoration through necessary monarchical concessions to ward off social protest and revolutionary threats rather than as an expression of a breakthrough of popular power. Europe in 1914 was mainly conservative and authoritarian. State-based paternalist social politics of stick and carrot integrated social protest in an approach where warfare and welfare went hand in hand through mutual reinforcement.[2]

Democracy arrived in Europe only after the two world wars between 1914 and 1945. After 1919, in reaction to the First World War, democracy broke through in parallel with totalitarian regimes of a new kind: communism, fascism, Nazism. The First World War brought the breakthrough of the masses into politics. After their hardships and sacrifices on the battlefield and on the home front, there was now no stopping the masses. Politics became more difficult to orchestrate than in the former society, with dreams of a European concert directed by a benevolent but more or less authoritarian state paternalism. The masses protested and rioted. The Russian Revolution was a direct consequence of the war. The breakthrough of the influence of the masses did not necessarily result in democracy, as we might want to believe, but could also easily end in fascism. A mass society presented as much a threat as a promise. The masses not only expressed their political preferences in bottom-up processes but could also be manipulated in populist and authoritarian top-down politics. This was the backdrop to the value crisis of the 1930s.

The value crisis began as an economic crisis after the collapse of the financial markets in October 1929. Mass unemployment haunted Europe, and political leaders seemed paralyzed before they began to act. They abandoned the gold standard and reacted to social protest with protectionism. Their concern was the economic crisis, which became a political crisis and a value crisis. They discerned a tension between economic liberalism and political liberalism, between capitalism and parliamentary democracy with the social question as the catalyst that turned the economic crisis into a political crisis and finally a general value crisis about the cohesion of industrial capitalist societies.

In his book *La rebellión de las masas* in 1930, Ortega y Gasset outlined how the advent of the masses contributed to the value crisis of the interwar period. Oswald Spengler, author of volumes about the decline of the Occident after the First World War, warned in *Man and Technics* (1931) against the destructive force of technology and industrial capitalism, while his bestseller *The Hour of Decision* (1933) – banned by the Nazi regime – criticized liberalism for its political and economic shortcomings and predicted a coming war that would destroy Western civilization. Other intellectual comments on the value crisis against the backdrop of economic depression and political turbulence were Dutch historian Johan Huizinga's *In the Shadow of Tomorrow* and the dystopian future vision of *Brave New World* by Aldous Huxley (Ortega y Gasset 1930; Spengler 1918–1922; Spengler 1931; Spengler 1933; Huizinga 1935; Huxley 1932). One aspect of the value crisis of the 1930s was the difficulty in distinguishing between democracy by the masses and totalitarianism for the masses in the wake of the failure of global capitalism.

The differences became visible only in retrospect, as Wolfgang Schivelbusch demonstrated in his book *Entfernte Verwandtschaft* ('Distant Relationship'). The value crisis of the 1930s began as an economic crisis after the collapse of the capitalist economic order in 1929, which became a general global political crisis. In the search for a solution to mass unemployment and social protest, a value crisis arose where democracy, fascism, Nazism and communism/Stalinism competed for solutions under relations of entanglement as much as demarcation. For example, US President Franklin Roosevelt was very interested in Mussolini's corporatism and Hitler's public employment politics in the design of his New Deal programme. Only after 1935, when Hitler and Mussolini began more systematically to connect the solution of the social crisis with expansive warfare for social integration, did the distinction between the democratic and totalitarian orders become clear (Schivelbusch 2005). Roosevelt was not only interested in solutions by what would later be seen as totalitarian regimes but also took to heart the book *Sweden: The Middle Way*, published by Marquis Child in 1936, which soon became a global bestseller. Child's argument was that Sweden had adopted an effective third-way compromise between the two political poles of the day: the United States and the Soviet Union, between wild, unruly and unmanageable capitalism, on the one hand, and coercive socialism, on the other (Childs 1936). In the same vein, the ordoliberal protagonist Wilhelm Röpke saw Switzerland as the model of a *dritter Weg* between laissez-faire liberalism and socialist collectivism (Röpke 1942: 43). No doubt connections existed between his search for origins in Swiss peasant community culture, which merged the ideals of individual and collective freedom, and the Nazi–Nordic myth, but Röpke nevertheless emphasized a distinctive Swiss character as clearly dissociative from the distorted Nazi fancies of the past.

Between the world wars, in economic and cultural terms, Germany was the European hub where crystallization of the crisis occurred. Economic development there between crisis and despair on the one side and expansion and reckless expectations of the future on the other, between depression and mania, exerted a great impact on Europe. The same goes for the cultural tensions in the Weimar Republic between futuristic cosmopolitan feelings of forward-thrusting pioneers and a xenophobic, narrow nationalism as a tool for revenge and new German greatness. The period was a general European oscillation between gloom and hubris; but in Germany this was amplified. After 1929, feelings of depression and crisis prevailed, with sentiments of economic, political and value crisis and lack of orientation and political control reinforcing each other. Germany was the centre of a storm brewing over Europe. Coudenhove-Kalergi's pan-European narrative broke down, as did the League of Nations as a kind of world government making the world safe for democracy after the First World War.

The philosophical debate at the end of the 1920s and in the early 1930s between Martin Heidegger, Ernst Cassirer and Edmund Husserl over what Husserl called 'the crisis of European sciences' was symptomatic of the search for orientation and a good illustration of the *Zeitgeist*. It was a moment when full social and political recognition seemed finally to be given to German Jews, who constituted a significant dimension of cultural life and intellectual debate in Germany. Cassirer became the first Jewish rector of a German university, in Hamburg. The moment was full of ambiguity and contradictions, however. It also contained a new turn in German nationalism, with anti-Semitism as a core dimension.

Heidegger had attracted attention with his book *Sein und Zeit* (Being and Time) in 1927 (Heidegger 1927). The book took issue with rationalism and emphasized authenticity from an existentialist perspective. Humans were not only thinking but in particular acting under conditions of being between life and death. The echo of Ernst Jünger's literary expression of his experiences of life at the front line during the First World War as a purifying 'storm of steel' is difficult to overhear (Jünger 1929; Jünger 1930). Heidegger was critical of the philosophical conception of truth and confronted the instrumental tradition of technology, with its treatment of nature as a 'standing reserve' on call for human purposes. The book was a radical existentialist-hermeneutic version of Husserl's phenomenology. However, as opposed to Husserl, it celebrated the 'will to power' and appealed to the prevailing mood of the time. The book quickly became a point of reference in the public debate.

Husserl had developed phenomenology at a time when the traumatic experiences of the First World War imposed doubts on reason and technology based on instrumental rationality. In particular, the doubts dealt with the scientific claim and conceptualization of truth. Husserl tried to open up the absolute closure of the term towards the *perception* of objects rather than objects as such. Perceptions offered not only one but many possibilities of interpretation. In his phenomenology Husserl focused on the issue of inter-subjectivity from this point of departure.

Husserl's *Crisis of European Sciences* was a last despairing appeal in a debate which was closing down and had begun as a much more open confrontation about clear alternatives in the wake of Heidegger's *Sein und Zeit*. Cassirer was the main opponent and the debate between him and Heidegger in Davos in 1929 was a catalyst. Cassirer mediated between natural and cultural sciences from a reason-based neo-Kantian perspective. He argued that Kant's critique of pure reason, 150 years before Heidegger, emphasized human temporality and finitude but also located human cognition and the capacity to use reason within a broader conception of humanity. With this reference, Cassirer challenged the relativism of Heidegger, arguing for the universal validity of truths discovered by the 'exact and moral sciences'. In the 1920s he developed his philosophy of symbolic forms, where he saw man as a symbolic animal. However, whereas animals perceive their worlds by instinct and direct sensory perception, humans create a reason-based universe of symbolic meaning with inter-subjective objective validity.

Husserl was a professor in Freiburg, where the young Heidegger was his assistant. Heidegger dedicated *Being and Time* to Husserl, who had retired in 1928, with Heidegger succeeding him. In 1933 the converted Lutheran Jew Husserl was suspended from the university and excluded from the library as well as other emeritus facilities. A few weeks after revocation of Husserl's emeritus status, Heidegger became rector of the university and joined the Nazi party. Husserl taught in 1935–6 in Prague and Vienna and in 1936 published *Die Krisis*, which described and analysed the crisis of European sciences around concepts such as truth, objectivity, reason and rationality (Husserl 1936). Two years later, Husserl died in Freiburg, intellectually isolated and abandoned. Only Gerhard Ritter, the nationalist-conservative historian, the biographer of Luther and the hagiographic portrayer of Prussia, went to his funeral. In his nostalgia for the German Reich as it had been before 1914, rather than as it had begun to take shape in a new version at this time, Ritter probably felt as alienated as Husserl. After less than a year as rector, Heidegger resigned after conflicts with colleagues from the political leadership of the university. The question of how much of a Nazi he really had been was one of the most contested issues after 1945.

Cassirer left Germany in 1933 for a few years in Oxford and from there to a chair at Gothenburg. After the German occupation of Denmark and Norway in 1940, he feared that Sweden might be Hitler's next target and left the following year for the

United States, where he died a month before the end of the war in 1945 (Cassirer 1936; Jeenicke 2012).

The value debate of the 1920s and the 1930s – against the backdrop of the experiences of the First World War, the Great Depression and the breakthrough of mass societies – dealt with the question of truth and objectivity. It also dealt with the question of sovereignty. Who was the sovereign that controlled and influenced the situation? The democracies had a clear answer: the parliamentary assemblies ruling and ruled by the constitutions. However, ever more people doubted that solutions to problems would be found there.

Politicians in the Weimar Republic began to circumvent domestic social problems in search of solutions via military expansion for new economic power. The geographer Karl Haushofer and the jurist Carl Schmitt laid the ground with the *Großraum* theory. The Nazi ideologue Alfred Rosenberg (1893–1946) used *Lebensraum* as a key concept in his book *Der Mythus des 20. Jahrhunderts* (1930). It must here be added that the view of a German mission of eastward expansion was conventional in Weimar. Gustav Stresemann was keen to keep Poland out of Locarno, for instance.[3]

The Catholic Schmitt was looking for community and identity at a time that felt lacking in both. In *Political Theology* (1922), Schmitt launched a Catholic-right revolutionary critique of the prevailing order. He focused on the power of the sovereign to declare a state of emergency, to explain that the law was no longer applicable. He rejected the layers of philosophical-political exegeses on the exercise of power that had been established over the centuries. What really mattered was control of the exceptional case, the moment when somebody has the power to stand up and declare that there is no alternative irrespective of what legal rules might apply. Schmitt's argument eventually came to rest on the issue of control of the exceptional situation in the political and legal arena. The agent who wields the power to proclaim the exceptional situation emancipates himself or herself from norms. Five years later, in *The Concept of the Political* (1927), Schmitt added a definition of what he considered to be the deepest essence of the political: the distinction between friend and foe (Schmitt 1922; Schmitt 1927).

Schmitt identified an obscure legitimacy in mere force of action. In so doing, he revealed a blind spot in liberal understandings of law as a universal order framing politics. However, although critically astute, Schmitt was unable to conceive of legislation by politics as a potentially progressive force and the possible source of positive normative developments through criticism of existing institutions. This was his blind spot. Politics does not stand above the law, and the law does not stand above politics. Rather, law is made and remade by politics; it deals with continuous political adjustment to and reformulation of legal checks. Proclaiming a state of exception is not the only response to a normative crisis.

The crisis of the 1930s, and reflections on it in philosophical and legal debates, and in fiction literature, constituted the framework of experiences when the search emerged, during and after the Second World War, for the origin in the past of a better European future. This was the framework of experience which made exiled German scholars of law and Paul Koschaker to seek firm ground for Europe in their imagery of Roman law. No doubt a dimension of escapism existed in the location of their intellectual asylum in such a distant past.

The search for stabilization through law: The ordoliberals against Schmitt and against the neo-liberals

Economists also reflected on the crisis of liberalism and capitalism. During the Second World War, Wilhelm Röpke became one of the champions in the outline of ordoliberalism as a response to the crisis of economic liberalism. Ordoliberalism was not so much about economic theory as about the legal and political framing of the economy. The Latin word *ordo*, 'order' in English, in its connection to liberalism can be translated as legal or law-based liberalism. In this enterprise Röpke also referred to Roman law. The German economist wrote in Swiss exile in the second volume of his trilogy on the crisis of his time (1944) that 'we owe to Roman and not to German law for a clear distinction between public and private law and are thus indebted to the former for the recognition of the individual as opposed to state rights'. On the other hand, he continued, 'The highly developed formal structure of Roman law may lend itself to the claims of a centralized absolutism.'[4] Röpke thus drew attention to the ambiguity of Roman law as a European point of reference.

In this respect, Röpke condensed what Wieacker would later say when discussing the legacy of Roman law, which in Röpke's view could be used to derive both fascism and private ownership in a liberal society. In order to bypass this ambiguity, Röpke developed a legal-political framework for the economy in a liberal capitalist order based on private ownership, a social-liberal version of the *Rechtstaat*, which had emerged in the nineteenth century to protect the new kinds of private contract in the industrial capitalist economy. The law-based ordoliberalism mediated between the *Rechtstaat* imagery and the growing claims by the labour movement since the end of the nineteenth century for a *Sozialstaat*, a welfare state.

Röpke did so in the framework of a debate among liberal intellectuals trying to come to terms with the crisis of liberalism. In August 1938 some twenty-five people, among them the philosophers Raymond Aron and Louis Rougier, along with the economists Röpke, Ludwig von Mises, Friedrich von Hayek, Jacques Rueff and Alexander Rüstow, met for a colloquium on the crisis of economic and political liberalism. Their discussions dealt with the likelihood and preconditions of a liberal renaissance, markets and crises, as well as the liberal state and an agenda of liberalism. They struggled for a new mobilizing concept for the intellectual movement they planned and which they defined as liberal, although demarcated from conventional liberalism, which had fallen into ever greater disrepute since the 1870s in a development that had accelerated during the Great Depression. The meeting discussed several concepts, among them neo-capitalism and constructive liberalism. In the final event it seems participants decided that neo-liberalism was the most attractive term, although no formal agreement or recorded unanimity was reached (Denord 2001; Denord 2008; Valpen 2004; Mirowski and Plehwe 2009; Jackson 2010).

From this point onwards, mainstream liberalism split into at least two tendencies. The German economists Röpke and Rüstow, and with them Walther Eucken (1891–1950), who was not among the participants at the Paris meeting, became the *Vordenker*, the 'pre-thinkers' of the German *soziale Marktwirtschaft*, based on a belief in a legal (ordoliberal) rather than political regulation of the economy. They turned Schmitt's argument upside down and set law, not politics, as the point of departure for social life and economic management.

In *Die Gesellschaftskrisis der Gegenwart* (1942) Röpke developed the ordoliberal programme on the basis of the argument about a pathological degeneration of occidental societies expressed in two dimensions: the intellectual moral and the political social economic. Mass societies driven by a borderless relativism called positivism and the technical- or technological-organizational orgy of big industry, big cities, mass production, proletarianization and extreme division of labour had deserted rural community life around free farmers, artisans and small entrepreneurs. The rootless masses had brought the crisis of democracy while big industry, oligopolies, cartels and monopolies had brought the crisis of capitalism. The crisis of socialist collectivism went hand in hand with the crisis of liberalism. Röpke argued for a third way, with Switzerland as the model, through a struggle on two fronts: against collectivism and against liberalism as it had developed, in need of fundamental revision towards competition but with a key role for the state in order to prevent both capital concentration and proletarianization. It did not make sense to reject collectivism politically without at the same time solving economic and social reform tasks. It was a catastrophic failure to regard the market as something autonomous, as a state of nature separated from the institutions of the state. Like pure democracy, the rule of the masses, undiluted capitalism is also unbearable and indigestible, so Röpke argued. It was wrong to ignore the deficiencies of the pure market economy translated into rationalistic doctrinism. He concluded,

> It in no way contradicts the market economy if the state with the coercive instruments at its disposal (in particular by means of taxation) with the purpose of more equal distribution undertakes a redistribution of property conditions, and as little, if it, let us say from taxation income pays allowances for worker housing or for water pipes in mountain villages. ... It in no way contradicts an economic policy standard that respects our economic constitution if the state on its own manages individual enterprises or whole production branches and itself performs as producer or trader in the market. The same goes for public work which the state undertakes in order to bridge or overcome a depression. (Röpke 1948: 306)

The ordoliberal version in response to the Paris meeting in 1938 – the term *neo-liberal* disappeared from their agenda after a while – sought distinction from laissez-faire liberalism, which Rüstow rejected as palaeo-liberalism.

Ordoliberal ideas had been developed even before the Paris meeting in 1938. Two manifestos were published in 1932 at the peak of the economic crisis: Eucken's *Staatliche Strukturwandlungen und die Krise des Kapitalismus* ('State Structure Transformation and the Crisis of Capitalism') and Rüstow's *Interessenpolitik oder Staatspolitik* ('Interest Politics and State Politics'). Franz Böhm's *Wettbewerb und Monopolkampf* ('Competition and Struggle against Monopoly') followed a year later (Eucken 1932; Rüstow 1932; Böhm 1933).

The ordoliberals confronted not only laissez-faire but also the conservative historicist school and the social democratic imagery of economic democracy founded in the era of

Bismarck, when organized modernity emerged in the 1870s. Ideas of corporate interest representation and conflict resolution continued to blossom in Weimar reinforced by the experiences of the planned war economy as well as by utopian ideas of organic community (Stråth 2016: 370). These ideas promoting big business and large-scale capital concentration were the target of the ordoliberals as much as laissez-faire liberalism. They saw it as their task to provide a legal framing, *ordo*, of the economy, an economic constitution that would safeguard it both from market self-destruction and from political conflicts. There was a critique of economic concentration and a commitment to strong antitrust law and the imagery of an impartial state monitoring the economy and preventing the political conflict spreading there.

The imagery of an economic constitution demarcated from politics was, of course, utopian. It nevertheless played an important role not only in Weimar but also in particular during the foundation of European integration in the 1950s. A clear social dimension was integral to the ordoliberal approach in the shape of the *soziale Marktwirtschaft*, the social market economy as it was to be called after 1945, based on the belief in legal (ordoliberal) regulation of the economy determining the scope for political intervention. The (West) German approach after 1945 should be seen against the backdrop of the experiences of the Weimar Republic as a democracy with strong anti-democratic opponents on both the radical right and the radical left. The ordoliberal social market-economic post-war order was a rupture in a German history of authoritarianism. Rule-governed technocratic monitoring of the economy would bring general welfare that would provide political allegiance.

Hayek, on the other hand, developed an alternative view and a theory for the liberalization and deregulation of the world economy, where regulation of social life would emerge through the market without the mediation of the state. In Hayek's view, regulation meant an inflexible doctrinaire legal framework for the economy, rejecting state mediation between social interests. The state should not intervene in the market in order to correct shortcomings and failures but should only guarantee strict application of market rules. After the German ordoliberals had abandoned the term *neo-liberal* suggested in Paris in 1938, Hayek became the protagonist in defining it in economic market-radical terms. In an essay in 1939, Hayek argued for neo-liberal market discipline through interstate federalism. In his brief article he drafted an economic and monetary federation that would function as a tool to do away with impediments on free movement of 'men, goods, and capital between the states', enabling creation of common rules of law, a uniform monetary system and common control of communications. All monetary policy would have to be a federal matter, as opposed to a state matter. The imposition of market rigidity was a matter of monetary policy as well as commodity and labour standards:

> While the states could, of course, exercise control of the qualities of goods and the methods of production employed, it must not be overlooked that, provided the state could not exclude commodities produced in other parts of the Union, any burden placed on a particular industry by state legislation would put it at a serious disadvantage as opposed to similar industries in other parts of the Union. As has been shown by experience in existing federations, even such legislation as

> the restriction of child labour or of working hours becomes difficult to carry out for the individual state. (von Hayek 1980 [1939])

Methods of 'raising revenue' (i.e. collecting taxes) would be 'somewhat restricted' for individual states. Greater mobility between states would necessitate avoiding all sorts of taxes 'which would drive capital or labour elsewhere', but there would also be considerable difficulties with many kinds of indirect taxation. In order to prevent evasion of guarantees of free movement of 'men, goods, and capital', the federation must have great power to impose restrictions on political intervention in the economies of the Member States. Limitations had to be placed not only on government policies but also on economic policies conducted by trade unions, cartels and professional associations. Once frontiers between the Member States were opened and free movement was secured, the monopolies of those organizations, and their power to control supply of their services or products, would cease.

Hayek provided a model of international capital against international labour. He did not, however, discuss why market union could not have a social dimension or a relatively high tax regime shared by all Member States. He did not discuss why unions could not cooperate across Member State borders instead of competing in a race to the bottom. Prevention of trade distortions could in his view only be a matter of keeping standards down. In religious metaphorical terms, Hayek indicated that a federal market could serve as a kind of cleansing purgative designed to make economies fit for competition. Purification in the name of 'progress' presupposed downward pressure on wages and social standards. Coercion and discipline were the key in Hayek's dream of liberty.

In *Der Gesellschaftskrisis der Gegenwart*, which Röpke published in Swiss exile in 1942, he argued for the third way between socialism and laissez-faire capitalism, although in a different way from Child in his book on Sweden, emphasizing legal rather than political primacy. Ordoliberalism was Christian in its design. The masters of the narrative were all Protestants but their appeal was trans-confessional and also attracted Catholics in Germany. In *Civitas humana* (1944), Röpke argued that Pius XI's papal encyclical *Quadragesimo Anno* in 1931 on the ethical implications of the social and economic order, issued against the backdrop of the Great Depression and mass unemployment, forty years after Leo XIII's encyclical *Rerum Novarum* addressing the conditions of workers around 1890, at heart came to the same conclusion as Röpke's own liberal–conservative socio-economic philosophy (Röpke 1948: xvii). The legal-political constructs of Röpke and Hayek, ordoliberalism and neo-liberalism respectively, were clearly quite different in their views on the connections between law and politics and in their search for meaning in the past: politics as a continuous correction of liberal economies, on the one side, and, on the other side, the rejection of politics in forms other than monitoring the rule of the market.

Since the 1980s, Röpke had, in the neo-liberal rhetoric, been linked to the protagonists of neo-liberalism, Mises and Hayek, as if they were all three thinkers of the same school. Röpke was co-opted into neo-liberalism despite the fact that he abandoned the term and argued for ordoliberalism with a social face. When ordoliberalism has been recognized in academic literature since the 1980s as the legal foundation of the

European integration project, the reference has been exclusively to competition rules. The fact that both ordoliberalism and the early phases of European integration involved a social component hand in hand with the competition rules in mutually reinforcing dynamics does not appear in the derivation of an ordoliberal European heritage.[5] The next section will comment further on the connection between social commitments and competition rules in both ordoliberalism and European integration.

The connection between Röpke, on the one side, and Mises and Hayek, on the other, is marked by differences rather than similarities. Röpke referred in the *Social Crisis* to the historical blindness of liberalism that created a false choice between socialism and capitalism. The choice was clear to Mises and Hayek, but Röpke was looking for a third way between the two theoretical approaches to the economy. This hijacking of ordoliberalism by the neo-liberals, and its later acceptance by ignorant critics of neo-liberalism, was an expression of the ideological force of neo-liberalism in its second wave between the 1980s and 2008.

One might argue that ordoliberalism inverts the relationship between the political and the economic in its plea for an economic constitution as a free-standing foundation of the polity, neglecting the concept of popular sovereignty. It is then important to emphasize that in early ordoliberal thought the economy involved a clear social dimension and an elaborated link to the social tasks of the state. It was neo-liberalism in the design of Hayek that radicalized the economic constitution and cut the social link. From neo-liberalism, a link emerged to liberal authoritarianism through economic fundamentalism with austerity as an instrument. But it is historically wrong to connect ordoliberalism to this development.[6]

Ordoliberal ideas were to influence the post–1945 European integration project in its early phases but not in the sense that the neo-liberals would argue in their post-Maastricht outline of the past.

Recreation of values: The European integration project, the modernization narrative, ordoliberalism and Keynesianism

The historical experiences that drove the reconstruction of European values after 1945 rejected the arguments of Schmitt. At the same time, though, the architects of the new Europe also had doubts about the capacity of the liberal alternative. They were looking for a legal rather than a liberal political alternative to Schmitt, a normative framework to prevent a reiteration of the liberal collapse. In Western Europe after 1945, Weimar served as a warning example, reinforced by the other warning example of the revolution that led to the Stalinist regime in the Soviet Union and its satellite regimes in Central and Eastern Europe. The insight in Western Europe was that democracy could be dangerous and therefore had to be controlled. The rule of the people could be the point of departure for politics in very different directions. Moreover, it could be manipulated. Memories were still fresh of how close to each other the various responses to the crisis in the 1930s had been before the differences became obvious.

The fragility of democracy was what the fathers of the European integration project wanted to change. They wanted to establish a stable and predictable political order. They wanted democracy based on rational rule instead of the charismatic and traditional leadership during the era of the world wars to stay with Weber's categories. Technocrats were expected to guarantee rational democracy. Their instrument was welfare for the allegiance of the masses, but differently from the Third Reich. From the beginning, the European integration project was designed as a rule-governed technocracy, not a democracy, with the aim of guaranteeing democracy in the Member States through the prospects of social citizenship. This was the policy of European rescue of nation states (Milward 1992).

Ordoliberalism in the design of Röpke, Rüstow, Eucken and other economists along with like-minded lawyers fitted well with this (West) European integration approach. In the early drafts of Jean Monnet, competition law to prevent cartels and capital concentration and to provide a legal framework for the market was linked to the issue of social standards. Although competition was considered to be the key to cheaper and better production, it would not occur through lowering labour standards. The plan was intended to appeal beyond narrow business interests and, to that end, it addressed the question of wages. Monnet's original idea was to give the High Authority, which in the Rome Treaty in 1957 became the Commission, wide-ranging powers in the area of wages but remained somewhat ambiguous as to the substance. Wage dumping was obviously to be prohibited, but Monnet also envisaged wages as an instrument for promoting better standards of living. The Dutch negotiators, supported by the Germans, rejected any such powers for the High Authority, whereas the Belgians, whose wages were the highest, solidly supported the social definition of the wage issue since, in practice, it would mean that the other Member States would have to promote higher wages. The French were split. The Italian position was more complicated because its steel industry, which was a low-wage sector with high unit-labour costs, was overmanned. In the end, Monnet's vision was narrowed down to a prohibition of wage dumping (Griffith 1986).

A European rule-governed technocracy defining the legal borders of the economy in terms of competition rules and securing democracy through provision of welfare by the Member States required the legitimacy of a convincing narrative. After 1945, US American historians and social scientists wrote the history of the victors around the theme of modernization. The functionalist narrative on modernization by the American social sciences described how superstition became reason, how backwardness became progress, how absolutism became democracy and how poverty became welfare. They established a development norm from which everybody could benefit in and beyond Europe. The United States was at the top of the development scale, constituting both the norm and the goal of economic and political development. Barrington Moore epitomized this narrative with his classic on the origin of dictatorship and democracy (Moore 1966). In his analysis, the key was treatment of the social question and class differences by the political system. Moore initiated a research trend under the buzzword of modernization. A narrative emerged where the final goal of modernization was democracy and welfare. It was now that democracy as a consequence of Enlightenment philosophy, not the world wars, became a core dimension of (West) European self-understanding. The modernization researchers built one bridge to the Enlightenment over the gap of the world wars and another between capitalism and democracy, political and economic reason and progress over the gap of the Great Depression and social destitution. This was the master narrative under which the European integration project evolved from fascism to (West) European unification.

The post-war necessity to re-establish a new Europe on its own ruins automatically created an expansive demand situation, in the shape of the reconstruction boom of the 1950s and 1960s. The emerging economies of growth and welfare, with full employment and a reasonable distribution of incomes and fortunes, created a basis for mutually reinforcing dynamics between mass consumption and mass production, demand and supply, in contrast to the people's democracies of Eastern Europe. The first priority and lesson from the experiences of the Great Depression in the 1930s, when the beginning of the (West) European integration project was negotiated in Paris in 1950 against the backdrop of the Korean War, was the connection between a strong welfare economy and democracy. The experiences of the economic crisis in the 1930s told how easily democracy could lose its way without a strong social commitment. These experiences were only some fifteen years old. Welfare was the currency for buying political allegiance, at least in the view that emerged in Paris. An economy based on a common market would provide resources for welfare. Through a general distribution of welfare, the European leaders created a contrast to the hardships in the Soviet system. General welfare generated by a rule-governed European market economy with a social face fitted very well with the ordoliberal imagery of Röpke, Rüstow and others. Economic growth through ordoliberal competition rules would provide the scope for an economically efficient social Europe.

John Maynard Keynes, too, contributed to the legitimizing economic theory that gave an interpretative frame for development in Western Europe. *The General Theory of Employment, Interest and Money* (1936), written in response to the Great Depression, was a theory for full employment policies in the industrial economies with a social psychological component emphasizing the importance of confidence in the future. Keynes argued that a new Great Depression could be avoided through political management of the economy, where a key political task was to infuse social feelings of certainty and security as a corrective to the experiences of precariousness and uncertainty that the capitalist system brought.[7] He argued that the economy was a polity, not the other way round, as would be strongly argued half a century later.[8] The technocratic application of his theory (*Keynesianism*) after the Second World War made him a mechanic provider of a toolkit for the maintenance of economic growth, where growth became permanent through political techniques and Keynes's insistence on uncertainty as the basic precondition of capitalism disappeared behind the imagery of permanent growth. In the political practices of Keynesianism, economic theory became like ordoliberalism: a kind of economic constitution, or at least convention, which provided the rules for political intervention in the economy.

This macroeconomic Keynesianism of political management and *dirigisme* (state control of economic and social matters) was clearly at odds with the ordoliberal imaginary which envisaged market competition with a microeconomic and legal focus. However, their attention to the social issue connected them, while the booming reconstruction economy hid the differences. The success of the West European economies, with growth and full employment, confirmed the Keynesian theory of full employment and belief in ordoliberal competition rules. A permanent solution to economic growth and full employment appeared to be a possibility. With a focus on social cohesion, ordoliberalism and Keynesianism emphasized legal and political primacy respectively under awareness of the fact that the two dimensions of social life are entangled. Overlapping interpretative frameworks linked the political, the social, the economic and the legal in a stable relationship, outlining a post-war (West) European utopia of political and social stability as well as progress through continuous economic growth.

The (West) European nation states were defined in civic and social rather than in ethnic terms, in close cooperation with other nation states, as national communities of destiny on the basis of welfare and (West) European cooperation ('integration'), and cohesion imposed by the Cold War.

The crisis of the 1970s

The crisis of the 1970s destroyed this (West) European political-legal-economic-social dynamic equilibrium of growth legitimized by and confirming the modernization narrative and the European heritage of Enlightenment rationalism. This dynamic equilibrium probably came rather close to the dreams of the exiled German scholars in Britain during the Second World War who mobilized Roman law for historical legitimacy. The arrangement was experienced as stable. The legal and political framing of the European economies promoted social peace through economic growth and redistribution of yields. This legal and political framing employed ever less Roman law à la Koschaker and Catholic religion as points of reference. The modernization narrative and belief in teleological progress moved the attention forwards rather than backwards.

The end of the 1960s brought strains to European full employment economies as workers radicalized their language in a struggle for a bigger share of the economic yield, better working conditions and a reduction in job-related stress. The conflict level grew and claims for economic democracy accompanied strikes, sits-ins and lockouts. Claims went beyond the mere issue of wages and developed into a struggle about the workplace more generally, centring on concepts such as economic democracy, co-determination, *autogestion*, *Mitbestimmung* and state ownership. This struggle, in turn, was intertwined with a larger generational revolt, which in Europe began in France and spread throughout Western Europe, but went beyond Europe as a worldwide escalation of social conflicts and peoples' rebellions against militarism and capitalism, bourgeoisie and bureaucracy. The Prague Spring was its East European version. The year 1968 also saw the birth of the environmental and anti-nuclear movements.

Against the backdrop of general internal radicalization, external factors began to undermine Europe's welfare economies during the first half of the 1970s. The post-war Bretton Woods order based on the dollar, agreed on in 1944, collapsed in 1971. The next blow came in the autumn of 1973 with the oil price shock, which initiated the beginning of a new international world order, a decrease in the power of the old European industrial economies and a growing scope of action for those third world countries producing raw materials.

Key industries such as coal, steel and shipbuilding broke down and mass unemployment occurred for the first time since the 1930s. The ordoliberal social market economy – based on competition rules and distribution of labour between the European market for economic growth and Member State responsibility for the distribution of social welfare – did not function. The same is true of the Keynesian toolkit. The development was generally considered impossible within the Keynesian interpretative framework which provided the toolkit for the management of full employment economies. Memories of the impact on the political system of social protests in the 1930s came back and alarmed European governments. They intervened with massive subsidy packages to stop or slow down industrial decline. Lobbyism and the corporatism of organized interests took on a new magnitude, bypassing the ordoliberal distinction between conform and non-conform state intervention in the economy. The accumulation of massive state debts accelerated inflation under conditions of economic stagnation, a development which ran counter to the theoretical economic wisdom of Keynesianism. The new phenomenon acquired a new name: stagflation.

Ordoliberal and Keynesian ideas progressively lost credibility in the wake of accelerating unemployment, growing public budget deficits and increasing inflation. The imagery of proactive management of the economy shifted to the imagery of political helplessness with only a *reactive* capacity. The development bypassed the ordoliberal framework, in particular the competition rules. A new economic orthodoxy emerged with deep roots in liberal philosophy, prescribing a lesser role for the state and promoting greater market freedom. The market would heal economies from corporatist sclerosis through state management. A new magic word – *flexibility* – promised a panacea. The neo-liberal turn occurred within a larger framework of ideological reorientation where many of the ideas of 1968 around the theme of de-hierarchization and co-determination were redefined by the political right and employers, who appropriated the priority of interpretation. They took over the 1968 language against hierarchies and channelled it in new directions where not least the trade unions became a target of attack.

The 1970s and 1980s saw a huge conceptual confrontation about the redefinition of key concepts such as freedom, equality, solidarity, economic distribution, welfare, state and market. A new semantic field emerged where government, which used to connote state hierarchy with legal and political guarantees of welfare and social standards, shifted to the softer and more market-oriented governance accompanied by terms such as *network* and *coordination*, signalling a retreat from ordoliberal legal prescriptions as well as political ambitions to steer and rule. The reform concept had come to mean social reform since the emergence of the social question as a political problem in the 1830s in particular. Now a redefinition began with the aim of cleansing the term of any social content. The Keynesian honorary term *full employment* disappeared from the political vocabulary like the concept of *welfare state*. Previously, the concept of *employment* was closely connected to rules of certain standards. This connection disappeared in the new vocabulary and the connection to social security eroded. New critical concepts, such as the two-thirds society, emerged in order to describe the development from the left. Social marginalization was the instrument to create political stability in a turbulent time.

A new labour market organization reflected the conceptual transformation. The labour force was increasingly divided between a core of company-loyal employees with fixed employment, on the one hand, and temporary employees, on the other. Around the core, new strata of temporary employment emerged in various forms through outsourcing or hiring and firing with far more precarious employment conditions and future prospects. The reserve army of labour that Marx and Engels had identified in the 1860s re-emerged.

The seeming breakthrough of working-class ideals about work in the late 1960s and early 1970s, with key terms such as *economic democracy*, *co-determination* and *state ownership*, coupled with the apparent step towards realization of the Marxist view of industrial society that it signalled, contained the germs of the dissolution of the working class in its historically established form. The end of industrial society in its centenary existence, where work provided social inclusion and existential meaning, shifted to social exclusion and loss of meaning for many without a workplace identification. State-guaranteed universal social citizenship rights split up in company-specific welfare arrangements and benefits for core employees and emergency relief for the marginalized part of the labour force with occasional work and pay. Employees doing the same job and having the same qualifications, working next to each other at machines and conveyor belts or in offices, could have very different wages and salaries. It is not difficult to imagine the long-term impact of this development on social cohesion and political allegiance.

The breakdown of national patterns of solidarity meant that mass unemployment did not represent the same political problem and threat to social stability as was first anticipated in the 1970s. Instead of social revolution, the period witnessed stabilization through social marginalization and a cultural retreat to old Darwinian metaphors, according to which it became generally accepted that only the stronger could expect to survive in the fight for survival in hardening markets (Stråth 2000; Wagner 2000). Economic liberalism sped up and political liberalism lagged behind in the wake of the growing tension between the national institutional framework of economies and the global performance of economies based on global component flows from regions with cheap labour to the labour-saving assembly of components in regions with higher labour costs. In the wake of this development, the question of social standards and employment security obtained a new dimension beyond the political control of national governments.

The 1970s and 1980s were a great divide in the history of modern Europe. After initial attempts to save collapsing industries, the fundamental transformation of rule-governed and politically managed welfare economies and labour markets went hand in hand with political exit from the guarantee of certain social standards and the decline of Keynesian welfare states and the ordoliberal imageries of social market economies. Keynes's emphasis on confidence in the future changed to experience of the opposite: general uncertainty about the future. This was a fundamental change.[9]

Propagation of a powerful neo-liberal economic vocabulary went hand in hand with a major ideological shift to neo-liberalism. Economic theory stood as the core of the new ideology. Hayek replaced Keynes and the German *soziale Marktwirtschaft*. Flexibility replaced welfare as the key socio-economic concept. The welfare state was put off as the tax-and-debt state. In the academic underpinning of the conceptual transformation, public choice replaced public finance as a field of investigation. This shift in academic-political perspective had four protagonists: Hayek, Milton Friedman, Margaret Thatcher and Ronald Reagan.

In the 1980s, Hayek and Friedman appeared with evermore convincing prescriptions for getting the economy on track again. The new neo-liberal language mixed Friedman's monetarist approach and Hayek's belief in the market process and the central role of prices rather than the state as regulator of the economy. Their argument was that if there was unemployment it was because wages were too high, and if there was inflation it was because governments spent too much. They contradicted Keynes's demand orientation where government spending was the right prescription in order to boost consumer purchasing power and consumer demand. To answer why Hayek's and Milton's neo-liberal narrative gained credibility, we must look at the great transformation that took place from the 1970s onwards. The new labour markets and the appropriation of the radical language of the 1968 movement by employers under the motto of 'small is beautiful' and 'flexibility' reinforced each other.

Even in 1939, Hayek's neo-liberalism, with his outline of the race-to-the-bottom customs union, was diametrically different from Eucken's, Rüstow's and Röpke's ordoliberal social market economy which, however, as we saw, did not prevent later neo-liberal thinkers as well as their critics from unhistorically incorporating the concept of ordoliberal in the neo-liberal vocabulary, which is an affront against Eucken, Rüstow and Röpke and their fellows (Röpke 1948: xvii). The Roman legacy and the ordoliberal imagery of a legal-political framing of the economy disappeared behind the neo-liberal hegemonic economistic view of self-regulating markets beyond political control.

The value crisis of the 2010s

The Lehman Brothers bankruptcy in September 2008 hit the financial world like a bolt from the blue. The collapse developed into a banking crisis which provoked massive state intervention under the motto of 'too big to fail'. This led to a state debt crisis and a new wave of speculation on the financial markets against state debts, which in turn hit the weak Southern Euro economies, Greece in particular. New state guarantees were mobilized to bail out speculating banks, German and French in particular, from their Greek commitments.

The awakening from the neo-liberal market dream in 2008 was abrupt. The experiences from the 1930s that the European leaders wanted to remember told that it was disastrous to let big banks fail. The experiences they forgot told that austerity politics breaks down political legitimacy and increases xenophobic nationalism. The belief of Merkel's Europe in austerity became a religious dogma with a strong moral message that defied empirical observations. The decline of Greek GNP by 25 per cent over a five-year period from 2010, with over half of its youth unemployed, did not alter this belief. Greece became a test case for political fundamentalism in the centre of Europe. The subtext of religious moralism around the concept of *debt*, which in German (*Schuld*) integrates the double meanings of debt and guilt, triggered a civilizing and disciplining education campaign against attempts to open up alternative approaches to political management of the economy. Hayek's theoretical construct had collapsed, but it nevertheless remained the central point of reference in the debate. The austerity campaign echoed his 1939 outline of the customs union with the goal of imposing financial discipline among the Member States, an economic constitution without flexibility, an economistic iron regime (von Hayek 1980 [1939]). The austerity approach extended the economic crisis to a political crisis and a value crisis.

Perhaps the most obvious parallel to Weimar is the crisis as mutually reinforcing dynamics between economic failure, political incapacity to manage what is ideologically imagined as a global economy without borders and the social crisis driven by the loss of existential orientation around work. Of course, the full employment societies of the 1950s and 1960s did not belong to the historical experience of Weimar. However, recurring feelings of uncertainty, precariousness, segmentation and divisions in the labour markets since the 1970s very much belonged to the Weimar experience. These dynamics have brought the breakdown of European core values with their origin in the Enlightenment project: breakdown in the sense of incapacity to communicate about their contentious meanings.

There is one difference. The value crisis in the 1930s dealt with the possibility of truth and objectivity. The solution to that value crisis was found through relativizing the imageries of truth and objectivity, the decline of positivism, and dissolution of the strong distinction between science and fiction. The present epistemological value crisis is deeper since it questions our imagery of human autonomy, the human as the gauge of everything, human responsibility for creation of the future and the capacity to shape it. In other words, the core message of human sciences is at stake against the backdrop of a powerful ideological language proclaiming that economic processes are driven by natural forces beyond human control. This was the belief that triggered austerity politics both in the 1930s and today.

Parliamentary representative democracy was an ideal but far from a European standard since Enlightenment philosophy and the American and French revolutions. The question is what the economic crisis since 2008 and, more generally, the rapid digital development of global financial capitalism has meant for the preconditions of representative democracy centred on legislative assemblies.

In his dictum 'the sovereign is the one who declares a state of emergency', Schmitt redefined 'sovereignty' from its original locus in theories of democracy in the legislature as representation of the people to the executive, which, after proclaiming a state of exception, used it to eliminate or restrict the ability of the legislative assembly to control the executive. The parliament-circumventing proclamation of a state of exception has become normal practice in contemporary democratic orders, not least in the framework of the politics of Euro rescue (Höreth 2008). The European legal order has lost the power of orientation and guidance with the consequence, in a strong argument by Dieter Grimm, that the Commission and the European Court of Justice have retreated to market activism in the only field where they still have interpretative power: competition rules (Grimm 2016; Grimm 2014; Grimm 2013). This Commission and ECJ market activism without a social dimension, coordinating and monitoring capital concentration and inviting lobby influence by big corporate business, is far from the ordoliberal market vision of competition rules for a social Europe in the formulation almost seventy years ago. And the imagery of a Roman law legacy is even more remote.

The reference by Angela Merkel to a decision of the Council in response to bank rescues and the Euro crisis as *alternativlos* is a case in point for the view that markets are beyond human control. In a contradictory but consistent way this argument goes hand in hand with the legal market activism that Grimm refers to. Even before the collapse of the financial markets in 2008, Giorgio Agamben had seen the development coming and argued that the distinction between democracy and dictatorship has disappeared.[10] This is a strong formulation without nuances, but authoritarianism is undoubtedly gaining ground in Europe and elsewhere. In Schmitt's view, the proclaimer of a state of exception appropriates the rights of the legislature generally, which is too strong a description of the present situation (Maus 2011: 7–8). However, the question is whether in practice, in the present parliamentary orders, the executive does not exert legislative functions. Of course, there is always the possibility of electing a new legislature and executive, but what difference would it make in attempts to react to global financial capitalism as in the Euro crisis? And is the execution of financial and monetary policies by the president of the European Central Bank, Mario Draghi, against the backdrop of the lack of a European fiscal regime, not an illustration of what Marx before Schmitt in the *Eighteenth Brumaire* described as *die Verselbständigung des Exekutivgewalts*, the emancipation of the executive authority? Or is it a silent delegation of power beyond constitutional cover due to a failure to agree on a common fiscal policy in the European Council?

Roman law as a legal legacy of Europe is no longer a relevant issue. European law – under ever fewer references to Roman law – has lost legitimacy under conditions of legal market activism. The same goes for ordoliberalism, after its incorporation into neo-liberalism. Röpke's second, negative interpretation of the Roman legal heritage as legitimacy of centralized absolutism fits with the present development of authoritarianism, although this development is occurring at the Member State rather than the European level. The alternative legacy binary in Röpke's interpretation, legitimization of individual private ownership rights, has shifted to legitimization of private corporate power and capital concentration, and mutated into his second Roman binary in the shape of 'centralized absolutism'. However, the imagery of a centralized Europe is rapidly losing contours, too. Europe is no longer a threat. The threat is the collapse of Europe itself.

The ongoing search for national identities is guided, not by a belief in progress and a wide horizon of expectations but by the narrow identification of enemies. Interest-based inclusive solidarity is no longer the key in the search for identity, but rather emotional exclusion. Accumulated experience since the 1830s of the need for interest-based social solidarity for the successful construction of community culminated in Röpke's ordoliberal social market-economic imagery and in post-Keynesian Keynesianism, which were abandoned in the 1970s. Hayek's neo-liberal market Europe has failed to develop an alternative framework for identification. Moreover, a narrow and exclusive ethnic nationalism is replacing the dissolution of the horizons of the 1990s after the end of the Cold War. Civic and socially inclusive national solidarity and feelings of community, constructed during the Cold War period before 1971, are declining. The crisis of the 1970s was a watershed in European history. And we are still living in the shadow of that crisis. Our ongoing crisis since 2008 can be seen as the second half of one long crisis. After the decline of the modernization and globalization narratives, no convincing, mobilizing and legitimizing European narrative has emerged to replace them.

Roman law, in a thick genealogy full of nuances, might – together with social market-economic ordoliberalism – have been a founding stone of the European integration project after 1945, a foundation myth that demarcated Europe from its Nazi and fascist heritage. However, this view of the Roman legacy is problematic and ambiguous in its oscillation between individual autonomy and centralized absolutism, as Röpke argued. Few today believe in the individual autonomy of European Union (EU) citizens. The EU as the incarnation of centralized absolutism was a horrifying picture earlier in the 1990s, when some critics feared a federalization of Europe, and occasionally linked their concern to Schmitt's *Großraum* theory as a warning example for the internal market (Joerges and Ghaleigh 2003). Recent developments towards de-Europeanization and renationalization indicate a general erosion of the legal foundation of the EU, so that questions of the Roman legacy seem less relevant. The EU is losing legitimacy both as a political and as a normative legal order (Tuori and Tuori 2014). In the present state of confusion and political paralysis, not only is the future unclear but also the past. Earlier crises triggered the search for roots and origins but only in connection with a search for new futures. The ongoing European muddling-through politics of presentism has little bearing on the future and little interest in the past. The search for new futures and pasts is taking place in nation states under a growing connection to authoritarianism.

Notes

1 'Definierbar ist nur das was keine Geschichte hat.' Nietzsche 1980 [1887]: 820.

2 Grotke and Prutsch 2014; Sellin 2014; Stråth 2016. For a problematization and historicization of teleological views, see Trüper, Chakrabarty and Subrahmanyam 2015.

3 Schmitt 1926; Schmitt 1928; Schmitt 1939. Concerning Stresemann, Locarno and Poland, see Stråth 2016: 276.

4 Röpke 1944. Quotation is from the English translation, Röpke 1948: xvii.

5 For a survey of this debate, see Solchany 2015: 11–33. Patel and Schweitzer 2013: 10 argue that ordoliberal ideas indeed influenced the evolution of European Union competition law during the foundational period following the Treaty of Rome in 1957, but that it was no simple transposition of ordoliberalism from the German setting to the Community. Only specific features of ordoliberal thinking such as individual rights and the rule of law provided a good fit. They are thus aware of the existence of other dimensions of ordoliberalism without naming them, but they do not mention the social political aim in Jean Monnet's design of the European Coal and Steel Community. Ramirez Pérez and van de Scheur 2013 connects ordoliberalism to the neo-liberal orbit: 'Competition law had thus become a goal in itself, and competition law became more Ordo liberal.' The merger of the two concepts is complete in Dale and El-Enany

2013: 614, 'The EU has displayed familiar characteristics: A lack of democratic method and a commitment to a neoliberal (or ordoliberal) doctrine.' Cf. also Wilkinson 2013: 543, 'Closely related to what is commonly now referred to as neo-liberalism, ordoliberalism is, one might say, simply more honest and straightforward about the role of the strong state in guaranteeing the "free economy", which is hardly free and ensuring "the rules of the game," which are bent when necessary.'

6 Cf. Wilkinson 2013: 554, who tends to discern a link between ordoliberalism and liberal authoritarianism.

7 An immense literature is available on Keynes and Keynesianism. See, for instance, Backhouse and Bateman 2011 and Skidelsky 2009. Cf. Magnusson and Stråth 2016: chapter 2.

8 Joerges, Stråth and Wagner 2005. See for Keynesianism Clarke 1998: chapter 10 and Magnusson and Stråth 2016: chapter 2.

9 For the great transformation in the 1970s, see Stråth and Wagner 2017: chapter 9. See also Stråth 2000; Wagner 2000.

10 Agamben 2005. For a critical comment on Agamben, see Maus 2011: 7–8.

References

Agamben, G. (2005), *The State of Exception*, Chicago: Chicago University Press.

Backhouse, R. E. and Bateman, B. W. (2011), *Capitalist Revolutionary*, Cambridge, MA: Harvard University Press.

Böhm, F. (1933), *Wettbewerb und Monopolkampf*. Berlin: Heymann.

Brunner, O., Conze, W. and Koselleck, R., eds. (1979–1997), *Geschichtliche Grundbegriffe. Historisches Lexikon zur politisch-sozialen Sprache in Deutschland*, Stuttgart: Klett-Cotta.

Cassirer, E. (1936), *The Philosophy of Symbolic Forms*, New Haven: Yale University Press (German original published in 1923).

Childs, M. (1936), *Sweden: The Middle Way*, New York Faber and Faber.

Clarke, P. (1998), *The Keynesian Revolution and Its Economic Consequences*, Cheltenham: Elgar.

Dale, G. and El-Enany, N. (2013), 'The Limits of Social Europe: EU Law and the Ordoliberal Agenda', *Regeneration Europe. Special Issue German Law Journal*, 14 (5): 613–49.

Denord, F. (2001), 'Aux origins du néo-liberalisme en France. Louis Rougier et le Colloque Lippmann', *Le Mouvement Social*, 195: 9–34.

Denord, F. (2008), 'Neoliberalisme et "économie sociale de marché": les origines intellectuelles de la politique européenne de la concurrence (1930–1950)', *Histoire, Economie et Société*, 27 (1): 23–34.

Eucken, W. (1932), 'Staatliche Strukturwandlungen und die Krise des Kapitalismus', *Weltwirtschaftliches Archiv*, 36: 297–321.

Griffith, R. (1986), 'The Schuman Plan Negotiations: The Economic Clauses', in K. Schwabe (ed.), *The Beginnings of the Schuman-Plan*, 35–71, Baden-Baden: Nomos.

Grimm, D. (2013), 'Zum Stand der demokratischen Legitimation der Europäischen Union nach Lissabon', in H. M. Heinig and J. P. Terhecht (eds), *Postnationale Demokratie, Postdemokratie, Neoetatismus. Wandel klassischer Demokratievorstellungen in der Rechtswissenschaft*, 105–22, Tübingen: Mohr Siebeck.

Grimm, D. (2014), 'Die Rolle der nationalen Verfassungsgerichte in der europäischen Demokratie', in C. Franzius, F. C. Mayer and J. Neyer (eds), *Grenzen von Recht und Politik*, 27–47, Baden-Baden: Nomos.

Grimm, D. (2016), *Europa ja – aber welches? Zur Verfassung der europäischen Demokratie*, München: C. H. Beck.

Grotke, K. and Prutsch, M., eds. (2014), *Constitutionalism, Legitimacy, and Power: Nineteenth-Century Experiences*, Oxford: Oxford University Press.

von Hayek, F. (1980 [1939]), 'The Economic Conditions of Interstate Federalism', in F. von Hayek (ed.), *Individualism and Economic Order*, 255–72, Chicago: Chicago University Press.

Heidegger, M. (1927), *Sein und Zeit*, Halle/Saale: Niemeyer.

Höreth, M. (2008), *Die Selbstautorisierung des Agenten. Der Europaische Gerichtshof im Vergleich zum US Supreme Court*, Baden-Baden: Nomos.

Huizinga, J. (1935), *In de schaduwen van morgen: een diagnose van het geestelijk lijden van onzen tijd*, Haarlem: H. D. Tjeenk Willink & Zoon.

Husserl, E. (1936), 'Die Krisis der europäischen Wissenschaften und die transzendentale Phänomenologie. Eine Einleitung in die phänomenologische Philosophie', *Philosophia: philosophorum nostri temporis vox universa*, 1: 77–176.

Huxley, A. (1932), *Brave New World*, London: Chatto & Windus.

Jackson, B. (2010), 'At the Origins of Neo-Liberalism: The Free Economy and the Strong State, 1930–47', *Historical Journal*, 53: 129–51.

Jeenicke, T. (2012), *Ernst Cassirers Philosophie der symbolischen Formen: Mythos, Sprache, Philosophie*. Saarbrücken: AV Akademikerverlag.

Joerges, C. and Ghaleigh, N. S. (2003), *Darker Legacies of Law in Europe. The Shadow of National Socialism and Fascism over Europe and its Legal Traditions*, Oxford and Portland, OR: Hart.

Joerges, C., Stråth, B. and Wagner, P., eds. (2005), *The Economy as a Polity*, London: Cavendish Press.

Jünger, E. (1929), *Storm of Steel*, London: Chatto & Windus (German original published in 1920).

Jünger, E. (1930), *Corpse 125: A Chronicle from the Trench Warfare of 1918*, London: Chatto & Windus (German original published in 1925).

Koschaker, P. (1938), *Die Krise des Römischen Rechts und die romanistische Rechtswissenschaft*, München: Beck.

Koschaker, P. (1947), *Europa und das römische Recht*, München: Biederstein.

Koselleck, R. (1959), *Kritik und Krise. Beitrag zur Pathogenese der bürgerlichen Welt*, Frankfurt: Suhrkamp.

Magnusson, L. and Stråth, B. (2016), *A Brief History of Political Economy: Tales of Marx, Keynes and Hayek*, Cheltenham: Elgar.

Maus, I. (2011), *Uber Volkssouveranitet. Elemente einer Demokratietheorie*, Frankfurt: Suhrkamp.

Milward, A. (1992), *The Rescue of the European Nation State*, London: Routledge.

Mirowski, P. and Plehwe, D. (2009), *The Road from Mont Pèlerin: The Making of the Neoliberal Thought Collective*, Cambridge, MA: Harvard University Press.

Moore, B. (1966), *Social Origins of Dictatorship and Democracy: Lord and Peasant in the Making of the Modern World*, Boston: Beacon Press.

Nietzsche, F. (1980 [1887]), *Zur Genealogie der Moral. Eine Streitschrift, Bd IV. Zweite Abhandlung: Schuld, schlechtes Gewissen und Verwandtes*, München [Leipzig]: Carl Hanser [C. G. Naumann].

Ortega y Gasset, J. (1930), *La rebelión de las masas*, Madrid: Revista de Occidente.
Patel, K. and Schweitzer, H., eds. (2013), *The Historical Foundation of EU Competition Law*, Oxford: Oxford University Press.
Ramirez Pérez, S. M. and van de Scheur, S. (2013), 'The Evolution of the Law on Articles 85 and 86 EEC [Articles 101 and 102 TFEU]. Ordoliberalism and its Keynesian Challenge', in K. Patel and H. Schweitzer (eds), *The Historical Foundations of EU Competition Law*, 20–53, Oxford: Oxford University Press.
Röpke, W. (1942), *Die Gesellschaftskrise der Gegenwart*, Zürich: Eugen Rentsch.
Röpke, W. (1944), *Civitas humana. Grundfragen der Gesellschafts- und Wirtschaftsreform*, Zürich: Rentsch.
Röpke, W. (1948), *Civitas Humana: A Human Order of Society*, London: William Hodge & Co.
Rüstow, A. (1932), 'Interessenpolitik oder Staatspolitik', *Der deutsche Wirtschaft*, 7: 169–72.
Schivelbusch, W. (2005), *Entfernte Verwandtschaft. Faschismus, Nationalsozialismus, New Deal 1933–1939*, Munich: Carl Hansner.
Schmitt, C. (1922), *Politische Theologie: Vier Kapitel zur Lehre von der Souveränität*, vol. 1, Berlin: Duncker & Humblot.
Schmitt, C. (1926), *Die Kernfrage des Völkerbundes*, Berlin: F. Dümmlers.
Schmitt, C. (1927), 'Der Begriff des Politischen', *Archiv für Sozialwissenschaften und Sozialpolitik*, 58: 1–33.
Schmitt, C. (1928), *Der Völkerbund und Europa*, Munich: Kösel.
Schmitt, C. (1939), *Völkerrechtliche Großraumordnung und Interventionsverbot für raumfremde Mächte. Ein Beitrag zum Reichsbegriff im Völkerrecht*, Berlin: Akademie der Wissenschaften.
Sellin, V. (2014), *Das Jahrhundert der Restauration. 1814–1906*, Munich: De Gruyter.
Skidelsky, R. (2009), *The Return of the Master*, London: Allen Lane.
Solchany, J. (2015), *Wilhelm Röpke, l'autre Hayek. Aux origines du néolibéralisme*, Paris: Publications de la Sorbonne.
Spengler, O. (1918-1922), *Der Untergang des Abendlandes*, München: Beck.
Spengler, O. (1931), *Der Mensch und die Technik*, München: Beck.
Spengler, O. (1933), *Jahre der Entscheidung. Deutschland und die weltpolitische Entwicklung*, München: Beck.
Stråth, B., ed. (2000), *After Full Employment: European Discourses on Work and Flexibility*, Brussels: Peter Lang.
Stråth, B. (2016), *Europe's Utopias of Peace: 1815, 1919, 1951*, London: Bloomsbury.
Stråth, B. and Wagner, P. (2017), *European Modernity: A Global Approach*, London: Bloomsbury.
Trüper, H., Chakrabarty D. and Subrahmanyam, S., eds. (2015), *Historical Teleologies in the Modern World*, London: Bloomsbury.
Tuori, K. and Tuori, K. (2014), *The Eurozone Crisis: A Constitutional Analysis*, Cambridge: Cambridge University Press.
Valpen, B. (2004), *Die offene Feinde und ihre Gesellschaft. Eine hegemonietheoretische Studie zur Mont Pèlerin Society*, Hamburg: VSA Verlag.
Wagner, P. (2000), 'The Exit from Organised Modernity: "Flexibility" in Social Thought and in Historical Perspective', in B. Stråth (ed.), *After Full Employment: European Discourses on Work and Flexibility*, 35–63, Brussels: Peter Lang.
Wieacker, F. (1990), 'Foundations of European Legal Culture', trans. E. Bodenheimer, *The American Journal of Comparative Law*, 38 (1): 1–29.
Wilkinson, M. A. (2013), 'The Specter of authoritarian Liberalism: Reflections on the Constitutional Crisis of the European Union', *Regeneration Europe. Special Issue of German Law Journal*, 14 (5): 527–60.

Index